META
YOUR
HEALTH
IN 45 DAYS

HOW TO HEAL YOURSELF
NATURALLY
CANCER WHAT'S THE ANSWER?
RESTORE YOUR HEALTH &
VITALITY & POWERS OF MIND
BODY TO SPIRIT IN 45 DAYS!
A NATUROPATHIC-
BIOENERGETIC - BIOLOGICAL-
HOLISTIC - SPIRITUAL-
ALTERNATIVE - APPROACH-
TO HEALTH & WELL - BEING
BY JEROME PLOTNICK, PH.D., N.D.

21st CENTURY ENERGETICS
LAKE of the WOODS, CA. 93225

DISCLAIMER NOTE!
This book is a reference work for educational purposes only and based on research by the author. The opinions expressed herein are not necessarily those, of or endorsed by the publisher, or book distributors. The information stated in this book does not attempt to heal, treat, or diagnose any disease. It is not a substitute for consultation with your health practitioner or duly licensed Medical Doctor. The health products enclosed in this book are not F.D.A. approved. "Exception is Liquid Needle"

Library of Congress Cataloging in Publication Data:

Plotnick, J.D.
Meta Your Health in 45 Days Book #1
Table of Contents. Page [7] Preface. Pages [4-6]
Includes Index. Pages:[132-139] Bibliography Pages:[167-174]

I. Plotnick, Jerome D. II. Title Meta Your Health in 45 Days
III. I.B.S.N.-10#-1451593171 & I.S.B.N.-EAN 13#:-9781451593174
IV. Published by 21st Century Energetics, Lake of the Woods,
California 93225 V. Distributed by Amazon.com/books, B&N.com
VI. Printed in the United States of America by Createspace.com

Afterwards For Cancer What's the Answer? Book #2

A Word From the Author
21st CENTURY ENERGETICS
"MENTAL-BODY-SPIRITUAL SPA"

~PRESENTS~

THE MENTAL-BODY-SPIRITUAL SPA PROGRAM
A BIOENERGETIC, NATUROPATHIC, HOLISTIC, SPIRITUAL APPROACH TO RESTORE VITALITY, POWERS OF MIND-BODY-SPIRIT, WHOLENESS, AND WELLNESS IN 45 DAYS. The program is designed specifically for professional athletes, martial artists, actors, stunt people, child athletes, other interested lay people, and professionals. Chapters-14 Afterwards-6-177 pgs. How to eliminate and prevent cancer holistically, alternatively, biologically, holistically. Afterward VII-160 pgs.-177-337 Cancer What's the Answer?

This book will explain in detail the why's and how's of the program. It will also give detail information on the program steps as well as the history, case studies, and other related information on the program. This program was developed and formulated by Jerome Plotnick, Ph.D., N.D. The program is 21st Century Cutting Edge Energetic Modern Naturopathic Medicine and Bio-energetic Technology Today combined with Natures Ancient Healing Wisdom.

The brain-mind is the highest center which we retrain through E.E.G. brainwave neurofeedback training. The body-brain is prepared for a safe detoxification called "Opening Channels" or Liquid Needle pre detoxification program. This is followed by a natural energetic detoxification program. The brain-body is energetically cleansed using a safe and natural energetic detoxification process. After detoxification we supply the brain-body with pure-natural vitamins, minerals, amino acids, herbs, elements, essential oils, energetic topicals, and O2-O3 for the necessary nutrients needed for optimum functioning. Once we renergixe and optimize your immunme system through the aforementioned you will able to protect yourself, resist from all disease invaders, increase energy, vitality, and balance.

Then we implement E.M.G. biofeedback training for stress reduction, muscle re-education, and coordination. We also perform E.E.G. brainwave training for mental fitness, focus, concentration, attention, alertness, relaxation, and peak performance.

A mind is a terrible thing to waste. Create success not stress. Stressors cause symptoms in the body's physiology. E.M.G. biofeedback teaches you new coping skills to alleviate of stressful symptoms. Mind-Body awareness through E.M.G. Biofeedback training=health and harmony. Gain your optimum potential, paint a new portrait, and create a new you. Restore your powers of mind. Re-balance your brain and increase focus, attention, concentration, relaxation, mental fitness, and peak performance through E.E.G. Neurofeedback training.

Health=A person is what they eat, drink, assimilate, think, and a free spirit. Heal the spirit, spirit heals the mind, and the mind heals the body. Dis-ease is caused by what their body cannot eliminate called toxins. Restore your brain-body with an energetic light photon frequency, safe fifteen day bath soak detoxification program. This is followed by supplying your body with the necessary nutrients needed for maximum performance.

Naturopathic prescription Rx-Take positive mental vitamins, super whole food supplements, organic vegetables, fruits, whole grains, seeds, nuts, pure water, pure air-03, ionic minerals, enzymes, amino acids, O2, spagyric herbs, flower essences, homeopathic, energetic light photon remedies, and topicals. Spiritual recovery through Bach flower essences, visage cards, affirmations, 12-13 Spiritual Steps, and meditation. Gain your optimum potential paint a new portrait and a new you.

The 21st Century Energetics Mental-Body-Spiritual Spa Program is specifically designed for professional athletes, martial artists, child athletes, actors, C.E.O.'s, and other professionals that require optimum performance, mental fitness, higher ability, a body capable of high peak performance, coordination, muscle leverage, and stamina required for performing difficult tasks.

After a 30 day detoxification and 9 day blood purification we replenish the body with the necessary nutrients to reinstate a healthy body. Once the brain-body is cleansed we implement the E.E.G. neurofeedback for relaxation, focus, attention, alertness, mental fitness, and peak performance. Then E.M.G. Biofeedback training is implemented for stress reduction, coping skills, muscle re-education, strength, and coordination. Elimination of all erroneous zero order cognitive core beliefs. Thereafter a maintenance program is implemented. The Tao of the Soul-Self-Slate audio. I use Chi Gong. ExStress, and L.N.T.B.

We hope you will join us and accomplish your dreams and achieve your highest potential. Create a new you with the 21st Century Energetics "Mental-Body-Spiritual Spa" Program. For program costs and schedules or for further information please e-mail, fax, write or call us today: 6132 Frazier Mt. Pk. Rd. #45, Lake of the Woods, CA. 93225 Web: 21stCenturyEnergetics.com Phone: (661) 245-3616 E-Mail:plotnickj@yahoo.com

This book is an adjunct to the "13 Steps From Illness to Health" AMNBPDR Alternative Preventive Naturopathic Bioenergetic Medicine Physicians Desk Reference book by Jerome Plotnick, Ph.D., N.D. See 21st Century Energetics books and ordering information on Page 128 Pages 116-117 to order this and other books by Jerome Plotnick, Ph.D., N.D., 21st CENTURY ENERGETICS, 6132 Frazier Mt. Pk. Rd. #45, Lake of the Woods, CA. 93225 Phone:(661) 245-3616 E-mail:plotnickj@yahoo.com Book(s)Avialable@amazon.com/books U.S, Amazon E.U., U.K., createspace.com direct, Libraries, and Academic Institutions, plus 20 or more online wholesale and retail book store outlets world-wide, & @ Barnes&Noble.com/nook/books Web:21stcenturyenergetics.com, Jerome Plotnick, Ph.D., N.D @ 21stCenturyEnergetics@Linkedin.com, Jerome Plotnick, Ph.D., N.D.@ 21st Century Energetics@face book.com

~FOREWORD~

This book is dedicated to all mankind to enable humanity to gain knowledge to transform and transpsycheate © the mind-body to spirit connection. Transform means going beyond your form or body. Transpsycheate(c) a new word I coined (created) means to go beyond your mind. Within a 45 day time period we are able to detoxify your body-brain energetically then replace the necessary nutrients for maximum rejuvenation, restore your powers of mind-body with both biofeedback, and neurofeedback training. Once re-established with brainwave balance, stress reduction, coping skills, muscle re-education, powerful energetic nutrients and substances that restore the brain-body with the necessary fuels that enable wholeness, and wellness. From a point of light from the mind of God let health, healing, and happiness return to the Earth's multitude. Let God's plan and will be done on Earth. Nature's ancient healing wisdom from the Great Physician, the 21st century modern cutting edge energetic medicine, and technology.

About the author Jerome Plotnick, Ph.D., N.D., C.B.F.Th., C.N.F.Th., C.C.D.C.S., C.T.F.H.I, and C.M.Hy.Th. Jerome Plotnick is a Naturopathic Physician, Behavioral & Counseling Psychologist, Biofeedback and Neurofeedback Therapist-Practitioner, Certified Chemical Dependency Counseling Specialist, Certified Acupressure-Touch for Health Instructor-A.K. Practitioner, Certified Master Hypno-Therapist, Psycho-Physiologist, and Pranic Healer that specializes in naturopathic (natural medicine), bio-energetic medicine, behavioral medicine, E.M.G. Biofeedback, and E.E.G. neurofeedback training for addictions, A.D.D., A.D.H.D., L.D., O.C.D., P.T.S.D., depression, anxiety, mental fitness, peak performance, stress reduction, coping skills, muscle re-ed, and pain control. Dr. Plotnick uses only physicians pure spagyric potent grade Asian, Ayurveda, Amazon, American herbal medicine, clinical and classical homeopathy, Bach flower essences, energetic light photon substances, energetic detoxification, and essential "A" oils. Dr. Plotnick is also a meditation instructor of both Eastern & Western disciplines. He uses creative visualization, guided imagery, autogenics, brain wave entrainment both audio-visual stimulation, scripting for life goals, and etc. Dr. Plotnick also uses an energetic needle-less acupuncture topical that is 1,000 times more powerful than normal needle acupuncture treatment. He also employs non-touch chiropractic an energetic

9

topical for all vertebra subluxation that reinstates a normal functioning vertebra, and spinal nerves such as L4, C2, etc. Dr. Plotnick is the author of several books called: "Meta Your Meditation," "Meta Your Nutrition", "Meta Your Mind," The 13 Steps from Illness to Health"-APNBMPDR-Alternative Preventive Naturopathic Bio-energetic Medicine Physician's Desk Reference, "Mind Memes-Miasms-Viruses Mind Takeover to a Mind Healing Makeover,""Bio-energetic, Mind, & Natural Medicine", "Meta Your Manifestation," Tao of the Soul-Self-Slate, and The 13th Step for Total Addiction Recovery." Dr. Plotnick also has designed several programs called 21st Energetics Mental-Body-Spiritual Spa mind-body-brain fitness and peak performance for professional athletes, actors, C.E.O.'s, and other professionals, Emmanuel- H.E.L.P. Drug-Alcohol-Processes Recovery program as well as formulating special herbal remedies called 21st Century Energetics: Mormon's Tea Herbal Detox, Can Kill, Can Cell, Gemma Stone Organic Radiation, Infection Fighter +, plus individual herbal extracts such as Olive Leaf, Pine Bark, Turmeric, Frankincense, Myrrh, Una de Gato-Cat's Claw, Milk Thistle, Rose Hips and Flowers, Chaparral, Lamb's Ear, Ma Huang, Sheep Sorrel, Burdock Root, Oregano, 7 C's Curry-Corriander-Cummin-Cloves-Cardamon-Cinnamon-Cilantro, Celtic Sea Salt, Pau d'Arco, Barberry, and Bee Pollen.

Jerome Plotnick, Ph.D.,N.D. is a consultant to all cancer patients wanting to perform alternative medicine and for those on conventional oncology treatment as an adjunct, addiction patients, mental fitness and peak performance for athletes, professional baseball players, martial artists, actors, stunt people, children athletes such as cheerleaders, acrobatics, and dancers, etc.

He is also a detoxification specialist, chemical dependency, process addiction, and a counseling specialist. Also a holistic health rest-oral naturopathic, bio-energetic counselor, and practitioner. A detoxification specialist. A wellness consultant. An Independent Professional Wellness Consultant, a holistic mind-body-spiritual guide, and counselor.

URGENT TOXICITY REPORT FROM THE E.P.A.!

During controlled studies, 100% of human body fat samples contained doses of chemicals including styrene (Styrofoam), diclorbenzene mothballs, household cleaners and (deodorizers) xylene, or benzene found in paints, gasoline, and D.D.T.,which has been banned since 1972. The five (5) most toxic metals are: lead, mercury, cadmium, beryllium, and antimony. These metals are involved in at least 50% of all deaths in the U.S. and much of the disabling diseases. Many of these are used in the chemical trails.

Possibly the most urgent need in your life is getting rid of heavy metals and chlorinated solvents from your cellular tissues. There are over 25,000 chemicals being used and released into our environment daily. All of them are extremely hazardous to your health. Recent studies have shown that one any combination of 3 chemicals are absorbed by the body the combined effect (toxic cocktail) is as much as 5,000 times more toxic than any one by itself. These chemicals take up residency and live in your body's fat and tissue linings. They can fool your body into believing they are hormones, create havoc with your emotions, and physical stamina. It takes your skin only 26 seconds to absorb any toxin.

Every year over 1,000 new chemicals are formulated and put into our environment by chemical corporations. Less than 5% are tested for safety or health concerns. In the U.S., state, and federal guidelines do not require testing prior to use. Most of the wealthy countries of the world are influenced by giant chemical corporations who continue to perpetuate their belief that the government should not "hamper or impede" scientific progress.

Possibly the truth may be that chemical companies are providing the answer to controlling the immense world population by the creation and utilization of these untested chemicals. It can take decades before physical evidence indicates a particular chemical or drug has been harmful. Around 99.99% of all chemicals are toxic. Consider glyphosate, formaldehyde, aluminum, and, mercury.

Governments have to deal with the "Greater or Common Good of ALL People." This means that anything that would potentially harm the country as a whole must be kept from the general population. This leaves us currently with the burden of using our common sense and learning to read between the lines.

Therefore, corporations will not inform you that their products are dangerous to your health and for you not to buy their products. The government can do nothing that would cause the nation's gross national economy to be compromised. It is really up to you to protect yourself and others with study, proper detoxification, derive protection against the unsafe concentration of chemicals, and heavy metal poisoning. Arthur Widgery President of D.N.R., Inc., Indiana 1991

21st Century Energetics offers you a 15 day program for eliminating heavy metal toxicity. It is safe, cost effective, and cutting edge technology. Rather than use the organs of elimination described later in the book we employ a natural energetic frequency detoxification that eliminates the toxins through the body's dermal (skin) and out into the bath water. That's right you take a series of 5-9 baths and take one internal remedy three (3) times per day. You will actually see after a few bath soaks the removed body's physical toxins enter into the bath water.

This energetic detoxification is suggested for heavy metal, chemo, radiation, lymph, chemical, virus, fungal, and bacterial toxicity. You may experience some symptoms such as sleepy, tired, fatigued, and light headed. This is a natural part of cleansing.

In the back of this book are listed all our programs and products and costs that will allow you to detoxify and restore, rejuvenate, re-establish, renew, replenish, resurrect your spirit, brain-mind, body-(immune-nervous-acupuncture-chakra-organ-gland systems), blood, brain, your being to a higher state of health, wellness, and wholeness.

The cost of our pre-detoxification program Liquid Needle E.V.B. is $137.00 followed by our natural primary energetic detoxification program cost of $500.00 Total program is $1000.00 and it takes 45 days. After which for $80.00-$200.00 you can purchase the finest health super whole food supplements available in the world, other energetic, and health related products. Is your health and well being worth spending money of $1000.00? Liquid Needle light photon energy products are now being implemented by myself, other Naturopaths, and Holistic Medical doctors. Illness can cost you thousands of dollars and even your life. It is up to you what do you choose health? or illness?

Look at yourself as a fine sports car such as a Ferrari, a fine expensive machine. Put in substandard fuel. Your Ferrari won't run as good as high octane fuel. Read this book for the energy fuel.

You will find the how's and why's and if you participate you will be able to restore your health, vitality, powers of mind-body to spirit connection of wellness, and wholeness in 45 days.

After you read this book and perform the 21st Century Energetics detoxification and maintenance program tell a friend about "Meta Your Health in 45 Days" it is the best favor you can bestow on anyone. Cancer patients read the chapter Cancer whats the Answer?

May Blessings Abound, Profound Peace, and Healing Permeate You.
Yours In Health, Love, Namaste.
Jerome Plotnick, Ph.D., N.D., N.C., H.H.C.

NOTE!
After Thoughts: With the current daily toxic poisons being dropped upon us from chem trails: Barium, Strontium, Aluminum, Lithium, and Cadmium. etc. Then the deadly toxic form of sodium fluoride and chromium valence-6 in our nations drinking water, toxic toiletries, fracking waste toxic chemicals in our ground water and oceans, glyphosphate "Roundup" another deadly chemical in our ground water and foods, factory farmed foods where heavy metals are used in growing, G.M.O.'s, E.M.F.'s, radiation coming from the recent Japanese Fukushima nuclear disaster on our farms, grazing fields, in our Pacific ocean, coal, aluminum, chromium valance-6, concrete manufacturing wastes that are airborne toxins, lastly the use of F.D.A. approved toxic synthetic drugs, and medicines that directly kill 300,000 people annually. It is imperative that every person becomes aware and knows that our government is no longer protecting us. We must take personal responsibility and learn how we can eliminate these deadly toxins (both the physical and frequency parts)in a safe, secure, successful manner, that is both quick, and cost effective. I have the antidote detoxification remedies listed in this book for your life saving and health restoration. Yours in Health, Jerome Plotnick, Ph.D., N.D.

<u>A 21st Century Naturopathic, Bio-energetic, Holistic, Spiritual Approach, and combined with Nature's Ancient Healing Wisdom. 21st Century Cutting Edge Energetic Medicine Today</u>! Brain-Body-Spa.

This program is designed to both restore the body (soma), the mind (psyche), the spirit (shen), and the vital energy (chi-elan vital) to be restored within 45 days. First the body is prepared for a detoxification called a pre-detoxification. This takes 3 days, followed by a series of 5 bath soaks, and every 3 days for a 15 day energetic natural detoxification.

A series of 5 bath soaks are usually implemented depending on what toxin you are removing and the taking of an internal energetic remedy. The body is initially prepared by restoring minerals, intestinal flora, amino acids, and vitamins. This allows the body to cleanse at a slow rate in a safe and secure manner. Once the body is re-established we implement a safe and natural energetic detoxification in a series of 3 bath soaks, 3 internal remedies, and the energetic remedy E.V.B. that initiates the energetic detoxification process. This energetic process actually pushes the toxins through the skin out of the body-brain into the bath water.

This is not a colon cleanse, colonic, homeopathic, or herbal normal detoxification using liver, lungs, colon, and kidneys to remove toxins. Toxins from the five toxic groups lodge themselves in the lipids (fat cells) and the extra-cellular fluid around the cells and intra-cellular fluid in the cell itself. This poisons the cell and its E.M.F. (electro-motive-force) is not able to function due to the interference caused by the toxins within intra cellular and outside the cell extra cellular that stop the normal cell-to-cell communications. Once the body is engaged in attempting to rid itself of the toxins and in most cases due to the amount of toxin, severity of toxin, location of toxin, emotional state, stress factors, and it cannot. This is the acute state of toxic disease which displays many symptoms and eventually the body compensates itself for the toxic load and enters a chronic state of disease. i.e. the polio vaccine is associated with C.F.S. There are 8 stages of bio-acumulation (toxicity).

Hence we have the modern-day symptoms of C.F.S. (chronic fatigue syndrome), autoimmune disorders (lupus, I.B.S. colitis, ulcers, cancer, diabetes, premature aging, and dementia (Alzheimer's),

14

etc. These are usually combined in the body to form a toxic cocktail. i.e. C.F.S. is associated with polio shots. Zoster virus "Shingles" with measles. D.P.T. vaccine with autism, and cancer.

This is called a "ping pong effect" that interferes with the cell communications and is called interference, causes a toxic condition that result in premature disease, and death. Most modern day illness is caused by this toxic interference. The cells cannot carry on their vital communications and functions. The electro-motive-force a cell's ability to do its assigned duty is disabled. There are many suppressive therapies that mask symptoms and drugs used to stop symptoms, but these are superficial treatments that do not get to the underlying cause(s) of all disease-illness. Today while billions of dollars are being spent on drugs and allopathic medicines our state of health in the U.S. is declining. You ask why? Because we are toxic from the five (5) toxic groups, eating substandard factory farmed, G.M.O.'s, non foods that are toxic, depleted of energy (frequencies)-vitamins-minerals-elements all of the nutrients needed to maintain a healthy body-brain, and wellness. While this is occurring we have a health care system designed to treat disease symptoms and not prevent or treat the cause(s) of illness. What can we do about it?

This book will explain the why's, how's, and what's. It will give you the necessary information to change your life simply, safely, in a short time period, and with proven dynamic results. While the so called health system costs are staggering with little results that allow for a drug free life and vitality. We offer an alternative that is cost effective and can be accomplished in a short time period. Once we rid the spirit-body-mind of toxins safely we restore vital nutrients in a spagyric, energetic, and ionic form. The body can absorb the nutrients easily for assimilation. Most over-the-counter vitamins, minerals, herbs are not assimilated due to the form there in, and especially people over forty years old cannot absorb them. These methods allow for the restoration of cells, tissues, organs, blood, lymph, and muscles, etc. Read: Dead Doctors Don't Lie by Dr. Joel Wallach, D.V.M., N.D., The 13 Steps From Illness To Health by this author.

Once accomplished and along with this process we restore brainwave balance with E.E.G. training which restores your powers of mind. Have you heard the mind affects the body and vice verse. Well it's absolutely true. It has been shown and research confirms that re-balancing or resetting the brains' waves at specific scalp sites can restore not only your mental functioning but also eliminate depression, addiction, anxiety, and hypertension. It will allow for relaxation, cognitive flexibility, maximum function, focus, concentration, mental fitness, and peak performance. We implement both E.M.G. biofeedback for self regulation of body functions, stress reduction, relaxation, muscle re-education, leverage, and pain control. We also implement an "Act of Forgiveness" allowing the participant to become an excretor of toxins, surrender, acceptance, and 12-13 Step program of recovery one day at a time. Also: Liquid Needle's: L.N.T.B., Chi Gong, ExStress,-pgs. 287-310

The best medicine is to give no medicine but rather to teach healing the mind-body to spirit through love, forgiveness, acceptance, modern bio-energetic technology, and nature. This is a bio-energetic, naturopathic, holistic, biological, a spiritual approach to wellness, and wholeness.

The doctor of the future will give no medicine but rather teach the patient care of the mind (psyche), the human frame (soma), and spirit (shen-spirit'us). To attain health-wellness one must study nature and its ancient wisdom. The mind-body to spirit must be detoxified and renewed. This program contains natural medicine, prayer, bio-meditation, organic food, positive mental vitamins, meaning and purpose, W.L.W.P.-work, love, worship, play, and exercise. To be or not to be that is the question? Be in Love with the creator-God, Be in Nature, Be in Love, Be Happy, Because-Be for a cause, Be all you can be, Be yourself, Be truthful, Become-Be your dreams, Be humble-humility, Be reverent, Be accepting, Be forgiving, Be thankful for your blessings, Be helpful and serve humanity, Be, and just Be called Being-ness. This book is dedicated to all who serve our creator May the Divine Universal Mind's will be done on Earth as it is in the Universe.

"God grant me the wisdom to change the things I can, the courage to accept the things I cannot change, and the wisdom to know the difference." Bill Wilson A.A. The meeting ending words.

Mind consciousness is the universal Law of Creation. Mind reproduces itself and creates your reality.

The Great Invocation.

From a point of Light within the Mind of God,
Let Light stream forth into the minds of men,
Let Light descend on Earth,
From a point of Love within the Heart of God, Let Love stream
forth into the hearts of men,
May Christ return to the Earth,
From the centre where the Will of God is known,
Let purpose guide the little wills of men,

The purpose which the Masters know and serve,
From the centre which we call the race of men,
Let the Plan of Love and Light work out,
And may it seal the door where evil dwells,
Let Light, Love and Power restore the Plan on Earth.

The Lord's Prayer.

Our Father who art in heaven,
Hallowed be thy name,
Give us this day our daily bread,
Forgive our trespassing as those who trespass against us,
Lead us from temptation and deliver us from evil,

For thine is the kingdom and the glory and the power,
Forever and ever. AMEN

CHAPTER ONE

Toxins the Major Cause of Disease.

The human system has the following sources of toxic disturbances:
1. Inherited Toxic Information (Miasms)-Genetic Disorders or Inherited Toxins and these can be removed by a certain homeopathic remedy. [Miasms, Meme's, Viruses, and Energetic Foci]
2. Spiritual Toxins-and the 7 Deadly Sins and the 11 Mental Terror States. The 7 Deadly sins are: Pride, Cruelty, Hate, Self-love, Ignorance, Instability, and Greed. The 11 mental terror states are: fear, worry, indecision, boredom, doubt, over-concern, weakness, self-distrust, uncertainty, impatience, and over enthusiasm. These can be eliminated by a 12 step spiritual program of recovery, shamanistic program for removal of passed down family inherited curses through a shaman and prayer, exorcism, flower essences (Bach remedies) called Fields of Flowers, or flower power, Rescue Calm, Chi Gong, L.N.T.B., ExStress, and E.E.G. neurofeedback alpha-theta deep states hypnogogic trance state training. The audio program "The Tao of the Soul-Self-Slate."
3. Physical Toxins-Metabolic Waste-Free Radical Waste-Digestive Waste-Natural Environment Pollutants-Immunizations-Biological Organisms (bacterial-viral-fungal) and their By-Products-Residues of Medicinal and Recreational Drugs. These can be removed through the 21st Century Energetics pre detoxification and detoxification program. This is a complete natural safe energetic detoxification program offered by Jerome Plotnick, Ph.D., N.D.
4. Mental-Emotional Toxins-Disease forming belief system-emotional-physical traumas-Negative-hurtful subconscious-Learned negative habit patterns. We remove them by E.M.G. and E.E.G. biofeedback-neurofeedback.[Alpha-Theta amd deep states training]
5. External Energy Field Disturbances-Geopathic Stress-WiFi-E.M.F.'s-Electromagnetic-Radiation-Frequency Disturbances. These are removed by 21st Century Energetics pre-detoxification and energetic detoxification program. Complete natural energetic detoxification program. Ongoing daily remedy(s) for prevention. When these toxins from the five (5) toxic groups are in a persons body-brain a toxic cocktail is formed called the "ping pong effect" causing serious effects on our immune, nervous, body systems, and brain. These can cause acute to chronic toxic disease symptoms and even death. This is why it is essential to use the 21st Century Energetics proven pre-post detoxification and natural

health restoral programs. The normal time period for this complete health restoral program is 45 days. The toxins are removed slowly, and safely out of the body-brain through your skin in fifteen (15) days in a series of five (5) bath soaks.

A nine (9) day inner cleansing blood purification program and diet are implemented to cleanse the blood. A lymphatic cleansing and toning program helps the lymph system remove toxins from the body as well. Despite the sincere efforts of the F.D.A., E.P.A., etc., our drinking water, food supply are extremely contaminated with toxic chemicals, and other toxins as mentioned previously in the five (5) toxic groups. In addition, there is excessive use of over-the-counter, prescription drugs, and medicines, etc. Most of which are petroleum, chemically based, and highly toxic to the brain-body. Some of these drugs prescribed have worse side effects than what they are being used for. Besides the building up of a tolerance to these drugs more is needed and this adds to the already toxic system. Also when combined for example with other drugs they form a toxic cocktail in the brain-body system. Note! Fluoride and Chlorine are highly toxic. Nitrites over 1 p.p.m, nitrates over 10 p.p.m. are highly toxic and carcinogenic.

Most of our modern day symptoms are caused by this toxic cocktail including auto immune disorders, etc. Is it any wonder why people are so sick today? And why they still continue down this pathway? People are creatures of habit and products of their environment, are easily mislead, and looking for a quick fix to their health problems. The pharmaceutical industry spends millions advertising. They earn billions on their drugs, medications half of which are useless, disease causing themselves, not to mention how expensive, and addictive. The answer to toxic disease is to remove the toxins, then treat your water, food, and environment including your spirit-brain-mind-body with light photon frequency substances that will counter the harmful effects of toxins.

This is accomplished by the following steps provided by 21st Century Energetics by Jerome Plotnick, Ph.D., N.D.
1. Avatar E.A.V. analysis or goEnergetix.com test kit. Discover minute bio-energetic disturbances before they become major and indicate what is needed for elimination of them. The Energetix's test kit indicates, tests one hundred and fifteen (115) remedies. A.K., T.F.H. acupuncture points, and meridian testing.

2. <u>Liquid Needle E.V.B.</u> pre detoxification program prepares the body so a slow, safe energetic detoxification can be implemented. Or O.C.consists of: (ReHydration-Amino Catalyst-7-Colon Clear-Pure Body-Flora Synergy-Spectramin). Thirty (30) days to complete.

3. Energetic Light Photon detoxification program-Energetically pushes the toxins out of the body and into the bath water after a series of five (5) bath-soaks and one (1) internal energetic remedy called E.V.B. The internal remedy helps break up the toxins for easy removal. It takes fifteen (15) days to complete.

4. Energetic Light Photon Substance for treatment of food, water, and brain-body daily detoxification. Keeps what you eat, drink, non-toxic, and safe for 32 hours. Taken internally, topically or soak your food in it. <u>Liquid Needle Yellow-Y-116EX</u>

5. Energetic Light Photon Substance for food, water, and nutrient enhancement up to a 4-6 time frequency increase in nutrient value. Energetic Light Photon Substance to increase energy, vitality, and balance of body-brain. Provides high stamina, energy, and vitality. <u>Liquid Needle E.V.B.</u> <u>Liquid Needle Green-G-120EX</u> for #5.

6. Daily herb-botanical, homeopathics, light photon solutions to remove radiation, electro-magnetic energy, and E.M.F.'s, etc. <u>Liquid Needle's Can-133</u> and <u>Coffee-130EX</u> Bath Soaks.

7. Energetic Light Photon Substance topically applied for re-energizing your chakras, acupuncture meridian system, and your biofields. <u>Liquid Needle Original</u> and <u>L.N.T.B.</u>

8. Daily homeopathic remedies for drainage, tonification, detoxification, and adaptation. Taken internally <u>Liquid Needle's H.B.H.</u> Series. Homeopathic, Bontanical, Herbal.

9. Daily whole food super supplements to eliminate and keep toxins and free radicals at a minimum level. A ¼ of a teaspoon a day keeps the doctor away and provides vitamins, minerals, herbs, phytomins, antioxidants, and essential oils, etc. This whole food super supplement contains everything needed for a healthy body-brain. The ingredients are organic and in the proper ratios so the compliment (synergistic) with each other as well as spagyric formulated. This is how the body wants its vitamins, minerals, herbs, and antioxidants. The body wants a natural state and at the high energy (frequency) potential. <u>Liquid Needle's Green G-112EX</u>

10. Daily Heart Studies Formula that supplies the heart with every nutrient it needs for maximum functioning, and health. Also N.O.

11. Daily ionic amino acids, cell salts-minerals, enzymes, and 02. <u>Liquid Needle Green, ENZ, MIN, VIT, Oxymoxy, Hydroxygen Plus, and Dr. Schusslers cell salts</u>. Taken internally.

How toxins interfere in cell-brain-body communications. A toxin is a negative frequency that interferes with your body cells communication system. This system keeps your spirit-brain-body functioning at its optimal potential. But just like a radio station that you are listening to when static or interference that block the normal operating frequency of the radio station you can't hear the sound. The same takes place within the brain-body. They respond to the highest frequency even if the frequency is a negative disturbance. We know that we can counter these harmful toxic frequencies by removing-blocking-countering them with higher frequencies, then by putting positive-resonant-beneficial frequencies back into the system, to restore, and re-balance the system. Use of <u>Liquid Needle's Original</u> to energize the biofield.

We operate on frequency this is how the body works. Even a medicine that is given alters, or changes the body's response to the condition, and illness, etc. This is called a signature frequency that all things in Nature resonate at. The immune system at 68-72 MHz then begins to heal the illness. This is how medicine whether allopathic or naturopathic works. Naturopathic medicine from nature works better because it is in harmony with your body. "Like cures like," or in Latin means "Similia-Similbus-Curentur." Allopathic medicine works against the body or unlike cures like. Natural medicine has no side effects. Unnatural medicine is poison and has side effects, and residues that are harmful to the body. Over time these are negative frequencies that cause illness. The toxins are hard to remove because they lodge in the lipids (fat cells) and the extra-cellular fluid around the cells. Normal colonics, colon cleanses, or even herbal detoxification just cannot remove all of these toxins. They only superficially act and remove only some of the toxins. <u>Only your body can heal itself</u>.

The detoxification program and protocol I employ and in this book removes all the toxins safely, and naturally within 45 days as advertised. There are no gimmicks and the program is the most effective in the world. Again the following four (4) steps must be employed to gain good health.
1. Reduce our susceptibility to toxins.
2. Detoxify the body. (21st Century Energetics 45 Day program).
3. Clean up our home, work, and recreational environments.(Purchase an electro (electric)-sensor).
4. Reduce or prevent future toxic exposure. Use Liquid Needle.

The 21st Century Energetics program deals effectively with all four of these steps ensuring a healthy, vital, energetic brain-body, and free of harmful toxins. Low level toxicity from a variety of sources can be very difficult to detect. The combined actions of these toxins create a "toxic cocktail" effect which can seriously weaken the spirit-mind-body connection making you extremely susceptible to stress and illness. Many of the symptoms of such toxins are usually not correlated to the presence of them. Most conventional medical testing often does not have an explanation for the symptoms. They diagnose many symptoms as "psychosomatic" disorders. Many people die because of misdiagnosis of symptoms. I know of a case where an ulcerated colon was misdiagnosed and a psychiatrist was prescribed instead of emergency treatment for a burst colon causing peritonitis. They told her it was in her head when it was in the colon. This lady died from the peritonitis. Peritonitis kills you if not treated immediately. So if the hospital doctors can misdiagnose peritonitis you can only imagine what they do for symptoms of toxic exposure. Some symptoms of toxicity may take years to manifest after the initial exposure, this makes it extremely difficult to correlate the toxins with the symptoms.

Conventional medical laboratory tests usually will not indicate the presence of toxins in the body unless an autopsy toxicologist is employed usually after you die. Only a duly qualified environmental toxicologist preventive medical doctor such as Dr. Murray Susser of Santa Monica, California or Dr. Stephen Edelson of Atlanta, Georgia can diagnose toxic disease. Bio-energetic practitioners can also diagnose toxic disease. Symptoms can be daily, on, off, or rarely. Ignoring these symptoms of failing to detoxify the body will eventually lead to chronic systemic toxicity (toxemia or septic dysbiosis), which eventually results in a (systemic infection or blood poisoning-peritonitis), causes severe damage to the internal organs, or tissues. When you detoxify you may encounter a "healing crisis." If flu like symptoms or any other symptoms manifest then you must stop for a day or so and then continue slowly. Sauna baths, massage, meditation, scrubs, dry skin brushing, deep breathing, and drinking distilled ozonated (03), hydrogen H-ion water, and with organic lemon juice will help the process.

Another issue is that some people are more susceptible to toxins than others. Amount of exposure, frequency of the exposure, state of their elimination, the filtering organs, and tolerance to a toxic substance determine the level of toxicity. The state of health, emotional state, and inherited constitutional-genetic weaknesses also play a role. An example would be that an alcoholic who already has a stressed liver. Alcoholics also have deep seated emotional problems. Exposure to a toxin to this person may have more serious consequences than for a person who is in excellent physical and emotional health. Metabolism that slows down can be dangerous as well. The sediment from metabolic waste can deposit in connective tissue and the outer walls of the blood vessels. This further progressive reduction of vital metabolic processes will alter the homeostatic capabilities of the body. Another problem is that substances outside the body such as by-products of metabolism, water, food, must be eliminated quickly to avoid depositing in the cells, and tissues. If the fluid that bathes the cells is congested, metabolic waste by-products will accumulate around their production sites. Heavy metals, chemicals, air, and water pollutants may deposit in the lipids, liver, kidney, reproductive organs, and nervous system. i.e. An overdose of ozone irritates the lungs, lead damages the brain, and pesticides cause liver, or kidney damage. Viruses, bacteria from infections killed by antibiotics also need to be eliminated, they will cause damage as well as existing micro-organisms that have by-products that enter extra-cellular fluid. or bloodstream can be distributed, and harmful throughout the body. i.e. L.D.L. arterial wall plaque.

The census among scientists is that the electromagnetic waves E.M.F. (frequencies) are more harmful than the biochemical reaction to the toxin. The energetic interference is distributed to the body's trillions of cells causing a breakdown in functions and causing severe symptoms. The outcome is cellular communication dysfunction. It goes through the eight stages of bioaccumulation.

The restoration of health and well-being. The human body usually has a remarkable capacity to neutralize and excrete toxins. In a healthy person when a toxin is present numerous enzymes, other molecules go into action, to prevent damage to cells, and tissues affected. Body mechanisms deactivate, chemically alter, and excrete toxins. i.e. lymphatic pus.

If the person is stressed, presently sick from bacterial, or viral infection, emotional trauma, high amounts of toxins, or a very noxious toxin. In this case the body's natural defenses become overloaded. When the body cannot detoxify itself the toxins tend to accumulate in and around the cells, causing direct, and indirect interference by accumulating in the extra-cellular fluid which slows down uptake, and release of cell metabolites that interferes with inter-cellular communications.

Normally the detoxification process is carried out by four (4) systems in the body which are respiratory, digestive, urinary, and dermal. These are supported by the blood and lymph systems. Kidneys excrete toxins in the urine, Liver through the bile, Skin from perspiration through the pores, Lungs from exhaled air. If a person is sad, suffering from grief, loss, and anguish this can block the lungs from excreting. The liver can block if a person is angry, or frustrated. The kidneys can block from excreting if a person is in fear or uncertainty. The dermal (skin) can block from excreting if a person is sad, and in grief. Fears and stressors.

Another important factor is called the toxic cocktail "ping pong effect." This is the redistribution of toxins from one tissue, cell, or organ to another. This is caused by toxins that dislodge, and instead of eliminating from the body, relocate, and cause reactions. This can occur when detoxification is premature and the body cannot handle the extra stress from stirred up toxins. Symptoms or suppressive treatments are used without eliminating the cause of the underlying pathology. Detoxification is performed while the organs of elimination organs are stressed, toxic, or sluggish. Deep level detoxification is performed before a pre or general detoxification program is accomplished.

To avoid the "ping pong effect" the following should be implemented.

1. Regulating the detoxification process as we provide in our natural energetic bath soak and internal energetic remedy. In a series of five (5) bath soaks the toxins are removed through the cells, tissues, blood, lymph, organs. and pushed out through the derma (skin) into the bath water. After the 2nd-3rd bath soak you can actually see the toxic residues in the water. The energetic light photon frequency internal remedy E.V.B. assists the body to

dislodge, and breakup for easy removal. This is a one of a kind process unique, unlike the traditional homeopathic, or herbal detoxification process. The removal of toxins does not stress out the system and works in a slow, safe, and positive manner. We also implement specific light photon frequency substances to support all organs of the body. We also use a light photon energetic frequency for calmness of mind while the detoxification process is implemented. This allows for an non-stressful period so the body can eliminate the toxins without adverse effects.(healing crisis) Proven results of this detoxification process are that since 1992 there have been no harmful effects, or problems noted by my self, and other health care practitioners. I have implemented and supervised the bath soak detoxification's from the manufacturer D.N.R., Inc. who has sold thousands of its detoxification products. No law suits or complaints to date have been noted. Liquid Needle is now F.D.A. approved. This is 21st century cost effective, cutting edge, energetic light photon medicine, and bio-technology today!

Bio-energetic Toxicology

1. As toxicity increases a person's digestion, absorption, and assimilation of nutrients is affected. Undigested food and their waste by-products in the toxic intestinal tract permit toxins to be absorbed into the blood, distribute throughout every cell including the brain, in some cases, and worsen an already toxic situation.
2. The body will attempt to defend itself and react through such health crises as colds, viruses, and bacterial infections. This forces us to slow down, rest to eliminate toxins through coughing, sneezing, runny nose, sweating, diarrhea, and fevers.
3. Oriental (Asian) medicine believes that all disease begins on an energetic level through life force (chi) disturbances. The chi is closely related to ones mental state. Once weakened a person begins to be affected by toxins, microorganisms, and disease. Toxins block the chi energy from flowing into the acupuncture meridians, and thus further weakening the system.
4. The chi energy acts like a compensatory system that allows the body to function even though it is in a state of acute or chronic toxic disease. Bio-energetic medicine of the West confirms the same findings of compensatory attributes that allow the body to minimally function in a toxic state. A toxic person may feel

25

somewhat normal even though they are experiencing a toxic condition as long as the chi energy remains strong. General fatigue, low vitality, mental confusion, or memory loss may be the only symptoms.
5. Severe emotional stress, traumatic injury, virus flu, death, or divorce of a loved one, and may suddenly cause an overload.
6. At this point the compensatory system will become ineffective and the patient will be more susceptible to disease and present a definite symptomatic picture. Also a low immunity W.B.C. count.

If the level of toxic bio-accumulation is high then there is pathology and symptoms. As it decreases the body restores to a healthy state and as it diminishes to almost or nothing then we have peak brain-body performance. In the "acute" symptoms state we may still have health.

1. <u>Homeostasis-health Homeostasis-elimination phase</u>: The body is detoxifying itself. It normally neutralizes the toxins in the liver and eliminates the through the feces, urine, sweat, menstrual flow, discharge from nose, mouth, and ears, etc.

2. <u>Acute Reaction phase</u>: The body does not succeed in eliminating the toxins by the elimination organs, but it will attempt to get rid of the toxins by acute reactions such as fever, vomiting, diarrhea, inflammation, flu, and eczema, etc.

<u>Energetic Disturbance-sub-clinical</u>:
3. <u>Bio-accumulation phase</u>: The body's elimination process fails to remove the toxin(s). The result is bio-accumulation and will lead to chronic cellular stress: benign tumors, gout, liver, kidney, and pancreas irritation, etc.

4. <u>Compensation phase</u>: This begins after the deposit of a toxin in or around the cell. This can take years, and depends on the body's compensatory capability.

5. <u>De-compensation phase</u>: The body can no longer compensate for the toxic disturbance. It will express its failure by symptoms: fatigue, acne, migraine and cluster headaches, chronic inflammation, P.M.S., allergies, and susceptibility to infections, etc.

<u>Biochemical disturbance-clinical</u>:
6. <u>Degeneration phase-1</u>: This is the result of the body's inability to effectively neutralize or eliminate the toxic disturbance. This is the beginning of the biochemical and histological changes caused by cell damage. This can result in osteoarthritis, emphysema, premature aging, and memory loss, etc.

<u>Histological disturbance-clinical</u>:
7. <u>Degeneration phase-2</u>: This is characterized by emotional and physical changes as the body reacts to degeneration and-or suppressive therapy (treating the symptoms not the underlying cause(s). The symptoms become unbearable and the usually the person will increase use of symptomatic remedies. Often they are depressed with increased mental anguish.

8. <u>Auto-immune neo-plastic phase</u>: In this phase depending on the persons genetics and immune system strength, the development of malignant tumors, or cancer may be present or in the precancerous state. Auto-immune reactions may also develop, and due to a furthered weak immune system. The body is in a severe disease state and becomes rigid and very difficult to help by any therapeutic program.

Enhance the detoxification process.
<u>The following can enhance the detoxification process</u>:
1. Exercise-Daily twenty (20)-thirty (30) minutes of exercise is recommended such as walking, any martial arts training, Tai Chi, Internal Kung Fu, swimming, jogging, cycling, dance, jump rope, and tennis, etc. Proper rhythmic deep breathing from the diaphragm controlled through the nose. See Meta Your Meditation Vol.1 & 2.
2. Nutrition-Removal of stress from the digestive system through good eating habits. Proper food combining is essential (see "Meta Your Nutrition") by Jerome Plotnick, Ph.D., N.D. for food combining or Dr. Gary Null's food combining book). Rotate foods for a variety such as protein, high complex carbohydrates, good fats, and whole grains. Eat simple foods not a wide variety at one time. Chew your food at least each bite ten (10) times until food liquefies. (See the eating meditation in "Meta Your Meditation" by Jerome Plotnick, Ph.D., N.D.). Do not drink liquids before the meal and wait 45-60 minutes after eating. People over 40 years of age should eat raw foods as much as possible, low cook foods under 118 degrees F. Take digestive enzymes such as Liquid Needle ENZ,

or Catalyst-U or, 7 a 21st Century Energetics distributed ionic enzymes to help digestion. Make your meal a meditation (see the "Eating Meditation") a spiritual feeding of your holy temple (body). Avoid junk foods, sodas, refined sugars, food additives, excess sodium (iodized salt), sweets, pies, cakes, cookies, processed, refined, and bleached foods. Test for food sensitive chemicals and usually do not eat any dairy products. Kefir or sauerkraut pre Biotics are highly recommended. Probiotics such as goEnergeix's FloraSynergy+, Dr. Nissel's-Mutaflor, and Oxymogen's-Glutaloemine are far much better. Keep vitamins and mineral supplementation at normal dosages. Use SpectraMin. Recommended is 21st Century Energetics distributed whole food supplements "Iredesca" or "Hydroxygen +" ionic amino acids, enzymes, and minerals. Celtic or Himalayan sea salt lightly sprinkled on food is beneficial to provide easy assimilated minerals and trace elements. Liquid Needle's-Green, VIT, MIN, and ENZ.

3. Other Adjuncts-Daily skin brushing. A weekly moist sauna or steam bath. Epsom salt added to a bath to remove toxins on the skin surface. Massage, Shiatsu, Jin Shin Do, Touch For Health, Acupressure, Internal Kung Fu, deep tissue, and lymph massage.

4. Emotional-Mental-Fields of Flowers, Rescue Calm, Bach Remedies such as Rock Rose, or Heather, or other mind calming essences such as Chi Gong topical, ExStress, aromatherapy, and essential oils. An "Act of Forgiveness," meditation, and self talk. Other factors to consider are: never suppress feelings and emotions, let it go, express emotions and frustrations constructively, direct, neutralize the negative energy in frustrations, negative thoughts through physical exercise, meditate, and pray. (see "Meta Your Meditation" by Jerome Plotnick, Ph.D., N.D.), cry, be patient, let go of pride, see other peoples perspective, change what can be changed, accept the things you cannot change, the wisdom to know the difference, do not attempt to control what cannot be controlled, have belief, faith, forgive, be pure in heart, unconditional acceptance, and unconditional love.

5. Relaxation-E.E.G. neurofeedback deep states alpha-theta brain wave training, a nap, and meditate. (see "Meta Your Meditation" by Jerome Plotnick, Ph.D., N.D.), breathing exercises, a walk in nature, listen to uplifting music, flotation tank, and laughter like watching funny movies. Things to remember: a negative thought is the absence of strength and immediately lowers your immune system function. Think positive thoughts always no matter what. The mind is the greatest healer. "See things as

already accomplished. Ask and ye shall receive."-Jesus Christ "Never, never, never give up."-Dr. Norman Vincent Peale. "Knock and the door shall be opened to you."-Jesus Christ. "The field of all possibilities is an invisible field that all things manifest from. So you can say that this is that, that is this, this is where you are, and that's it."-Deepak Chopra, M.D. "A golden thread runs through everything in existence and connects all together." "The best therapy is to awaken the healer within." Dr. Albert Schweitzer All is one, one is all, and all one GOD. Say and see in your mind's eye what it is you want. Be careful what you wish for as you might just get it. Manifest wisely.

NOTE! It is advised to receive your supplements in the form of super whole food supplements such as Liquid Needle's- Green, Vit, Min, Enz, Iredesca, Biomatrix, Etherium Super Energized Blends, Youngevity, and Greening Powder. These are specially formulated by nutritional experts that are totally natural, organic, spagyric, synergistically prepared for easy assimilation, and utilization. There are on the market presently copycat products which are not even close to the aforementioned products. Don't believe the hype they tell you as the product can never deliver a complete detoxification nor can it give you all the nutrients your body needs. Always consult with your licensed medical or alternative practitioner before you perform any detoxification. You should always be under the supervision of a detoxification specialist. If you believe the market ploys or pyramid marketing companies selling you inferior products you will be greatly disappointed. Remember if it's to good to be true it's not. Claims that cannot deliver the promised results. Also laughter called geotology is a great healer, body, gland, and organ harmonizer. Hugs increase a neurotransmitter that elevates moods and is an anti-depressive. Hug a tree also for increased life force energy. Earthing or walking barefoot on the earth increase the life force energy as well. Be in the sunshine daily as well as it also provides the cosmic prana energy. Deep Tibetan breathing exercises brings in the air globule prana. Spiritual exercises such as Tai Chi, Chi Gong, Internal Kung Fu, martial arts, or exercises like Tae Bo. Just a half ½ to one (1) hour in nature will increase your elan vital (life force energy) by ten (10) fold. The best therapy is no therapy. Rather training ones self such as cognitive behavior modification, meditation, self hypnosis, E.M.G. Biofeedback, E.E.G. Neurofeedback called self regulation, Oriental-Asian Acupuncture-Herbs. The ultimate therapy is none, its Mama Nature.

CHAPTER TWO

Pre-detoxification Program.

"Opening Channels" is the pre-detoxification Brain-Body Spa program that consists of the following: Rehydration, Amino-gest, Spectramin, Colon, Body Clear, Catalyst-7, and Flora Synergy. This is a specially formulated to provide the body with the necessary nutrients to provide a complete detoxification without any interference. If the body is prepared then the process goes smoothly without any problems. These cutting edge health detoxification products are from goEnergetix's.com

Rehydration provides the body with electrolytes necessary to prevent dehydration. It consists of: Adrenal 3x-6x-12x, A.T.P. 4x-6x—12x, Taraxacum Officinale 1x, Gaba 6x-12x-30x, Germanium Sesquiooxide 4x-6x-8x, Hypothalamus 3x-6x-12x, Kidney 3x-6x, Coffea Crude 1x, Serotonin 12x, Silica Tera 4x-6x-8x, Hypericum Performatum 3x-6x-12x, Distilled Water 70%, Glycerine 15%, and Ethanol 15%. For dehydration A.D.D.-A.D.H.D., depression, chiropractic adjustments not holding, corrects the left spinning and switching, elevated blood pressure, muscle cramping, P.M.S., menopausal disorders, chronic fatigue syndrome, adrenal mineral cortoid support, eczema not pitting, and photo phobic renal support.

Amino-Gest provides the body with predigested proteins from fish that provide the necessary amino acids. It consists of: Concentrated deep ocean white fish protein with Omega-3 fatty acids. For Irritable Bowel Syndrome-leaky gut, "Pre digested" protein Fibromyalgia, multiple digestive problems, heart support, increase H.D.L.'s, reduce L.D.L.'s, reduces cholesterol and triglycerides, intense protein. Supplementation easily assimilated immune insufficiency, Chronic Fatigue Syndrome, chronic wound skin healing, adjunctive cancer support, herpes lysine deficiency, hypertension nutritional support for digestive dysfunction, tissue damage, and protein-related conditions.-180 capsules.-$24.95

Spectramin provides the body with easily assimilated minerals and trace elements. It consists of: Magnesium, Chloride, Potassium Sulfate, Lithium, Sodium, and the following in naturally occurring amounts: Bromide, Calcium Carbonate, Fluoride, Silicon, Nitrogen,

Selenium, Phosphorous, Iodine, Chromium, Iron, Manganese, Titanium, Rubidium, Cobalt, Copper, Antimony, Arsenic, Molybdenum, Strontium, Zinc, Nickle, Tungsten, Scandium, Tin, Lanthanum, Yttrium, Beryllium, Silver, Uranium, Gallium, Zirconium, Vanadium, Beryllium, Tellurium, Bismuth, Hafnium, Terbium, Europium, Gadolium, Sonarium, Cerium, Cesium, Dysprosium, Holmium, Lutetium, Thallium, Erbium, Neodymium, Prasedymium, Hirmium, Niobium, Tantalum, Thorium, Thallium, Rhenium, and plus other elements found in sea water. For right spinning ionic trace minerals. Element depletion. Stress sustains custom imprint. 4 oz.-$19.50

Colon Clear provides the body with fiber that cleans the digestive-intestinal tract. It consists of: proprietary blend of organic wild crafted herbs in vegetarian capsules: Turkey Rhubarb, Cascara Sagada, Sage, Aloe, Barberry, Ginger, Black Walnut, Dandelion, Slippery Elm, Pure Body Clear, Colon Clear. all come together as a cleansing, and purification program. For: Intestinal cleansing and detoxification of Parasites, Candida, Diarrhea-Constipation, and Heavy Metals. Works in conjunction with Pure Body Clear. Opens the channels. 90 capsules.-$16.50

Pure Body Clear: It includes Pure Body Clear and Colon Clear. New Formula contains the following proprietary blend of organic or wild crafted herbs in vegetarian capsules: Milk Thistle, Turmeric, Artichoke, Schizandra, Rosemary, Dandelion, Yellow Dock, Gentian, and Barberry. For systemic cleansing and detoxification. Works well in conjunction with Colon Clear. Opens the channels.-$41.50

Catalyst-7 provides the body with protease, amylase, lipase, cellulose, lactase, inverase, maltase, and alpha-galarosidase in an herbal base containing barley grass, marshmallow, papaya, ginger, gentian, fennel, and anise.

Catalyst-U: This product has similar properties and action as Catalyst-7, however it is Protease free. 100% organic and gastric soothing, utilize it in the treatment of Gastritis, Chron's Disease, Ulcers, Heals the Mucosal Lining, Irritable Bowel Syndrome (I.B.S,), and Digestive Lesions.
Ingredients:
<u>Amylase</u>-aids in the digestion of starch and sugars.
<u>Lipase</u>-aids in the digestion of fats.
<u>Cellulase</u>-aids in the digestion of plant fiber.

<u>Lactase</u>-aids in the digestion of milk sugar.
<u>Sucrase</u>-aids in the digestion of sucrose.
<u>Maltase</u>-aids in the digestion of malt sugar.
In a proprietary blend of certified organic botanicals:
Marshmellow, Calendula, Chamomile, Slippery Elm-Traditionally used to heal, and soothe the mucous membranes.
Gentian-supports digestion; pH regulator; gastric relaxant; and promotes bile flow.
Ginger-antiviral; antibacterial; pH regulator; and may be indicated in H-Pylori bacteria in stomach.
Licorice-research shows it aids in gastric mucosal healing.
Lavender-anti-bacterial; anti-parasitic; anti-inflammatory; and gastric relaxant.
Gamma Oryzanol-a naturally-occurring component of rice bran oil. Significant research has determined significant therapeutic efficacy in gastrointestinal disorders such as ulcers, gastritis, and irritable bowel syndrome.
Flora-Synergy provides the body-intestinal tract with pro-biotics the necessary flora that promotes a healthy intestine and colon.
NOTE!
Don't be fooled by marketing ploys advertised as the super energy detox and nutrient drinks. Pure hype and absolutely no authentic double blind studies to prove their claims. There is absolutely no evidence that these products do what they claim. They have a pyramid marketing scheme and it is purely a money making venture. It cannot and doesn't compare to what I have in the 21st Century Energetics Health Rest-oral program. We first prepare the body for complete detoxification thereafter we begin to slowly remove all the toxins from the five (5) toxic groups. They offer a drink which will not remove the toxins in the lipids, and collagen, etc. Neither do they remove the spiritual toxins nor do they realign the brains frequencies necessary for a complete bio-field balancing. My method is proven authentic and not hype. Also if it's to good to be true it's not. Common sense should tell you that a drink or these advertised detoxiication foot pads won't be able to remove toxins from your system that are like glue. Only a pre program that supports, allows the cells to be able to release the toxins as well as a way to completely eliminate them safely, and become an excretor. This is described in my program. Many other researchers have designed along with my expertise the 21st Century Energetics 45 day detoxification and health rest-oral program. There are so many fads that are unproven that claim to do

what they are claiming but they are unproven placebos. My program is what is called an active placebo as it has an energetic action as well as a placebo action. I could take anything that I strongly believe in. Again to restore health, and detoxify properly: 1. prepare the body cells 2. minerals, vitamins, amino acids, enzymes, and probiotics 3. then begin to clear the body and colon 4. remove the spiritual toxins the seven (7) deadly sins & the eleven (11) mental terror states, etc. 5. then a fifteen (15) day Liquid Needle energetic detoxification that pushes the toxins out through your largest elimination organ your skin in a series of five (5) bath soaks. Elimination of the five (5) toxic groups. It is one hundred percent (100%) guaranteed and safe. It is also cost effective. F.D.A. approved through clinical trials.

CHAPTER THREE

The Detoxification Program.

After the pre-detoxification program is completed we proceed with the primary (post) detoxification program. This consists of taking an energetic light photon frequency internal remedy three (3) times per day and a series of five (5) baths every three days until fifteen (15) days have passed. After the second (2)nd-third (3)rd bath you will begin to actually see in the bath water the toxins removed into the water from out of your body.

While you accomplish the detoxification you should also drink distilled or purified water with lemon juice, dry skin brush, mild exercise such as walk, etc., meditate, massage, lymph tone homeopathic remedy, diet containing alkaline raw vegetables, fresh fruits, whole grains, fiber, complex carbohydrates, extra virgin olive oil, amino acids such as fermented soy, mushrooms, and beans, etc. Also mandatory is energy based Liquid Needle E.V.B.

Perform an "Act of Forgiveness" on pages 100 & 269 described in the back of this book so you may let go spiritually and therefore eliminate physically. Also suggested is a walk daily in nature, Fields of Flowers, Bach remedies, Rescue Calm Flower essence remedies that promote removal of the seven (7) Deadly Sins, and the eleven (11) Mental Terror States. Energetic Light Photon Chi Gong for calmness of mind. Perform E.E.G. brain wave neurofeedback. Perform alpha-theta for relaxation and deep states training. Perform E.M.G. biofeedback training for stress reduction management. Also recommended are: Chi Gong, Tai Chi, and yoga. Listen to spiritual music and daily meditation. M.P.3/C.D.'s-Rest, Journey by the Sea, and Tao of the Soul-Self-Slate. These are all natural anti-depression. Also advised is L.N.-Chi Gong & ExStress.

Heal Your Spirit & Emotions.

An adjunct method to heal your emotions is with the Bach Flower essences and various herbs. Dr. Edward Bach, M.D., an English physician stated, "There are seven (7) primary causes of disease which are: Pride, cruelty, hate, self-love, ignorance, instability, and greed." There are eleven (11) mental terror states, "Fear, terror, worry, indecision, boredom, doubt, over-concern, weakness, self-distrust, impatience, and over enthusiasm." Dr. Bach believed that all disease comes from the ills of the heart and spirit. The body's physical ills are just symptoms. These aforementioned seven (7) causes and eleven (11) mental states cause the suppression of the immune system and the life force which subjects us to the invasion of illness.

He discovered that certain flower essences produced high frequencies that were able to counter and neutralize the seven (7) primary causes of disease as well as the eleven (11) mental terror states. He produced them by extracting the essence substance and by a potentization method that is done as in preparing homeopathic remedies. He experimented on himself first and then on his patients and found his discovery very successful in treating all illnesses. In fact he gave up his medical practice and just implemented his newly discovered remedies which he named; The Bach Flower Essence Remedies."

Dr. Bach made a medical connection between feelings and actual physical illness. This has been backed up by recent research findings that indicate if you think positive, center upon health, then you will stay healthy, stimulate the immune function, and live longer. The fact is that your mind can heal your body.

This new branch of science is called "Psycho-somatic-neuro-immunology or mind-body-nervous system-immune system. Your secret weapon against disease and aging is your mind. The mind rules the body and the immune system. Your emotions definitely affect your body's ability to heal, defend, and preserve itself. i.e. An experiment was performed by scaring a person which put them in fear and caused an immune system reaction. Afterward a blood test was performed and it was found that a large decrease in white blood cells occurred. White blood cells are your immune system's first line of defense. See page: 258

Even if you eat right, exercise if you let fear, and anger in you will depress your immune system, and your health will decline. On the other hand laughter invigorates all the glands, makes you feel happy, this stimulates your immune system, and heals your mind. The negative emotions that dominate your mind will depress the immune system and surely compromise your health. There is a direct link between hypertension caused by low level stress called duress and your emotions. Stress causes excessive secretion of nor-epinephrine a stress hormone, then high blood pressure, stroke, arteriosclerosis, and heart attack failure.

It was found by Norman Cousins that laughter can heal you and is the best medicine. Laughter invigorates all your glands, makes you feel happy, this stimulates your immune system, and heals you. Norman Cousins healed himself of a serious illness when he was hospitalized for it. He was getting sicker and sicker, much weaker until he finally decided to watch the three (3) Stooge's movies, and he laughed himself back to health. He even wrote a book about his experience called, "Anatomy of an Illness" in it is healing through laughter. Laughter is called gelotology.

Illness is no accident it is the direct alienation of you from the universal energy. This means love and creation. The opposite is hate and destruction. The Law of Cause and Effect called karma. i.e. Have you ever heard the expression "He died of a broken heart?" It is known that heart problems are linked to unfulfilled drives for significance such as an executives heart trouble and the feeling of being not loved is an underlying factor. People who smoke are putting what the Chinese call "Evil Heat" into their lungs to warm an non-loved heart. Each part of the body that is affected by disease will produce evidence of defects of the personality that are manifesting on the physical level. For all defects of disease there exists permanent antidotes which is high frequency extracts of non-poisonous flowers and now Liquid Needle.

The greatest healing force is Divine Law of Unconditional Love. This is the "I AM" which is the everlasting source of love and power in the universe. It provides us with power for life and love. Love to share with our fellow humans, animals, plants, all of humanity, and life. Dr. Edward Bach discovered that all illness is psychologically induced. These could be restored by using flower essences, etc. He said, "There were states of imbalance which could be healed with these essences and create a spiritual way of life." This is Divine Unconditional Love and the "I AM."

The Seven (7) Deadly Sins are:
1. Pride is the lack of recognition of the smallness of the Ego personality and it is pride the utter dependence on the soul. In its lesser capacity it assumes too much for itself like a

spoiled child. Pride refuses to recognize that success in the world is not due to pride itself but is the blessings bestowed by the Divinity within. It is sometimes referred to as the "Counselor Within." Actions contrary to the will or self will. This produces mental rigidity, you become prone to stiffness, and rigidity of the body. Hence the diseases: Arthritis, rheumatism, back, and joint pain. These symbolize the need for mental flexibility. The Bach remedies indicated are: Water Violet, Vervain, Chicory, Mimulus, and Impatiens.

2. Cruelty is the denial of unity of all and failure to understand that any negative action adverse to any person is in opposition to the whole and hence against universal unity. Love thy neighbor as thy self!-Jesus. This cruelty can become physical or mental pain. The Bach remedies indicated are: Chicory and Impatiens.

3. Hate is the opposition of love and is the reverse of the Law of Creation and the Divine plan of nature. It creates loneliness, a violent and uncontrollable temper, mental nerve problems, hysteria, repressed fear, resentment, selfishness, and a predisposition to cancer. The Bach remedies indicated are: Holly and Willow.

4. Ignorance is the refusal to learn and observe the truth as it occurs in and around us. The results are impaired vision or hearing, short sighted, learning difficulties, speech problems, and deafness. The Bach remedies indicated are: Gentian and Cerato.

5. Instability is when the Ego personality refuses to be ruled by the higher self and leads us to betray others such as Judas against Jesus. The lack of seeing people all the way through a problem by only partially helping them. These are accident prone people. The Bach remedies indicated are: Impatiens, Agrimony, Scleranthus, Cerato, and Clematis.

6. Greed is a lust for power and ignoring the rights of others to develop their own pace, according to their karma of the soul. It is the opposite of freedom of individuality of every soul. It causes domination, addictions, and gluttony. The Bach remedies indicated are: Chicory, Heather, Cerato, Vervain, and Rock Water.

7. Self-love is where the person is truly separate from the whole which is unity. "God." Imagine ourselves separate and we deny our self access to the one true power. This chokes the power (life force) from our connection with the universe, we weaken, wilt like a dying plant without sunlight, and die. The Bach remedies indicated are: Impatiens, Agrimony, Scleranthus, Clematis, and Cerrato.

The Eleven Mental Terror States and indicated Bach remedies are:

1. <u>Fear</u>-Mimulus
2. <u>Terror</u>-Rock Rose
3. <u>Worry</u>-Agrimony
4. <u>Indecision</u>-Scleranthus
5. <u>Boredom</u>-Clematis
6. <u>Doubt</u>-Gentian
7. <u>Over-Concern</u>-Chicory
8. <u>Weakness</u>-Centaury
9. <u>Self-Distrust</u>-Cerato
10. <u>Impatience</u>-Impatiens
11. <u>Over-Enthusiam</u>-Water Violet

I use a product called "<u>Fields of Flowers</u>" that contains all of the Bach flower essences at 30C power in one remedy. It is cost effective and works well. The brain-body will only use what it needs. Flower Power in one bottle. See product under goEnergetix's.com to order. Don't believe the hype you see advertised as these are pure hype, they can never remove the toxins in your lipids, and collagen, etc. These so called products may have some beneficial nutrients but are not going to completely remove all toxins. The only proven method is the one I have described to you. I also use and recommend <u>Miasm-tox</u> a homeopathic remedy that eliminates miasms the passed on inherited multi-generational spiritual toxins. Its available at Apex Energetics in Santa Ana, California and they are online @ ApexEnergetics.com also available @amazon.com and other websites. See pages 260-261. I begin all my light photon frequency energetic detoxification fifteen (15) day bath soaks with 1. <u>Liquid Needle Lympha L-105</u> for the detoxification and re-balancing of the lymphatic system. 2. This is followed by <u>Liquid Needle Coffee-130-EX</u> for for detoxification and elimination of carcinogens, radiation, heavy metals, parasites, chemicals chemotherapy cleansing, and bio-field balance. 3. This is followed by <u>Liquid Needle Gold-105-EX</u> for detoxification and elimination of stress, emotions, yeast, fungal, candida, cleansing, and relaxation. 4. Then next is Liquid Needle Blue Soak-105 for vitality, balance,energy, pain elimination, and fatigue. 5. For cancer patients using chemotherapy is <u>Liquid Needle CAN-133-EX</u> for elimination and detoxification of chemotherapy chemicals, dead cancer and other cells killed, carcinogens, radiation, free radicals, enhancing T-Killer cells, and enhancing the immune system. 6. Also L.N. VIR-513EX for virus and bacteria infections. Note! Before use of any <u>Liquid Needle bath soaks, topical, or oral solutions the use of E.V.B. for 4-7 days is required. This prepares the body for detxification and raises the bodys electrical frequency biofield four (4) to six (6) times higher than its normal operating biofield frequency.</u>

CHAPTER FOUR

Re-establishing the Brain-Body Nutrients.

The 21st Century Energetics program utilizes the following nutrients to replenish and reinstate nutritive balance to the brain-body.

Super whole food supplement-The body-brain requires natural whole food supplementation so it may assimilate and absorb the required necessary vitamins, minerals, herbs, essential oils, compounds it needs to restore optimum balance, vitality, and life force energy to all the trillions of body-brain cells. I have researched and found one Super Whole Food Supplement that was formulated from the world's finest, purest, natural, and spagyric nutrients. It contains 150+ wild crafted, organically grown nutrients blended in the proper ratios. It is Iredesca. We use that to nourish your body after it is completely cleansed and free of all toxins. To order go to the product information in the back of this book for cost. For the heart advised is Heart Studies Formula by Exsula.com

Brain nutrients.-The brain requires certain vitamins, minerals, amino acids, water (H20), and herbs to help it maintain its optimum performance. I use Brain Fuel-Support products and a light photon frequency topical L.N.T.B. that provides vitamins, minerals etc., and maximum nutrition for the brain. Also the cell salt potassium phosphate, the mineral boron, choline, and zinc balanced with copper. We also use Physiologics brain nutrients. See on pages 40-41. I advise daily melatonin, B6 folic acid, and N.A.D.H.

Body nutrients.-The body requires vitamins, minerals, amino acids for cell E.M.F. (electro-motive-force) operation so cells do their assigned duty. FACES: folic acid, vitamins: A, C, E, and selenium. I use ionic enzymes, amino acids, minerals, and O2. Celtic Sea salt is also used for easily assimilated minerals. I use light photon frequency energetic topical for vitamin and minerals. I treat all foods and water, etc. with a special light photon energetic frequency substance that completely detoxifies anything eaten or drank for thirty two (32) hours. It renders everything that enters your body safe. I also use a light photon energetic frequency substance that enhances all nutritive values of food up to two hundred percent (200%) higher. I use a light photon energetic frequency remedy E.V.B. added to pure water that will increase body-brain chi-energy-vitality-balance daily six times higher. See on page 38. Liquid Needle Green and Yellow.

Spiritual nutrients.-These are called positive mental vitamins. We use flower essences products such as Fields of Flowers, Bach remedies, Rescue Calm, and a light photon energetic frequency product called Chi Gong to calm the spirit. See on pages 34-38.

Physiologic's physician only products can be ordered through Jerome Plotnick, Ph.D., N.D.@ 21st Century Energetics.com
Brain nutrients advised are as follows:
5-H.T.P. Complex 50 mg.-precursor to melatonin. A neurotransmitter that sends messages through the nervous system, which contributes to mood and well being. Contains B-6 to assist the formation of seratonin, niacin, magnesium which play an important roles in the nervous system, and valerian root to help promote relaxation.-$31.99
Aceytl L-Carnitine-250 mg.-promotes memory and cognitive function.
D.M.A.E.-100 mg.-promotes the synthesis and function of certain neurotransmitters.-100 mg.-$28.49 1000 mg.-$53.99
Eleuthro Siberian Root-50 mg.-adaptogenic support to promote well being.-$8.49
Ginkgo Alert Formula-combines a range of nutrients and botanicals that work synergistically to promote alertness, support memory function, and mental performance. Increases oxygen to the brain, delivers D.M.A.E., choline, the amino acids, L-glutamine, L-tyrosine, L-pyroglutamic acid, which promote the synthesis, and function of certain neurotransmitters. Panax ginseng as an adaptogen.-$25.49
Huperzine A Complex-advanced memory formula. Huperzine A supports cognitive functioning.-$31.99
L-Theanine-100 mg.-supports mood centers of the brain. A phytochemical in green tea. Is present in the brain and studies indicate that it interacts with the neurotransmitter G.A.B.A. known for it's importance in nervous system functioning, works with the brain's mood centers.-$18.49
Lecithin Choline-1200 mg.-promotes mental function and nerve cell health.-$15.49
N.A.D.H.-5 mg.-found in every living cell acts as an antioxidant and is an energizing co-enzyme.-$33.99

Phosphatidylserine Complex-100 mg.-supports brain function, sharpens mental focus, concentration, and helps memory.-$49.99
SAM-e-200 mg.-supports mood and emotional well being.-$33.99
Vinpocetine-10 mg.-supports cerebral circulation.-$19.99
Melatonin-1 or 3 mg.-supports sound sleep.1 mg.-$4.99 3 mg.-$7.99
B Basic or B Complex-100 mg.-supports nervous system health.-B Basic $6.49-B Complex.- $13.99
Liquid Needle's-ExStress or Chi Gong-brings user into a relaxed state of being. See in this book to order.-$45.00 for either one.
goEnergetix's-Relax Tone and Fields of Flowers-removes 7 deadly sins and 11 mental terror states. See Pgs.-38,110 to order.
Apex Energetics-various homeopathic and flower combinations.
Lifetree Aromatix-essential oils-heather, lavender, etc.
To see Apex Energetics or Lifetree Aromatix products see AMNBPDR the 13 Steps From Illness To Health by Jerome Plotnick, Ph.D., N.D. see on pages: [128,129] of this book to order.
NOTE! As I have previously stated there are hypes and claims made by many new companies that produce products advertised on T.V. The claims made are no truer than me selling you the Brooklyn Bridge. It is these money making hype company's that I have seen before. The product(s) may be okay and contain some nutrients herbs, etc. But here is why it can't deliver a complete necessary detoxification. 1. The product does not prepare the body for a detoxification. 2. It cannot remove the toxins contained in your lipids, collagen, combined toxins called "toxic cocktail," etc. 3. It does not prepare the user to become an excretor on a mental and spiritual level. 4. It is another type of company and is not the real deal. Remember if it is to good to be true it's not.

Again don't buy into hype as we in the alternative preventive health field hear dozens of claims daily. They are not true and cannot deliver the claims. Always see a reputable Naturopathic or Bio-energetic Practitioner or Preventive Medical Doctor in your area. Just use your common sense only health products that are specifically tested and proven through careful study and sold to health care alternative professionals should be used. You should also be under the care and supervision of a health care professional. As an example when you detoxify you may experience a healing crisis. In this case immediately stop the detoxification and wait until the symptoms subside. Thereafter consult with your physician and resume at a much lower dose of the detoxifier. Again as I have stated don't believe those who make statements unless they produce authentic double blind studies and a proven track record. Airborne, Genesis, other advertised colon cleanses do not detoxify your body completely nor your mind, and spirit. The 21st Century Energetics detoxification program is authentic, proven by reliable research, and study. It is also completely safe but should be performed under the supervision of a qualified physician or practitioner. The hype is for money. It is not your best option for really accomplishing a total detoxification, and re-energizing your cells with a complete nutritional rejuvenation. Also the mind and spirit are not taken into consideration. The claims of energy and mood uplifting cannot be accomplished at the level that our professional program provides. Nor do they brain-train or take the spirit into consideration.

CHAPTER FIVE

Re-balancing the Brains' Waves with E.E.G. Brainwave Neurofeedback Training.

E.E.G. neurofeedback is a client centered training. It is used to balance brainwaves that may be oscillating faster or slower than normal. When the brainwaves are operating within their normal range there is an increase in focus, attention, deep relaxation, mental fitness, and peak performance. E.E.G. training provides both an auditory, and visual feedback based on parameters derived from spectral analysis of the E.E.G. signal at specific brain-scalp sites.

The brainwave frequencies delta (1-3 Hz.), theta (4-7 Hz.) alpha (7-11 Hz.) low beta S.M.R. (12-15 Hz.), beta (15-20 Hz.), high beta (20-38 Hz.), gamma (38-42 Hz.), user (4-20 Hz.) resonate at specific frequency ranges. At specific brain scalp sites sensitive electrodes are placed that pick up micro volt electrical signals. These signals are fed into the neurofeedback device. Here at the device the signals can be set at certain training thresholds called parameters. The signals are sent back to the trainees scalp-brain sites. Certain training protocols are set for specific training outcomes such as increase alpha, and thereby increase relaxation.

The E.E.G. neurofeedback training is used for deep states relaxation training by providing both visual-auditory signals that correspond to the trainees increase in the alpha frequency as an indicator of achieving a relaxed state. Other benefits include reducing theta while raising low beta S.M.R. which enhances concentration that results in reduction of errors, greater attention to detail, increased self-control, sustained attention to tasks, and ability to shutoff environmental distractions.

Increase the percent of alpha brainwave enhances creativity that provide increased decision making capabilities, increased generation of new ideas, accuracy improvement, and general relaxation improvement. The duration of training ranges from ten (10)-eighty (80) sessions from one time per week to ten times per week per the trainees goals and needs. During an E.E.G. training session the trainee should relax, allow the system to teach the brain when the E.E.G. shows the desired amount of brainwave energy, and when it does not.

All beneficial effects are a result of the learning your brain will experience as a result of the visual-auditory signals that are provided. The trainee should not "try" to relax. Trying may defeat the beneficial effects that are desired. The trainee should just relax and allow the brain learning to begin. It may take one initial session to nine repeition sessions of the brain learning to begin. The two main effects of E.E.G. neurofeedback training that can be seen are:
1. The number of points that can be scored during a training session may increase over every session.
2. The levels of the E.E.G. signals may increase in order for the benefits of training to increase. The effects of E.E.G. neurofeedback training are primarily in the improvement of relaxation in the trainee over the course of E.E.G. training.

The trainee can learn to change brainwave patterns with neurofeedback training. The following conditions have been proven to respond well to training depression, stress, anxiety, A.D.D., A.D.H.D., L.D., O.C.D., P.T.S.D., addictions of substances, and processes. The E.E.G. brainwave training normalizes brainwave patterns in specific areas of the brain that influence both our emotional, attention, and cognitive performance. It can also balance out electrical distribution in the brain. It is a client-centered-training and a learning model method.

Brain parts and presenting profile or function:
Left Hemisphere-logic and planning details.(logic-math
Right Hemisphere-emotional and social awareness.(holistic-art)
Parietal lobes-ability to do complex grammar and problem solving.
Temporal lobes Right Hemisphere-facial recognition and word recognition.
Cingulate gyrus-smooth transitions-cooperation and attention.
Sensorimotor cortex-fine motor skills and calm motor system.
Occipital lobes-visual memory pattern recognition and spatial orientation.
Frontal lobes-creative function—working memory and attention.
1. Alpha-theta training opens the door to healing ones-self, the reclamation of repressed feelings, and memories. With a predominance of theta 4-7 Hz. focus is on the internal world. This

is the hypnogogic state where the inner healer is to be encountered. Alpha brainwave 8-13 Hz. is considered a bridge from the external world to the inner world and vice-verse.

2. Alpha-theta training promotes twilight states that eventually evoke hypnogogic imagery. In the hypnogogic state we can use audible suggestions, or visualizations that enter, go deep into the mind, and they become reality. i.e. scenes of abstinence to alcoholics have been proven to alter their desire to drink. After 10-30 sessions of training can make the alcoholic sick if they consume alcohol. An (alcohol allergic reaction called the "Penniston Effect"), and eventually become sober. Several studies confirm this such as: Penniston-Kulkosky (1989-90), Scott, Brod, Siderof, Kaiser, and Sagen et al. (2000-02) Plotnick (2001).

3. During the 1960's and the inception of E.E.G. neurofeedback training alpha was the predominant, the first brainwave to be named, and trained.

4. Alpha enhancement and alpha synchrony training have many non-clinical applications such as peak performance, cognitive flexibility, creativity, athletic control, hemisphere synchrony, and inner awareness.

5. Alpha-theta is more efficient than talk therapy for the treatment of personality disorder, substance abuse, and P.T.S.D.

6. Alpha-theta training requires only thirty minutes per session.

7. Alpha-theta training can be performed daily or three times per week with thirty sessions normally with three-eight minutes of visualization, or suggestion, and a possible debriefing period of fifteen-twenty minutes for P.T.S.D., etc.

8. Sensor placement is always at the posterior location(s) Either R/H, CZ (center line), or if in doubt PZ.

9. Assessment is performed by two channel assessment one scalp electrode placed at P3, the other at P4, and the reference at P7.

10. If the client is depressed then P3 electrode placement is contraindicated.

11. Five (5) conscious responses to alpha-theta training:

1. The client with negative experiences such as painful imagery of body sensations.

2. The client with frustrations who remarks "I just can't get deep."

3. The client who goes to sleep.

4. The client with no experiences, but who reports a state of deep relaxation.

5. The client with excellent experiences, such as insight, and the unlocking of repressed memories.

Alpha-theta brainwave neurofeedback training for addictions is a holistic and spiritual approach to re-balance your brainwave frequencies through the Penniston-Kulkosky protocol. This is a client-centered-training that requires a minimum of 20 sessions with a 65-85% percent success rate in several studies. Penniston-Kulkosky (V.A. & the Univ. of So. Colorado) (100%), Scott, Sagen, Kaiser, Brod, et al. (Cri-Help-E.E.G. Spectrum Institute)(65%), Dickson (Univ. of No. Texas), Plotnick (21st Century Energetics) (100%), Walters, Fahrion, and Green & Green (Menninger Clinic).

It is usually used with 8 diaphragmatic breathing sessions and temperature pre training (94 degrees for ten minutes).

This followed by script containing alternative responses to problematic behaviors, (alcohol-drug rejection scenes), and personal-interpersonal "ideal self" images. This is followed by thirty (30) sessions of alpha-theta brainwave training, unless high baseline theta levels suggest at least ten (10) initial sessions of beta enhancement-theta inhibit, and (S.M.R. low beta training).

When the brainwaves are brought back into normal balance the desire for addictive substances, or processes is diminished, thereby creating a maximum of increasing the outcome to eighty five percent (85%) for a successful recovery. The addict's brain waves are out of normal balance causing psycho-physiological dependence on alcohol-drugs to allow their brainwaves to come into balance. When they drink or take drugs they feel normal. It is a perverted way to attain spirituality. Substitution of E.E.G. neurofeedback training allows the addict to bring their brain waves back into normal balance without the use of alcohol or drugs. When this occurs there is also a release of repressed negative emotional feelings. These are the cause of the psychological imbalances. This training is approved and used by the V.A., Menninger Clinic, E.E.G. Spectrum Institute, University of North Texas. University of Colorado at Pueblo, Colorado, and 21st Century Energetics, etc. This alpha-theta brain wave training for addiction, combined with a 12 step A.A., or N.A. spiritual program of recovery greatly enhances permanent sobriety.

Several studies confirm a high success rate from the aforementioned:

They are Penniston-Kulkosky Study V.A., Pueblo, Colorado and the University of So. Colorado, Cri-Help-E.E.G. Spectrum Institute, Menninger Clinic, University of No. Texas Drug Rehabilitation Center, and 21st Century Energetics. To see the double blind study of E.E.G. neurofeedback brainwave training on A.D.D., A.D.H.D. children and the use of topically applied L.N.T.B. Liquid Needle Total Balance you will see the double blind study, and results thereof in this book on pages: 309-310, and on page 418 of The 13 Steps From Illness To Health-APNBMPDR book by Jerome Plotnick, Ph.D., N.D. The study performed was using L.N.T.B., on A.D.D. Children, and the results thereof. For information on Jerome Plotnick, Ph.D., N.D. you can also go to 21st Century Energetics web site: 21stCenturyEnergetics.com

Jerome Plotnick, Ph.D., N.D. is an expert and authority in alternative preventive Naturopathic and Bioenergetic Medicine. He is also highly qualified in E.E.G. Neurofeedback and E.M.G. Biofeedback training and a clinician. He is a Master Hypnotherapist. He is a consultant on Energetic Detoxification, Nutritional, Herbal, Homeopathic, Aromatherapy, Flower essences, Vita Flex, Light Photon Frequency Energized Solutions called "Liquid Needle" as well as a Needle-less Acupuncturist, Acupressurist, A.K.-Touch For Health Practitioner, Touch & Non Touch Healer, Shiatsu, Chi Gong Practitioner, Jin Shin Do Practitioner, Hypnotherapist, Mind Control De-programmer, N.L.P., Guided Imagery and Visualization Practitioner, Author, Instructor of Eastern & Western meditations, Pranic Healer, Pranic Psychotherapist, Shamanistic and Spiritual Healer, Ayurveda, Asian, Amazon, American Herbal Medicine, and Chemical Dependency Recovery Specialist. Biofeedback and Neurofeedback Entrainment/Empowerment Clinician, Psycho-Physiloogist, Pranic Healer, and Remote Distance Healer.

CHAPTER SIX

What is Biofeedback?

E.M.G. Biofeedback is biological-body information feedback which uses an electronic instrument to feed back measurements of bodily processes. The person is normally unaware, and which may be brought under voluntary control. A person can receive immediate information about their biological conditions such as muscle tension, skin surface temperature (S.S.T.), brainwave activity, galvanic skin response (G.S.R.), blood pressure, and heart rate. It is a learning method that enables the trainee to be an active participant in the functioning of their own body and its health.

Biofeedback is a recent health technology, developed through a combination of psychological technique, medical knowledge, and electronic response. It uses specialized instruments as simple as a hospital thermometer and as sophisticated as an electroencephalograph a device which measures brainwave patterns.

At any instance of time there are numerous minute physiological changes driven psychologically usually occurring in our bodies. I.e. Fluctuations in brain activity, brain wave patterns, heart rate, blood flow, hormonal, and gastric acidity. Most of these changes are related to psychological factors, such as stress, emotional arousal, fear, sexual excitement, anxiety, and physiological relaxation. This is the interaction we monitor of the mind and body which is the focus of biofeedback training.

Most changes that do occur in our bodies are normally beyond our awareness. Biofeedback is a method to become aware of signals from one's body reactions. Modern electronic technology has developed biofeedback instruments which amplify these signals so that they may be heard over the internal and external noise. Through deep states relaxation training, trainees can learn to "quiet" down their bodies to minimize internal, external distractions so that they can "hear," and feel their tiny feedback signals. They can also learn coping skills in stressful situations, lower heart rate and blood pressure, re-educate muscle groups, and minimize pain, etc. It only takes a short time of biofeedback training to "quiet" the body to hear these signals.

Most of the psycho-physiological processes a trainee can learn to control with biofeedback training were in the past believed to be beyond voluntary control. Biofeedback research has clearly shown that consciously controlled changes in muscle tension, blood flow patterns, brainwave patterns, heart rate, emotional arousal can be learned in a short time period of training, and repeated thereafter without further need for instrumentation.

After twenty five (25) years of research and application of health methods in biofeedback. The Association for Applied Psychophysiology, Biofeedback Society, the American Holistic Association, and they all state that more than fifty percent (50%) of illnesses can be avoided by biofeedback training called psycho-physiologic self regulation.

Doctors across the U.S. all agree that between fifty 50%-eighty 80% of all health problems are psychosomatic. That means the majority of percent medical problems are unconsciously self generated. It has been found that these problems can be reversed with proper psycho-physiologic training. i.e. Raynaud's disease, low blood pressure, migraine headaches, high blood pressure, tension headache, chronic muscle tension in neck, back, head, hypertension, addictions, depression, imagined stress and stress response, A.D.D., A.D.H.D., O.C.D., and P.T.S.D., etc.

These so called diseases are simply subconscious or unconscious bad habits in the sub-cortical nervous system. These negative involuntary behaviors, which often are unconscious reactions to stress, may be accompanied by acute pain, or pathological symptoms that seem to the public to be illnesses. Most knowledgeable health practitioners know that this is incorrect.

Hard to believe? But true. We know in the field of biofeedback from thousands of studies, that the same is true of psychosomatic diseases. These are not diseases, they are behavioral consequences. Dr. Pellitier put it this way in his book. "Mind is a Healer Mind is a Slayer." Dr. Wayne Dyer puts it this way in his books "Pull Your Own Strings", "If you believe it, you will see it." Norman Cousins put it this way: "The greatest force in the human body is the natural drive of the body to heal itself-but that force is not independent of the belief system, which can translate expectations into physiological change." Nothing is more wondrous about the fifteen billion neurons in the human brain than their ability to convert thoughts, hopes, ideas, attitudes into chemical substances such as beta endorphins, and other poly peptides. Everything begins, therefore, with belief. What we believe is that most powerful option of all." "If you believe it you will see it."

Learning theory and visceral learning within experimental psychology states that "learning" is a permanent change in behavior due to past experience. Usually some type of reinforcement is considered necessary for operant conditioning called instrumental learning to occur. Both overt and covert behavior made up of thoughts, feelings, and physiological responses. The C.N.S. was considered responsive to instrumental learning or operant conditioning. The A.N.S. was considered to function unconsciously. In 1978 Miller stated the possibility of the A.N.S. could be trained instrumental conditioning model. Later in 1974 Kimmel, Harris and Brady indicated that instrumental learning could both produce increases and decreases in vasomotor responses, blood pressure, salivation, galvanic skin response, heart rates, and rhythms. Most research concerning instrumental conditioning of visceral responses controlled by the A.N.S. provided the development of the clinical applications of biofeedback and the argument over whether such conditioning is a legitimate phenomenon.

Clinical biofeedback is based on the premise that it can assist trainees improve the accuracy of their perceptions of their own visceral events i.e. (blood pressure, heart rate, and rhythm) thereby allowing them greater self-regulation of these events. This lead to other views of biofeedback: Learning and visceral learning, psycho-physiology, behavior therapy, stress, relaxation management research techniques, bio-medical engineering, electromyography E.M.G., diagnostic E.M.G., single motor unit control, consciousness, altered states of consciousness, cybernetics, cultural factors, and professional developments.

Primarily biofeedback is viewed as instrumental learning, but with added cognitive, mental dimensions, and environmental re-enforcers. Cognitive learning includes: thinking, visualization-imagery, foresight and planning, and problem solving strategies.

Psycho-physiology is the scientific study of inter-relationships of physiological and cognitive processes. As a form of applied psycho-physiology, clinical biofeedback assists trainees to alter their own behavior through systematic feedback of such physiological responses as E.M.G., peripheral blood flow, electrocardiograph E.K.G., sweat gland activity, E.E.G. brainwave rhythms and patterns, and blood pressure. Some professional providers refer to themselves as clinical psycho-physiologists.

Behavior therapy and behavioral medicine. Behavior therapy developed in the 1950's as an alternative to traditional theories and therapies for various mental disorders. This model is largely considered the educational model. Behavioral medicine is focused on the learning theory and therapies, to medical, dental disorders, other health disorders under psychopathology, or mental disorders. Sometimes it is referred to as health psychology, that treats chronic diseases, and mal adaptive behaviors. It places a greater emphasis upon the role of the patient in both the prevention, the recovery from organic diseases, and conditions. The same emphasis is evident in applied biofeedback. Many practitioners consider clinical biofeedback a specialty within the field of behavioral medicine.

Stress research, relaxation therapies and other stress management techniques. Hans Seyle (1974), Cannon (1932), Bernard quoted by Pi-Suner (1955) all developed the concept of physiological homeostasis as a major process by which the body maintains itself in health and balance. Cannon named it the innate stress response and Seyle named it the "fight-or-flight" response. The stages are alarm, resistance, and exhaustion. Langley (1965) noted that physical, mental, and social disorders occur because some homeostatic feedback mechanism is malfunctioning. Stress seems to be a major effect in imbalance. One of the first forms of physical relaxation was called Hatha yoga. Then Jacobsen "Progressive relaxation", Maharishi Yogi "Transcendental meditation", Schultz Autogenics, Progoff's "Process meditation", Silva "Silva's Mind control", Shealy's "Biogenics", Mesmer "Animal magnetism", Erikson, Barber, Tart, Liebault, Charcot, Freud, Hilgard, Weitzenhoffer, Boyne, Kappas, Krogen, Bryant, Plotnick "Clinical hypnotherapy, and "Benson "Relaxation Response."

Bio-medical engineering develops instruments to measure physiological events accurately and reliable without which there would be no biofeedback. These scientists have developed skin temperature, respiration, cardiac, heart rate and rhythm, sweat gland, electro-dermal, brainwave, peripheral blood flow, muscle activity, angles of limbs, muscle force measurement instruments. Prior to W.W.II the equipment was not sensitive enough for measuring most of the body's internal electrical impulses. After the war progress occurred that made it possible to record multiple and simultaneous channels of physiological information. With the advancement in computer and software programs there is greater storage capability, statistical analysis, and graphic displays.

Electromyography, Diagnostic electromyography, and single motor unit control. In 1929 a classic paper written by Adrian and Bronk who showed that the electrical impulses in individual muscles provided an accurate reflection of the actual functional activity of the muscles. Reports as early as 1934 appeared that state voluntary conscious control of individual motor unit potentials were possible. Smith (1934). Marinacci and Horande (1960) added case reports of the potential value of displaying E.M.G. signals to patients in order to assist in neuro-muscular re-education. Basmajian (1963-1979) also reported on the control of single motor units.

Consciousness, Altered states of consciousness and E.E.G. feedback. Theorists Tart (1969), Krippner (1972), Ornstein (1972), Pellitier and Garfield (1976), Schwartz and Beatty (1977), and Jacobson (1982) are among those who have made significant contributions to the understanding of human consciousness. There have been numerous studies of altered states of consciousness, whether induced by hypnosis, drugs, or meditation, have contributed to our knowledge and understanding between brain functioning, and human behavior. This research has stimulated the development of neurofeedback, which involves the relationships between brain, and behavior. In the early 1960's studies of alpha (8-12 HZ) biofeedback reported the relationship between emotional states and certain states of consciousness. Alpha was reported as a relaxed but alert state. Kamiya (1969) reported that alpha waves previously believed to be out of conscious control could be volitionally controlled. These findings were reported by others. Brown (1877), Hart (1968), and Orne (1979). But Basmajian (1983) reported that alpha feedback had become an absolute scientifically defensible tool and it returned to the research laboratory from which it should not have emerged so prematurely. In recent years specialized E.E.G. biofeedback of selected brain areas and carefully selected parameters of E.E.G. activity have produced sensor motor rhythms, a 3-8 Hz slow wave activity have been investigated in well controlled studies, and have emerged as effective therapeutic approaches for selected patients with C.N.S. disorders such as epilepsy. Doctors: Lubar and Sterman (1982, 1983). Currently E.E.G. neurofeedback applications for addictions, A.D.D., A.D.H.D., O.C.D., L.D., P.T.S.D., mental fitness, and peak performance have produced proven results in various studies such as addictions Penniston-Kulkosky (1992) Scott, Brod, Sagen et al. (2000-03), and Plotnick, (2001). Various practitioners in the field such as Jerome Plotnick, John Demos, Jennifer Cochagne, Bill Scott, Sue Othmer, Herschel Toomin (R.I.P.), Marjorie Toomim, (R.I.P.) Thomas Collura, Brain Master Technologies, Bill Scott, E.E.G. Spectrum-Institute, and Biofeedback Institute of L.A. et al. report successful results in E.E.G. neurofeedback training for a variety of brain disorders including anxiety, depression, deep states relaxation, focus, concentration, and alertness. There are now methods to perform a total brainwave assessment with Brain Master Technologies-Mini Q, a two (2) channel assessment, and Bio Comp's system, etc. There are computerized training protocols, comparative training capabilities with norm standards, ability for individualized training programs via creating personal software. At the present time the potential is unlimited for what can be accomplished with computer technology and the advanced neurofeedback training devices now available.

Cybernetics means the study of biological controlled mechanisms. The field that deals with information processing and feedback is called cybernetics. Principles of cybernetics are is that a variable cannot be controlled unless information about the variable is available to the controller. The information is called feedback. Ashby (1963); Mayr (1970). In biofeedback trainees are provided with direct concise feedback from their physiological functions, which is feedback through an instrument enabling them to learn to control (self regulate) these bodily functions. A principle of cybernetics is that feedback makes learning possible. In this way muscle tension, heart rate, blood pressure, breathing, etc., and can be re-educated to perform satisfactorily.

Operant conditioning is one form of feedback which can be provided in a form of either positive or negative consequences of a particular behavior. The information processing model is derived from research in cybernetics. Brown (1977, Gardner, Montgomery (1981), Anliker (1977), and Mulholland (1977). For further information on cybernetics read Psycho-Cybernetics by Maxwell Maltz. Dr. Maxwell Maltz was a plastic surgeon who performed rhinoplasty's (nose job). He performed one such rhinoplasty on a middle aged woman. He gave her a cute Za Za Gabor type nose after surgery. In a few weeks when the bandages were to come off he sat the woman in his office in front of a mirror. He asked are you ready to see your beautiful nose? She replied, "Yes I am." He began removing the bandages and when the last bandage was off she looked in the mirror at her new nose. At that point she began screaming Oh! How ugly it is! How ugly I am! Dr. Maltz was amazed that she really believed her noise and her-self was ugly. From this he actually within some time researched and formulated what is now called the field of psycho-cybernetics. It states that what you believe on the inside of yourself or your inner cognitive beliefs called the zero order beliefs are what you will project on the outside. Psycho-Cybernetics is mind over biological systems.

Cultural factors have also contributed to the development of biofeedback. The merging of traditions of the East such as acupuncture in the 1960's and meditations of Tai Chi Chuan, Yoga, T.M., and Zen, etc., have merged with the West's techniques of biofeedback, hypnosis, relaxation response, and autogenic exercises, etc. Biofeedback has been called the Zen or Yoga of the West or electronic Zen. In the U.S. another contribution is a Zeitgeist due to the escalating cost of health care, prevention awareness, unnecessary use of pharmacology, the growing awareness of fitness, diet, exercise, meditation, and yoga. These all have contributed to the development of biofeedback training as a viable method of health enhancement and relaxation. In biofeedback you can actually see graphic images of any changes made or your innate bodily functions moment by moment. Therefore wellness and wholeness are the individual's responsibility. So it stands to reason that a client-centered training program to reduce stress, pain, muscle tension, create a relaxed, focused, calm, and an alert mind is on the cutting edge. Biofeedback training is believed to facilitate self regulation of body-brain functions thereby creating wellness, health, homeostatis, and spiritual growth. Biofeedback is a form of bio-meditation.

Professional developments such as the organization of professional certification, research, and clinical education have greatly contributed to the development of biofeedback. Organizations such as B.C.I.A. Biofeedback Certification Institute of America, B.S.A. Biofeedback Society of America, B.R.S. Biofeedback Research Society, A.A.B.C. American Association of Biofeedback Clinicians, A.A.P.B. Association of Applied Psychophysiology and Biofeedback have contributed enormously. Much to the credit of Mark Stephen Schwartz, Ph.D. Also Menninger Clinic, Doctors. Stephen Fahrion and Dale Walters, Elmer and Alyce Green, Martin Mutke, E.E.G. Spectrum Institute, Siegfried and Sue Othmer, Biofeedback Institute of L.A., Doctors. Marjorie and Herschel Toomin, Eugene Penniston and Kulkosky, V.A. and The University of Colorado, Doctors. Bill Scott, Kaiser, Sagen, and Brod. Cri-Help and E.E.G. Spectrum, Dr. Thomas Collura, Brainmaster Technologies, Doctors: Joel Lubar, Barry Sterman, Barbara Brown, Budzynski, Cannon, Fehmi, Elmer Green and Alyce Green, Kimmel, Marjorie Toomin, Joe Kamiya, Orne, Luthe, Kenneth Pellitier, Schwartz, Hans Seyle, Silva, C. Norman Shealy, Charles Tart, Wickramaeskera, Tarler, Smith, Nowlis, Mayr, Dupont, Marinacci, Hart, Gardner, Greenfield, Fox, Brundy, Binder, Daley, Basmajian, Adler, Anchor, Andrews, Annent, and Beatty. Also many practitioners including Doctors. Victoria Ibric, Jennifer Cochagne, John Demos, Robert Dickson, and Jerome Plotnick. Non doctor practitioners, Sam Odom.

Summary.

The field of biofeedback is on the threshold of spectacular achievements in the prevention of most modern-day illness and disorders without drugs, medicine, or needless surgery. It is a self regulation learning process that allows for the client-trainee to take responsibility, re-educate, or relearn how to take control, normalize certain body-brain functions, thereby creating wellness, wholeness, and a healthy you.

Biofeedback is a group of experimental procedures in which an external sensor is used to provide the organism with an indication of the state of bodily process, usually in an attempt to effect change in the measured quantity.

Biofeedback is psycho-physiological feedback.

Biofeedback is physiological measurement monitored with sufficient sensitivity to detect moment-by-moment changes. These changes are reflected immediately to the person attempting to control the process. The trainee is motivated to learn to effect physiological changes.

Biofeedback is a process or technique for learning voluntary control over automatically of regulated bodily functions.

Biofeedback is training for learning psychosomatic self-regulation.

Biofeedback is the use of sensitive instrumentation or monitoring devices that detect, amplify internal physiologic processes, and feed it back to the trainee.

Biofeedback is the process of making one aware of very subtle changes in physiological states in the hope of bringing those states under conscious control.

Biofeedback a technique using sensitive instruments to measure and process, indicate feedback the ongoing activity of various body processes of which the trainee is usually unaware so that the trainee may be able to change and develop beneficial control over these body processes.

These may be in the form of auditory or visual signals that indicate normal or abnormal events in order to teach them to be able to manipulate these otherwise involuntary events by manipulating the display signals.

Stress, Stressors, and the Stress Response.

A stressor is any challenging stimulus.

A stress response is the integrated cognitive emotional, behavioral, and physiological response to a stressor. All stress responses are designed to protect the individual and ensure survival.

56

These are learned patterns. Through repetition as anxiety-reducers, through stimulus-response generalization, and classical conditioning (Smith, 1987, p. 12), these patterns may become fixed and inappropriately used (Smith, 1987, p. 6). Previously functional patterns become dysfunctional. The same coping style, behavior pattern, or defense mechanisms can be highly functional, or severely dysfunctional depending on the problem.

Stress may be defined as "A relationship between the person and the environment that is appraised as taxing, or exceeding his, or her resources, endangering his, or her well-being (Lazarus, 1984). The relationship may also be intra-psychic, i.e.., internal conflict, and illness.

<u>Positive stress</u>: The stressor challenges coping skills but does not overwhelm them. Positive stress is experienced as pleasure, excitement, learning (i.e., exercise, sex, games, interest in work etc.; also useful anger, sadness, and fear, etc.
<u>Negative stress</u>: The stressor threatens to overwhelm some aspect of the individual's perceived capacity to cope, (fights, crowded freeways, and not enough money, etc.).

<u>Types of stressors</u>: Environmental pollutants, extreme temperature, electric shock, prolonged exercise, bodily injury, and disease.

Normally-conscious voluntary domain-cortical and craniospinal:
1. sensory perception of outside-the-skin (outs events)
2. emotional and mental response to outs events
3. limbic response
4. hypothalamic and pituitary response
5. physiological response
6. sensory perception of inside-the-skin (I.N.S.) events, via biofeedback
7. emotional and mental response to (I.N.S.) events
8. limbic response
9. direct perception of inside-the-skin (I.N.S.) events normally-unconscious involuntary domain-sub cortical and autonomic

<u>"Self regulation" of psycho physiological events and processes</u>: Sensory perception of outs events, stressful leads to a physiological response. If the physiological response is picked up

and fed back to a person who attempts to control the behavior of the feedback device, resulting in a "new" limbic response. This response in turn makes a change in "signals" transmitted and modifying the original physiological response. A cybernetic loop is thus completed and the dynamic equilibrium (homeostasis) of the system can be brought under voluntary control. Biofeedback practice, acting in the opposite way to drugs, increases a person's sensitivity to I.N.S. events, and developments. External feedback is eventually unnecessary because direct perception of I.N.S. events becomes adequate for maintaining self regulation skills. Physiological self control through classical yoga, is one method as in meditation as T.M., and self hypnosis, etc. But for control of specific physiological and psychosomatic problems biofeedback training seems more efficient.

The cutting edge E.E.G. neurofeedback brain-train is now being used for all addictions, A.D.D., A.D.H.D., L.D., P.D., P.T.S.D., O.C.D., B.P., Epilepsy, Anxiety, Hypertension, and Depression with amazing results. No drugs or psychotropic medicines that are the cause of severe toxicity and poly drug addiction and are worse than what were taken for initially. Side effects can be life threatening. Again the E.E.G. brain-train is a learning method, the brain resets itself into normal parameters, and eliminates the symptoms aforementioned. Usually ten (10)-twenty (20) one (1) hour sessions are required. The normal hourly fees and are $85-$125 per hour are are the present industry professional costs. Compared to a life of taking dangerous psychotropic drugs and medicines that have serious side effects, high costs, and may cause a poly drug addiction. The cost of E.E.G. neurofeedback brain-train are cost effective. From $850.00 to $2,000.00. The cost of a psychiatrist office visits from $50-$125 and the prescribed lifetime of Xanax as an example @ $40-$100 per prescription which lasts a month. i.e. Psychiatrists office and evaluation over a year estimated @ $2,500. Also note that if you were given a Xanax prescription @ 1 mg. initially due to its effectiveness it will require a higher dosage to accomplish the relief of Panic attacks. Eventually you will require a dosage of 2 mg. three times (3x's) daily and may even require a higher dosage. This is both dangerous, highly addictive, and can be life threatening. As the intake of the drug increases its effectiveness becomes diminished and many users also may drink alcohol to calm themselves down. The mixture of Xanax and alcohol is both dangerous and deadly, it can cause neuropathy,

58

incontinence, dizziness, fainting spells, falling down from interrupting motor functions in the nervous system that controls your muscle actions, folic acid folate, and potassium depletion. It also can cause schizophrenic mimicking episodes. This is life threatening and has killed patients. E.E.G. neurofeedback brain-train is completely safe, cost effective, and a non drug natural method to accomplish elimination of all the aforementioned disorders. Once your brain resets itself you may require a tune up one (1) session one (1) to two (2) times per year. You can also purchase a home unit and train yourself thereafter.

Note! It has been confirmed that a twenty (20) minute session of E.E.G. Neurofeedback alpha-theta brain wave training is equal to several months of daily one hour of any meditation practice sessions. It also is equal to four (4) hours of R.E.M. restful sleep. It also was recently confirmed that a twenty (20) minute session of either E.E.G. Neurofeedback training or any meditation practice will increase your body's frequency of your bio-field by 20 MHz. A state of illness is measured at around 42-52 MHz. A health body state is measured at around 58-62 MHz. A healthy brain wave state is 72-90 MHz. So if you perform either E.E.G. Neurofeedback training session for twenty (20) minutes or a twenty (20) minute meditation session you will automatically raise your bio-field frequency into a health state. This also helps your immune and nervous systems. You can also use three (3) light photon energetic frequency solutions called L.N.T.B. (Liquid Needle Total Balance), Liquid Needle E.V.B. (energy-vitality-balance), Liquid Needle Original topical applied solution to re-balance the bio-field, acupuncture meridian system, nervous system, lymphatic system, and eleven (11) major chakras. See on pages 87, 258-307. Also recently discovered by Tanio Technologies is that a 20 minute session of meditation raises the body biofield frequency by around 20 MHz. A sick body is measuread at around 42-52 MHz. Therefore, daily meditation can increase your biofield frequency to the health range of around 68 MHz. See pages 284-307 for all D.N.R., Inc. Indiana for Liquid Needle light photon frequency solutions.

CHAPTER SEVEN

<u>Nine (9) Day Inner Cleansing & Blood Wash & Gravizon</u>.

<u>Cell Stagnation</u>. Since the blood circulates throughout the body and to every cell it requires cleansing. If the blood is toxic then these toxins are carried to all your cells causing stagnation and toxic disease. Many factors cause this condition such as fatigue which depletes your nervous energy and impairs your glandular secretions. Another factor is overeating because it will cause a sluggish elimination of cell wastes. These will inhibit the cells from necessary nutrients it needs for the electro motive force (E.M.F.) and proper elimination of cell respiration waste products to be sent to the blood. Cell stagnation can contribute to a cancerous condition and especially breast cancer. See Cancer What's the Answer? CHAPTER VI on pages 177-337.

Many toxic diseases originate and are directly connected to the cells. A stuffed nose, chest and lung congestion, sinus, bronchitis, asthma, colitis, and are the result of stagnation. Arthritis is also a toxic accumulation in the body. Lastly skin eruptions such as acne, eczema, candida yeast, hives, or pimples indicate faulty drainage, and deficient nutrition.

When this condition is occurring we have organ disorders, loss of muscular tone, chronic fatigue syndrome, a general feeling of illness with a variety of symptoms that range from temperature, weakness, nausea, dizziness, vomiting, sleep problems, memory loss, infections, and a low immune resistance. This is caused by poisons in and around the cells and poor blood circulation and sluggish elimination. These are the warning signs that nutrition, cell drainage are impaired, and cell destruction is occurring. Unless steps are taken to reverse this situation then the person affected will have premature aging and a decline in vitality, energy, body function leading to serious deterioration of health leading to premature aging, and premature death.

<u>Cell Rejuvenation</u>. To correct the nutritional deficiency and proper elimination of toxic wastes one must supply your body with live natural foods rich in nutrients, minerals, vitamins, and fiber, etc. in order to restore and replenish the cells. According to nutritionist and author Helen Houston you must first heal the

body. She explained that all disease was an outgrowth of poisonous toxic waste that have accumulated, clogged the intestinal wall causing poor elimination, and re-circulating these dangerous wastes back into the body through the intestines. I also strongly concur with her. This causes toxemia, septic dysbiosis, systemic infection, blood poisoning, peritonitis, and premature aging, etc.

The nine (9) day cleansing diet. It is best to implement in the late spring but in fact any time will suffice. For the first 4 days you will only eat the following foods: fruits and vegetables. On the 5th day you will drink certain fruit juices I will describe shortly. On the 6th and 7th day you will eat an abundance of green salads and green vegetable juices loaded with chlorophyll. On the 8th and 9th day you will be drinking fruit juices again.

All fruits and vegetables will be thoroughly clean and detoxify the foods using special light photon substances that detoxify and enhance the nutritive values of the food two hundred (200%) higher. Four (4) to Six (6) MHz increase. Use <u>Liquid Needle's-E,V.B.,Yellow, and Green</u>. After these are the foods you will eat:
1. Apples-provide blood oxidation and prevent intestinal putrefaction, regulate calcium metabolism, retard aging, and render the urine normal. "An apple a day keeps the doctor away."
2. Asparagus-cell growth normalizer. High iodine, sulfur, and silicon. Contains proteins called histones which control cell growth. Contains vitamin A, B complex, C, calcium, phosphorus, iron, iodine, sulfur, and silicon.
3. Banana-high in potassium. Helps muscle tone, liver, and kidneys. Called a "poor mans food."
4. Beets-a high potassium and sodium content provides a good solvent for calcium deposits. They regulate menstruation, low vitality, low blood sugar, blood building, liver tonic, anemia, and blood alkalizer. They are a good source of magnesium, iron and calcium. Maintain a healthy blood stream especially helpful in low blood pressure.
5. Cranberry-contains citric, malic, and benzoic acids. Acts as a intestinal antiseptic and aids digestion It is helpful in obesity, poor complexion, liver disorders, pimples, diarrhea, asthma, catarrh, and goiter. Immune system enhancer.
6. Celery-is a mild diuretic, laxative, and stimulates circulation. The stalks contain potassium, vitamin A, and B. It is good for arthritis, gout, sciatica, high blood pressure,

rheumatism, obesity, insomnia, urinary disorders, chronic appendicitis, hyper-acidity, headaches, neuritis, neuralgia, cystitis, and dropsy. Body builder and vitality.

7. Carrots-Rich in Vitamin A, blood cleansing and alkalizer. Contain most minerals and vitamins required daily. Protects the eyes, treats ulcers, anemia, hay fever, colitis, asthma, emphysema, rheumatic conditions, constipation, digestion, and respiratory tract. Prevents rickets, good for diabetics, builds healthy bones, and teeth.

8. Cabbage-rich in vitamins A, B and C. Helpful for kidneys and bladder disorders, obesity heart trouble, skin eruptions, scurvy, deficiency diseases of thyroid and adrenal glands, and constipation. A blood cleanser and detoxifier. Helps teeth, gums, hair, and bones. Minimizes insulin requirements. Can be used in juice form mixed with carrot juice one (1) part cabbage to three (3) parts carrot.

9. Cucumbers-promote urine flow, and mild diuretic. High potassium helps both high and low blood pressure. High in vitamin C used for neuritis, fevers, obesity, rheumatism, nervousness, pyorrhea, skin eruptions, and acidosis. Contains Vitamins K, A, and Potassium.

10. Coconuts-provide complete protein loaded with natural amino acids and electrolytes. High in vitamin B. Helpful in digestive disorders, colitis, gastritis, stomach ulcers, sore throat, liver complaints, nervous exhaustion, indigestion, constipation, and underweight.

11. Grapefruit-high in vitamin C, 3 1/2 ounces of grapefruit juice yields 650 mg. of vitamin C. It also contains 7% fruit sugar. Helpful in reducing diets, acidosis, gall stones, high blood pressure, sluggish liver, malaria, and poor complexion. Prevents colds, mild diuretic, mild laxative, and replenishes vitamin C lost during fevers. Note! Do not use in cases of colitis or digestive tract inflammation.

12. Grapes-fat burner, sugar balancing, blood and body builder. Helpful in liver disorders, anemia, jaundice, pimples, and skin diseases. Stimulate circulation, mild laxative, nervousness, reducing aid, and low blood pressure. Note! Not recommended for diabetics, diarrhea prone, and hyper-acidity.

13. Lemon-contains 6% citric acids, high in vitamin C, 3 ½ ounces of lemon juice contains 1000 mg. of vitamin C. Helps minimize hemorrhage. Helpful in colds, gout, jaundice, obesity, rheumatism, and liver disorders. It is also a cell scrubber and blood

cleanser. Note! Do not use in cases of colitis or digestive tract inflammation. Note! Use the lemon rind as its high in C.

14. Lettuce-source of vitamins A, E, C, and B. Helpful in urinary disorders, insomnia, acidosis, obesity, catarrh, anemia, dyspepsia, goiter, and stimulates circulation. Mild diuretic and laxative.

15. Orange-high in vitamin C, 3 ½ ounces of orange juice contain 900 mg. of vitamin C. Excellent source of calcium and phosphorous. Blood cleanser, high blood pressure, diabetes, arthritis, obesity, scurvy, bone and teeth building, liver disorders, and reduce acidity of urine. Take in A.M. for best results.

16. Onion-antiseptic, source of sulfur, mild diuretic, and phlegm expectorant. Helpful with sinus trouble, cystitis, dyspepsia, catarrh, colds, insomnia, nervousness, pimples, skin eruptions, and stimulating circulation. Mix with celery juice.

17. Parsley-high in organic iron, chlorophyll, calcium, and vitamin A. Helpful in menstrual and malaria disorders, anemia, halitosis, nephritis, congested liver, rheumatism, high blood pressure, gall stones, urinary tract disorders, and asthma. Combine with celery, carrot juices. 7:1 Parsley ratio.

18. Pears-contain citric and malic acid. Helpful in indigestion, high blood pressure, colitis, catarrh, skin eruption, and decrease acidity of urine. Note! Pears are not recommended for diabetics.

19. Spinach-gland harmonizing, high in vitamin A, iron, and chlorophyll. For high blood pressure, functional heart trouble, anemia, goiter, acidosis, eyes and optic nerve and muscles, nervous exhaustion, obesity, dyspepsia, neuritis, tumors, and constipation.

20. Pineapple-contains 12% fruit sugar, 78.9 mg. of Vitamin C, high chlorine content, digestive aid, antiseptic, and contains the enzyme bromelean for protein digestion. Helpful for gland regulation, dyspepsia, sore throat, bronchitis, obesity, goiter, tumors, catarrh, arthritis, high blood pressure, and diphtheria. Reduce urine acidity, mild diuretic, and normalizes menstruation.

21. Tomatoes-high source of vitamin C and A. Blood purifier, gall stones, acidosis, sinus trouble, dyspepsia, jaundice, decrease urinary acidity, and biliousness

22. Turnip-high in vitamin A and C. 3 ½ ounces of turnip juice contain 1000 mg. of vitamin C. High in organic calcium, phosphorous, iron, and sulfur. Leaves are high in chlorophyll. Blood purifier, anemia, high blood pressure, sluggish liver,

acidosis, poor appetite, bladder disorders, bone, and teeth building.
23. Watermelon is a Native American healh tonic for most illness. Watermelon is a detoxifier and helps cleanse the body.
24. Purple grapes are used for detoxification and are high in antioxidants and an alkaline 9.0 pH content.
25. Black, blue, raspberry berries are used for immune system enhancement, and cleansing.

Calcium for Health.

Calcium deficiency causes a loss of body energy. The nervous system suffers and the body cannot convert food to energy. Around 25% of the food's potential energy and 23% of its protein value are lost when calcium is deficient. An excellent easily assimilated high content calcium vegetable is Kale and California Figs. Also phosphorous, boron, MK-7-K2 and vitamin D3 are associated needed factors for calcium. The mineral Boron is also required for calcium assimilation. Take CA.4:1 ratio with MG. Note! Currently in the U.S. We are Magnesium deficient.

Foods to Absolutely Avoid.
During the 9 day blood purification and diet, you should eat no oils, fats, starches, or meats.

THE NINE (9) DAY INNER CLEANSING AND BLOOD PURIFICATION.

First Day.
Eat only fresh vegetables and fruits organic is preferred by not necessary if unavailable. Treat all vegetables and fruits with our light photon energetic detoxification and nutrient value enhancer. Liquid Needle's Green & Yellow. Raw food consumed is better.

At night, drink a glass of garlic broth made of the following:
1. Cut fine slices of raw garlic. Cook for 7 minutes is a small pan in 1/3 of a glass of purified water. Pour the cooked garlic and broth into an 8 oz. glass and fill the glass with skimmed milk. Coconut milk is preferred. Drink before going to sleep. Take a minimum of the daily requirement of calcium lactate in the mid-afternoon.
2. Second Day.
Repeat the entire procedure of the First Day.

3. <u>Third Day</u>.
Repeat the entire procedure of the first and second day.
4. <u>Fourth Day</u>.
Drink an 8 oz. glass of sauerkraut juice first thing on an empty stomach. This supplies lactic acid, which aids the intestinal friendly flora. If elimination does not take place, follow up ½ hour later with an 8 oz. glass of warm fresh grapefruit juice, or an herbal laxative, enema, or vitamin C. Continue eating fresh vegetables and fruit. Take a minimum daily requirement of calcium lactate in the mid-afternoon.
5. <u>Fifth Day</u>.
Repeat the entire procedure of the 4th day, with sauerkraut juice, etc. Continue with fresh vegetables and fruit. Take the minimum daily requirement of calcium lactate in mid-afternoon.
6. <u>Sixth Day</u>.
Repeat the procedure of the 4th and 5th days with sauerkraut juice, etc. Take the minimum daily requirement of calcium lactate in mid-afternoon. Eat an abundance of green salads, greener the better. Dressing should be pure apple cider vinegar, honey, paprika, and water. Shake well and serve cold. Drink an abundance of green vegetable juices such as the Green Drink sold at Trader Joe's, Whole Foods, etc. The following green vegetables are recommended: celery, lettuce, spinach, parsley, cucumber, onion, cabbage, rhubarb, and papaya. Also goEnergetix's.com "Greening Powder."
7. <u>Seventh Day</u>.
Take a minimum of the daily requirement of calcium lactate in the mid-afternoon. Eat an abundance of green salads, the greener the better. The dressing should be sesame oil, pure apple cider vinegar, honey, paprika, and water. Shake well and serve cold. Drink an abundance of green vegetable juices, the greener the better. The following green vegetables are recommended: celery, lettuce, spinach, parsley, cucumber, onion, cabbage, rhubarb and papaya. Also goEnergetix's.com "Greening Powder."
8. <u>Eighth Day</u>.
Continue with fresh vegetables and fruits. Take the minimum daily requirement of calcium lactate to mid-afternoon. Drink all you can of the following fresh juices: orange, grapefruit, apple, papaya, pineapple, coconut, blackberry, raspberry, and cranberry.
9. <u>Ninth Day</u>.
Continue with fresh vegetables and fruits. Take the minimum daily requirement of calcium lactate in the mid-afternoon. Drink all you can of the following fresh vegetable juices: carrot and celery

combined, parsley and spinach combined, cabbage and cucumber combined, and papaya.

Blood Wash.

Start the day with a quart of fresh orange juice.
Take a quart of grape juice (unsweetened) around noon time.
Take a quart of pineapple juice (unsweetened) around 3 P.M.
Finish the day with a quart of fresh orange juice in the P.M.

Blood Wash Remedy.

The blood wash remedy consists of the following: organic non-sulfured black strap molasses, organic raw honey, organic apple cider vinegar, organic maple syrup, garlic, turmeric, beet powder, carrot powder, cayenne pepper, and Celtic sea salt. Mix equal amounts of molasses, honey, cider vinegar, and garlic in a quart jar. Let garlic sit for a few days before drinking. Add a teaspoon of turmeric, cayenne pepper, M.S.M., and Celtic sea salt. Also to replenish blood electrolytes coconut milk or water. Take a healthy sip every few hours during the day. Sea Weed contains our blood constituents. Note! all Pacific sea weed and etc., are radiated.
Organic Non-sulfured black strap molasses contains potash, iron, calcium five times higher than milk, B complex vitamins, copper, potassium, phosphorous, and chromium. Helpful against all cancers, sinusitis, menopause, anemia, varicose veins, and erysipelas.
Organic maple syrup is a detoxifier and anti-cancer.
Organic apple cider vinegar-helps oxidation of the blood, prevents intestinal putrefaction, regulates calcium metabolism, anti-aging, normalizes urine, blood consistency, regulates menstruation, and promotes digestion. Helpful for appetite suppressant, heart problems, hemophilia, nose bleed, sore throat, cough, laryngitis, asthma, vigor, digestive problems, frequent urination, and promotes digestion.
Honey-contains practically all of the vitamins, potassium, copper, sulfur, iron, magnesium, calcium, sodium, silica and chlorine. It kills bacteria on contact. Helpful for various heart conditions, diabetes, hay fever, colitis, arthritis, neuritis, and gastric ulcers. High in B1, B2, and C. Note! Glyphosate is in honey.
Garlic-contains allicin, iron, potassium, sulfur, iodine, zinc, manganese, phosphorous, copper, fluorine, vitamin B, C, and D. It has anti-bacterial, anti-parasitic, anti-viral, and anti-cancer

properties. Helpful for high blood pressure, bronchitis, asthma, emphysema, colds, gas, gallstones, arteriosclerosis, mucus, elimination, sinus problems, and increased vigor.

Turmeric-contains high antioxidant properties and scavenges free radicals. Prevents anti-aging, metzymes, keeps cells producing, and replicating as they were originally with no damage from free radical, etc. It is used as a medicinal herb in Ayurveda medicine.

Cayenne Pepper-contains high detoxifying compounds that cleanse the cells.

Celtic Sea or Himalayan Salt-easy to assimilate, contains all of the minerals, and trace elements.

Foods To Absolutely Avoid.

1. All enriched, bleached, refined, processed white flour products.
2. Any products made from white sugar or corn. Artificial Sweeteners.
3. Hard water. Chlorinated, Fluoridated.
4. Old vegetables (4 days old).
5. Coarse matured meats.
6. Pork.
7. Muscle meats.
8. Fatty foods. Hydrogenated Fats, Margarine, Poly Saturated, etc.
9. Iodized salt.
10. Food high in animal fats.
11. Adulterated foods. G.M.O., Factory Farmed, Boxed, Canned, and Preserved, etc.
12. Carbonated drinks.
13. Processed foods. Refined, Enriched, Chemical Added, Canned, etc.
14. Alcoholic beverages. Except organic Vis-Vercera red wine.
15. Coffee. Exception organic coffee and the green coffee bean.
16. Tea except herbal. Green and black if not chemically treated.
17. Rich sweet refined white granulated sugar deserts.
18. Ice cream.
19. Sweets of all kinds refined white sugar, (cookies, pies, cakes, and candy).
20. Condiments (all kinds).
21. Sauces.
22. Gravies.
23. Saccharin.
24. Synthetic sweeteners. Aspartame, Nutri-sweet, etc.

25.Black Pepper. An over dosage.
26.Synthetic pills. (Drobinol, opiates, and anti depressents).
27.Drugs (laxatives and sedatives).
28.Homogenized pasteurized cows milk. Milk of any kind even organic. (All milk is being radiated, glyphosated, other toxins).
29.Foods cooked over 118 F degrees. (destroys enzymes).

Health Restoral Nutrients.

1.Everyday take vitamins F-A-C-E-S for cell E.M.F. Electro-motive-force a cells ability to function properly. These are:
a) Folic Acid. 0.5 mg.
b) Vitamin A beta carotene activity. 25,000 I.U.
c) Vitamin C Ester or natural C with Rose hips, rutin, bioflavonoid and hisperidin, etc. 5,000 Mg.
d) Vitamin E Natural d-alpha-tocopherol from organic non G.M.O. Soybean Oil. 400 I.U. {GAMMA}
e) Selenium from Brewers yeast 50 Mcg. Silica adult dosage 40 mg.
2.Minerals especially chromium and G.T.F. (Glucose Tolerance Factor).
3.Honey-Apple Cider Vinegar-Non-sulfured Black Strap Molasses-Garlic.
4.Celtic sea, Himalayan salt contains all minerals for ionic easy to assimilate minerals and trace elements.
5.Whole grains such as Buckwheat (kasha-brown rice-quinoa-spelt-millet-aramanth-steel cut oats).
6.Sunflower seeds, sesame seeds, chia seeds, flax seeds, watermelon, and pumpkin seeds. Pumpkin seeds are anti-parasite.
7.Carob. Natural Chocolate substitute.
8.Kelp or Nori and all other seaweeds. Note! No Pacific Seaweeds.
9.Lecithin.
10.Fish-Krill Oil and Flax seed oil for E-fatty acids. Note! No Pacific Krill Oil.
11.Cayenne Pepper natural detoxifier.
12.Turmeric natural antioxidant. (anti-cancer and anti-inflammatory).
13.Ghee butter with cream removed (Ayurveda remedy).
14.Cinnamon produces chi energy, alkaline, and anti-inflammatory.
15.Clove energy to organs.
16.Papaya aids digestion. Alkaline fruit @ 9.0 pH
17.Sea weed, chlorella, dulse, algae, and spirulina sea vegtables.

18.Root Vegetables-ginger, dandelion, radish, beet, red, galandal.

Other Health Tips.

1.Elimination Recipe: 2 cups of celery, 2 cups of
carrots, 1 cup of spinach, and 1/2 cup of parsley. Grind up
vegetables and save the juices. Add 1 quart of purified water
and simmer 15-20 minutes. Serve warm.
2.Deep breathing exercises A.M.-P.M. we are oxygen creatures
that need clean fresh air for cell respiration and oxidation.
3.Sunshine at least 15-30 minutes per day after 3 P.M. and wear a
natural sun screen. Coconut oil, Olive oil, and Avacado oil are
advised.
4.Water. We need a minimum of 8 glasses per day of purified or
distilled water. (Ozone 03, and made alkaline with water wands).
5.Rest and meditate or nap 20-30 minutes per day.
6.Walk ½-1 hour per day in Nature if possible.
7.Bath 15-30 minutes before sleep skin brush, add Epsom salts,
baking soda, and lavender to clean pores of skin.
8.Visualize and see yourself the way you want to be and
that it already has been accomplished. (Believe it &
you will see it-Dr. Wayne Dyer).
9.Meaning and Purpose in life (goals, work, and dreams). "Dharma."
10.W.L.W.P. stands for work, love, worship, and play.
11.Affirm say, self talk what you want. I Am A-Z., i.e. A=affluent
12.Script and write a life script for goal achievement.
13.Exercise (bicycling-walk-martial arts especially Tai Chi,
 Internal Kung Fu or Chi Gong, Tantra, Yoga, and swimming, etc.

Spiritual Tips.

God does not dwell in an Unclean Temple.
Cleanliness is next to Godliness. The cleaner you are or your
machine which is a Ferrari the smoother and more power you have.
You are made of water, minerals, organic chemicals, and the air
you breathe. We are mostly free space energy, the cosmic light
photon life force. Your body is a loaned holy temple while you are
here on Earth. Your covenant reads as long as you keep it in good
condition, you stay in it. God does not dwell in an unclean or
broken temple. As long as your body is chemically and spiritually
perfect, you have the power to attract prosperity, and goodness to
yourself. "Cleanliness is next to Godliness."

1. <u>Live organic alkaline food attracts life</u>. Especially (buds, shoots, roots) Dead food attracts death. Avoid as much as possible all cooked and fried foods. Remember raw food is live food. Clean or detoxify your holy temple your body, clean, or detoxify your mind, and spirit.
2. <u>Pray and meditate</u> to Divine Universal Mind "God" for guidance and Divine Will to be done in your life. The Power of Prayer.
3. <u>Intention</u> of what you intend to do or accomplish in your life. The Power of Intention.
4. <u>Meaning and Purpose</u> your <u>Dharma</u> what you stand for and your life's work. If you don't stand for something you'll fall for anything.
5. <u>Unconditional Love</u> the <u>Unity</u> for everyone and everything in your life.
6. <u>Blessings</u> in your life as you are where you are supposed to have. Count and be thankful for what you have.
7. <u>Humility</u> and be humble in your life. Eat, Pray, Laugh, and Love.
8. <u>Acceptance</u> for things you cannot change, change the things you can and the wisdom to know the difference.
9. <u>Laughter</u> is a great healer. Laughter harmonizes the glands.
10. <u>Thinking positive</u> attracts positive in our life.
11. <u>Surrender</u> the EGO and let go and let GOD control your life.
12. <u>Belief and faith</u>, if you believe it you will see it in your life.
13. <u>Eliminate Ego</u> become desire-less for release of negative Karma.
14. <u>Attitude</u> how you react to negative situations.
15. <u>Be in the now</u> this very moment and let go of the past.
16. <u>Let go</u> of toxic people, places, relationships, and situations.
17. <u>Be in Nature</u> daily and become one with it. You are Nature.
18. <u>Exercise</u> daily. Internal Kung Fu, Tantra, Yoga, and walk, etc.
19. <u>Drink</u> 8-8 oz. glasses of purified alkaline and 03 water daily.
20. <u>Forgiveness</u> let go of resentments or getting even with people.
21. <u>Dharma</u> discover your life's meaning and purpose.
22. <u>Arma</u> perform service to humanity daily.
23. <u>Karma</u> elimination of negative debts from wrong spiritual actions.

<u>Gravizon. Amazon Herbal Formula</u>.

Gravizon guidelines. Gravizon is an herbal support formula formulated by Amazon Herb Company using the spagyric process. In addition to Graviola (a known cancer killing herb that is reported to be 10,000 times more powerful than chemotherapy with no known side effects, it only kills cancer cells), other herbs which help the body to support immune function, to detoxify, and too drain toxins. It is suggested to take at least one eight (8) ounce bottle of Gravizon along with Shipibo Treasure Tea, Fiberzon, and Aquazon. Take four to aix (4 to 6) weeks. Depending on an individual's response, a second eight (8) ounce bottle may be beneficial to an individual consuming this support formula. All of these products can be taken in larger amounts as the body tolerates them.

A word of caution: causing cellular detoxification without adequate drainage may result in a "healing crisis." Symptoms are similar to flu. Itching and skin rash may also occur. Gravizon is an herbal support classified as a dietary supplement. If Hippocrates were alive, he would almost certainly have indicated this as one that fits his quote: "Let food be your medicine and medicine be your food."

<u>Ingredients</u>.
<u>Proprietary Herbal Blend</u>.

1. Graviola-anti-cancer and anti-mutagenic.
2. Una de Gato-phytochemical alkaloid, anti bacteria, viral, and fungal.
3. Pau D'Arco-anti-cancer and immune enhancer
4. Jatoba-decongests the urinary tract, cystitis, bladder, prostate infections, and energizer.
5. Jurubeba-stimulates digestion, anti-inflammatory, for liver, spleen, and rich in alkaloids and used for uterine tumors.
6. Sangra De Drago-heals the lining of the digestive system assists in stomach and intestinal ulcers, anti-viral, and antioxidant.
7. Camu Camu-highest Vitamin C source in the world, astringent, and antioxidant. Note! Pine Tree Needles are also very high Vitamin C.
8. Dong Quai-used for female disorders, menstrual balance, assists liver to utilize more oxygen, and stabilizes blood pressure.
9. Quebrea Pedra-liver, gallbladder, and immune system enhancer.
10. Alfalfa-high in minerals, vitamins, chlorophyll source, detoxifier, and neutralizes acids.
11. Boldo-treats liver and intestinal dysfunctions, neutralizes acids, and aids digestion.
12. Artichoke-helps neutralize and stimulate bile.

13. Soy-isoflavones, adaptogens, protease inhibitors that are anti-mutagenic, anti-cancer. Genestein and Daidzein phyto-estrogens.
14. Safflower-supports heart, liver and promote circulation.
15. Tangerine Peel-helps clear the lungs of mucus, aids appetite, and digestion.
16. Aqularia-enhances cerebral function, balances mind-body connection, and nervous system.
17. Samambala-detoxifies body enhances the immune system.
18. Sarsaparilla-promotes rejuvenation, circulation, clears toxins, balances the glandular system and stimulates metabolism.
19. Peach Kernel-promotes circulation, dissolves accumulated blood clots, and opens blocked liver.
20. Dalergia Wood-enhances skeletal/muscular reflexes and mobility.
21. Bitter Orange-digestive tonic and anti-tumor.
22. Manaca-stimulates lymphatic system, anti-cancer and anti-inflammatory.
23. Tayuya-flushes excess fluids from tissues, reduces edema, and swelling.
24. Catuba-increases circulation, stimulant for the nervous system and brain.
25. Suma-contains 11% saponins which contain anti-cancer compounds, used for leukemia, blood pressure, and high cholesterol.
26. Iporuru-relieves symptoms of osteoporosis and increases flexibility.
27. Abuta-balances hormones and heals internal hemorrhaging.
28. Espinheira Santa-soothes and heals stomach ulcers, supports adrenal glands, increases energy, immune response, and digestion.
29. Muira Puama-tones nervous system, gastrointestinal disorders, used for stress, and traumatic conditions.
Gravizon-#GVZN-$75.00 ea. Two (2) bottles required $150.00
Shipibo tea-#ST-$19.99 Fiberzon-#FZN-$29.99 Aquazon-#AZN-$4.99

Note! In reference to Item #13 aforementiond. Soy isoflavones such as Genistein and Daidzein if isolated can be taken, but all soy food products should only be eaten if they are fermented. Also absolutely no G.M.O. or factory farmed soybeans. Eat only certified organic fermented soy foods only.

CHAPTER EIGHT

Whole Food Super Supplements.

IREDESCA.

Superior super food concentrate with hundreds of High Powered Nutrient Factors in a balanced full spectrum Spagyric blend. Contains 100% plant-life created ingredients. Providing vitamins, minerals, ionic elements, enzyme pigments, phytonutrients herbs, antioxidants, energy and longevity factors, pycogenols, probiotics, anti-parasitics, assimilation factors, essential oils plus metabolic, and digestive antioxidant enzymes plus much more. 60 mg. Co-enzyme Q10 etc.

Iredesca is a wild-crafted whole food, herb, essential oil, and plant formula that contains everything your body needs in a special blended formula. The blend is made from natural substances from around the world. Organic wild crafted spagyric nutrients that the body can assimilate easily. When you begin taking Iredesca you only take one (1) one quarter (¼) of a teaspoon daily. After a few months you can build up to a teaspoon. Iredesca supplies all you need for maximum vitamin, mineral, trace elements, plant phyto nutrients, antioxidants, essential oils, and fiber, etc.

Every patient I have that takes Iredesca remarks how much energy and vitality they have after a short time taking it. It is a remarkable formula that can after my pre-post detoxification change your level of endurance, vitality, and stamina. After age forty regular isolated vitamins, minerals, etc., cannot be absorbed, or assimilated. Your body requires whole foods for easy assimilation and absorption. This is why your food and supplements should be in a whole food regimen. In fact most all of your vitamins and minerals can cause toxic conditions in your body. Most are made with fillers and binders that are toxic. Besides you can't digest these isolated. or multi-vitamins. and minerals.

Iredesca is a food so perfect your cells begin to awaken and restructure themselves according to your ideal cellular plan, A food so complete it provides abundant resources for your body's every nutrient need including the needs of all your other foods and supplements you have ignored. A food so cleansing decades of accumulated toxins and unwelcome invaders are gently ushered away leaving your cells cleaner, happier, and more energetic then they have been since childhood. A food so satisfying and it abolishes cravings for foods you have been trying to avoid. It puts you back in charge of your appetite and diet. A food so nutritionally powerful and energetic that it surpasses the effectiveness of hundreds of dollars a month in supplements, convenient by replacing handfuls of vitamin, herb, and mineral pills.

Iredesca is the world's most complete and perfect food. It has a tropical fruity taste yet it is about one thousand (1,000) times as nutritious as ordinary food. Iredesca's life created nutrients will feed your cells better in ways they have ever been fed before. This will allow them to clean, remodel, repair faster than destructive forces, and disease are trying to erode them. Within a few months time and your cells will have literally created a new body. A body more as your body blueprint intends.

Iredesca is made from certain plants that accumulate nutrients and create phyto nutrients at amounts dozens of times greater than other plants. Its formula contains one hundred and fifty plus of the best of these super food nutrients to create a perfect food. It contains hundreds of vitamins, minerals, trace minerals, phytonutrients, and enzymes, etc. All of Iredesca's nutrients are genuinely natural. It is 100% plant life created. This is the most natural form for any nutrient and far more desirable from a cellular standpoint than either chemical nutrients or so called "natural" isolates.

Underlying the physical manifestation of each cell is a conscious life energy matrix that instructs each cell as to what role it should take. Heart, brain and liver, etc., healthy or weak. If this was not so we would develop from conception as a mass of undifferentiated cells, each a clone of our original first cell. By clarifying the signal of our life energy matrix which is influenced by our thoughts, and by making the correct building materials available to our new cells in transition called re-differentiated, we make a superior realization of our health, appearance inside and out, vitality, and well being.

In Iredesca these new breakthroughs are achieved in part by phyto nutrient colors, life frequency energy fields, and ethereal fragrances concentrated by plants from solar energy light. Iredesca gets its name from the iridescent light as color qualities of these ingredients. Exsula Iredesca manufacturer gathers the rare and precious ingredients from every continent except Antarctica.

Scientists believe that dietary nutrients out perform natural one isolate supplements because they contain naturally occurring substances. Iredesca contains dozens of trace minerals including several of the sources of non-atomic (non-radioactive) rhodium, iridium, iodine, and strontium. There is 630 mcg. of life created chromium which is three times as much as contained in supplements. Iredesca delivers extraordinary levels of enzymes and enzymatic pigments. A typical supplement may have only 25 mg. of its star nutrient in a 250 mg. Capsule, or tablet, and that translates to ninety percent filler. If you take two of this and three of that of a dozen different supplements, or even one of a metallic, or ascorbate you are paying for swallowing fillers which are after nine weeks become extremely toxic, produce toxic substance radiation frequencies that interfere with the cells communication system to cause illness, but not in the case of metallic and ascorbates as you are not even absorbing them into your system, and they are without life force. Iredesca supplies 100% functional ingredients without filters, binders, and synthetics. A day's supply of Iredesca powder which is three teaspoons in a glass of water or juice provides the equivalent of ninety loose 250 mg. capsules. Because of the absence of fillers, etc., Iredesca delivers several times the total nutrient equivalent to hundreds of capsules per day. Dead Doctors Don't Lie by Dr. Joel Wallach.

Certain nutrient accumulator plants cannot be concentrated without disrupting their inherited valuable qualities. This in energetic terms with the frequency signature as a whole off all its constituents (parts). i.e. Foxglove an herb used with great success for heart problems was shown to have no harmful side effects. But the extracted substance (compound) digitalis one of its compounds and added to synthetic fillers in order to pass an F.D.A. standard dosage has been shown to cause further heart problems such as convulsive heart failure and cause death due to prolonged use.

Nature has in its wisdom created the foxglove herb to be used as the whole plant with all its life force frequency constituents called synergists. With no synthetic fillers. Because it cannot be patented in its natural state nor adhere to an F.D.A. standard dosage, it has been altered for a profit so it can be patented as digitalis, pass a standard dosage yet remain toxic, and cause more harm than good over prolonged use. Unfortunately if it is prescribed for long prolonged use it eventually contributes to further disease and even eventual death. Iredesca contains the precious portion of all the whole herb ingredients and its synergists from the antagonistic or useless bulk in a created life form. Iredesca's ingredients cost $2,000.00 per pound but allow Iredesca to pack an outstanding volume of phyto nutrient power.

Iredesca is a synergistic blend of one hundred and fifty plus super foods in one bottle. All foods are compatible with each other. It's vegetarian, gluten free, and non-dairy. It is mostly organic or wild crafted. It is hand harvested in the wild in a way to assure future harvests from the natural growing sites. Some ingredients like Co-enzyme Q10, nutritional yeast, spirulina are scientifically cultured in carefully tended growing environments. Iredesca contains no chemicals, coloring's, flavorings, preservatives, or chemical additives of any kind.

If interested in Exsula's Iredesca you will find ordering information in the appendix section in the back of the book.

Nutrition facts:

The amount per serving is 88 calories or 37 fat calories.
Total fat 4 gr., 5% daily value of saturated fat from lecithin 0.8 gr., 4% cholesterol 0 mg., 0%, and potassium 300 mg. or 10%
Total carbohydrates 10 gr., 4%,
Dietary fiber 1.5 gr., 6%,
Sugars 8 gr.,
Protein 5.5 gr., 11%,
Vitamin A 1700% (1600% as beta carotenes),
Vitamin E, 620%,
Iron 25%,
Vitamin D 100%,
Vitamin C 630%,
Thiamine 530%,

Riboflavin 300%,
Niacin 120%,
Vitamin B6 330%,
Calcium 10%,
Vitamin B12, 1380%,
Biotin 125%,
Panotothenic Acid 150%,
Iodine 130%,
Phosphorous 25%,
Zinc 105%,
Magnesium 11%,
Copper 100%,
The ingredients in mg. per serving are:
High tech "Hypo-Allergic Enzyme-digested nutritional yeast (35 specific complexes) 4,641 %.
Xtra Pure "Soya Lecithin" 3,721%,
Juice extracts of grape, beet, elderberry, lyceum, cranberry, purple cabbage, carrot, and tomato. 3,393%
Silymarin (30:1) extract, 61%,
Co-Enzyme Q10 99.97% pure 60%,
Astragalus (4:1) extract 58%,
Ethereal Essence of Tangerine orange, Lemon, Cardamon, Ylang Ylang, Grapefruit, Thyme L, Nutmeg, Clove, Rosemary, Siberian Ginseng, Lavender, Rock Rose, and Iris. 57%
Siberian Ginseng (10:1) extract.
Pycogenols extract of grape, persimmon, and pine bark 50%.
Madagascar centella extract 49%.
Ampalya (Bitter Melon extract) 47%
Nettle leaf (1-2% silica) 39%.
Ginkgo Biloba (50:1 extract) 45%.
Swedish Bilberry (100:1) extract) 33%.
Pau de Arco (4:1 extract) 33%.
Rue plant powder 30%.
Odorless garlic powder 27%.
Echinacea purpea E (7:1 extract) 22%.
Grape fruit seed essence 19%.
Saffron (stigmas of flowers) 11%.
Hawaiian Spirulina 1,500%.
Juices of Barley, Wheat, Alfalfa, Watercress, Parsley, Broccoli, Kale, Kamut, Cauliflower, Celery, and Green Pepper 1,253%.
Nutraflora (F.O.S.) 1,000%.
High Pectin apple fiber 700%.

Green Papaya, Noni, Pineapple bromelain, and digestive enzymes 616%.
Bio-dynamic (S.O.D. Super oxide dismutase/catalase), mung, soy, wheat, and lentil sprouts 550%.
Green wild oat seed and tribulus 370%.
Cracked cell chlorella 360%.
Citr Max tamarind extract 333%.
Acerola cherry concentrate 267%.
Dunaliella carotene complex 250%.
T.F.A. and brown rice membrane 222%.
Schizandra (9% schisand, A, & B) 207%.
Soymatto cultured soy 200%.
Probiotic micro flora & S.B.O.'s (32 types), 8 billion cells 180%.
Chicory and/or dahlia inulin 160%.
Red clover flowers 155%.
Spinach octacasanol 152%.
Extracts of champignon, reishi, coriolus, matake, cordyceps, and shitake mushrooms 147%.
Yukon bee pollen 140%.
Ginger (4%) volatile oils 139%.
Hawthorn berries (2% vitexim) 137%.
Nova Scotia dulse, Icelandic kelp, and Northern pacific red algae 129%.
Aloe Vera (freeze dried extract) 120%.
Saw palmetto 34-35% free F.A. 111%.
Coriander, paprika, and cayenne 107%.
Royal jelly (lyophilized 5.9%) 10 HAD equivalent to 350 mg. raw 100%.
Turmeric 95%.
Curcumin/cats claw vine bark (4:1) extract) 90%.
Churchuhasi extract 88%.
Citrus pectin enhanced 77%.
St. Johns Wort (0.3% hypericum) 73%.
Suma (pfaffosides A, B, C, D, E, and F.
Olive leaf extracts essence 62%.

This blend of organically grown and hand harvested nutrients, herbs, anti-oxidants, vitamins, and minerals are imported from all over the world, then made into a powdered blend in the right synergistic balanced portions which then is bottled and comes to you in the product called Iredesca. This is Exsula's finest product and will provide you with everything that your trillions of cells need for optimum performance. It maintains the detoxification, intestinal flora needed for a healthy colon, and a balanced biological terrain. Your metabolism balances, assimilation of these nutrients into the system provides a constant source of pure nutrients from these whole food sources, that provide optimum health rest-oral, and maintenance. IREDESCA-#IRDSC-$85.99

I also endorse the following whole food super supplements: Etherium all the energized supplements, Youngevity, Biomatrix, and Greening Powder which are listed in the products addendum. These are also spagyric, organic, wild crafted, synergistic formulated for high utilization, nutrient, and micro nutrient abundance. The manufacturers of these outstanding products have thoroughly researched and tested the products for safeness, effectiveness, purity, and assimilation. When as example Iredesca is formulated it is in the proper dosages and therefore it's synergistic action of the nutrients. See on pages 76-78.

I have repeatedly pointed out inferior products that make claims. There are no authentic studies to back up their claims and also these products are no more than hype and marketing ploys to fool you. Money is the root of all evil and it is the motivator in this case. I challenge any product against the 21st Century Energetics detoxification program. Let any independent laboratory test their users of Genesis or other products against users of 21st Century Energetics users and a group that does nothing to detoxify. This will verify my claims that our products are the best in the world.

Note! If Iredesca is temporarily out of stock due to unforeseen problems in it's manufacturing. In its absence Etherium's super energized blends are highly recommended. GoEnergetix's.com Greening Powder and Biomatrix are also highly advised too.

I also advise Dr. Joel Wallach, D.M.V., N.D. liquid whole food supplement formula "Youngevity."

I also advise D.N.R.'s Liquid Needle-Green, Vit, Min and ENZ. Liquid Needle's-E.V.B. Energy-Vitality-Balance to increase your bio-electric field four to six (4-6) times higher. See further information about all Liquid Needle products on pages 284-307.

CHAPTER NINE

Ionic Minerals, Enzymes, Amino Acids, and Stabilized O2.

You cannot live very long without oxygen. It stands to reason that most people who live in urban cities are breathing deficient amounts of O2. In fact our natural supply of oxygen is slowly diminishing. There is also the problem of shallow breathing. Environmental pollutants as well as cigarette, marijuana, cigar, and pipe smoking all contribute to a clogged respiratory system. This diminishes greatly the necessary oxygen intake necessary to sustain a healthy brain and body. Cells need O2 to carry out cell respiration, the oxidation of nutrients necessary for the cell metabolism, and function.

Pollutants from automobiles (exhaust gases and tire disintegration), fast food restaurants (exhaust fumes), (smoke, pollutants), industrial plants (chemical pollutants into air, water, and ground), and paint (oil based fumes) are the leading polluters. This in turn causes toxins to enter the lungs and block oxygen uptake. We are oxygen starved and toxic. This combination weakens and causes many of our modern day symptoms seen by many physicians. New illnesses such as chronic fatigue syndrome and others are on the rise. People feel weak and cannot function at their intended level of performance. What can we do about the present situation? Note! Also coal, aluminum, and concrete.

We can pass legislation for cleaner air less chemical production and live in harmony with Nature. How to accomplish this?

Get involved in your own life and do something to target anyone of the aforementioned causes. One person can make a difference. Be aware of your own particular lifestyle and what can be improved.

Another powerful way on increasing one's oxygen intake is to supplement your self daily with the following stabilized oxygen supplements. These products include: Hydroxygen Plus- 02, ionic enzymes, amino acids, and minerals, Oxygen Elements Plus, Dynamo2, and Oxy-Moxy, etc. These oxygen products enable the lungs to put more oxygen into the bloodstream with every breath. One 2.36 ounce bottle of Oxy-Moxy can put more oxygen into the bloodstream than a medical tank of oxygen (used with a breathing tube placed in the nose) can every day and for two months.

1. Oxy-Moxy and the other aforementioned products help free the body of waste gases and toxins. They speed the elimination of carbon dioxide (CO2) and other by-products of living. This makes more room available on our hemoglobin for more oxygen.

2. Oxygenates the blood stream naturally. They help the lungs get more oxygen out of the air we breathe, directly into the bloodstream, and to benefit all of our body's cells. Other products start with limited amounts of oxygen in the bottle and deliver it to the digestive systems.

3. Sub-lingual Application. They are the only enhancing products made specifically for oral absorbing which is seven (7)-thirty (30) times more effective than absorbing nutrients by digestion.

4. Measurable results are so effective that increased blood oxygen levels can be measured within a few minutes, on an oximeter.

5. It is excellent for athletes. It helps people with high physical demands. They increase oxygen and this increases endurance with translates to increased performance. It does the same for extended exercise, or those who have to do physically demanding work.

6. Excellent for anyone with impaired lung function. They reduce the need for inhalers for asthmatics, people with emphysema, and help those with pneumonia, and bronchitis.

7. Excellent when the local air supply is lacking sufficient oxygen to meet the body's demands. These are ideal for people exposed to smog, any airborne pollutants, or breathing exhaust fumes while trapped in traffic; for people who fly in jet planes, or work in modern air conditioned buildings where the same air is constantly recycled, and for people visiting high altitude places until their bodies acclimate to the thinner air that's there.

8. Helps reduce "Jet Lag". These help to prevent the oxygen debt that's a major factor in causing the feelings of tiredness and fatigue.

Working out in high altitudes? These aforementioned oxygen products can help. You don't have to be scientist to know that the higher up you go, the less oxygen there is. At seven thousand (7,000) feet up there's about half the amount of oxygen there is at sea level.

So what, you say? So try down hill or cross country skiing, snow boarding, hiking, or biking in the mountains without acclimating first, and see how miserable high altitude sickness can make you feel.

When your body is deprived of the oxygen it's used to, it can't perform right. You feel exhausted. Headaches and nausea are common. It's hard to sleep. Your heart beats faster and your feet move slower. High altitude sickness can be very serious and even fatal. If you're a high altitude exerciser you're probably familiar with the common advice. Allow your body a few days or even weeks to acclimate to high altitude before you do strenuous activities. Drink lots and lots of water. Avoid alcohol and other dehydrators. Go to lower altitudes immediately if you experience serious symptoms, such as gurgling in the lungs.

And now there is a bit of uncommon advice, an oxygen enhancer called Oxy-Moxy, Hydroxygen Plus, Oxygen Elements Plus, and Oxy-Moxy developed by Abraham Chaplin, M.D. and Ph.D, who has studied the benefits of oxygen enhancement for more than fifteen years. Dr. Chaplin claims that his product enables the lungs to put more oxygen into the body with every breath.

Dr. Chaplin made his discovery in 1963 while researching oxygen enhanced formulas and their under-the-tongue application with Dr. Carl Pfeiffer at the Princeton Brain Bio Center.

Here is a simplified explanation of how Oxy-Moxy works: Each of us normally breathes about 5,000 gallons of air per day. With massive deforestation, loss of rain forest, the overwhelming increase of pollutants, photosynthesis is markedly reduced on a global level, and the percent of oxygen in the air we breathe is dropping.

Years ago, our air consisted of 30%-35% oxygen. Now it's down to 18%-20% and in some highly industrial cities even less. For many people, this shortage is compounded by other factors, such as reduced lung capacity from anemia, or smoking, increased metabolism due to hyperactivity, or stimulants (coffee, alcohol, etc).

The bottom line is, each breath delivers less oxygen to our bloodstream. Now there is Oxy-Moxy. It is a blend primarily of

Norwegian seaweed, a mix of enzymes proven effective in enabling the lungs to get more oxygen into the body with every breath. Chaplin, drawing on repeated tests done with a standard Nelcor 100 oximeter measuring the level of O2 in arterial blood, says that Oxy-Moxy can increase the amount of oxygen extracted from these 5,000 gallons of air by 2 to 3%, enough to pump about 150 gallons of extra oxygen into the body every day.

Dr. Chaplin says he is very careful not to extol it's value in treating or preventing asthma, emphysema, or even high altitude sickness. "We're a food supplement. I'm careful not to make any medical claims. I don't want to be an over-the-counter drug, because it costs at least $10 to $12 million to document. So we just call ourselves a respiratory oxygen enhancer and that way we stay under the radar."

My own personal radar got very burned on Chaplin's low-key approach. It is completely safe and has no known side effects, he says. And over the past 15 years, he's used it with thousands who wanted a breathing boost for all sorts of reasons, from boosting athletic performance to avoiding jet lag (which is really oxygen deprivation).

What about a double-blind, super-scientifically-controlled studies" "I don't feel that's necessary," says Dr. Chaplin, whose company, En Garde Health products, has been selling Oxy-Moxy, and other oxygen related dietary supplements since 1984.

"It works, simple." I'm going to take it to Tibet with me and see. Dr. Chaplin suggests I start taking it a few days before I leave. The way I take it is to put 10 to 15 drops under the tongue, leave it there for 30 seconds, and then swallow. One dose will begin to boost my oxygen intake in one to two minutes; the booster effect will last a few hours, and I can continue taking it without side effects. One bottle costs $ 24.95 and contains 2000 drops. It has a slightly mint flavor.
OXYMOXY-#OXMOX-$24.95 available @amazon, herbal health, luckyvits
DYNAMO2-#DYMO2-$24.95 available @amazon, herbal health, luckyvits
COLO2ZONE-#CO2ZO-$24.95 available engarde, amazon," "
HYDROXYGEN PLUS-#HP+-$59.99 contains ionic enzymes, amino acids, minerals and O2 available @amazon,zapata, bestdeals, luckvits
OXYBLAST-#OXB-#39.99 OxiLife-OXL-$8.17 OxyMax available @ walmart

We are oxygen (02) breathing water (H20) beings with earth which are the minerals mainly then add amino acids. It stands to reason that oxygen (02) and our breathing lower oxygen (02) levels contained in our atmosphere and environment can and does effect our cellular respiration. This is the cells ability to produce energy, carry out its life electro-motive-force, promote our health, and vitality. We need a higher content of oxygen (02) to carry out these functions, since the air we breathe, the way we breathe is not adequate, so we must supplement our bodies, and brains with the oxygen (02) supplements aforementioned. It is the same way our depleted soil does not give us our required nutrients so it is essential to supplement ourselves with whole food supplements for optimum health, energy, and vitality. Water is also an essential element for we are 85% water. Water becomes toxic with the toxins we absorb, so this to must be frequently hydrated, and drink a minimum of 8-8 ounce glasses of pure distilled water daily. Tip: Add 02, Energetix's Rehydration, L.N.T.B., L.N.-E.V.B. to the water for maximum strength, and 03 charged water. Remember you are what you think, drink, eat, breathe, digest, assimilate, and metabolize. Daily oxygen (02), ozone (03), Hydrogen ions (H-ions), Liquid needle-E.V.B. charged water, whole food supplements (Liquid Needle-Green, Yellow, Youngevity, Iredesca, Biomatrix, Greening Powder, and Etherium Energized Blends). This combined with thinking positive healthy thoughts are your foundation for health, well being, energy, vitality, and balance. Also advised is The A2Z Aqua6 ozone (03) air, water, and oil ozone generator. Available @Amazon.com or on ebay.com. Also advised is a Turapur hydrogen ion maker (H-ion) with a tourmaline 3 stage water filter. Available at Turapur.com. For alkaline water use alkaline water wands available @ amazon.com.

CHAPTER TEN

Light Photon Solutions Internal, External Topicals Applied on Specific Acupuncture Points, Chakras, and 15 Day Detox Soaks.

Our bodies respond to frequency. Each human, animal, plant, and all living things contain a signature frequency. This determines at what frequency it resonates at. Light travels at 186,000 miles per second. Light contains all the known frequencies we see. If you take a fluid such as water and impose certain light wave photon frequencies upon the molecules you can charge the water with thousand's of frequencies. These are considered positive high frequencies. Our body is composed of billions of cells that make up our organs, glands, muscles, blood, bone, and brain, etc. These when they are in a homeostasis balance or healthy operation operate at frequencies that are in certain parameter balanced alignments. When stressed and toxic or out of frequency balance the aforementioned cannot operate to function properly. We call this a variety of terms ranging from cell interference, toxicity, bio-accumulation, and degeneration, etc. When this happens we have symptoms which warn us something is not functioning properly. We usually are in a state of ease and when not we have acute to chronic symptoms resulting in what we call disease. See pgs. 25-27

In bio-energetic and naturopathic as well as behavioral medicine-psycho-physiology we look at frequencies operating in normal parameters for healthy outcomes. Naturopathic medicine gives natural medicine in the form of herbs, homeopathic remedies, and flower essences, etc. These are made up of frequencies that when given to a sick person change the body's bio-field an energy field that can be measured. A sick person has a lower energy field [42-58 MHz]. The natural remedy raises the frequency, helps the immune system, so eventually you will return to the frequency producing health, and no symptoms. "Like cures like." The body always will respond to the highest frequency even if it's producing illness. Light photon frequency solutions or remedies are produced by high frequency light photons, (energetic frequencies of the light spectrum band being superimposed, (imprinted) on molecules of minerals), and suspended in mineral water. The minerals capture thousands of these light photons on each mineral particle. When this is either taken internally, externally, and topically on certain acupuncture points, or food soaked in it will render toxins harmless for 32 hours, increase food nutritive values 200%, detoxify toxins, energize, vitalize, and balance the bio-field, etc. Another factor is that all body organs, skin, lymph, blood, and vertebra's, etc., all resonate at certain frequency as well. When in a healthy and normal state these can be measured and if we produce a matching frequency by imposing (imprinting) these frequencies on the mineral molecules we then can produce the same in the body. "Like cures like."

The Sun's rays of light photons race towards the Earth millions of miles in minutes and energize all living things. They produce energy and grow plants that feed us. The energy in the plant, fruit, nut, seed, legume, herb, and vegetable, etc., is then consumed by us, and energizes us. Each has a signature frequency. It gives us life energy for our body operation. Without these frequencies we would die. Without the Sun the planet Earth would become cold, barren, and produce no life.

It stands to reason that these same light photons E.M.F.'s can be produced in a laboratory, be imposed on, or in mineral water, consumed by us, and produce a healthy balance in our body. We can utilize these frequencies to accomplish an increase in energy, vitality, and balance. The body always seeks homeostasis or balance for health. Once negative frequencies caused by toxins replace the positive frequencies we have illness, first the acute, or alarm state, then chronic, or the compensation state.

We can change the frequencies back to normal and our symptoms will diminish. The body can return to the intended frequencies and we can restore balance. Once in balance we have a healthful state. Light photons are the cutting edge of bio-energetic medicine and technology.

We can now completely detoxify safely and naturally with light photons in mineral water. These frequencies push the toxins right out of the body into bath water. Placed on acupuncture-points they can energize the body's organs, defense, or compensatory system. They can be taken internally and produce energy-vitality-balance. They can revitalize food, detoxify food, render harmful toxic chemicals safe, re-energize your organs, brain, body constituents, and produce a calm mind state, etc. This is the 21st century energetic cutting edge medicine, technology, and combined with Natures healing wisdom. This is called Liquid Needle.

I have personally used all of the light photon energetic substances since 1992 with great success and no complaints from patients. I have performed a study with light photon Liquid Needle Total Balance that actually brought the E.E.G. brainwave frequencies into balance and helped hold them in desired parameters on pages: 309-310. I have also used the detoxification bath soaks for addiction, to remove toxic residues from the brain with success, and wellness. Arthur Widgery and Ken Widgery, N.D, of D.N.R., Inc.com and Jerome Plotnick, Ph.D., N.D. of 21stCenturyEnergetics.com The following on page: 87 is a list of light photon energetic products. See on pages: 287-310 Liquid Needle products and their protocols. Topical substances placed on acupuncture points or chakras:

PRODUCTS & ORDERING INFORMATION:

Original-1 oz.-$35.00 re-balance acupoints, chakras, and bio-field
Original Extra-Strength-1 oz.-$40.00
Brown-1 oz.-$35.00 hormones, vitamins, minerals.
Brown Extra-Strength-1 oz.-$45.00
Green-1 oz.-(vits, mins, herbs vitalize 200% higher nv)-$40.00
Green Extra-Strength-1 oz.-$45.00
Yellow-1 oz. (detox all known toxins in food, water, etc.)-$40.00
Extra-Strength-1 oz.-$45.00
Total Balance-1 oz.-$45.00 re-balance bio-field and brainwaves
Chi Gong-(calm, Chi Gong meditative state)-1 oz.-$45.00

Detoxification Protocols-Body Soaks

Gold Extra -Strength-(detox-yeast, fungus candida toxins all)-32 oz.-$70.00 Internal-8oz.-$50.00
Coffee Extra-Strength EX-(detox-heavy metals, chemo, parasites, chemicals-colon, cleansing, and balance)-32 oz.-$70.00 Drops 1/2 oz.-$40.00
Cig-131,522 Cigarette-(detox-nicotine)-32 oz.-$70.00 Drops-1/2 oz.-$40.00
Tab-32 oz.-$70.00 Drops-1/2 oz.-$40.00
Can-133-(detox-chemo-radiation-cancer)-32 oz.-$70.00 Drops-1/2 oz.-$40.00

Par (parasites)-32 oz.-$70.00 Drops-1/2 oz.-$40.00
Lympha L-105(lymph)-32 oz.-$45.00 Drops-1/2 oz.-$30.00
Res (respiratory)-32 oz.-$70.00
Lvr (liver)-32 oz.-$70.00
Blue (energize all of the acupuncture points)-32 oz.-$45.00
Clear-32 oz.-$45.00 (balance, stress, emotions, hormones, sleep)
Amber Plus-32 oz.-$70.00 (cleansing, pain, fluid balance)
Foot Soak-32 oz.-$45.00 (balance, vitality, pain, stress, hormones)
Ex Stress Soak-105-Ext-(eliminate stress)-32 oz.-$45.00
Ex Stress Extra Strength Soak-105-Ext-Ex-32 oz.-$70.00

Miscellaneous

Shampoo Drops-(protect brain from chemicals)-1 oz.-$40.00
CheckMate-(pain, toxicity, balance, joints, and inflammation-32 oz.-$45.00
Liquid Triggers Pain Gel-(eliminate pain)-1 oz.-$45.00
Fabric Shield-(protect fabrics from chemicals)-8 oz.-$30.00
Neutra-Spray-(protect brain from chemicals)-8 oz.-$30.00
Total Balance-(balance entire body bio-field)-1.1 oz.-$45.00
E.V.B. or EX-(energy-vitality-balance)-32 oz.-$125.00 $135.00
E.V.B. Extra Strength-(energy-vitality-balance)-8 oz.-$45.00
E.V.B. Oral Spray-(energy-vitality-balance)-1.1 oz.-$45.00

Liquid Signals Oral Supplements

DHE-(D.H.E.A.) 501-1/2 oz.-$30.00
MEL-(Melatonin) 502-1/2 oz.-$30.00
PRO-(Progesterone, Estrogen, P.M.S., and Menopausal) 503-1/2 oz.-$30.00
BAR-(Barley) 504-1/2 oz.-$30.00
VIT-(Vitamins all) 506-1/2 oz.-$30.00
PYC-(Pycogenol) 505-1/2 oz.-$30.00
ENZ-(Enzymes all) 507-1/2 oz.-$30.00
HEA-(Heart) 508-1/2 oz.-$30.00
HEA-(Heart Extra Strength) 508EX-1/2 oz.-$40.00
WAL-(Walnut antiparasitic) 509-1/2 oz.-$30.00
CAN-(Cancer Extra Strength) 509EX-1/2 oz.-$40.00
ALL-(Allergies) 510-1/2 oz.-$30.00
ALL-(Allergies Extra Strength) 510EX-1/2 oz.-$40.00
VIR-(Virus) 513-1/2 oz.-$30.00

VIR-(Virus Extra Strength) 513EX-1/2 oz.-$40.00
KBL-(Kidney-Bladder-Liver) 514-1/2 oz.-$30.00
KBL-(Kidney-Bladder-Liver Extra St.) 514EX-1/2 oz.-$40.00
COL-(Colon) 515-1/2 oz.-$30.00
COL-(Colon Extra Strength) 515EX-1/2 oz.-$40.00
STA-(Stamina) 516-1/2 oz.-$30.00
CEL-(Cells) 517-1/2 oz.-$30.00
TOX-(Toxins) 518-1/2 oz.-$30.00
GLA-(Glands) 519-1/2 oz.-$30.00
GLA-(Glands Extra Strength) 519EX-1/2 oz.-$40.00
MIN-(Minerals all) 521-1/2 oz.-$30.00
SKN-(Skin) 524-1/2 oz.-$30.00
SKN-(Skin Extra Strength) 524EX-1/2 oz.-$40.00
ENC-(Endocrine) 527-1/2 oz.-$40.00
NUTRITION PAK-NP-3-$65.00
EX COLD/FLU/SINUS PAK-CFPEX-$95.00
EX HEART/CIRCULATION PAK-HCPEX-$95.00

Ex Stress Products

EXSTRESS ORAL DROPS-STR-525-1 Oz.-$40.00
EXSTRESS ORAL DROPS-1/2 oz.-$30.00
EXSTRESS EX ORAL DROPS-STR-525EX-1 oz.-$45.00
EXSTRESS SOAK-105-EXT-32 oz.-$45.00
EXSTRESS EXTRA STRENGTH SOAK-105-EXT-EX-32 oz.-$70.00

H.B.H. (Herbal-Botanical-Homeopathic) Products

STO (Stomach)-601-8 oz.-$35.00
INT (Intestines)-602-8 oz.-$35.00
CLN (Colon)-603-8 oz.-$35.00
LVR-(Liver)-604-8 oz.-$35.00
JNT (joints)-605-8 oz.-$35.00
NRV-SYS (nervous system)-606-8 oz.-$35.00 NRV-SYS-EX-8 oz.-$40.00
END-SYS (endocrine system)-8 oz.-$35.00 RND-SYS-EX-8 oz.--$40.00
CAR-SYS (cardiovascular system)-8 oz.-$35.00
RES-SYS (respiratory system)-8 oz.-$35.00
URI-SYS (urinary system)-8 oz.-$35.00 URI-SYS-EX-8 oz.-$40.00
CLN-603-EX Strength-8 oz.-$40.00 CAR-SYS-EX-8 oz.-$40.00
LVR-604 Ex Strength-8 oz.-$40.00 RES-SYS-EX-8 oz.-$40.0

Liquid Triggers (rebalance energetically all cervical-thoracic lumbar vertebras)

C1 vertebra-1/2 oz.-$30.00
C2 vertebra-1/2 oz.-$30.00
C3 vertebra-1/2 oz.-$30.00
C4 vertebra-1/2 oz.-$30.00
C5 vertebra-1/2 oz.-$30.00
C6 vertebra-1/2 oz.-$30.00
C7 vertebra-1/2 oz.-$30.00
C8 vertebra-1/2 oz.-$30.00
T1 vertebra-1/2 oz.-$30.00
T2 vertebra-1/2 oz.-$30.00
T3 vertebra-1/2 oz.-$30.00
T4 vertebra-1/2 oz.-$30.00
T5 vertebra-1/2 oz.-$30.00
T6 vertebra-1/2 oz.-$30.00
T7 vertebra-1/2 oz.-$30.00
T8 vertebra-1/2 oz.-$30.00
T9 vertebra-1/2 oz.-$30.00
T10 vertebra-1/2 oz.-$30.00
T11 vertebra-1/2 oz.-$30.00
T12 vertebra-1/2 oz.-$30.00
L1 vertebra-1/2 oz.-$30.00
L2 vertebra-1/2 oz.-$30.00
L3 vertebra-1/2 oz.-$30.00
L4 vertebra-1/2 oz.-$30.00
L5 vertebra-1/2 oz.-$30.00
Coccyx vertebra-1/2 oz.-$30.00
Sacrum vertebra-1/2 oz.-$30.00
Liquid Triggers Kit contains all aforementioned vertebra-LTKIT-1/2 oz. all-$425.00

Dynique & Draw

Dynique Solution-(face lift) D106-32 oz.-$30.00
Dynique Liquid Pearls-DLP-1/2 oz.-$25.00
Draw-W108-(wound healing)-32 oz.-$30.00 Draw Extra Strength-W108-Ex-32 oz.-$45.00 DrawPlusSpray-W109-S-8 oz.-$30.00

Sports Topicals

Sports Topical Silver (Mental)-ST-M-1 oz.-$40.00
Sports Topical Gold (Physical)-ST-P-1 oz.-$40.00
Sports Soak P (Physical)-SS-P-32 oz.-$45.00
Sports Soak M (Mental)-SS-M-32 oz.-$45.00
NOTE!
When the Sports Topicals are used with our E.E.G. & E.M.G. biofeedback training program it is highly effective for professional athletes. Aids by keeping the training outcomes in place longer, then permanently for optimum performance physical, and mental fitness.
1 day Priority overnight: $25.50
2 day Priority: $17.50
3 day Priority: $9.50
Drop Ship: $13.60
C.O.D. U.P.S. Charge: $13.60 please check for current prices.
To order call: (661) 245-3616 leave your name, shipping address, zip code, phone number, credit card number and expiration date. If pay by check or money order send to: Jerome Plotnick, Ph.D., N.D., 6132 Frazier Mt. Pk. Rd., #45, Lake of the Woods, CA. 93225 Include shipping, handling, and method you want order sent to you. Include cost with your product cost. Please make your money order out to Jerome Plotnick if sending check make it out to Jerome Plotnick and when check clears we will send out your order. If paying by C.O.D. add an extra fee to U.P.S. of $6.50 if drop ship adds $12.50 U.P.S. only accepts cash for payment so please have the exact amount on hand to receive your order. Thank you for your cooperation and your order.

I use Liquid Needle Light Photon Energized solutions as the foundation of all my healing programs including detoxification, E.E.G. neurofeedback brainwave training for A.D.D., A.D.H.D., L.D., and addictions, etc. Liquid Needle products have been researched and proven for their energy enhancement, ability to balance, assist the body to restore energy-vitality, and balance. Liquid Needle products have been clinically tested, trialed and now are F.D.A. approved as of 2017. See my double blind study in this book on pages 309-310 and the study results also on page 418 of The 13 Steps From Illness To Health-APNBMPDR book by Jerome Plotnick, Ph.D., N.D. Also see pages: 287-310 in this book.

CHAPTER ELEVEN

E.M.G. Biofeedback for Stress Reduction, Coping Skills, Muscle Re-education, and Pain Control.

E.M.G. Biofeedback training is a client-centered-holistic-approach to re-balance your body's musculoskeletal system, to control body functions, learn coping skills to reduce stress, eliminate pain through E.M.G., G.S.R., and Temperature Biofeedback training. This is a client-centered training which allows one to become aware of their stressors that affect your body's physiology, then learn new coping skills, and to remove their effects.

It also alleviates associated pain by re-balancing the body's stress points. It retrains muscle groups so the musculoskeletal system operates at its optimum performance with strength and leverage. Learning the causes of symptoms, removing them alleviates pain, and suffering. The stressors are learned, can be re-learned, by developing new coping skills, and self regulation.

Learning the causes of symptoms, removing them with E.M.G. biofeedback training alleviates stress, pain, muscle tension, and improper body function. The stressors are learned and affect your body's physiology in many symptomatic ways. These can be re-learned by developing new coping skills to eliminate, or reduce significantly stress, anxiety, muscle, tensions, and pain, etc. The biofeedback training brings the muscles, body functions back into balance creating harmony, wellness, and wholeness.

When this is achieved healing occurs. Biofeedback is used to treat chronic pain, carpal tunnel syndrome, Raynaud's disease, high blood pressure, hypertension (the leading cause of heart problems), heart rate, headaches all, neuromuscular tensions (N.M. re-ed), T.M.J., bruxism, cerebral vascular and Palsy, motor tics, epilepsy, respiratory disorders, panic attacks, anxiety, peripheral nerve damage, and spinal chord injury, etc.

Biofeedback has been accepted by most insurance companies as an adjunct to treatments being received by insured patients. Most V.A. Hospitals have used it to treat various veteran disorders. President Clinton strongly approved its use in the V.A. system. The Mayo Clinic, Menninger Clinic, hospitals, Universities such as

Univ. of No. Texas, Univ. of So Colorado, U.C.L.A., Institutes such as E.E.G. Spectrum, Biofeedback Institute of L.A., and Brain Master Inc., etc., nationwide employ it in their treatment, and research. It is applied psycho-physiology and falls into the category of behavioral health, health psychology, and medicine. Unlike meditative techniques, hypnosis, yoga, and relaxatio techniques, biofeedback can be seen, heard by the trainee, and can also be recorded. This allows an accurate record of progress to be shown for medical, psychological, and chiropractic treatment. Insurance company's can also see successful progress in an insured patient.

The trainee can also benefit because they can hear, see, and review their training outcomes. This makes a trainee more apt to gain rewards when they can see their training outcomes.

Biofeedback usually begins with temperature training sessions where an thermistor electrode is placed on the forefinger and is hooked to a thermometer, The trainee learns auto regulation by increasing their body temperature 1-3 degrees, and holding it for a time period. A visualization of the trainee sitting in front of a fire or putting their body in a hot bath usually is employed. Once the trainee masters this they can move to other biofeedback training applications such as G.S.R. galvanic skin resistance. This is a method that measures skin resistance in micro volts, is used to measure tension, nervousness, and stress, etc. This is fed back into the measuring instrument and the trainee attempts to lower it by developing new coping skills per the imbalance. Once the trainee develops coping skills they can relearn the learned negative behavior and change it to a more positive outcome.

Biofeedback is a mind body interplay also called a psycho-physiological interplay. Mind affects the body's physiology. An example would be fear when someone is in a fearful state then we have fight, flight, and sleep state. This is a normal reaction when there is a real d anger. But if the fear is imagined in the mind then we have fight, flight, and exhaustion when there is no real danger. We have this on a subconscious level so the person is not aware of the fear. The body responds with panic, action, and exhaustion, etc. This can be eliminated once the person is made aware of the fear and relearns to effectively diminish it. On the other hand we may have a person that has muscle tension and this can be eliminated by using the mind to self regulate that tension by telling one's self that it is reducing it. It is like behavior modification one little step everyday until it is eliminated. Hypertension is a major cause of death in the U.S. today. He died of a broken heart is a true statement. When you are tense in a nervous state where the nervous system is operating when it should not then we have hypertension. The heart rate, blood pressure is adversely affected, this can cause heart attacks, and strokes. Have you ever felt heart palpitations and there didn't seem to be any known immediate cause. This is hypertension in action. Usually though the person doesn't even know it's happening until they suffer a major problem. Note! May also be a Calcium deficiency.

Biofeedback training can measure the imbalance in the body's psycho (mind), physiology (body), to teach the trainee to self regulate heart rate, blood pressure, vascular blood circulatory system, respiratory, muscle tensions, urinary incontinence, and hypertension, etc. Most people are unaware of these imbalances until they begin training areas of dysfunction. Once recognized the trainee begins a slow process to re-learn and change these unwanted imbalances. The symptoms usually are eliminated in a short time period and they no longer need the biofeedback instrument. If needed a trainee can thereafter also purchase a cost effective E.M.G. Biofeedback self training device.
Note! Low Calcium can also cause heart palpatations and muscle cramping. Rx: Needed for proper Calcium distribution is Vitamin D3-5000 mg. in extra virgin oil non G.M.O. capsules and Vitamin K-2 MK-7, 100 mcg. non G.M.O. vege capsules. The element Boron is also needed for Calcium assimilation and absorbtion.

CHAPTER TWELVE

E.E.G. Neurofeedback Training for Relaxation, Focus, Alertness Concentration, Memory, Mental Fitness, and Peak Performance. Elimination of Anxiety, Depression, all Addictions of Substances and Processes, O.C.D., P.T.S.D., A.D.D., A.D.H.D., and L.D., etc.

E.E.G. neurofeedback is a client-centered training I call a mental spa. Just as you relax in a body spa the E.E.G. training helps you to relax your mind in a mental spa. It is used to balance brainwaves per their normal wave frequencies. This helps to increase focus, attention, relaxation, mental fitness, and peak brain performance. It eliminates P.T.S.D., A.D.D., A.D.H.D., O.C.D., B.P.D., P.D., addictions, depression, anxiety, and tensions, etc.

The E.E.G. training provides both audio and visual neurofeedback based on parameters derived from spectral analysis of the E.E.G. signal at specific brain sites.

The brainwave frequencies are delta (0Hz.-4Hz.), theta (4Hz.-7Hz.), alpha (7 Hz.-12 Hz.), low beta-S.M.R. (12Hz.-15Hz.), beta (15Hz.-24Hz., high beta (24-Hz.-32Hz.), and gamma (32Hz.-44Hz.). These are located at specific brain (scalp) sites where sensitive gold plated electrodes are placed that can pick up micro volt electrical signals. These signals are fed into a neurofeedback device that can amplify and block the signals as are desired.

Here the signals can be set a certain training thresholds and then feedback to the trainee's scalp site. Certain protocols are set for specific training such as relaxation, mental fitness, peak performance, addictions, and all brain disorders aforementioned.

The E.E.G. training is used for relaxation training by providing a visual-auditory signal that corresponds to the trainee's increase in alpha frequency as an indicator of achieving a relaxed state. Other benefits include reducing theta while raising S.M.R. low beta waves, it enhances concentration that results in reduction of errors, greater attention to detail, increased self-control, sustained attention to tasks, and ability to shutoff environmental distractions. This is the elimination of all outside distractions.

Increasing the percent of alpha brainwave enhances creativity that provides increased decision making capabilities, increased accuracy improvement, and general relaxation improvement. The duration of training ranges from thirty to eighty (30-80) sessions. From one (1) time per week to ten (10) times per week depending on the trainee's goals, needs, and ability to learn.

During an E.E.G. training session the trainee should relax, allow the system to teach the brain, when the E.E.G. shows the desired amount of brainwave energy, and when it does not.

All beneficial effects are a result of the learning your brain will experience as a result of the visual-auditory signals that are provided. The trainee should not try to relax. Trying may defeat the beneficial effects that are desired. The trainee should just relax and allow the brain learning to begin. It may take a 1-10 initial sessions of the brain learning to begin.

The two main effects of E.E.G. neurofeedback training that can be seen are:
1. The number of points that can be scored during a training session may increase over every session.
2. The levels of the E.E.G. signals may increase in order for the benefits of training to increase.

The effects of E.E.G. neurofeedback training are primarily in the improvement of relaxation in the trainee over the course of E.E.G. training sessions that I call the "Mental Spa" © 2009-2017

An Example of E.E.G. neurofeedback brainwave training application for Holistic Addiction Recovery. A total holistic and spiritual approach to re-balance your brainwave frequencies through alpha-theta training called the Penniston-Kulkosky protocol.

This is a client-centered training that requires a minimum of twenty sessions. Most studies show a 65%-85% outcome for successful drug recovery. There have been four (4) such studies performed by Menninger Clinic-Steven Fahrion and Dale Walters, Ph.D., Cri-Help, and E.E.G. Spectrum-Bill Scott Ph.D., Kaiser, Sagen, Brod, et al., University of Colorado and V.A. Hospital at Pueblo, Colorado Eugene Penniston and Carl Kulkosky Ph.D., Martin Mutke, M.S., C.D.S., Robert Dickson, L.C.D.C., L.P.C., and Jerome

Plotnick, Ph.D., N.D., C.C.D.C.S. It is used as an adjunct usually with a 12 step spiritual program of recovery (A.A., N.A., C.A.), or other group programs. The studies show that the experimental group that received the E.E.G. neurofeedback alpha-theta brainwave training showed a higher recovery rate then just a 12 Step program. After receiving the alpha-theta training over 20-30 sessions even if the addict took a drink of alcohol would suffer from the Penniston effect. It makes the sober trainee sick. It also shows a dramatic elimination of P.T.S.D. in Vietnam era veterans that received alpha-theta for stage four alcoholism. They all remained sober (abstinence) in over six years of review. Recent studies at Cri-Help recovery center also confirm this outcome.

When the brainwaves are brought back into normal balance the desire for addictive substances, or processes is diminished, thereby increasing the outcome to 65%-85% for a successful recovery, and when used in conjunction with a 12 Step program of recovery. An addict's brainwaves are out of normal balance causing psycho physiological dependence on drugs. The training allows their brainwaves to come into balance. Substitution of neurofeedback allows the addict to bring their brainwaves back into normal balance without the use of drugs. The use of drugs (alcohol) is viewed as a perverted way to gain spirituality according to Dr. Carl Jung, Dr. Silkworth, and Bill Wilson. When this occurs there is also release of repressed negative emotional feelings that are the cause of the psychological imbalances. Addicts medicate themselves to numb their feelings and emotions. E-motions also trigger drug use. Again, the alpha-theta training for addictions is on the cutting edge of technology and is proving itself effective in the treatment of all addictions.

The training is approved by the V.A., University of No. Texas, Menninger Clinic, E.E.G. Spectrum Institute, B.C.I.A., and other treatment facilities. Some chemical dependency recovery specialists in the field are Robert Dickson, Martin Mutke, Bill Scott, Eugene Penniston, Carl Kulkosky, Dale Walters, Steven Fahrion, and Jerome Plotnick. If interested in alpha-theta training for addictions call or write 21st Century Energetics and contact Jerome Plotnick, Ph.D., N.D. Contact address and phone is in the back of the book.

Note! We refer to addicts as aforementioned to include alcoholics. Alcohol is a drug just like any other known addictive substance. The original research study (Penniston-Kulkosky) was performed with 12 stage IV alcoholics who were also Vietnam P.T.S.D. afflicted combat veterans. The experimental group who received the Penniston-Kulkosky protocol were all shown to remain sober, whereas the control group who received only the standard 12 step program model, and they all returned to alcohol, etc. There was utilization review for six (6) years thereafter and the experimental group remained sober. One of the groups participants died of cirrhosis of the liver. Another study was then performed at Cri-Help in No. Hollywood drug rehabilitation program. Dr. Bill Scott and Dr. Sagen et al. had similar results in their double blind study. There was previous and continuing study of the Penniston-Kulkosky protocol at the Menninger Clinic by Doctors Walters and Fahrion, University of No. Texas Rehabilitation Center by Dickson, E.E.G. Spectrum Institute by Dr.Scott, Biofeedback Institute of L.A. by Dr. Toomin, and 21st Century Energetics by Dr. Jerome Plotnick. See Dr. Jerome Plotnick's 13th Step For Total Addiction Recovery-a holistic, spiritual, bio-energetic, nutritional, approach book, and program.

I also employ the use of light photon frequency energy-based solutions from D.N.R., Inc. Indiana called Liquid Needle Total Balance (L.N.T.B.), a detoxification bath soak called CIG-131 as aids to eliminate addictions, drug residues from the brain, and body. L.N.T.B. is also an adjunct in re-setting (re-balancing) the brain waves of alpha-theta-beta. Read my study utilizing L.N.T.B on pages:309-310 in this book and on page 418 of The 13 Steps From Illness To Health-APNBMPDR

CHAPTER THIRTEEN

21st Century Energetics "Mental/Body/Spiritual Spa" Program Summary

21st Century cutting edge holistic, ,bio-energetic, naturopathic medicine, and technology today! Nature's ancient healing wisdom presents: 21st Century Energetic's-"Mental/Body/Spiritual Spa"

The brain-mind is the highest center which we retrain through E.E.G. brainwave neurofeedback training. The body-brain is energetically cleansed or detoxified using a safe natural energetic cutting edge program. Once detoxified we supply the brain-body with pure spagyric vitamins, minerals, amino acids, enzymes, herbs, light photon energetic internal and topical substances, ionic stabilized oxygen O2 for the necessary nutrients, and elemnets needed for optimum functioning.

Then we implement E.M.G. biofeedback training for stress reduction, muscle reeducation and coordination. We perform and implement further E.E.G. neurofeedback training for mental fitness, focus, concentration, attention, alertness, relaxation, and brain peak performance.

A mind is a terrible thing to waste. Success not stresses. Stressors cause symptoms in the body's physiology. E.M.G. biofeedback training teaches you new coping skills to eliminate stress symptoms. Mind-Body awareness through E.M.G. biofeedback training equals health and harmony. Gain your optimum potential and create a new you.

Restore your powers of mind. Re-balance your brain and increase your attention, focus, concentration, relaxation, mental fitness, and brain peak performance through E.E.G. neurofeedback training. Health=You are what eat, think, and what your body cannot eliminate (toxins). Once you eliminate the toxins from the five (5) toxic groups, replenish the life force energy then your body will be able to begin to heal, and repair itself. Note! Only your body has the ability to heal itself. Note! Your mind-body-spirit are all interconnected.

SUMMARY

AN ACT of FORGIVENESS

This is to be initiated by the person that is implementing our detoxification program. By letting go and not holding on to resentments, anger, or fear the detoxification process will be successful. Letting go on a mental, emotional, and spiritual level will allow your physical aspect to release as well.

"I forgive now, and forever all persons, places, situations where I had resentments, anger, and fear. I am holding a rope that is between me and those people. I see each person I resented, and now there is a rope between me and that person, place, or situation. I am now going to cut the rope that binds me to them or it, when I do, I release for now and forever all resentments between us, or it. I cut the rope, now I let them, or it go in peace, and blessings. They prosper and so do I. And I now let go, now and forever, all negative thoughts towards them, or it. They go in peace and harmony as I do too. I forgive, let all things go, so that the greatest good for all concerned manifests. May My Life be filled forever with Unconditional Love, Profound Peace, Harmony Happiness, Health, and May Blessings Abound."

MEDITATION & "PRAYER of LIGHT"

Father-Mother GOD,
I just ask now, once again for the Light of the Holy Spirit,
The Light of the Christ, and the Light of GOD the Universal Father to be present here with Me.
I ask that this Light, Surround, Fill, Guide, Protect, Uplift Me, and allow Only That Which is for the Highest Good to be brought forward to Me.
Now, and throughout this Day,
I ask for the Presence, the Love, the Guidance of the Mystical Traveler, Preceptor, and Consciousness.
That would Guide, Assist, and Uplift Me.
I ask for Healing and Balancing on all Levels of my Being-ness, and that any Curses and Negativity which can be released, be taken, and Trans-muted Into the Highest Realms of Light.
Father-I ask All in Perfect Love, and Perfect Understanding, Keeping Clear My Destiny on the Earth.

I am always willing and grateful to be of Service-And, I ask for
More Opportunities to be of Service.
May I perceive and manifest that service. And have a Loving
Consciousness.
Though, Ever Thy Will Be Done,
And I ask that My Will be as yours,
And that the Christ God Consciousness Dwell in My Being-ness-Now,
and all the days of My Life
SO BE IT. SO MOTE IT BE. A-MEN.

LORD'S PRAYER

Our Father who art in Heaven,
Hallowed be thy name,
Give us this day our daily Bread,
Forgive us our Trespassing and Transgressions,
As those who Trespass and Transgress against us,
Lead us out of Temptation,
Deliver us from Evil,
For Thine is the Kingdom,
And the Glory,
And the Power Forever,
A-Men

BUDDHIST ACT OF FORGIVENESS

" If I have harmed anyone in any way either knowingly or
unknowingly through my own confusion I ask for forgiveness,

If anyone has harmed me in any way either knowingly or unknowingly
through their own confusion I forgive them,

And if there is any situation I AM not yet ready to forgive I
forgive myself for that,

For all the ways I harm myself negate, doubt, belittle myself,
judge, or be unkind to others, or myself through my own confusion
I forgive myself."

THE AMERICAN NATIVE INDIAN TEN (10) COMMANDMENTS

1. Treat the Earth and all that dwell therein with respect.
2. Remain close to the Great Spirit.
3. Show great respect for your fellow beings.
4. Work together for the benefit of all Mankind.
5. Give assistance and kindness wherever needed.
6. Do what you know to be right.
7. Look after the well-being of Mind and Body.
8. Dedicate share of your efforts to the greater good.
9. Be truthful and honest at all times.
10. Take full responsibility for your actions.

HIPPOCRATES OATH

I swear by Apollo The Healer, by Hygieia, by Panaces, and by all the Gods and Goddesses, making them witnesses, that I will carry out, according to my ability and judgment, this oath, and this indenture.

To hold my teacher in this art equal to my own parents, to make him partner in my livelihood, when he is need of money to share mine with him, to consider his family as my own brothers, and to teach them this art, if they want to learn it, without fee or indenture, to impart precept, oral instruction, and all other instruction to my own sons, the sons of my teacher, and to indentured pupils who have taken the physicians oath, but to nobody else.

I will use treatment to heal the sick according to my ability and judgment, but never with a view of injury and wrong-doing. Neither will I administer poison to anybody when asked to do so, nor will I suggest such a course I will not give a woman pessary to cause abortion. But I will keep pure and holy both my life and my art. I will not use the knife, not even, verily, on sufferers from stone, but I will give place to such as are craftsmen therein.

Into whatsoever houses I enter, I will enter to help the sick, and I will abstain from intentional wrong-doing and harm especially from abusing the bodies of all. And whatsoever I see or hear will not be divulged. Now I carry this oath, and break it not, may I gain forever reputation among men for my life and for my art, but if I transgress it and for swear myself, may the opposite befall me.

Hippocrates...Unfortunately today this oath is not being done...

Bibliography.

Short Condensed Version

Getting Started with Neurofeedback-John N. Demos, M.A., L.C.M.H.C., and B.C.I.A.-E.E.G.-2005-W. W. Norton & Co.

Alpha Theta Training-Robert M. Dickson, L.P.C., L.C.D.C., B.C.I.A.-E.E.G.-2001

BrainMaster System Type 2E Module & B.M.T. Software for Windows-Release 1.9-BrainMaster Technologies, Inc., Thomas Collura, Ph.D.-2001

Biofeedback a Practitioners Guide-Mark S. Scwartz & Associates-1987-Guilford Publications, Inc.

Nine Day Inner Cleansing and Blood Wash for Renewed Youthfulness and Health-I. E. Gaumont and Harold Buttram, M.D.-1980-Parker Publishing Co.

The Bach Flower Remedies-Edward Bach, M.D. and Harold Wheeler, M.D.-1931, 33, 52, 79-Keats Publishing, Inc.

Elementary Treatise in Herbology- Dr.Edward E. Shook-1978,80,84,93-Enos Publishing Co.

E.M.G. Blue Prints-Biofeedback Institute of Los Angeles, Marjorie Toomin, Ph.D., and Herschel Toomin, Ph.D.- B.C.I.A. E.M.G.-1998-B.F.I.L.A.

Meta Your Meditation-Jerome Plotnick, Ph.D., N.D.-21st Century Energetics Publishing, Co., Lake of the Woods, CA.-2001

Meta Your Nutrition-Jerome Plotnick, Ph.D., N.D.-21st Century Energetics Publishing, Co., Lake of the Woods, CA.-2002

The 13 Steps from Illness to Health-APNBMPDR-Jerome Plotnick, Ph.D., N.D.-21st Century Energetics Publishing, Co. CA.-2009-2015-2016

Meta Your Mind-Jerome Plotnick, Ph.D., N.D.-21st Century Energetics Publishing, Co., Lake of the Woods, CA.-2015-2016

Biofeedback-Barbara Brown

Futureplex-Anti Homeopathic Formulas-Professional Reference Guide-1988, 89,94-Roy Martina, M.D., K. Lenia Scanlon, M.S., Armond Simonian, D. Hom. Apex Energetics, Inc., Santa Ana, CA.-1988-89-1994

Energetix-Clinical Newsletter for Healthcare Professionals-Volume 1-10-2006 Ciel Walko, L.Ac., N.D., Dohionega, GA.-2006

Gravizon Guide-Amazon Herb Co.,FL.-Linda Hegstrand, M.D., Ph.D.-2002

Oxygen Elements Plus, Oxy-Moxy-Resonance and Global Health Inc.,

EnGarde Health Products, V.N., CA.- Dr. Chaplin, M.D., Ph.D.-2000

Beyond Biofeedback. N.Y.: Delacorte Press, Elmer E. Green and Alyce M. Green., Ph.D.'s.-1977

Gravizon, The Amazon Herb Co, Juniper, Fla.-2000

Iredesca, Exsula Co, Federal Way, Washington.-2000

Energetix's, Inc. Products, Dohionega, Georgia.-2000

D.N.R., Inc. Products, Indianapolis, Indiana.-2000

Apex Energetic's Products, Santa Ana, CA.-2000

LifeTree Aromatix Products, Sherman Oaks, CA.-2000

Bag of Pearls-Institute of Traditiional Medicine-Sabhuti Dharmananda-Portland , Oregon-1989

Chinese Healing Arts-Internal Kung Fu-Translated by Dr. John Dudgeon, M.D. and Edited by William Berk-Unique Publications, Burbank CA.-1986

Marijuana Chemistry-Genetics, Processing & Potency by Michael Starks,Ronin Publishing, Berkeley, CA.-1977 & 1990

The Eye of Revelation by Peter Kelder, Borderline Sciences,Garberville, CA.-1989

Elementary Treatise in Herbology by Dr. Edward Shook, N.D., Enos Publishing Co., Banning, CA.-1993

Jude's Herbal Home Remedies by Jude C. Williams, M.H., Liewellyn Publications, St. Paul, Minn.-1996

Pranic Healing by Master Choa kok Sui,Samuel Woser, Inc., York Beach, Maine-1989

Relaxation Response by Dr. Herbret Benson, M.D. Avon Books, New York-1974

Pyramid Power by G. Pat Flanagan, Ph.D., DeVorss & Co.,Santa Monica, CA.-1973

Nine day Inner Cleansing for Renewed Youthfulness and Health by I.E. Goumant and Dr. Harold E. Buttram, M.D., Parker Publishing, West Nyack, N.Y.-1980

Natural Cures by Kevin Trudeau, Alliance Publishing Group., Rlk Grove Village, IL.-2004

Healing With the Mind's Eye by Dr. Michael samuels, M.D., Summit Books, New York, N.Y.-1990

The Book of Secrets by Bhagwan Shree Rajneesh, Harper Colophon Books, New York, N.Y.-1972

Imagery in Healing Shamanism and Modern Medicine by Jeanne Achterberg, Ph.D., New Science Library, Boston, Mass. -1942, 1995

PRODUCT PRICE LIST & ORDERING INFORMATION:

Core Botanicals (2 oz.)

01010 Core Artemisia Blend-$18.50 (Anti parasitic-worms)
01015 Core Berberina Blend-$18.50 Alterative (anti bacterial, intestinal parasites, ocular infections, chlamydia, tricomonas, urinary, herpes, blood purifier, and mouth ulcers)
01020 Core Bilberry-$18.50 (Vision enhancer)
01030 Core Black Radish Blend-$1850 (Hiatal hernia, gastric reflux, hemorrhoids and varicosities)
01040 Core Borage Blend-$18.50 (Blood builder, adrenal vitality, circulation thyroid support, thymus immune builder, liver & pancreas support, and ringworm expulsion)
01050 Core Burdock Blend-$18.50 (Alterative, tonic, diuretic, depurative, laxative, inhibits tumor growth, antibiotic, anti fungal, liver-gall bladder detox, spagyric essiac, blood purifier)
01060 Core Cardus Blend-$18.50 (Liver & gall bladder decongestion, increases glutathione by 45%)
01070 Core Cat's Claw-$18.50 (Antibacterial, viral, fungal, increase blood circulation to brain-heart, plaque inhibitor, G.I. disorders, arthritis, cystitis, herpes, and radiation support-chemo-X-ray-E.M.F.'s)
01080 Core Cilantro Blend-$18.50 (Mercury detox-brain-kidney & liver support, takes mercury from intra cellular to extra cellular tissues-use with lymph tone 2 or 3)
01090 Core Cohosh Blend-$18.50 (Female hormonal, menstrual, vaginitis, anemia, increases sexual energy, and underdeveloped breasts)
01100 Core Condurango Blend-$18.50 (Leaky gut, hiatal hernia, lymphatic drainage of the breast, gastic reflux, hyperacidity of stomach, colitis, and gastritis)
01115 Core Convalaria Blend-$18.50 (Angina, heart palpitations, high blood pressure, arrhythmias, lowers pulse rate, irregular heart beat, heart tonic for smokers, and erectile stimulation)
01120 Core Dandi Blend-$18.50 (Hepatitis, liver problems, cirrhosis, jaundice, gout, fatty liver, thyroid hormones are conjugated in the liver, spleen congestion, psoriasis, hypoglycemia, blood purification, and rheumatism)
01130 Core Dong Quai Blend-$18.50 (Female Hormonal, painful or absent periods, after use birth pill, lack of breast milk, skin and acne problems, cramps, anti spasmodic, relaxant to nervous

system, blood thinner, tonic for reproductive, and nervous system-contraindicted in pregnancy)

01140 Core Echina-B-$18.50 (Powerful immune response to bacteria)

01150 Core Echina-C-$18.50 (Powerful immune response to candida)

01160 Core Echina-V-$18.50 (Powerful immune response to viral)

01170 Core Feverfew-$18.50 Febrifuge (Anti inflammatory, relaxant, vaso dialatory decreases blood vessels response, digestive stim.)

01180 Core Gen 2 Blend-$18.50 (Spagyric hoxsey, stagnant blood, lymph cleanser, liver & bowel cleanser, swollen lymph glands, congested spleen, liver disease, arthritis, and eczema)

01190 Core Ginkgo Blend-$18.50 Circulation enhancer (peripheral circulation, increases oxygen uptake, depression, senility, dementia, memory enhancer, inhibits aggression, dizziness equilibrium, head injuries, tinnitus, headaches, allergic crisis)

01195 Core Guggulipid Blend-$18.50 (Cholesterol L.D.L., triglycerides reducer, free radical scavenger, cardio protector, reduces blood pressure, and improves circulation)

01200 Core Hawthorn-$18.50 Heart tonic (heart weakness, high blood pressure, angina, palpitations, rapid heart beat, dilation of blood vessels, and lowers cholesterol)

01210 Core Hydrangea Blend-$18.50 (Diuretic, cathartic, tonic, stimulates bile flow, cleans biliary tree, gallstones, kidney stones, gout, illocecal valve, calcium spurs, and assists converting blood fats to blood sugar)

01220 Core Juniper Blend-$18.50 (Diuretic, stimulant, and carminative, prostate hypertrophy, increases sexual energy-men, nocumia-bed wetting, male hormonal imbalances, vitality, impotency, and urinary bladder congestion-stimulates)

01230 Core Lapacho Blend-$18.50 (Antibacterial, viral, fungal, candida, immune system enhancer, E.V.B.-C.M.V.-mono, flu, spleen congestion, thymus support, and lymph drainage)

01240 Core Licro Blend-$18.50 (Laxative, demulcents, C.F.S., exhaustion, reactive hypoglycemia, allergies, heart palpitations, candida, thyroid-pituitary axis, P.M.S. menopause, arthritis, hay fever, and lung problems)

01245 Core Meca Blend-$18.50 (P.M.S., increases libido, resolves menstrual symptoms, female hormone balancer, anti depressant, C.F.S., natural alternative to anabolic steroids, increases stamina, mental clarity, memory enhancer, immune-stimulant, fertility support, and hypothalamus support)

01248 Core Mycelia Blend-$18.50 (Immune enhancer, respiratory inflammation, systemic & specific infections, immune support, T-cell stimulant, Lyme's disease, anti viral, hepatitis A-B-C, anti tumor, antioxidant, hypertension, cardiovascular support, and N.K. cell increase)

01250 Core Myrrh Blend-$18.50 (Antibacterial, lungs and sinus congestion, respiratory problems, mucus remover, bronchial relaxant, and colds-flu)

01260 Core Olive Leaf Blend-$18.50 (antiviral, anti microbial, anti viral, anti bacterial, anti parasitic, anti fungal, herpes, intermittent claudication, and heart-circulatory)

01263 Core Para-V Blend-$18.50 (Anti parasitic, round,tape, and pin worms)

01266 Core Queen of the Meadow Blend-$18.50 (Diuretic, nervine, gout, rheumatoid arthritis, and high blood pressure-kidney related

01270 Core Sambucus Blend-$18.50 (Removes mucus, antiviral, bacterial, and lymph drainage)

01280 Core Sarsparilla-$18.50 Alterative, depurative, anti toxin from joints and skin, psoriasis, cleansing, and balancing)

01290 Core Scrofulara Blend-$18.50 (Spleen, lymph,,liver congestion, and spagyric Eli Jones remedy)

01300 Core Solidago Blend-$18.50 (Antibacterial, kidney congestion, repair, and support)

01310 Core Saint John's Wort Blend-$18.50 (Anti anxiety and depression)

01320 Core Trifolo Blend-$18.50 (Lymph, breast, spleen drainage, and arthritis)

01330 Core Valerian-$18.50 (Anodyne, nervine, antispasmodic, tension, nervous disorders, anxiety, and headaches)

01340 Core Phyto Lavage (Herbal douche Candida, Thrush, Chlamydia, and vaginal pH)-$15.70

ATTENUATER NOSODE DETOXIFIERS (2 oz).

02020 Addicide-Chord-$17.10 (Insecticide, pesticide fertilizer detox)

02030 Aller-Chord 1-$17.10 (Multiple food allergies detox)

02040 Aller-Chord 2-$17.10 (Multiple air borne allergies detox)

02050 Amoeba-Chord-$17.10 (Multiple water borne bacteria)

02060 Bacteria Chord-$17.10 (Multiple dimensional bacterial detox, and Lyme disease detox))

02070 Chem-Chord $17.10 (Multiple pharmacological detox and multiple recreational drug detox)

02080 Colo Chord-$17.10 (Intestinal)

02090 Dental-Chord-$17.10 (Dental toxic chemicals)
02100 Gyne-Chord-$17.10 (Female sex organ detoxify, herpes, chlymidia, gonorrhea, syphilis, papilmo, trichiomonis, and candida thrush))
02110 Hepata-Chord-$17.10 (Liver-hepatitis)
02120 HZ Chord-$17.10 (Herpes all strains detoxify)
02125 Inflamma-Chord-$17.10 (Any all inflammations)
02130 Lipo-Chord-$17.10 (Fatty lipid detoxify)
02140 Merabolic-Chord-$17.10 (Enhances metabolic rate, geographic stress detox, and radiation poisoning))
02150 Metal-Chord-$17.10 (Heavy metal toxins detox isodes)
02160 Mono-Chord-$17.10 (Mononucleosis, Epstein-Barr, and cytomutagenic detox)
02170 Myco-Chord-$17.10 (Mycotoxin, fungal, and multiple molds detoxify)
02180 Mycocan-Chord-$17.10 (Candida all strains detoxify)
02190 Neuro-Chord-$17.10 (Nervous system detox, heavy metals detox, viral detox, heavy metal isodes, viral isodes, and insecticides isodes))
02200 Para-Chord-$17.10 (Parasites expulsion detox round, pin, and flat worm detox)
02210 Pneuma-Chord-$17.10 (Lung detox, pneumonia, industrial, environmental, beauty salon, and tobacco detox)
02220 Rena-Chord-$17.10 (Kidney, bladder detox, and heavy metal isodes @1M)
02223 Sinus-Chord-$17.10 (Sinus-sinusitis drainage, colds, flus, coughs, and allergies)
02225 Thyro-Chord-$17.10 (Thyroid-pituitary support, coxsacie virus and virus, heavy metals, and vaccination isodes)
02230 Vaccin-Chord-$17.10 (Multiple vaccinations detox)
02240 Viru-Chord $17.10 (Multidimensional viral detox and coxsacie-multiplicity of the most common viruses)

DRAINAGE & TONIFICATION (2 oz.)

03010 Adrenal Tone-$17.10 (Adrenals enhancer)
01315 Drainage-Tone-$17.10 (Spleen, thymus, lymph drainage)
03020 Flu-Tone-$17.10 (Antiviral colds, flu's, coughs and E.V.B.-C.M.V.-Mono_Coxsacie)
03030 GB-Tone-$17.10 (Gallbladder drainage, tonic, and liver drainage secondary)

03040 Kidney-Tone-$17.10 (Kidney drainage, kidney stones, and cystitis) tonic)
03050 Liver-Tone-$17.10 (Liver drainage all conditions and tonic)
03060 Lymph-Tone 1-$17.10 (Lymphatic drainage, acute conditions initial stage of homotoxicology, and tonic)
03070 Lymph-Tone 2-$17.10 (Lymphatic drainage cellular secondary stage of homotoxicology and tonic)
03080 Lymph-Tone 3-$17.10 (Lymphatic drainage, compensatory third final stage of homotoxicology, and tonic)
03090 Rehdydration-$17.10 (Rehydration for dehydration, A.D.D., A.D.H.D., P.M.S., and C.F.S.)
03100 Relax-Tone-$17.10 (Nervine, anxiety, depression, nervous tension, pain control, and white coat syndromes, etc.)
03110 Surgical-Tone-$17.10 (Wound healing pre & post surgeries, speeds healing, pain control, dental, injury treatment for cuts, and bruises, etc.)
03120 Throat Spray-Tone-$15.50 (Antibacterial, coughs, laryngitis tonsillitis, and swollen glands)

SARCODES

04005 Adaptopath-$17.10 (Adaption C.F.S. , exhaustion, hormone imbalance, menstrual, and menopausal disorders)
04010 Adrenopath-$17.10 (adrenals, C.F.S. , adrenal weakness, allergies, and low energy)
04020 Circulopath-$17.10 (Circulatory, supports heart, angina, and heart timing)
04030 Endopath-F-$17.10 (Endocrine hormonal support and restores sexual energy female)
04040 Endopath-M-$17.10 (Endocrine, hormonal support, prostate, and restores sexual energy male)
04050 Hypothalmapath-$17.10 (Hypothalamus support, A.D.D.-A.D.H.D. and pituitary, and pineal disorders)
04060 Lymphopath-$17.10 (Lymphatic drainage, lymph builder, and seven (7) endocrine sacrodes)
04070 Renapath-$17.10 (Kidney support for infections, congestion, kidney stones, and cystitis)
04080 Thyropath-$17.10 (Thyroid balances hyper-hypo thyroid patterns)

FLOWER REMEDIES (2 oz.)

06010 Fields of Flowers-$17.10 (All Bach flower essences to counter 7 deadly sins & 11 mental terror states))
06020 Rescue Calm-$17.10 (Nervine spagyric "rescue remedy", traumas, shocks, accidents, injuries, and stressful events)

PHENOLICS (2 oz.)

07010 Isopathic Phenolic Rings-$17.10 (Contains 37 phenolics I.e. candida and allergy desensitizer)

TOPICALS

09010 Mycoderm (2 oz.)-$16.00 (Fungal skin and athletes foot)
09020 Healing Gel (2 oz.)-$16.00 (Herpes, poison ivy bruises, and cold sores)
09029 BioCatalin Lotion (4 oz.)-$16.00 (Muscle injuries, bone spurs, ligaments, joints, arthritis, and connective tissue)
09030 BioCatalin Lotion 8 oz.)-$24.00 (Same as above)

HORMONAL

10008 D.H.E.A. Liposome-$23.00 (Adrenal hormonal support, C.F.S., memory loss, and reduce body fat)
10015 Melatonin Liposome Spray-$14.00 (Resets the circadian rhythm, hormonal support, and sleep disorders)
10020 Phyto Pro-G-(Progesterone cream female hormonal imbalance, P.M.S., and menopause)-$27.50
10030 Prenenolone Liposome-$23.00 (Memory, mental fatigue, arthritis, and concentration)
10070 Somatotrophin h.G.H. (1 oz.)-$37.50 (Restore muscle mass, increases hair growth, increases sexual stamina, sharpen vision, boosts cardiac output, and improve mental condition)

IONIZED TRACE ELEMENTS

11010 Bismuth-$12.00 (Intestinal ulcers, frontal headaches)
11020 Cobalt-$12.00 (Anemia, migraine, and peripheral disorders of blood flow)
11030 Copper-$12.00 (Exhaustion and susceptibility to infections)

11050 Iodine-$12.00 (Exhaustion, glandular disorders, and labile blood pressures)
11060 Lithium-$12.00 (Depression, nervousness, anxieties, and neurotransmitters)
11070 Magnesium-$12.00 (Neuritis, arrhythmia, and chronic colitis)
11080 Manganese-$12.00 (Pituitary support, Parkinson's, and ligament trauma)
11090 Molybdenum-$12.00 (Hair loss, candida, allergies, depression, osteoporosis, and migraines)
11100 Phosphorus-$12.00 (Nervous, allergies, weakness after infections, and osteomalacia)
11110 Potassium-$12.00 (Muscle weakness, cardiac insufficiency, tachycardia, fatiguem and catarrh)
11120 Selenium-$12.00 (Angina, precancerous, free radicals, cardiac risk, and immune deficiency)
11130 Sulfur-$12.00 (Acne, psoriasis, eczema, and diminished reactions)
11140 Zinc-$12.00 (Impaired brain function, nervous, alopecia, prostatis, and low concentration)
11150 Manganese-Cobalt-$12.00 (Circulatory disorders and climacteric problems)
(11160 Manganese-Copper-$12.00 (Asthma, fatigue, colitis, respiratory infections, and arthritis)
11170 Manganese-Copper-Cobalt-$12.00 (Anemia, C.F.S.)
11180 Copper-Gold-Silver-$12.00 (Poly arthritis, lymph disorders, seplicsemia, and premature aging)
11190 Copper-Zinc-$12.00 (Endocrine disorders, fatigue, low vitality, and pituitary hypothalamus disorders)
11200 Zinc-Nickle-Cobalt-$12.00 (Pancreas disorders and hypothalamic disorders)
11210 Multi-Somaplex 21-$29.00 (Combination of all trace elements in synergistic balance, stress, C.F.S., and depletion)

NESTMANN

12040 Contessa Female Tonic (8 oz.)-$16.00 (Menopausal-hot flashes, mental exhaustion, depression, irritability, insomnia, and kidney detox))
12060 Acusine Nasal Spray-$13.70 (Chronic rhinitis, allergy, blocked nose, sinusitis, nose bleed, and throat congestion)
12070 Luvos (7 oz.)-$13.70 (Parasites, digestive problems, absorbs pathogens and toxins, ulcers, colitis, dysbiosis, and candida)

12090 Peppermint Oil Drops-$10.00 (Bile production, asthma, breath freshener, breathing problems, fainting, and dizziness, antispasmodic and analgesic, effect on coughs, flu, and stomach cramps)

12100 NemaBase (120 tablets)-$14.00 (Breaks down acid deposits in connective tissues, arthritis, gout, muscle pain, increases alkaline reserves in blood, increases the amount of hydrogen carbonate in the blood, counteracts the acidic effects of harmful diets, stress, toxins, excess bloating, over exertion, shortens recuperation after illness, reduces oxidation stress in liver, lungs, kidneys, hyperactivity in muscles, and tendons)

NUTRITIONALS

13005 Adrenal Force (60 capsules)-$16.00 (Powerful adrenal support-natural D.H.E.A. hormonal support, compliment estrogen-NOTE! Do not use for more than 3 months at a time-after support with botanicals and homeopathics)

13010 Alka-C (buffered Vit. C powder) (180 grm.)-$20.50 (Buffered Vit-C powder, non-toxic tolerance of Vit. C, alkalizing mineral drink, reduces stress, immune enhancer, trace mineral loss, protection, and accompanies therapy

13020 Allicin-G (90 capsules)-$15.00 (Heavy metal detox for kidneys support, chleation therapy, sclerotic plaquing tendencies, hypertension, arthritis, natural "antibiotic" anti-fungal, mycotoxin, parasitic, eczema, increases circulation, memory loss, cardio protective, protects against carcinogenic chemicals, heavy metals and pollutants, pain from insect bites, high B-1-B-12 vitamins, moves lymph system, lowers blood cholesterol, strengthens blood vessels, rectal insertion for hemorrhoids, asthma, bronchial, and lung expectorant)

13025 AminoGest (180 capsules)-$39.90 (Irritable bowel syndrome, leaky gut, "pre digested" protein, fibromyalgia, immune insufficiency, C.F.S., chronic wound healing, adjunctive cancer support, herpes (lysine deficiency), hypertension, nutritional support for digestive dysfunction, tissue damage, and protein related conditions)

13030 Artic Alginate (120 capsules)-$36.00 (Removes heavy metals from intestinal tract, dental toxins, X-ray exposure, radioactive exposure, E.M.P.'s exposure, psoriasis and other metal based skin problems, poor water supply, chemotherapy, radiation therapies, radioactive strontium, industrial chemicals, tobacco, hypothyroid)

13035 B5 (90 capsules)-$14.00 (Panotothenic acid, anti stress, adrenal hormone function, synthesize of neurotransmitter acetylcholine to support neuromuscular function, allergies, headaches, arthritis, psoriasis, teeth grinding when asleep (bruxism), and alcoholism)

13040 BioBalancer (120 capsules)-$27.00 (Complete male-female endocrine support, C.F.S., fibromyalgia, and safe for children to take)

13042 BioGest Powder (925 gm.)-$55.00 (Digestive and liver support during detox, ongoing digestive liver maintenance, and support in the presence of chronic xenobiotic exposure)

13045 BioMatrix (60 capsules)-$22.00 (Full nutritional, phyto-nutritional, and mineral support)

13047 BioMatrix (120 capsules)-$36.00 (Same as above)

13050 Catalyst-7 (90 capsules)-$26.00 (Full enzyme support, part of Opening Channels pre detox program, alpha-galactosidase for bean and legume digestion, anti-inflammatory if taken between meals, mix with healing gel for herpes and canker sores, high chlorophyll content, and bad breath),

13060 Catalyst-7 (180 capsules)-$47.00 (Same as above)

13070 Catalyst-U 90 capsules)-$44.00 (Protease free digestive enzymes, part of Opening Channels pre detox program, systemic cleansing and detox, works in conjunction with Opening Channels)

13085 Colon Clear & Pure Body Clear Set with-manual-$73.00 (Opens the channels, intestinal cleansing, and detox, part of the Opening Channels detox program, parasites, candida, diarrhea-constipation, heavy metals, and works in conjunction with Opening Channels Pure Body Clear)

13095 Colon Clear 990 capsules)-$23.00 (Same as above)

13097 CoQ10 Liposome Tincture (2 oz.)-$35.00 (Antioxidant, heart and immune enhancer, reduces L.D.L., and energy production)

13100 Flora Synergy (60 capsules)-$19.90 (Same as above provides intestinal friendly flora)

13110 Flora Synergy (150 capsules)-$40.00 (Same as above)

13121 Flora Chewable (60 wafers)-$19.90 (Same as above right spinning intestinal flora support, candida, parasites, digestive pH support, digestive overload, diarrhea-constipation, C.V., survives antibiotics, survives gastric acids and juices, milk free, and allergy free probiotic)

13126 Galt-Immune (90 capsules)-$39.90 (Gut associated immune issues, stimulates interleukin-2cytokines and macrophage action, poly peptides, amino acids, omega 3's, Beta 1, 3 glucens, organic bovine colostrum and predigested white fish protein, essential hemoglobin's and other immune factors, anti-viral, bacterial of digestive tract, lungs, increases white blood cells, stimulates phagocytes, and elevates non-specific antibodies.

13130 Greening Powder (180 capsules)-$28.00 (Green super food-chlorophyll, antioxidant support, phyto nutrients, adaptogens, liver and immune support, digestive support, and does not contain algae due to toxic contamination-neurotoxicity)

13140 Greening Powder (10 oz.)-$48.00 (Same as above)

13160 Inflamma Force (60 capsules)-$24.00 (All inflammatory conditions, plaque buildup in the arteries, compliments chleation therapies, joint conditions, osteoarthritis, gouty arthritis, SLE, musculoskeletal disorders, rheumatoid arthritis, chronic sinusitis, fibrocystic breasts, carpal tunnel syndrome, dissolve clots, and pain control. Use 2 caps mixed into Bio Catalin)

13168 Pancrea Force (60 capsules)-$20.70 (Reactive hypoglycemia diabetes, pancreatic insufficiency, C.F.S., fibromyalgia, recurrent yeast infections, migraine, arthritis, and prostate hypertrophy)

13170 Phyto Cal-Mag Plus (90 capsules)-$19.90 (Easily ionized calcium and magnesium replacements 5:1 Boron for assimilation accurate assimilation (pH5.2)

13180 Phyto Rad Antioxidant (2 oz.)-$28.00 (Highly stabilized spagyric antioxidant, anti-free radical, anti-mutagenic, (bacteria), anti-coagulant, reduction of L.D.L., anti-microbial, anti tumor, systemic inflammation, reduces $rH2$ (B.T.A.) in liver, kidneys, and lymph)

13185 Spectramin (4 Oz.)-$29.00 (For right spinning ionic trace minerals, contains 62 trace elements plus others found in sea water for element depletion, and stress,)

13190 Thyro Force (60 capsules)-$25.00 (For functional hypothyroid support, energy depletion, weight gain, loss of later third of eyebrows, hormonal support, and cross check with liver Core Dandi Blend as thyroid hormones are conjuncted in liver)

13200 XenoForce (90 capsules)-$16.50 (Strong immune support, prostate, pancreatic (insulin), mucous membrane balance, lung protective factors, motion sickness, renal support, long term healing cystitis, bruising, eye and renal development, chronic tensions, skin conditions, and allergic reactions)

OPENING CHANNELS PROGRAM

O.C. 1 month supply 1 each of the following products)-$246.00
(Opening Channels a pre detoxification program for xenobiotic
accumulations that opens channels allowing for detoxification
Failure to do so is like throwing a bucket of water against a
closed door which is pointless and damaging. The program gently
yet thoroughly provides for the lymphatic, liver, biliary tree,
kidney, digestive, colon pathways to be open, and draining. During
this process the program replenishes lost minerals, comprised of
amino acids and essential fatty acids, reseeds beneficial
intestinal flora, re-hydrates cells, and tissues. Supports and
fortifies the healing pathways within the patient which may be
compromised if a detoxification protocol were commenced
immediately)
03090 ReHydration (2 oz.)-$17.10
13025 AminoGest (180 capsules)-$29.10
13060 Catalyst-7 (180 capsules)-$47.00
13085 Colon Clear 7 Pure Body Set with-manual-$73.00
13110 Flora Synergy (150 capsules)-$40.00
13185 Spectramin (4 oz.)-$29.00

SPECIALTY ITEMS

15010 MycroSurge (2 oz.)-$46.00 (12 Chinese mushrooms in a
liposome spray for anti viral, respiratory inflammation,
infections systemic and specific, increase immune support, and
anti tumor)
15020 Sea Cure (180 capsules)-$39.90 (Concentrated deep sea ocean
white fish protein with omega-3 fatty acids for irritable bowel
syndrome, leaky gut. "predigested" protein for fibromyalga,
multiple digestive problems, heart support, increases H.D.L.'s
decreases L.D.L.'s, reduces cholesterol and tri gylcerides,
intense protein supplementation easily assimilated immune
insufficiency, C.F.S., chronic wound healing, adjunctive cancer
support, herpes, lysine deficiency, hypertension, nutritional
support for digestive dysfunction, tissue damage, and protein
related conditions)
15030 Sea Vive (90 capsules)-$39.90

Hormone Screening

(Includes saliva test, and customized phyto-hormone cream, and 2-way shipping from patient to lab, and lab to practitioner)

30010 Female Comprehensive Panel-$399.00 (Test for n6 hormones saliva test for corticoid, D.H.E.A., Melatonin, Progesterone, Estrogen, and Testosterone from test results we formulate a custom phyto-hormone herbal homeopathic liposome cream for your specific needs)
30020 Female Circadian Panel-$300.00 (Same as above but 10-1 collections and further analysis of menstruation cycle time periods from which further remedies can be made on an individualized needs basis)
30030 Male Comprehensive Panel-$300.00 (Saliva test for male hormones and from test results a customized phyto-hormonal herbal-homeopathic liposome cream is made per your specific needs)
30060 Hormone Retest Panel-$225.00 (Retest per above)
Note! Please ask us for all current prices for goEnergetix's.com physician only health rest-oral products.

Homeopathic Properties:

Nosodes-Isopathy-are dilutions from pathological tissues and substances
Sarcodes-Organotherapy-are derived from healthy organs, glands, and tissues, etc.
Cell salts-are derived from basic chemicals of body minerals.
Orthomoleculars-are potenized dilutions of naturally occurring substances.
Gemotherapuetics-are derived from embryonic tissues of fresh plants.
Animal Kingdom-are derived from animal sources.
Phytotherapuetics-are derived from herb and botanical extracts.
Oligotherapuetics-are derived from minerals.

Shipping & Handling:
1 day overnight: $25.50
2 day Priority: $ 17.50
3 day Priority: $9.50
Optional Drop Ship: $12.50
C.O.D.: $6.00 U.P.S. charge

To order phone: (661) 245-3616 leave your name, shipping address, zip code, credit card number, securuty code, and expiration date.

To contact Jerome Plotnick, Ph.D., N.D., C.C.D.C.S., C.N.F.B. TH. "Penniston-Kulkosky Addiction Protocol" for 21st Century Energetics-Specialized addiction treatment, energetic non drug detoxification, counseling, and alpha-theta training for addictions with a probable 65%-85% success rate. Call for further information.

Phone: (661) 245-3616 for an appointment. I hope you enjoyed this book and if you have any questions pertaining to anything in this book part one please write me @:

21st Century Energetics,
"Mental-Body-Spiritual Spa",
c/o Jerome Plotnick, Ph.D., N.D.
6132 Frazier Mt., Pk., Rd. #45,
Lake of the Woods, CA 93225-9200 or
Phone #@ (661) 245-3616 M-Sa. 9-5 P.S.T.
Websites: 21stcenturyenergetics.com or @linkedin.com, bing.com, jeromeplotnickphdnd@facebook.com manta, or biopharma.com jerome plotnick, ph.d., n.d @google.com, and @aol.com

E-Mail: plotnickj@yahoo.com

May Spiritual Blessings Abound, Peace Profound, Yours In Health, Jerome Plotnick, Ph.D., N.D.

PRE-ACKNOWLEDGMENT

Thank you Duke Zelinski, President of Sportform, Inc. Without your help and encouragement I would not have been able to write this book. May the future for both of us be filled with blessings and prosperity. May we help the many who need our guidance.

ACKNOWLEDGMENTS

I wish to express my sincere appreciation for their precious time, consideration, knowledge passed on to me by many professors, instructors, consultants, authors, doctors of allied health professions, and researchers in the fields of the aforementioned writings. To all past and present persons living or passed on I owe an extreme debt of gratitude. Thanks to Joseph Hough, N.D.,

Ph.D., D.C., M.D.-R.I.P., for Naturopathic Medicine, John Thie, D.C., for Touch for Health-A.K., Robert Singer, D.C., Chiropractic Touch Healing, Professor James Daley, Ph.D., Psycho-Social Psychology & Biofeedback-Ortho Molecular Medicine, Professor Mildred Henry, Ph.D., Humanities & Psychology, Marshal Ho, R.I.P. Lic. Ac., Acupuncture & Herbs, Master Pei, Chi Healer National Treasure of Korea, Don Williams, D.C., B.E.S.T.,A.K.-Spirituality, Allan Solomon, Ph.D., Behavior Management Psychology-Family Counseling, Allan Greenspan, M.D., Osteopathic Medicine, Cheryl Teague, P.T., Lic. Ac., Acupuncture, James Julian. M.D., Holistic Preventive Medicine, Gil Boyne, B.A. C.M.H.Th.In., R.I.P. Certification for Hypnotherapy Practice, Bill Scott, Ph.D., Internship for Alpha-Theta E.E.G. B.W. training for Addictions-Practice, Sue Othmer, B.A., T.O.V.A. & Neurofeedback Theory & Practice Internship, Marjorie Toomin, Ph.D., R.I.P., Biofeedback E.M.G. Theory & Practice Internship, Herschel Toomin, Sc.D., R.I.P., E.M.G. Biofeedback Instrumentation, Jennifer Cochagne, Ph.D., E.E.G. Neurofeedback Training-Theory-Practice-Internship, Professor James Crossan, Ph.D., M.F.C.C., C.C.D.C.S., R.N., Certified Chemical Dependency Counseling Specialist-C.A.D.D.E.-Theory-Practice-Internship-Certification, Greg Schafer, B.A., C.C.D.C.S., Addiction Theory, History and Counseling-for Practice, Peter Kraus, Ph.D., Prof. U.C.L.A.-Interwoven@earthlink.net Consultant-Book Covers for 13 Steps & Meta Your Mind-Business Practice-Promotion, Carol Meshberg, R.N., Holistic Preventive Medicine-Homeopathy-Herbs-A.K., Marianne Jones, R.I.P. Nutrition-Chiropractic-Massage John St. John, Meditation & Spirituality, Naud Robinson, Consultant Business-Finance, Sharon Frazier, Spiritual Advisor, R.I.P., Stephen Co, Pranic Healing & Pranic Psychotherapy, Grand Master Yong Yu, Tae Kwan Do & Meditation, Philip Selinsky, ,C.M.H.Th., C.M.Th., Massage, A.K., Hypnosis Practice, Mary Marks, D.C., Touch for Health, James Brown, J.D., Consultant Legal, Donald Lucien, J.D., Consultant Legal, Arden Edwards, J.D., Consultant Legal, Vera Greenland, Spirituality, Walt Clark, Common Sense and Course of Miracles and Mind Science, Martin Gilbert, M.A., R.I.P., Childhood friend, U.S.N., Pan Am, John DeMoran, R.I.P. U.S. Navy Navy friend, Craig Mica, G.M.1, Retired Navy Seal, Friendship-Courage-Honor. To my childhood friend Ron James Sorrenson, U.S.M.C. veteran an American patriot and hero, made the constitutional amendment against flag burning, a protector of the U.S. flag, created a flag MIAOON for "missing in attack on our nation," for those who lost their lives on 9-11, and flown on the yard-on of the U.S.S. Wasp on memorial day 2007. Presently flown in the forward Operating Base Shank in Logar Province, Afganastan 2009. Also he is the executive director of the United States Citizens Alliance and activist for veterans causes. To my first and true love that I always loved throughout my life Beverly "Junior" Miangalara. To my sons Jamie Plotnick & Jon Plotnick thanks for making me proud of two fine men. To my spiritual daughters Keeley and Julianne and granddaughters Tessie and Adrianna may your lives be filled with many blessings. My grandsons Nathan, Justin and Jayden. Love to my daughter-in-laws Maryann and Sherrie. Thanks for the loving memories. Last but not least my mother Tessie for her giving me all she had, my father Frank Murray for his kind and gentle ways and to my grandmother Sarah who loved me and helped to raise me. R.I.P. Thank you GOD the MASTER DIVINE MIND PHYSICIAN UNIVERSAL SPIRIT for your everlasting love, wisdom, and guidance through my life. Sometimes the road was so hard I wanted to give up, but then I asked you for strength, guidance, and I received your blessings. "I AM" A-MEN

Honorable Mention to: Dr. Wayne Dyer-R.I.P.-Spirituality, Deepak Chopra, M.D.-Ayurveda, and Gary Null, Ph.D.-Nutrition, K.P.F.K. radio programs over the years such as K.P.F.K. radio and Allan Watts,R.I.P. Jack Garrish-R.I.P. Biomeditation, Hearts of Space, Mind-Body Connection K.I.E.V. radio, Karen Williams, Healing Music-"Rest," "Journey by the Sea," Don Williams, D.C. and Bernd Friedlander, D.C., Gerard Joseph, Ayurveda Practitioner, et al. Also my grandson Nathan in No. California and grand daughters Adrianna who is a mother married with four children who works as a medical technician and Tessie attending community college and employed as a construction manager in No. California. Many blessings of prosperity. My two sons Jamie and Jon Plotnick. My son Jamie who has been actively helping many disadvantaged girls in his non profit organization the Bay Point Cheers with the help and assistance of my daughter-in-law Maryann, and grand daughter Tessie the cheer leading Coaches. Many thanks and much love.

Abbreviations:

A.K.-Applied Kinesiology (muscle testing)
B.A.-Bachelor of Arts
D.C.-Doctor of Chiropractic
M.A.-Master of Arts

M.D.-Medical Doctor
Lic. Ac.-Licensed Acupuncturist
C.C.D.C.S.-Certified Chemical Dependency Counseling Specialist
C.A.D.D.E.-California Alcohol Drug Dependencies Educators
N.D.-Naturopathic Doctor
Ph.D.-Philosophy Doctor
R.N.-Registered Nurse
C.M.H.Th.-Certified Master Hypnotherapist
C.M.H.Th.In.-Certified Master Hypnotherapist Instructor
J.D.-Jurist Doctorate (Doctor of Law)
G.M.1-Gunner's Mate 1st Class, U.S.N.
M.S.-Master of Science
E.E.G.-Electroencephalograph
E.M.G.-Electromyograph
T.O.V.A.-Test of Variable Attention
P.Th.-Physical Therapist
St.-Saint
CA.-California
Inc.-Incorporated
Mtn.-Mountain
Pk.-Park
Rd.-Road
A.A.-Alcoholic's Anonymous
N.A.-Narcotic's Anonymous
C.O.D.-Cash on Delivery
U.P.S.-United Parcel Service
B.C.I.A.-Biofeedback Certification Institute of America
B.F.I.L.A.-Biofeedback Institute of Los Angeles
B.F.S-Biofeedback Society
A.P.P.B.A.-Applied Psychophysiology Biofeedback Association
C.Bf.Th.-Certified Biofeedback Therapist
C.Nf.Th.-Certified Neurofeeedback Therapist
L.C.M.H.C.-Licensed Clinical Mental Health Counselor
META-Going Beyond, Above,
S.B.A.-Small Business Association
S.V.E.D.C.-San Franando Valley Economic Development Corporation
A.M.P.D.R.-Alternative Medicine Physician's Desk Reference
C.E.O.'s-Corporation Executive Officers
E.g.-Example
I.e.-Example
?-Question
A.D.D.-Attention Deficit Disorder

A.D.H.D.-Attention Deficit Hyperactivity Disorder
L.D.-Learning Disability
O.C.D.-Obsessive Compulsive Disorder
P.T.S.D.-Post Traumatic Stress Disorder
P.D.-Panic Disorder
APNBMPDR-Alternative Preventive Naturopathic Bio-energetic
Medicine Physician's Desk Reference
02-Oxygen
03-Ozone
Gelotology-to laugh

Herbal Properties:

Anondyne-reduces nerve sensitivity.
Antiacid-reduces stomach and intestinal acidity.
Anthelminites-helps destroy intestinal worms.
Antarthritics-relief of gout and arthritis.
Antiperiodics-reduce body temperatures.
Antiseptics-prevent putrefaction.
Antispasmodics-relief of fits and spasms.
Antisyphilitics-rid system of syphilis.
Antizmotics-eliminates germs.
Apierents-mild purgatives.
Aphrodisiacs- increase sexual power.
Aromatics-stimulate gastro-intestinal mucus membranes.
Bitters-stimulate digestion.
Cardiac Depressants-lower heart's action.
Cardiac Stimulants-increase heart's action.
Carminitives-excite intestinal peristalsis and eliminate gas.
Cathartics-purgatives
Chologogues-promotes bile flow.
Demulcents-soothe and protect irritated mucus tissues.
Deodorants-eliminate foul odors.
Detergents-cleanse wounds.
Diaphoretics-promote perspiration.
Digestants-ferments and absorption of food.
Disinfectants-destroy toxic decaying organic matter.
Diuretics-increase urine secretion.
Drastics-cause irritation.
Ecbolics-produce abortion.
Emetics-producevomitting.
Emmenagogues-stimulate menstruation.

Emullients-soften and protect tissues.
Errhines-promote nasal secretion.
Expectorants- eliminate thick mucoid matter.
Galaciagogues-increase breast milk.
Haemosiatics-stop hemorrhages.
Hydragogues-cause large water discharges.
Hypnotics-cause sleep.
Laxatives-mild purgatives
Local Anestheics-local anesthetic.
Mydriatics-dialation of the eye pupil.
Myotics-contraction of the eye pupil.
Narcotics-powerful anondyne hypnotics.
Nutrients-promote nutrition.
Sedatives-lower functional activity.
Sialagogues-excite salivary glands.
Soporifics-cause sleep.
Stimulants-increase functional activity.
Stomachics-stimulates the stomach.
Stytics-stop hemorrages.
Sudorifics-produce profuse perspiration.
Taenicides-kill tapeworms
Tonics-stimulate nutrition
Vermicides-kill intestinal worms.
Vermifuges-expel intestinal worms
Vulnerary-promote healing.

AN ANSWER AND MY OPINION TO DR. ANDREW WEIL, M.D. IN REFERENCE TO HIS COMMENTS ABOUT NATUROPATHIC MEDICINE AND CHIROPRACTIC ON PAGES. 135-142 in his "HEALTH AND HEALING" book.

Dear Dr. Weil, M.D.,

First sir read my books and then comment. Naturopath's most of the doctors I know have broad knowledge in herbal medicine, homeopathic medicine, Chinese medicine including acupuncture theory and practice, and Chinese herbal medicine, Ayurveda medicine, Bio-energetic medicine, chiropractic muscle testing,A.K., acupressure, touch healing, massage-Shiatsu, Jin shin do, Thai, etc. Some of us like me are educated in acupuncture theory and practice, applied kinesiology also educated in herbology, homeopathy, anatomy, physiology, biology, chemistry, physics, psychology, humanities, arts, liberal studies, social science, life science, physical science, computer science, neutraceuticals, chemical dependency studies, hypnotherapy, healing, biofeedback, and neurofeedback. Some naturopath's as Dr. Michael Murray in Washington State have advanced the practice to a higher level of educational standards. Naturopath's in Washington work with M.D.'s and some can write prescriptions as well. Naturopathic Colleges such as Bastir College, in Washington state and Clayton College of Natural Health, in Birmingham, Alabama founded by Dr. Lloyd Clayton, N.D. There is also Dr. Robert Cass of goEnergetix's in Georgia an expert in bio-energetic medicine. He also runs a college for E.A.V. bio-energetic medicine. There are also many Naturopathic medical doctors such as Dr. Julian Whitaker, M.D. There are many doctors who use natural medicine because allopathic is deadly and for the most part does not work. Where are the scientific studies that back you're so called allopathic medicine? According to Gary Null, Ph.D. an authority on nutritional medicine there are well over 960 scientific studies that support alternative medicine including naturopathic. There are many scientific studies that support herbal, Chinese medicine, and doctors that have written many books supporting naturopathic medicine such as Dr. Ken Widgery, N.D., Dr. Roland Thomas, N.M.D., Dr. Rudolph Ballantine, M.D., Jude C. Williams, M.H. Dr. Ronald Klatz, M.D. Dr. Bernard Jensen, D.C., Dr. George Goodheart, Errol Korn, M.D., Efrem Korngold, O.M.D., L. Ac., D.C., Dr. John Thie, D.C., Dr. Joseph Hough, N.M.D., Dr. James Julian, H.M.D. Dr. Edward Bach, M.D., Dr. Harold Buttram, M.D., Dr. Michael Samuels,

M.D., Dr. Edward Shook, N.D., Dr. Richard Gerber, M.D., Dr. Roy Martina, M.D., Dr. James Balch, M.D., Gary Null, Ph.D.., Dr. Deepak Chopra, M.D., Dr. Wayne Dyer, Ph.D., Dr. Hans Nipper, M.D., Rudolph Skelnar, M.D., Dr. Paov Airola, N.D., Dr. James Tyler Kent, M.D. homeopath, Dr. Bernie Segiel, M.D., Dr. Steven Edleson, M.D. Dr. Robert Morse, N.D., Dr. Murray Susser, M.D., Environmental toxicology, Dr. Ken Widgery, N.D., C.E.O. of D.N.R., Inc. Liquid Needle light poton bioenergetic frequency solutions, Jerome Plotnick, Ph.D., N.D. biofeedback, bioenergetic-frequency detox-healing, neurofeedback, and ayurveda, etc. Read Dr. Deepak Chopra, M.D. and Dr. Wayne Dyer, Ph.D., R.I.P. et al. Are they quacks too? I don't rely on hair analysis as a method of diagnosis. Hair analysis could indicate the use of drugs and heavy metal toxicity only. Another comment you made about chiropractic educational requirements is absolutely untrue. Chiropractors take more courses than medical doctors as yourself. They have higher standards as well. You believe in allopathic that is your training so how can you render an unbiased opinion. You're brainwashed as an M.D. So you write books and grow herbs does that make you an authority on alternative medicine? I think not. Although I like some of the things you state, I do respect your knowledge and opinions, but I don't agree with you on Naturopathic medicine, and some of your other opinions on Chiropractic. By the way before your allopathic drug and needless surgery medicine becomes a dinosaur without any scientific proof whatsoever start reading the alternative medicine scientific studies that Dr. Gary Null speaks about. Your allopathic medicine is a modern day heroic mutate. Doctors prescribe drugs and medicines that are worse than if you took nothing at all. Michael Jackson, Lindsey Lohan, Heath Ledger, Anna Nicole Smith are a prime example, or Elvis Presley, etc. Psychiatry another bankrupt profession is in my opinion just for the most part legalized drug pushing. I know we couldn't live without the genuine medical doctors that perform miraculous trauma, and surgical life saving medicine. But as for treating symptoms and an organ no way Jose! That's not how a human being operates. We are a mind-body-spirit. Treat patients not symptoms. Treat with natural medicine not with side effects and poisons. Treat the mind and not with psychotropic drugs but with flower essences, relaxation, E.M.G. biofeedback training, E.E.G. neurofeedback training, love, and understanding. Most of all keep your holy temple clean with detoxification, eat right, breathe right, drink pure water, think right, exercise, meaning and purpose, prayer, and meditation. No drugs, just love, and hugs. Do no harm. Remember Hippocrates Oath?

Here sir is how I run my naturopathic counseling practice. <u>First</u>. Before anything I prepare the patient for a pre detoxification to prepare the body for detoxification. <u>Second</u>. Then I implement an energetic detoxification and have the patient on a special detoxification diet. I support their mind with Bach flower essences and have them do an "Act of Foregiveness" It takes a period of around 45 days to cleanse and re-energize. Afterward I will do pulse diagnosis and determine if there are energy excessive or deficiencies in the acupuncture system. I will treat with light photon needle-less acupuncture. If organ-meridians are in need of support I administer herbal and nutritional remedies. <u>Third</u>. I also offer biofeedback training for patients in need of relaxation, elimination of muscle tension, hypertension, pain, stress reduction, coping skills, heart rate, and blood pressure, etc. <u>Fourth</u>. I also offer neurofeedback training for anxiety, depression, O.C.D., P.D., A.D.D., A.D.H.D., L.D., addictions both substance and process, mental fitness, and optimum performance.

<u>Fifth</u>. I get patients on the right diet for them, teach meditation, relaxation techniques, super whole food supplement, oxygen therapies, herbal, light photon remedies as necessary including both classical, and clinical homeopathics. <u>Sixth</u>. I also offer for those who need it drug detoxification, counseling and neurofeedback training for addictive disease. It has a proven track record and backed up by scientific studies such as Menninger Clinic, University of No. Texas Drug Rehabilation Center, V.A. in Pueblo, Colorado, the University of Southern Colorado, Cri-Help Rehabilitation Center and the E.E.G. Spectrum Institute, Medical doctors, neurologists, Ph.D.'s in Psychology performed the research studies confirming a high success rate using E.E.G. neurofeedback Penniston-Kulkosky Protocol on addicts. Basically I know you're a good man and I respect you as a doctor. For the most part your books are good but in some areas I believe you just don't have your facts right. This is my humble opinion. Respectfully,

Jerome Plotnick, Ph.D.., N.D., C.N.F.Th., C.B.F.Th., C.C.D.C.S.-C.A.D.D.E., C.M.H.Th., C.T.F.H.I., C.P.H. Cert. Pranic Healer, M.I., Meditation Instructor

Weight Loss Information

There are a multitude of weight loss products on the market. Don't be fooled by their claims. There are absolutely no scientific studies that prove their claims. In my opinion they are all not what you should do to lose weight. Most are over-the counter-products just like products that claim to grow hair. Only Propecia a prescription drug has shown to grow hair. Weight loss products are temporary fixes for a problem that you can accomplish with life style changes. If you want to lose weight it takes time and you want to lose weight slowly. You want a permanent fix which requires a proper diet, exercise, smaller balanced meals, prayer, meditation, and visualization.

The 21st Century Energetics 45 day health rest-oral program outlined in this book is what you really need for a permanent weight loss.

Another one of my books The 13 Steps From Illness To Health, Meta Your Nutrition, and Meta Your Mind will be extremely helpful in any weight loss program.

So don't be fooled by quick fixes they just won't work over the long haul. For a permanent weight loss there are changes necessary. Remember if it's too good to be true its not. There is a sucker born every minute. Don't waste your time and money on T.V. advertised weight loss products. If you believe it you will see it. Everything begins in the mind. Then take action through diet and exercise. Visualize it and create the new you.

Remember it's what's going on inside that's most important. See it, say it, and then do it. Getting healthy is the most important factor. You can lose weight if you detoxify yourself, eat the proper organic vegan alkaline diet, and exercise daily. Drink 8 oz. glasses of distilled water. If you are lipid heavy you need to burn fat (convert to energy) this is done by taking an enzyme called Lupron (lipase), B-12, and mental exercise using your mind during the day burns calories or by physical exercise that burns calories. If your body has an excess of water then under a physician's supervision hydrate and use of herbal diuretics are advised. The pre and post detoxification programs in the 45 day health rest-oral program are advised.

Water and fat are the enemies especially if toxins occupy the cellular fluid and are in the lipids of your body. That is why you must perform a detoxification so these toxins can be removed safely.

Remember patience is a virtue. If interested in further information on a permanent weight loss please contact me Phone: @ (661) 245-3616 M-F 9-5 P.S.T.

<u>Smoking and Alcohol-Drug Addiction</u>.

If interested in a permanent stop smoking program or alcohol-drug recovery program please read my other books on Meta Your Recovery, the 13th Step For Addiction Recovery. Pre-Post Detoxification Program, homeopathic, flower essences, light photon remedies and bath soak for stopping smoking, as outlined in this book. This along with E.E.G. alpha-theta (Penniston-Kulkosky protocol) brainwave training for addictions (several studies confirm a very high success rate using this training), 12 Step Program, and daily meditation are essential. Also you must discover what your soul-spirit wants for you rather than what you want. As long as you are in an out-of-alignment with your soul you will have disharmony and suffering. Recommended are Bach Flower remedies-Fields of Flowers. MP3/C.D.'s the Tao of the Soul-Self-Slate-Rebirth, Celestine Prophecy by John Redfield go into nature, ask to be led to the right path for you, and your soul. Wait and you will be led and have your answer. Rest and Journey by the Sea by Karen Mitchell. Read the Meta Your Meditation, 13 Tao's from Ancient to Modern Spiritual Masters, perform meditations, and spiritual Tao's. Also as an adjunct Potentials Unlimited videos and audios for self healing, stop drugs, alcohol, smoking, and weight loss, etc. I also use Liquid Needle's: CIG-131 bath soak & Cig-522 drops and Liquid Needle Total Balance-L.N.T.B. For brainwave re-balancing for addictions, O.C.D., P.D., A.D.H.D., depression, and A.D.D. See pages 414-415 in The 13 Steps From Illness To Health-APNBMPDR book. See pages: 287-310 in this book.

If you are smoking or drinking alcohol please take the smokers remedy and the alcohol remedy listed on pages 92-93 Step 6 of The 13 Steps from Illness to Health book by Jerome Plotnick, Ph.D., N.D. Since drinking and smoking depletes your body of its vitamin and mineral reserves it is essential that you supplement yourself

with what I have outlined (also Liquid Needle Green Vits, Mins in the aforementioned book daily. Also advised is L.N. Cig-131,522. If interested in further information and participating in my programs for addiction recovery please call me.
Phone: (661) 245-3616 Leave your phone number, message, and best time to call you. Thank you. Yours In Health,
Jerome Plotnick, Ph.D., N.D., C.B.F.Th., C.N.F.Th., C.C.D.C.S.-C.A.D.D.E.-C.A.A.R.D.-N.A.C., C.M.Hyno Th., C.T.F.H.I. Behavioral-Counseling-Psychologist-Biofeedback-Neurofeedback Therapist specializes in addictive disease-Psycho-Physiologist-Naturopathic Practitioner-Counselor-Addictionologist Certified Chemical Dependency Counseling Specialist(C.C.D.C.S.)-Member-Counselors Alcohol Drug Dependency Educators (C.A.D.D.E.)-Counselors Alcohol And Related Dependencies (C.A.A.R.D.)-National Alcohol Counselors (N.A.C.).21st Century Energetics formulate and manufacture herbal health restoral products, distribute retail and wholesale products listed in this book and the 13 Steps From Illness To Health-APNBMPDR-repertoire of products catalog, publish health-wellness-wholeness, spiritual, addiction recovery books, and F.D., M.P.3/C.D.'s. Promote and teach programs based on Jerome Plotnick's books.
Jerome Plotnick, Ph.D., N.D.
Author of the following books:

META YOUR MIND-$30 order #101
META YOUR MEDITATION-$40 order #102 coming in Dec. 2017
META YOUR NUTRITION-$30 order #103 coming in May 2018
META YOUR HEALTH IN 45 DAYS-Holistic Healing Cancer-$30 order #104
META YOUR MANIFESTATION-$30 order #105 coming in Dec. 2107
MIND MEME'S MIASMS TAKOVER TO MIND HEALING MAKEOVER-$20 order #106
BIOENERGETIC, MIND & NATURAL MEDICINE-$30 order #107
THE 13 STEPS FROM ILLNESS TO HEALTH 155 pg-$20 order #108 13 Steps + ANBMPDR 828 pg-$40 F.D.-#19.99 order # 109 or #109A
THE TAO OF THE SOUL-SELF-SLATE-$20 order #110 coming in Nov. 2017
THE 13 TAOS FROM ANCIENT TO MODERN SPIRITUAL MASTERS-$30 order #111
THE 13th STEP FOR TOTAL ADDICTION RECOVERY-$10 order #112
FAST FOOD IN THE FAST LANE-$10 order #113
MIND-BODY CONNECTION RADIO SHOW LIVE CD-$10 order #114
THE TAO OF THE SOUL-SELF-SLATE-REBIRTH MP2/CD-$20 order #115
JOURNEY & REST KAREN MITCHELL MP3/CD-$30 order #116
SELF HEALING CD-$20 order #117

TWIN HEARTS MEDITATION-MASTER CHO KOK SUI CD-$20 order #118
CHONDRIANA & LIFE CRYSTALS, GEORGE MERYKL Ph.D.-$20.00
ROYAL RIFE-EXPERIMENTAL FREQUENCY ULTRASOUND GENERATOR-Call for price.
Shipping-3 day priority add $ 9.50 U.S.P.S.
Overnight Express add $15.75 U.S.P.S.
U.P.S. call for rates.
Send-check-or Postal Money order to:
21st Century Energetics
Jerome Plotnick, Ph.D., N.D.
6132 Frazier Mt. Pk. Rd. #45, Lake of the Woods, CA. 93225-9200
Pay by Pay Pal-Visa or Master Card only call (661) 245-3616 for acceptance have credit card or debit card #, Name on Card, expiration date, and the security code # on back of card. Leave information on message if no answer. We are busy and we will take the information you leave and process your order as soon as possible.

If you call after 12 P.M. your order will be shipped the following day. We are on Pacific Time Zone.
If interested in ordering John Steel's Lifetree Aromatix's Grade "A" Essential Oils see in the 13 Steps from Illness to Health Practitioners P.D.R. pages. 551-564 or please call for product information (661) 245-3616
To have our complete herbal,homeopathic, light photon-botanical whole food super supplement reference guide, and product information catalog order "THE 13 STEPS FROM ILLNESS TO HEALTH" + (APNBMPDR)"Alternative Preventive Naturopathic Bioenergetic Medicine Physician's Desk Reference"-$40-828 pages..-#109 available on a F.D., or Soft Cover book, or #110 available WiFi e-book @ Amazon.com/-kindle-e-books $20

To the U.S. Presidents, Obama, Trump, the U.S. Senate, and U.S. Congress: If the average citizen could be covered for alternative-holistic-preventive-Naturopathic-Bioenergetic medicine testing-pre-post detoxification program and then the appropriate whole food supplements, light photon remedies, herbal, homeopathic remedy maintenance support. The government could save billions of dollars, the citizen-taxpayer could have a healthier life without most of the unnecessary drugs, medicines that are strangling the economy, and the user. Natural medicines have no or little side effects are much more cost effective and in most cases are not used for a lifetime. i.e. Chinese medicine costs for treatment $1,000 compared to a 3 day stay in a hospital for the same medical illness is $5,000. The success outcomes are 85% for Chinese medicine treatment that treats the cause of the illness compared to 0% for the allopathic hospital suppressive treatment that only treats the illness symptoms. If you want a truly excellent health care program for Americans then invest in the aforementioned program in natural preventive medicine. A program such as aforementioned in this book or the 13 Steps from Illness to Health book can give the American public the very best in the world, save lives, money, and allow the government to get out of the immense financial instability currently taking place.

Again, as stated by Benjamin Franklin, "an ounce of prevention is worth a pound of cure." If we combine the alternative natural preventive medicine with conventional allopathic medicine the U.S. would lead the world in the best health care system anywhere. We don't need the life time drug treatment and unnecessary surgery, etc. If you can diagnose disease before it occurs then treat it with low cost natural medicine and other preventive treatments.

i.e. The cost of the Meta Your Health in 45 Days program would be around $1,500.00 and would thereafter cost $1,000.00. Compare that to a hospital stay, ongoing treatments for a lifetime on drugs, and in most cases does not heal the patient. Cancer as an example can cost thousands of dollars with loss of the patient's life.

NOTE! DISCLAIMER also on Page 2
This book does not claim to diagnose, prescribe medicines, treat, heal, or cure any disease. Always consult with your

physician or licensed health care practitioner. This program is not intended to replace your medical treatment. It is an adjunct to any medical program. The F.D.A. has not approved the statements or the health products contained herein.

NOTE!

This book is an adjunct to "The 13 Steps to Illness" APNBMPDR-Alternative Preventive Naturopathic Bioenergetic Medicine Physician's (Practitioners) Desk Reference.
To order online go to: createspace.com, amazon.com, amazon.com e-books/kindle, Barnes&Noble.com/nook/books, Borders, in the San Fernando Valley: Valencia, Santa Clarita, Santa Monica, Redondo, Pacific Palasades, Malibu, O.C. Beach cities Laguana, Newport, Huntington, San Diego, Bay Area: Walnut Creek, Danville, Sausilito, Tiberon, Mill Valley, San Francisco, and N.Y.C., or any city. Call the stores in your area and ask them to order these exclusive cutting edge books. You may also
Phone: 21st Century Energetics @ (661) 245-3616.
Website: 21stcenturyenergetics.com E-mail: plotnickj@yahoo.com
Jerome Plotnick, Ph.D., N.D-21st Century Energetics,
@ facebook.com, Jerome Plotnick, Ph.D., N.D. @Linkedin.com,
@ Manta.com, Biopharma.com, Google.com., Bing.com, Aol.com,
jeromeplotnickphdnd@facebook.com, @amazon.com/books, B&N.com.

NOTE!

B

blood purify-60,61-67,
blood wash-60,66
body-brain spa-4-6
boldo-71
boredom-38
boron-64
botanicals-105
Boyne, Gil-51
Brady, Dr.-50
brain/body nutrients-39
brain/body spa-4,14-15,30-31
brain functioning-54
Brain Master Tech.-53,55
brain mind-4,12
brain wave-15
brain wave frequencies-59
Brod, Dr.-45-46,55
Brody, Dr.-50,55
Bronic, Dr.-52
Brown, Dr.-52,54
Brundy, Dr.-55
Bryant, Dr.-51
bruxism-113
Budzynski, Dr.-55

C

cabbage-62
calcium-64
camu-camu-71
Cannon, Dr.-51
carrots-62
carpel tunnel-92
catalyst-19,28,31,113
catuba-72
celery-61
cell diseases-60
cell restoration-15,89
cell rejuvenation-60,89
cell stagnation-60

C

Celtic sea salt-10,68
chronic fatigue syndrome-14,
30
Chaplin, Dr.-82-84
Charcot, Dr.-51
chemical pollutants-18,82
chi-16,,25,28,34,40
Chi Gong-16,25,28,34,40,87
chlorophyl-63,114
chronic pain-92
Christ-28
cingulate gyrus-44
Cochagne, Dr.-53
coconut-62,64
cognitive beliefs-6
cognitive flexibility-16,51
Collura, Dr.-53,55
colon & colon cleanse-14,31
colon clear-31
colonic-14
common good-11
compensation phase-26
concentration-12,41
oonscious response-45-46
conventional medicine-22
cranberry-46,61
Cri Help-46,98
cruelty-34,37
cucumber-62,65-66
cybernetics-53-54

D

daily botanicals-20
dalergia wood-72
decomposition phase-27
deep states relax-28,43,47
degeneration phase-27
dehydration-30
Demos, John-53,55

T

toxic four & eleven step detox-18-20
toxic frequencies-13
toxins-11-13,15,18-27
turmeric-66,68
turnip-63
twelve steps-5,97-98,
Twenty 21st Century Energetics-3,5,14,
16,19,28,40,46

U

una de gato-71
urinary-26,94
unconditional love-36,70
Univ. of So. Colorado-46,97
Univ. of No. Texas-46-47
un-sulfured molasses-66

V

V.A.-55,96-97
vascular disease-50,92,94,106
viral toxins-25-26,38,71
Vitamin D3-64
voluntary control-49,56

W

Walters, Dr.-46,96-97
weakness-23,25,35
weight loss information-126
wellness-4,12
whole food supplement-21,28-29,39,58-59,61,68-69,73-79,83
white blood cell count-26
Wickraneskara, Dr.-55
Wilson, Bill-16,97
W.L.W.P.-16
worry-34

X

Y

yoga-51

Z

Zietgeist-54
Zen-4,54
zero order beliefs-6

AFTERWARD I

THOUGHTS TO THINK ABOUT & PONDER

In the universe and in our lives the only thing you can count on
is change. It is constant. One must realize that only you can
create a healthy prosperous life. No one else besides you and the
creator. Your mantra should be that "I am a wave of tranquility
(Peace of God) in a sea of chaos." The universe is managed chaos.
God created it, a divine plan for each one of us. and in creation.
You must go with the Universal Divine Mind's plan and not yours.

Here is a question you may or not have heard. How many
psychiatrists does it take to change a light-bulb? Answer: It
takes one but the light-bulb has to want to change. Change is
inevitable in this life. How we do it is the important factor. I
believe on Earth we are headed for Nirvana. Nirvana means "Heaven
on Earth," or the Golden Age.

Anyway my belief probably differs from yours especially if you go
to church and believe that is the only way to God. I believe most
churches are a business, money making entities that are tax free,
and mainly social affairs. I believe anyone can get to, connect
with God consciousness, without going to any one church, or
religion. This is not to say that churches or pastors, etc. are
bad. I just don't think that Jesus Christ who cast out the money
lenders and money makers wants anyone to attend that kind of
church. He also stated no stone churches. Yet what do we have?
Million dollar pastors with immense stone buildings called
churches. I just don't believe that is right or what a Universal
Divine Creator God wants from me. On the other hand I do not
condemn those who believe they must attend church. It is just not
right for me. When the rich pastors donate 90% of their monies to
charity, give up their airplanes, mansions, boats, and expense
accounts then maybe I will believe them. Otherwise I am convinced
they are somewhat like the Hebrew pharisees that had Christ
crucified for upsetting their apple cart.

I believe the living God of this world and Universe wants exactly
for us what he had. Did he have wealth? No. He had followers,
comradeship, loyalty, brotherhood, and giving always. Not
receiving. Give up your lavish life styles as well and prosper all

140

those around you. That's what Jesus did for his followers. Again churches are money making businesses that are tax free. While the multitude have to pay their fair share. These churches and rich pastors need to pay their fair share as well in my opinion. I believe in spirituality an individual connection to God not a group religious, and dogma concept. Therfore nature is my church.

God is an abundant Creator so ask for a barn full of blessings, live by spiritual divine laws, and it will be granted to you. God created you in as a super deluxe model. Ask and ye shall receive. Knock and the door shall be upon unto thee. Prosperity means peace of God, health, wholeness, love, and harmony. Just don't let money become your God. I believe the spirit of God is within.

Lastly, we don't need a national health care plan what we need is a health care prevention plan. These medical doctors are just as much the problem as the health care insurance providers. Allopathic medicine is a killer. We need to get away from this brain-washing, move to prevention through alternative, holistic, naturopathic, bio-energetic medicine as I have entailed in this, and my other books "Bio-energetic, Mind and Natural Medicine," The 13 Steps from Illness to Health." Alternative Preventive Naturopathic Bioenergetic Medicine Physician's Desk Reference,"- APNBMPDR, "Meta Your Mind," "Meta Your Nutrition," "Meta Your Meditation, and "Meta Your Health in 45 Days."

The Republican conservatives want you to keep the status quo, are in bed with the allopathic doctors, and insurance companies who donate lots of money for their election to office. The Democrats want you to have more of the same on the backs of the taxpayers.

But again, it's the same old, same old deal. I haven't heard prevention in their plan as the main goal. Yes we do need allopathic for surgery, trauma, and emergency medicine. We don't need more of the same drugs, needless surgery, chemotherapy, radiation, and three to four hundred thousand deaths per year caused by these barbaric practices.

What we really need is change you can count on from your creator who created nature and natural medicine. Not your government that promotes man-made artificial pharmaceutical, petroleum, drugs, and unnatural medicine. We are both taxed and petroleumed © to death.

141

These synthetic medicines are worse for you than your illness. Once you become addicted to them you are also suffering from toxemia. You are just as hooked, addicted, and more sick than when you began taking them. There is a natural solution and a spiritual solution for every health problem.

For health care do not depend on the government, depend on yourself, prevention through healthy lifestyle choices, your creator for nature the ancient healing wisdom, our modern "cutting-edge" 21st Century energetic medicine called bio-energetic naturopathic, holistic, alternative, and preventive medicine. Remember what Benjamin Franklin stated, "An ounce of prevention is worth a pound of cure." Jerome Plotnick, Ph.D., N.D.

AFTERWARD II

HOW TO DEAL WITH MODERN-DAY PSYCHO-SOMATIC STRESS, DURESS, FEAR, WORRY CAUSING TENSION, HYPERTENSION, ANXIETY, AND PAIN.

We suffer in our modern day of ongoing stress caused by a toxic environment. In the ancient past when we saw a tiger, our primitive brain would cause us to fight-flight, and then play dead. That is how we coped. If we go to the zoo, see a tiger behind the bars we don't fight, or flight. But when our brain's neo cortex does not communicate with our old reptilian brain it causes our sympathetic nervous system to create fight, or flight, and even when there is no danger. This causes a stress that creates tension, pain, anxiety, hypertension, worry, and fear. Stressful situations in our life whether real or imagined. Because of this continual stress, the sympathetic nervous system remains engaged, causes adrenalin to flow, and prepares us to fight, or flight as if the tiger we saw in the zoo was out of the cage. Due to this it cannot communicate back to the para-sympathetic nervous system which normally brings us back to normal functioning. This causes us to have muscular tensions, anxieties, aches, pain, worry, and fear. This also allows adrenalin to be in our system when it is really not needed. This causes a high heart rate, high blood pressure, hypertension, and many other symptoms. The end result is a toxic mind, or body, or both causing symptoms that are being experienced by the majority of people in our society. The mind might not be able to focus and it may have racing thoughts. The body may have tensions, aches, and pains. They both might occur simultaneously or individually.

Part of the problem lies in the ego or the "I." Your sense of self, how you look, dress, your style, car, where you live, and perform, etc. This is the idealized self image we project out to the world. When we cannot meet our expectations of the "I" the ego we cause a dissonance a stress which then causes anxieties, worry, fear, tension, hypertension, aches, and pains, etc. This also compromises our immune system function. If we are not able to maintain our ego it keeps the sympathetic nervous system active and a cause of the aforementioned problems. The other problem is caused by how we handle the stress of our environment which is our modern day life in many problems of survival of basic needs which is the main cause of the high divorce rate, then worry, and fear.

If you live in the big city the traffic, crime, and stress of big city life. Modern day society is so stressed out that for many of us the sympathetic nervous system is in the fight or flight mode continuously and we suffer due to it. The way to turn the sympathetic nervous system off and allow the para-sympathetic nervous system to bring about normal functioning is to find out what type we are. i.e. a mind conscious cognitive anxiety malfunctioning, or body somatic anxiety spasms, or both. Then how to change our situation through one or more of the bio-meditation processes.

The idea is to discover the following then take the appropriate action in the form of the various types of relaxation training practices whether for mind, body or both. These are the questions you need to ask yourself to change your present state.

What type are you? Do I have a racy mind full of anxiety, fear, and worry. Do I have a body full of aches, pain, muscular tension, and etc,? What form of bio-meditation do I need? What should I do?

You could have a body somatic reaction causing aches, pain, and muscular tension, etc. Or you could have a reaction that causes your mind to be not able to concentrate or focus. A problematic negative thinking mind sometimes called the monkey mind.

If you suffer from cognitive anxiety then you probably need and want to engage in a mantra, counting breath meditation, mandala, sound, or a single point meditation. This will engage your mind in the appropriate relaxation training.

If you suffer from somatic body anxiety causing spasms, aches, pains, muscular tension then you will probably need, and want to engage in Hatha yoga, or E.M.G. biofeedback training for the specific area of tension, etc. Biofeedback E.M.G. specifically treats through the training of one's self, taking conscious control of these areas, and of specific body muscular tensions, etc.

If for example you should have a high anxiety causing tension in both mind and body then what would be advised is Tai Chi. This is the mind involved in body movement. Another suggestion would be to play the game of tennis or inner tennis. Also Internal Kung Fu.

If you suffer from low anxiety for tension in both mind and body then what would be advised is conventional Eastern and Western meditations, such as the Zen of Doing, and Anything, etc. There are also the following: Progressive Relaxation by Dr. Edmund Jacobsen where you begin at your toes and work all the way up your body to the top of your head and scalp. You tense the muscles and then relax them. This would be a body process meditation.

If you suffer from both mind an body low anxiety then what would be advised is Autogenic exercise by Dr. Jon Schultz where you integrate your mind and body. A mind-body interplay. This would be for both mind and body. For example you concentrate on your body such as your lungs, breath, and breathing. Then involve the mind by saying, "it breathes me." Focus your mind on your lungs. An Autogenic exercise. On page 278 for an autogenic exercise.

If you suffer from a low anxiety of mind and body then what would be advised would be hetero hypnosis where a hypnotist relaxes you through suggestion and imaging is used to actively engage the person through their senses. Here you organize your inhibitory processes to be induced into the hypnotic state. Physical-Emotional-Intellectual. On page 270 for self hypnosis instruction.

If you suffer from a high anxiety of mind and body then what would be advised would be self actualized or self hypnosis where you through disorganizing your inhibitory processes to hypnotize yourself. Physical-Emotional-Intellectual. See pages: 269-270

If you suffer from both mind and body anxiety then what would be advised would be Hatha yoga where you do yoga exercises that involve your mind. This is similar to Tai chi.

If you suffer from body anxieties then what would be advised would be E.M.G. biofeedback training for muscular tensions, heart rate, and blood pressure, etc. Here you are made aware of and are taking control of your bodily functions, and muscles, etc. You are taught to relieve tensions, relax muscles, and as an example control your heart rate. It is a learning model. Self Regulation.

If you suffer from mind anxieties then what would be advised would be E.E.G. neurofeedback training for nervous, anxiety, fear, worry, lack of focus, concentration, and racy thoughts. A definite need to calm the mind to deep states of relaxation. E.E.G. training is used for the following: A.D.D., A.D.H.D., L.D., Dyslexia, P.T.S.D., O.C.D., P.D., B.P., Addictions, Mental Fitness, and Peak Performance. It is a learning model.

Breathing exercises are used as a precursor to prepare to enter relaxation or whatever bio-meditation you are going to perform.

If you suffer from body or mental muscular pain, and tension then a Touch For Health meditation by running of the acupuncture meridians, or acupressure massage, or acupuncture touch would be advised. If interested call the Touch For Health Foundation or Thie Chiropractic Offices in Pasadena, California for an appointment, or referral to a certified Touch For Health practitioner in your area. In California there are many chiropractors that use the Touch For Health techniques. Also recommended is a Licensed Acupuncturist that also performs physical therapy and massage. The one I know personally that is outstanding is Cheryl Teague, L.Ac., L. Phy. Th. She is in the Medical Office of Dr. Mark Greenspan, M.D. located on Van Nuys Blvd. in Sherman Oaks, California. Also needle-less acutherapy.

If you suffer from body anxieties causing muscular aches, pains, and tensions a Touch For Health treatment, or a full body massage is also highly advised from a qualified certified massage therapist. Recommended is Pranic Healing, Jin Shin Do, Shiatsu, Acupressure, Internal Kung Fu, Tai Chi, and Thai style of massage.

If you suffer from low anxieties in mind, body, then what would be advised would be both Western, and Eastern meditation. There are many meditations to perform such as: Single Point where you concentrate on a single object, Breath to Breath where you concentrate on each breath as you inhale and exhale. Thought to Thought where you concentrate on each thought as it comes and goes, Mantra, or T.M. where you concentrate on a particular or general word, etc. Zen here you concentrate on what your doing or anything occurring becomes the meditation, A-Z where you on each letter of the alphabet, for each letter you state a desire of peace, or prosperity. The 1,000 petal lotus where you concentrate on a lotus as you drop each petal into a river and watch it disappear, etc.

An old Indian statement is that a Fast Mind is a Sick Mind; a Slow Mind is a Healthy Mind; a   Still Mind is a No, or Divine Mind. By the aforementioned bio-meditation processes you will be able to let go of fear and guilt. When this occurs then there is a shift in perception that allows unconditional love to be fully realized. I highly recommend along with the aforementioned practices that you read the "Course of Miracles" or attend the course. There are audios available. Tao of the Soul-Self-Slate.

I also highly recommend along with your bio-meditation used that you use the following naturopathic-bio-energetic remedies, etc. They are as follows:
Physiologics-Mental Function & Mood & Relaxation Support-5HTP-COMPLEX-#5318-Nervous system-relaxation, ACEYTL L-CARNATINE-#55236-Promotes memory & cognitive function, DMAE-#1864-Promotes synthesis of neurotransmitters, ELEUTHRO SIBERIAN ROOT-#12066-promotes well being, GINKGO ALERT FORMULA-#55134-Promotes mental performance, HUPERZINE A COMPLEX-#10361-Advanced memory formula, L-THEANINE-#12882-Supports mood centers of the brain, LECITHIN CHOLINE-#355052-Promotes mental function & nerve cell health, NADH ENADA-#6535-Fights free radicals and energizes, PHOSPHATIDYLSERINE COMPLEX-#10006-Supports brain function, sharpens mental focus, and helps memory, SAM-e-#7116-Supports mood and emotional well being, VINPOCETINE-#12764-Supports cerebral circulation, MELATONIN-#7915-Nutritionally supports sound sleep, B-BASIC-#12045-supports brain function, B-COMPLEX-#10288-Supports nervous system health.
Liquid Needle's-Light Photon bio-energetic's-Heals the mind/body-ExStress Ex, Anti-stress, Chi Gong-meditative state, E.V.B.-energy, vitality, balance, L.N.T.B.-bio-field balance, Shampoo Drops-Calmness, NRV-SYS-EX-Anxiety, grief, and depression, etc.-#'s-E.V.B., L.N.T.B., Chi Gong, S.D., Original, ExStress, and NRV.
Energetix's-Heals the spirit-Fields of Flowers-removes 7 deadly sins & 11 mental terror states-balances spirit, Rescue Calm-Calmness.-#'s-F.O.F.,R.C. Also Heather and Rock Rose.
Amazon Natural Treasures Herb's-Heals the mind/body-Uri-depression, Catuba-Hypertension, Amarelo-Anxiety.-#'s-UR-1007PA-$99.00,CAT-00419PA-$16.99,AMLO-300419PA-$120.90
Lifetree Aromatix or Young's Living Essential Oils-Heals the mind-body-Basil-mental fatigue, Cedarwood-Tension, Chamomile-Anti-stress, Frankincense-Stress and depression, Geranium-Release negative memories, Lavender-Relaxation, Orange-Promotes peace and happiness, Rose-Promotes balance and harmony, Sage-Cope,

depression and mental fatigue, Spruce-Helps release emotional blocks, Tangerine-Calms nervousness, Valerian-Nervousness, Vetiver-Anti-stress.#'s-B,CE,CH,F,GE,LAV,OR,RO,SG,TA,and VA.

21st Century Energetics Herbs-Heals the mind-body-Heather, Chamomile, Celery, Conchona bark, Dill, Fit root, Skullcap with Goldenseal. Hysopp, Lobelia, Peach tree leaves, Pennyroyal, Queen of the meadow, Red clover, Rosemary, Rue, Sage, Skunk cabbage, Spearmint, Squaw vine, St. John's wort, Thyme, Twin leaf, Valerian, Wild cherry, Wood betony, Blue violet, Sanicle, Buchu, Red sage, Catnip, Peppermint, Marshmellow root, and Mugwort tincture-Nervousness and calmness.-#'s: H,CH,CE,CO,D,FR,SC,RC,R, RU,SA,SK,SP,SQ,STJ,TH,TW,V,WC,WB,BV,S,BU,RS,C,AT,PEP,MR, and MUT. Lobelia, Boneset, Pennyroyal tincture, Queen of the Meadow-Relaxants.-#'s-BO,PRT,and QM.

Blue cohosh, Catnip, Cayenne, Fit root, Masterwort, Red clover, Sasafras, Skunk cabbage, Spearmint, Twin leaf, Wild yam, Red root, Fennel, and Cedon-Spasms.-#'s: BC,CAT,VAY,FR,MST,RC,SAF,SC,SP,TL, WY,RR,FE,and CED.

Apex Energetic's-Heals the spirit-all of their flower Essence Combinations and Visage Cards to extensive to list. They are included on pages [200-207] of APNBMPDR Alternative Preventive Naturopathic Bioenergetic Medicine Physicians Desk Reference by Jerome Plotnick, Ph.D., N.D.

I also highly recommend the following audios available from 21st Century Energetics:

"The Tao of the Soul-Self-Slate" by Jerome Plotnick, Ph.D., N.D. hypnotic as well as a spiritual talk, frequency tones, music, lecture on side one, and on side two spiritual enlightenment, re-birthing, relaxation, and self healing.-#-21CETSSS(4-90 min.pgms.)

"Journey by the Sea" and "Rest" by Karen Mitchell a spiritual enhancing healing music and narration on one side that allows the listener to enter the alpha-theta relaxation mind state.-#-LJKMJBS,R

"Self Healing" by Barrie Konikov a hypnotic on side one and subliminal on side two for mind/body healing.-#-PUSH

"Relieve Stress & Anxiety by Barrie Konikov a hypnotic on side one and subliminal on side two for relieving stress & anxiety-#PURSA

"Open Focus" by Shakti Duane a hypnotic relaxation audio for dissolving pain.-#-OFSD

"Creative Visualization" by Shakti Duane for spiritual affirmations to heal the mind and body.-#-CVSD

"Meditation on the Twin Hearts" by Master Choa Kok Sui, Pranic Healer for a spiritual balancing and upliftment.-#-IISMCKSMOTH
"Enhancing Massage" by Steven Halperin for healing music to enhance any massage you and receive.-#-AASHEM
"Course of Miracles" by Dr. Gerald Jampolsky and Anette Cerinceroni for lessons to attain the peace of God, spirituality, and love. Mini Course for healing relationships.-#-COMFFIP
"Metaphysical Meditations" by Sri Kriyananda meditations for inner peace, samadhi, silence, light, joy, and love.-#-MMCCSK

HERBS, VITAMINS, AMINO ACIDS, NATURAL CHEMICALS

5-HTP COMPLEX-#5318-$29.99-PHYSLG
ACEYTL-L-CARNATINE-#55236-$53.99-PHYSLG
D.M.A.E.-#1864-$10.99-PHYSLG
ELEUTHRO SIBERIAN ROOT-#12066-$8.49-PHYSLG
GINKGO ALERT FORMULA-#55134-25.99-PHYSLG
HUPERZINE-A-COMPLEX-#10361-$31.99-PHYSLG
L-THEANINE-#55233-$6.99-PHYSLG
LECITHIN CHOLINE-#55052-$15,49-PHYSLG
N.A.D.H. ENADA-#6535-$33.99-PHYSLG
PHOSPHATIDYSERINE COMPLEX-#10006-$49.99-PHYSLG
SAM-e-#7116-$33.99-PHYSLG
VINPOCETINE-#12784-$19.99-PHYSLG
MELATONIN-#7915-$7.99-PHYSLG
B-BASIC-#12045-$6.49-PHYSLG
B-COMPLEX-#10288-$13.99-PHYSLG

FLOWER ESSENCES

FIELDS of FLOWERS-#06010-$17.10-ENX
RESCUE CALM-#06020-$17.10-ENX

LIGHT PHOTON BIOENERGETICS

EXSTRESS-EX-$70.00-DNRLN
EXSTRESS-DROPS-$40.00-DNRLN
NRV-SYS-EX-$40.00-DNRLN
E.V.B.-$45.00-DNRLN
S.D.-$40.00-DNRLN
L.N.T.B.-$45.00-DNRLN
CHI GONG-$45.00-DNRLN

ESSENTIAL OILS-AROMATHERAPY

BASIL OIL-#3-$17.50-LTA
CEDARWOOD OIL-#24-$7.50-LTA
CHAMOMILE OIL-#16-LTA
FRANKINCENSE OIL_#224-$30.00-LTA
GERMANIUM OIL-#226-$30.00-LTA
LAVENDER OIL-#243-#25.00-LTA
ORANGE OIL-#261-$40.00-LTA
ROSE OIL-#266-$25.00-LTA
SAGE OIL-#287-$30.00-LTA
SPRUCE OIL-#137-$16.00-LTA
TANGERINE OIL-#140-$12.15-LTA
VALERIAN OIL-#3548-$33.60-YLO
VETIVER OIL-#151-$14.00-LTA

AMAZON HERBS

URI HERB-#1007PA-$99.00-ANT
AMERLO HERB-#1811PA-$120.90-ANT
CATUBA HERB-#00419PA-$16.99-ANT

HERBS

BLUE COHOSH HERB-#5034-$14.75-21CE
BLUE VIOLET HERB-#5145-$12.00-3204-$21.60-21CE
BUCHA HERB-#1230-$36.00-21CE
CATNIP HERB-#5022-$15.85-21CE
CAYENNE HERB-#1310-$17.65-21CE
CELERY HERB-#5024-$12.75-21CE
CHAMOMILE HERB-#5025-$12.25,#1316W-$19.70-21CE
DILL HERB-#1470C-$26.65-21CE
FENNEL HERB-#5051-$12.75-21CE
FIT ROOT HERB-#3202C-$16.20-#1227C-$17.30-21CE
GOLDENSEAL HERB-#5067-$26.25-$16.25-21CE
HYSOPP HERB-#1811-$17.50-21CE
LOBELA HERB-#2212C-$16.20-21CE
MARSHMELLOW ROOT HERB-#2301C-$19.80-21CE
PEACH TREE LEAVES HERB-#2509C-$18.00-21CE
PENNYROYAL HERB-#2610C-$13.50-21CE
PEPPERMINT HERB-#2515C-$16.20-21CE

QUEEN OF THE MEADOW HERB-#2702C-$13.25-21CE
RED CLOVER HERB-#2803C-$26.10-21CE
RED ROOT HERB-#2804C-$13.50-21CE
ROSEMARY HERB-#2814C-$14.40-21CE
RUE HERB-#5122-$12.75-21CE
SAGE HERB-#5124-$12.50-21CE
SKULLCAP HERB-#2911C-$15.00-21CE
SKUNK CABBAGE HERB-#2922C-$27.00-21CE
SPEARMINT HERB-#2928C-$13.00-21CE
ST. JOHN'S WORT HERB-#2903-$12.50-21CE
SQUAW VINE HERB-#2932-$13.00-21CE
THYME HERB-#3003C-$16.20-#5130-$13.50-21CE
TWIN LEAF HERB-#3007C-$15.70-21CE
VALERIAN HERB-#3200C-$12.00-21CE
VIOLET, BLUE HERB-#5145-$13.00-21CE
WILD CHERRY HERB-#1320C-$20.70-21CE
WILD YAM HERB-#3400C-$18.00-21CE
WOOD BETONY HERB-#1212C-$11.75-21CE

AUDIOS

TAO OF THE SOUL/SELF/SLATE-JEROME PLOTNICK, PH.D.-#21CETSSS-$20
JOURNEY BY THE SEA-KAREN MITCHELL-#JBSLJKM-$10
REST-KAREN MITCHELL-RLJKM-$10
SELF HEALING-BARRIE KONIKOV-#PUSH-$10
OPEN FOCUS-SHAKTI DUANE-#OFSD-$10
CREATIVE VISUALIZATION-SHAKTI DUANE-#CVSD-$10
MEDITATION OF THE TWIN HEARTS-MASTER CHOA KOK SUI-#MOTH-$20
ENHANCING MASSAGE-STEVEN HALPERIN-#AASHEM-$10
COURSE OF MIRACLES-GERALD JAMPOLSKY & A. CERINCERRONI#COMFFIP-$10
METAPHYSICAL MEDITATIONS-SRI KRIYANANDA-#CCSKMM-$10

VIDEOS

RELIEVE STRESS & ANXIETY-VCR-DVD-BARRIE KNOIKOV-#PURSA-$
SELF HEALING-VCD-DVD-BARRIE KONIKOV-#PUSH-$35.00
PHYSIOLOGICS-PHYSLG   AUDIO ACTIVE STEVEN HALPERIN-AASH
ENERGETIX-ENX   COURSE of MIRACLES FOUNDATION FOR
DNR,INC.-DNRLN   INNER PEACE-FFIP
LIFE TREE AROMATIX-LTA   SHAKTI DUANE-SD
YOUNGS LIVING OILS-YLO   CRYSTAL CLARITY-KRYIYANANDA-CCSK
AMAZON NATURAL TREASURES-ANT   INSTITUE OF INNER STUDIES-IISMCKS

AFTERWARD III

HOW TO REVERSE AGING, DISEASE, ENERGY-LESS STATES CAUSING PRE-MATURE HEART DISEASES, DIABETES TYPE II, PROSTATE CANCER, OTHER METABOLIC, AND ASSOCIATED TOXIC DISEASES

The latest research from scientists from around the world that are studying mitochondria related to aging, illness, and energy bankruptcy. It is about how we age, how we become energy-less with organ, and muscle weakness. This can be reversed with the use of high powered anti-oxidants: E.V.B., L.N.-Green & Yellow, B-12, vitamin D3, K2, E, glutathione, turmeric, pomengrante juice, and P.Q.Q. The problem lies with our energy motors within the cells, organs, and muscles, etc. called mitochondria. We can reverse our mitochondia degeneration causing depleted energy states and even regenerate them. The difference between your children and yourself is the state of your mitochondria. These are the energy producers in your body. In children they are powerful but as we age, our predetermined genetic profile [passed on deficient genes, miasms, meme's, etc.], nutrient, anti-oxidant deficiencies, as we become weaker, and illness of various types consume us. This can all be reversed with the proper total energetic detoxification pre and post programs I have introduced, with the proper supplementation, with the use of the aforementioned vitamins, and anti-oxidants. Also with the use of Super Bovine Colostrum such as "NOW" brand with 1-I.G.H. factors, astragulus, olive leaf, and larch. Vitamin E Gamma triatholone, Vitamin D3, K2, CoQ10, glutahione, D.H.E.A. [dehydropieandrosterone], CA.4:1 Mg., pomegranate, panax ginseng, eleuthro ginseng, folic acid, selenium, Vitamin A, Ester C, bee pollen, vitamin B complex [brewers yeast], Life Crystals, and hyularonic acid. Again just taking the aforementioned nutrients [antioxidants, etc.] without properly detoxifying the body is useless. Toxins are within the lipids [fat cells], intracellular and extracellular fluids, blood, etc. It causes cell communication interference, associated toxic disease, and symptoms. There is also the "ping-pong effect" where the toxins compound and move from one place to another within the body. Therefore merely taking the aforementioned mentioned antioxidants and nutrients, etc. will not render completely the desired regeneration, elimination of the aforementioned conditions, and diseases. Therefore I have designed a program that will be 100 times more potent and will enable you to reverse your disease state to a health state. The following 13 Steps are:

Step 1. Pre-Detox Prepare the body for detoxification with "Opening Channels." or now preferred is Liquid Needle's E.V.B. Pre detox. Thereafter the E.V.B. pre detox it is followed by:

Step 2. Post-Detox Liquid Needle 15 day Bath soaks energetic detoxification with Lymph, Coffee, Gold, and Cancer, etc.

Step 3. Supplement with super whole food supplements such as Iredesca, Life Crystals "Renaissance," Vibrogen Plus, Etherium, Biomatrix and all of the aforementioned vitamins, minerals, and nutrients. *Use Liquid Needle's Green, VIT, MIN, and ENZ.

Step 4. Brain-train E.E.G. brainwave training for mental fitness, and peak performance, etc.

Step 5. Needle-less acupuncture and chakra re-balance with Liquid Needle "Original and Blue" topically applied solutions.

Step 6. How to Deal with Modern-Day Psycho-Somatic Stress, Duress, Fear, Anxiety, and Worry causing Tension, Hypertension, Anxiety, Depression, Panic, and Pain. See on Pages: [143-151]

Step 7. Prayer, meditation, yoga, tantra, and spiritual exercises.

Step 8. Exercise, aerobics, Chi gong, Tai chi, walk, jog, Tae bo, martial arts, and internal Kung Fu, etc.

Step 9. Massage, touch for health, acupressure, Jin shin do, etc.

Step 10. Aromatherapy with essential oils.

Step 11. Arma, Dharma, and Karma. Arma volunteer for charity, etc, Dharma-discover your life's meaning and purpose or the Divine Gods Will, Karma-what ever goes around comes around or as you act and thing will be returned to you. Eliminate desire, EGO, fears, negative acts, and karma, etc.

Step 12. Removal of the 7 deadly sins and the 11 mental terror states, meme's, mind viruses, energetic foci disturbances, miasms-passed on generational gene information, and genetic deficiencies, etc. Use of Bach essences-Fields of Flowers from goEnergetix.com

Step 13. Make God #1 in your life through Higher Power belief, 12 step program or other spiritual program. Christ-Buddha-Divine Mind Consciousness. Giving is Receiving, There is a spiritual solution for every problem, If you believe it you will see it. Dr. Deepak Chopra, Dr. Wayne Dyer, and Dr. Jerome Plotnick books and audio programs. Deepak Chopra's "7 Spiritual Steps for Success," Dr. Wayne Dyer's "Transformation," "There is a Spiritual Solution for Every Problem." Dr. Jerome Plotnick's "Tao of the Soul-Self-Slate," "Meta Your Meditation," "Meta Your Mind," "Mind, Memes,

Miasms, Virus Takeover to a Mind Healing Makeover," "Meta Your
Manifestation," and Bioenergetic, Mind, & Natural Medicine."
To reverse diabetes, prevent and eliminate cancer, the following
anti-inflammatory alkaline foods, and herbs are highly advised.
Also recommended is a body pH of between 7.35-7.45 pH and a blood
pH that is below 7.56 pH the following foods are advised:
Watercress, No. Atlantic Kelp, Shitake Mushroom eaten raw, Papaya,
Blueberry, Broccoli, Sweet Potato eaten with the skin, Purple
Grapes, Mango, Spirulina, cracked cell Chlorella, Blue Green Algae
(Neurotoxin free), Adzuki, Extra Virgin Olive-Castor-Coconut-Hemp-
Cannabis Oil, Garlic, Ginger Root, Bitter Melon Herbs advised are:
Turmeric, Basil, Nutmeg, Guggul, Tropical Rose Mallow, Cat's Claw,
Ginger, Rosemary, Cinnamon, Parsley, Cardamon, Chives, Boswella,
Licorice, Cayenne, Dandelion Root, Burdock Root, Pau d' Arco, Red
Root, and Graviola (Annona Muuricata). Also advised is G.T.S.com
Kombucha and ProNatura Kombucha: Dr. Skelnar, M.D. Germany 555 mg.
caps.

Elements advised: 03, OxyMoxy, Dymano2, Colo2Zone, and Hydroxygen
Plus

D.N.R., Inc.com Indiana. Light Waves Photon Photanicals Liquid
Needle formulations which includes all of their energy-based
solutions topicals, detoxification bath soaks, and rebalancers,
etc. See Liquid Needle information, protcols, and products on
pages 85-91,162-163,183,208-09,240,260,284-307,309-310

AFTERWARD IV

LYME DISEASE (BORRELOSIS) A NATIONAL UNDETECTED EPIDEMIC

There is a silent epidemic going on in the U.S. called "Lyme" Disease" caused by the bite of an infected tic. According to Jessie Ventura on his T.V. show "Conspiracy Theory" a whistle blower that worked on the Plum Island in the Long Island Sound where the U.S. government has a biological warfare laboratory. He claims that that they were experimenting with tics putting biological agents on them and letting the infected tics bite animals they had contained at the secret facility. Only what happened is that these infected tics escaped quarantine to became airborne and landed in a place in Connecticut called Lyme, Connecticut, and where the first cases of the disease were discovered in the 1970's.[hence the name Lyme Disease was given to this infectious tic bite]. It appears that the government has unleashed a horrible disease upon the citizens of the U.S. It is a disease that has spread all across the country. The government disclaims they are responsible for Lyme disease. This disease also called "borrelosis," is similar to G.W.S. Gulf War Syndrome symptoms, and pathology, I believe the Lyme microbe are the product of the U.S. government's secret bio-warfare program and has been covered up. Same as the current chem trails and HARRP.

The G.W.S. according to Doctors: Nicolson's of the University of Texas Medical Center was caused by mycotoxins, biological warfare agents produced by the U.S. government, used against the Iraq Republican Guard troops, and also infected our own troops in the Gulf War. It also appears that the Lyme disease symptoms are very similar to the G.W.S. I believe they are the one in the same or very close to the symptomology. The only difference may be the delivery system used. In Lyme disease the use of tics in G.W.S. the use of explosive devices unleashing the biological agents. There are probably in the U.S. hundreds of thousands of non diagnosed cases of the disease. The symptoms are often called C.F.S. Chronic Fatigue Syndrome. I strongly believe the U.S. government black operations section who are unnamed and who have at their disposal multi billions of dollars all undisclosed. The government has covered up their mess and lies as they did with troops returning from Vietnam infected with agent orange. The V.A. and D.O.D.claimed the illness that returning troops from the Gulf

War where, quote, "all in their heads" as they did with troops returning from the Vietnam War. But when the troop's families became ill there was an outcry for action. Both of the Nicolson's did research and cured many of the ill troops but around 6,000 died from the G.W.S. unnecessarily according to them. Their families are still becoming sick and children also. Many have died from it. Is that "all in your head." For shocking information on the true causes of our governments cover up and their direct involvement in the death of our troops see the movie called "Beyond Treason." You can get a copy of this documentary by going to: beyondtreason.com. If you are a veteran you can receive a free copy.

* I viewed the documentary and was shocked as a former veteran myself. So there appears to be sufficient evidence that "Lyme Disease" called "borrelosis' is a U.S. government created biological agent, that was placed on tics, was allowed into the environment by accident, or on purpose? Either way the spread of the disease and transmitted by tics is now nationwide. All five (5) species of tics can carry this disease agent. We have an epidemic because it is nationwide, covered up by the government, and cannot be diagnosed by regular medical laboratory testing. In many cases it remains in limbo hiding in the host person undetected and then springs up without any indication. Extremely hard to diagnose it remains an unnamed disease usually called C.F.S., Fibromyalgia, and unspecific symptoms that are all related to Lyme Disease "borrelosis." Recently new D.N.A. by P.C.R. in plasma or cerebro-spinal fluid after an interval of 4-8 months with an electron microscope is being used to correctly diagnose Lyme disease. I know of a case that had the infection in their D.N.A. Hopefully physicians nationwide will be able to recognize the symptomatic picture, be able to do testing to determine whether, or not a patient exhibiting symptoms is infected with the disease. In the meantime both conventional antibiotic treatment, detoxification, and alternative treatment are highly advised.

G.W.S., I.M.O., F.M.S./C.F.S.D.S., and borrelosis-Lyme disease all have similar pathogenesis, which is T.L.R. the triggering by the B.L.P.'s, or L.P.S. of pathogenic microbes. Borrelosis also attacks the endothelia; cells of the blood vessels. This triggers inflammation in these infected blood vessels wherever they are located in the body. In other words once the borrelosis infection infects these cells that in turn stimulate vascules of the blood vessels. Vascules of the nervous system, skin, muscles, tendons, connective tissue explains the disease, and it's symptoms. Borrelosis is hard to destroy, it can reside, grow intracellular (within cells), and out of the reach of the infected persons immune system. The microbe borrelosis rotate their filament body so they can corkscrew throughout the hosts body by invading tissue, penetrate cells, replicate, and destroy the host cells they infect. I believe that the use of olive leaf extract should be used as it prevents from replicating by surrounding the cell walls with a protein called "oleopein" which prevents viruses from being able to penetrate the cell wall and replicate themselves. This borrelosis agent seems to be akin to a virus in this respect. The borrelosis spirochetes hide their flagella, which are normally antigenic, from the host immune system defenses. They can also wrap themselves with the membrane of the host cell, thus concealing themselves from the hosts immune system. But the borrelosis is considered a bacteria.

This makes borrelosis hard to eradicate, since it grows slowly, and has this ability to escape immune system detection. This is why I implement the aforementioned alternative protocols 1-18 and indicated as steps 1-9. Early detection and immediate treatment are necessary to prevent permanent damage to the patient. Also borrelosis can remain dormant in the host for a long time periods, but can return to activity at any time.

If a person is bitten by any tic species immediate medical attention and treatment is imperative. The tell tale signs of the bulls-eye-rash. This bulls-eye-rash will appear 3-30 days after the initial tic bite. The rash grows concentrically over 5-10 days and without treatment may last several weeks, Note! The rash can mimic such skin problems as hives, eczema, sunburn, poison ivy, and flea bites, etc. Also the rash can be tiny or large up to 12" in diameter. It can itch, feel hot or have, even no symptoms. All rashes should be photographed and checked by a knowledgeable L.D. experienced physician immediately. Note! Not all rashes are L.D. associated. Non L.D. tic bites will produce E.M. skin rashes called E.M. multiple lesions 2-4 weeks following the initial bite.

Thereafter 4-6 weeks following the tic bite, the first symptomatic signs will manifest such as flu like symptoms or malaise. Symptoms include: sore throat, severe headaches, neck aches, severe fatigue, chills, fever, and swollen glands (lymph nodes). Usually the symptoms subside but may relapse as the disease spreads and continues. Some time later in advanced cases the person may experience myalgia, (muscle, and joint pain). Mainly in large joints such as hips, knees, elbows, and shoulders. Small joints such as wrists, fingers, and toes may be involved. The pain is often described as severe, jumping from joint to joint, and may be present for short periods of time. There can be pain in teeth and in temporal-mandibular joints (jaw) that is common. There may be neurological involvement with symptoms such as: muscle twitching, burning sensations, prickling-shooting pains, and numbness. It can also cause palsy of the affected areas but usually causes neuro-sensory signs before neuro-motor disease. Facial nerve (Bell's palsy) is another neurological symptom of L.D. Encephalitis (encephalopathy) may manifest as cognitive dysfunction which includes short term memory loss, psychiatric symptoms such as panic, anxiety, and depression.

Other symptoms may include the following: blurred vision, uvetis, ringing of the ear (tinnitus), hearing loss, shortness of breath, palpitations, or tachycardia (rapid heart rate), chest pains, abdominal pains, diarrhea or irritable bowel syndrome, testicular or pelvic pain, urinary incontinence, dizziness, tremors, and dysautonomia, or hepatitis.

Since the L.D. can exhibit many symptoms it is an infectious and toxic disease. It mimics symptoms of fibromyalgia, C.F.S., arthralgias, muscle, tissue, and tendon pain. It can mimic a neurological disorder. There are hundreds of symptoms that are caused by L.D.

If a person goes not diagnosed or misdiagnosed and is not treated immediately the symptoms may appear as other diseases such as Bell's palsy, arthritis, tachycardia, joint, and tendon pain, etc. In 11% of infected persons L.D. causes erosion of the cartilage or bone. Also noted are neurological disturbances such as memory loss, sleep, mood disturbances, numbness, and tingling sensations in the hands, or feet. The L.D. is progressive, destructive, and debilitating. In severe untreated cases may be fatal.

Other causative factors of the disease may be degenerative skin disorder called arocdermatitis chronica atrophicans (A.C.A.). It can cause metabolic-endocrine dysfunctions that lead to weight gain or loss. It affects women much worse than men. There is also the possibility of passing the disease to spouse, etc. Almost the same as H.I.V. is contagious through body fluids, etc. The G.W.S. is also passed on to other family members in the same manner.

SYMPTOMS:
HEAD: headache, neck pain, facial pain or paralysis, teeth pain, dry mouth, loss of taste-smell, numbness in tongue-mouth, and peculiar metallic taste.
BLADDER: frequent or painful urination, repeated urinary tract infections, irritable bladder, and inter-intestinal cystitis.
LUNG: respiratory infection, cough, asthma, pneumonia, pleurisy, and chest pains.
EAR: pain, hearing loss, ringing in ear (tinnitus), sensitivity to noise, dizziness, and equilibrium disorders.
EYES: pain due to inflammation, (scleritis, uvetis, optic neuritis), dry eyes, light sensitivity, drooping of the eyelids (ptosis), conjunctivitis, blurry or double vision, swelling around the eyes, and bags below the eyes.
THROAT: sore throat, swollen glands, cough, hoarseness, and difficulty in swallowing.
NEUROLOGICAL: headaches, facial paralysis, seizures, meningitis, stiff neck, burning-tingling-prickling sensations (parathesia), loss of reflexes, loss of coordination, equilibrium problems-dizziness-mimic M.S., A.L.S., and Parkinson's.
STOMACH: pain, diarrhea, nausea, vomiting, abdominal cramps, and anorexia.
HEART: weakness, dizziness, irregular heart beat, myocardia, pericarditis, palpitations, heart block, enlarged heart, fainting, shortness of breath, chest pain, and mitral valve prolapse.
MUSCLE & SKELETAL: arthralgias (joint pain), fibromyalgia, (muscle inflammation, and pain).
OTHER ORGANS: liver infection, hepatitis, elevated liver enzymes, enlarged spleen, swollen testicles, and irregular ceased menses.
NEUROPSYCHIATRIC: mood swings, irritability, anxiety, rage, poor concentration, cognitive loss, memory loss, appetite loss, mental deterioration, panic, depression, and insomnia.
PREGNANCY: miscarriage, premature birth, birth defects, and still birth.
SKIN: E.M., single or multiple rash(s), tags, hives, and A.C.A.
NERVOUS SYSTEM: increased susceptibility to electrostatic shock.

If the infected patient is on long term antibiotics then a probiotic is necessary to reestablish intestinal flora. Also it may be necessary to use antibiotics for extended periods up to one year or more. Since the B.L.P.'s (borrelosis lipo-proteins) trigger harmful responses in tissues and organ systems which cause symptoms including: fybromyalgia, arthritis, neurological symptoms, psychiatric symptoms, immune system dysfunction, and endocrine deficiencies. The B.L.P.'s cause immune system dysfunction and trigger complex imbalance of chemical immune system modulators called (cytokines). If over stimulated they cause reactions such as pain, inflammation, and cell death called (apoptosis). Some of the cytokines include: tumor necrosis factor alpha (T.N.F.-a), interleukins- (I.L.6), Fatty acid products (eicosanoids such as inflammatory prostanglandins, thromboxanes, a leukotreines), and these have potent inflammatory-physiological properties. The B.L.P.'s have a key component (Pam3cys), which triggers innate immune response that cause the disease. B.L.P.'s are the lipid-protein and the structural part of the borrelia cell membrane. These are extremely potent immune modulators even in small amounts. Thereby, a few borrelia can produce enough B.L.P.'s, to cause significant disease, and resulting symptoms.

According to Doctors: Trevor Marshall, Liz Marshall of the Los Robles Regional Medical Center, located in Thousand Oaks, California (Sarcinfo.com). Called the Angiotensin Hypothesis. As the circulating concentration of 1,25-D increases in the inflamed tissue caused by sunlight which fuels the inflammation, via 1,5-D, and Angiotensin II. This increases the quantity of hematapoetic stem cells differentiate to produce monocytes. Monocyte differentiation into macrophages and epitheloid giant cells is enhanced. The differentiating macrophages and giant cells release Angiotensin II (A-II). The A-II then binds at A-II type 1 receptors on the macrophages, activated lymphocytes, stimulating Nuclear factor-kappaB (N.F.-kB), and to signal the release for a cascade of Th1 cytokines. At least one of these cytokines, Gamma Interferon, increases the amount of 25-D being converted to 1,25-D in the macrophages, which in turn catalyses the differentation of monocytes into even more macrophages, and giant cells.

Naturopathic-Bioenergetic Protocol for the Alternative Medicines Treatment of Lyme Disease (Borreliosis).

In order to kill the Borreliosis pathogen, detoxify dead pathogens, enhance the immune system function, support energy, clear inflammatory responses, and calm the mind-body-spirit the following is recommended: Note! Essential pre treatment with 7 Forests White Tiger Chinese herbal formula SPIROX.

Pre 1. ITM-7 Forests Chinese Herbal Formula "SPIROX" for barricated toxins that eliminates the borreliosis biofilm. This enables many natural killing remedies to destroy it.

1. Atlantean Alchemy Collodial Gold @60 p.p.m. taken for 3x's per day 12-18 drops under the tongue held for 1-2 minutes then swallowed. This is followed the next day with Etherium True Colloidal Silver or Amino Acid & Botanical Supply @ 1200 p.p.m. taken for 3x's per day 12-18 drops under the tongue held for 1-2 minutes then swallowed. Thereafter drink 8 oz. of distilled water. This should be taken for 1 ½ weeks. Also while taking the colloidal silver drink 8-8 oz. glasses of distilled water daily. [Anti bacterial, fungal, viral, and cancer, etc.]

2. Una de Gato "Cats Claw" a phyto alkaloid in caps or tea form 3x's per day at a min. of 500 mg. [Anti-bacterial, fungal, viral.]

3. Pau d'Arco "Taheebo" phyto chemical alkaloid in caps or tea form 3x's per day at a min. of 500 mg. [Anti-bacterial, fungal, viral, and cancer.]

4. Olive Leaf in capsules or extract Three (3) times (x's) per day at a minimum.of 500 mg. [oleopein a protein that prevents viruses from replicating ("budding") themselves.]

5. Hydroxygen Plus-ionic enzymes, amino acids, minerals, and 02 use as directed on bottle. [Anti-bacterial, fungal, viral, and cancer, etc. Provides necessary enzymes, amino acids, and minerals plus 02 (Oxygen).] Ozone 03 made by an A2Z aqua6 ozone generator.

6. Kombucha Fungus Tea for bringing the blood pH under 7.56 Sip during the day. [All mammals have a polymorphic microbe called mauve-psora-cancer causing bacterial, fungal, viral microbe that causes cancer when the blood pH exceeds 7.56 pH.]

7. Goldenseal Root extract or powder caps at a min. of 500 mg. 3x's per day. For decreasing inflammatory responses of the borrelosis infection throughout the body. Note! F.D.A. Listed toxic herb.

8. Annoa muricata "Graviola" an anti-cancer Amazon herb that has been researched and found to be ten thousand (10,000) times (x's)

more powerful then any of the chemotherapy agents used to kill cancer cells. It only kills cancer cells so it is non toxic and does not destroy the immune system. ["Gravizon" a synergistic formula can also be used.] Amazon Herb Co.com

9. Energetix's-"Opening Channels" prepares the body for a complete detoxification.

10. Liquid Needle's-E.V.B., Lympha, PAR, NRV, Blue, Gold, Coffee, Liver Bath Soak, and internal remedies energetic detoxification.

11. Energetix's Galt Immune, Somatotrophin 1-I.G.H., Lympthtone II-III & Fields of Flowers. Provides immune enhancement, provides elimination of mind-body-spirit toxins.

12. Medi-Val's-Vibrogen Plus for nutritional support and Chleated Cell Salts for cell support.

13. Herbs: Elderflower-Echinacea (3)-Hyssop, Goldenseal, Astragalus, Eleuthro for immune, and general support.

14. Black Garlic (Allicin) for anti-bacterial.

15. Apex Energetic's-Miasm Can-Miasm Tox-Bacterio Tox for energetic foci associated with bacterial pathogens.

16 7 Forests Chinese Herbs-Paris -7, I.S.6, C.O.G.L., C.O.A.-Tonify chi, vitalize blood, clear toxins, inflammation-anti-cancer, bacterial, and viral, etc.

17. Fenugreek herb that clears mucus.

18. Bioplasma-Hyland Homeopathic Co. Cell salts at various potencies.

19. Sleep under and meditate in a true scaled pyramid of any material. Preferably non metal for increased psychotronic energy.

STEPS: pre step SPIROX 1-9 Protocol is designed to do the following:

1. Atlantean colloid Gold, Etherium's-Colloidal Silver, Pau D'Arco, Una de Gato, Annona Muricata "Graviola," Hydroxygen Plus, and R.S.O full extract T.H.C.-C.B.D. oil to kill the borrelosis pathogen-B.L.P.'s infection. Liquid Needle-E.V.B.

2. Energetix's-Opening Channels pre detox program followed by Liquid Needle's-Bath Soaks, Internal Remedies to energetically detoxify the killed off microbes, and toxic wastes.

4. Medi-Val-Vibrogen Plus, Chlelated Cell Salts, Iredesca, Etherium Super Blends, Greening Powder, Biomatrix for nutrition supplementation. and high powered cell support.

5. Energetix's-Somatotrophin 1-I.G.H., or NOW's-Super Bovine Colostrum with oleopein for immune system support.

6. Liquid Needle's-ExStress, Chi Gong, E.V.B. L.N.T.B. to provide anti-stress, and energy-vitality-balance.

7. Energetix's-Lymphtone II, III for lymphatic support and detoxification.
8. Energetix's-Fields of Flowers all of Bach's flower essences @ 30 C in one bottle for removal of the 7 deadly sins and the 11 mental terror states.
9. Apex Energetic's- Miasm Tox, Bacteria Tox, Miasm CF-Paraclenz-Extracellular Blood Terrain for removal of miasms associated with the borrelosis infection, and vitalize the blood.
10. 7 Forests Chinese herbal formulas-for anti-bacterial-cancer, toxin elimination-provides chi tonification, clear toxins, vitalize blood. Paris-7, Astragalus, Ganoderma, Tang-kuei, etc.
11. Ukrane a celandine based and other synergistic natural herbs given intravenously along with Hydrogen peroxide and Vit C.
12. Ozone 03 water made by an A2Z aqua6 ozone generator.
13. Hydrogen ion water mand by a Turapur water maker and filter.
14. Stabilized oxygen 02 OxyMoxy, Dymano2, and Colo2zone
15. Liquid Needle: EVB, Yellow-118EX, Green-120EX, Original-116EX

CONVENTIONAL ANTIBIOTIC TREATMENT:

Early diagnosed cases can be treated with doxycycline, minocycline, penicillin, or amoxicillin. Chronic cases can be treated with amoxicillin, tetracycline, doxycycline, minocycline, clarithomycin, metronidazole, co-trimoxazole, sulfamethoxazole-trimethoprim, and anzithromycin. Depending on how long the patient is infected is how long the antibiotic treatment is necessary. Early detection treatment should be for 2 months. Later detection or relapse indicates months of treatment with the antibiotics aforementioned. Chronic or undetected for years may require years of antibiotic treatment. Generally, treatment for chronic borrelosis L.D. usually requires a period of time equal or greater than the time the patient has had the disease. Note! After every antibiotic panel or continually during the antibiotic treatment the patient must take pre and probiotics to reseed the intestinal flora killed off by the antibiotic treatment. Also suggested are sauerkraut and kefir.

ALTERNATIVE TREATMENT:

The aforementioned of the eighteen (18) indicated natural medicines, herbs, and vitamins, etc. alternative treatment is also advised for chronic cases as the antibiotics alone may not be enough to kill the borreliosis infection. Note! The use of the alternative protocol steps 1-9 will not have any toxic or adverse effects used with the antibiotics. Always check with your duly licensed medical and alternative physician before taking and conventional or alternative medicine treatments. Again both the conventional and alternative treatment can be used in conjunction and are quite effective to eliminate the borrelosis L.D. infection.

Bibliography: Lyme Disease (Borreliosis) A Plague of Ignorance Regarding the Ignorance of a Plague by Dr. Scott Taylor, D.V.M. Encarta Encyclopedia information on borreliosis, tics, L.D.

NOTE! Updated Important Information.
Recent information concerning treating Lyme Disease. One of the most important factors that blocks the current conventional and alternative treatment is that the Lyme Disease microbe had a cuspid or what is called a bio-film that encapsulates it, protects it, from the conventional antibiotics, and alternative herbs from killing it. Recently 7 Forests Chinese Herb Company has a product that is a Chinese herbal formula that will eliminate the bio-film protection and renders the Lyme Disease microbe to be destroyed. To order the 7 Forest's SPIROX formula. Go to: www.snhc.com Stonington Natural Health Center (860)-536-3880 also check @naturalnutritionals.com
Also according to medical doctors and researchers Trevor and Liz Marshall, M.D. of Lyme disease of the Los Robles Regional Medical Center, Thousand Oaks, CA. Lyme patients should not be in the sun as it accelerates the disease according to their findings. See page 160 for their research findings. Their conclusion is No Sun.

NOTE! Updated Important information.
Order an Inner Fire.com copper portable pyramid for $135.00 plus $25.00 shipping also they give a 40% discount on any pyramids costing over $130.00. Total price is $106.00 plus tax for a 6 foot base portable copper pyramid. It has been researched and discovered that no microbes can survive under a pyramid. In fact, maggoted meat was placed under a pyrmaid, the maggots fled the meat they were in, and to die rather than remain under the pyramid. So I suggest you purchase the Inner Fire Pyramid to sleep and meditate under it for any Lyme Disease infected patient.

ORDER

To order any of the aforementioned go below to the order blank and insert the herb, homeopathic or naturopathic remedy, light photon bio-energetic remedy, flower essence remedy, book, or audio you wish to order. Follow the easy instructions. Thanks for your support. V/MC PayPal Credit Card/P.O. Money Order/Check/ accepted

----

Name of Product   # of Product   Amount-ea.   Cost

_____

_____

_____

_____

_____

_____

_____

_____

_____

_____

_____

_____

_____

_____

_____

_____

_____

_____

_____

_____

_____

_____

_____

_____

_____

_____

_____

TOTAL_____ $_____

SHIPPING & HANDLING ADD $12.60 U.S.P.S.

PRIORITY_____$_____

TAX IF APPLICABLE CA.ADD 8.5%_____ $_____

GRAND TOTAL_____ $_____

DISCLAIMER NOTE!

This book is produced, published, 21st Century Energetics, 6132 Frazier Mt. Pk. Rd. #45, Lake of the Woods, CA. 93225-9200 Available on a F.D. for download to your P.C. at websites: 21stCenturyEnergetics.com jeromeplotnickphdnd@facebook.com or e-mail:plotnickj@yahoo.com or write to the above address. This book is printed and distributed by createspace.com to order go to amazon.com/books $40.00 If you want an e-book go to: amazon.kindle.com $20.00 To order in printed book form go to createspace.com, amazon.com, for download @amazon.com/e-books/kindle, or Barnes & Noble and Borders Book stores et al. and online will carry it also if you ask for it. To order any of the aforementioned and listed audios,natural herbs, homeopathics, light photon frequency remedies, essential oils, books, etc. go to websites: 21stCenturyEnergetics.com, manta or biopharma.com 21stCenturyEnergetics.com 21stcenturyenergetics@facebook.com or Amazon.com/books, Createspace.com/books Jerome Plotnick, Ph.D., N.D. or write: 21st Century Energetics, In CA.   6132 Frazier Mt. Pk. Rd. #45, Lake of the Woods, CA. 93225-9200 or E-mail:plotnickj@yahoo.com or Phone: in CA.: (661) 245-3616 If you use mail send the order form or copy of it on page 165 with your order. We look forward to serving you. Thanks for your order.

BIBLIOGRAPHY

Chinese Herbal Formulas Second Revised Edition=Huang-yen Hsu, Ph.D. And Chan-shin Hsu, Ph.D.-Ohai Press/Oriental Healing Arts, Long Beach, CA.-1997

A Bag of pearls-1996 Edition-Subhuti Dharmananda, Ph.D.-Institute for Traditional Medicine and Preventive Health Cure-Portland, Oregon-1996

Physician's Clinical Reference Guide-Dr. Robert Cass, N.D., Alice Bello, DiHom-Energetix's-Dahionega, Georgia-1999

Physicain's Clinical Repertory-Dr. Robert Cass, N.D., Alice Bello, DiHom-Energetix-Dahionega, Georgia-2001

Liquid Needle Product Information-Arthur Widgery-Developmental Natural Resources, Inc.-Indianapolis, Indiana-2001-2016

Back to Eden-Jethro Kloss-Back to Eden Books-Loma Linda, CA.-1982

Natural and Medicinal Cures-Editors of Prevention Magazine-Rodale Press-Emmaus. Pennsylvania-1994

Clinical Bio-energetics-Michael Galitzer, M.D.-Santa Monica, CA.-2001

Physiologics Basic Core Health, Bone and Joint Health, Anti Aging Health-Thorton, Colorado-2001

Apex Energetics-Catalogue-Santa Ana, CA.-2001

Apex Energetics-Professional Reference Guide-Santa Ana, CA.-1994

Apex Energetics-Homeopathic and Bio-energetic Products-Santa Ana, CA. 1994

An Introduction to Young's Living Essential Oils-Ninth Edition-D. Gary Young-Payson, Utah-2001

New Vistas Products-Medival-Denver, Colorado-1998

Dr. Recommends-MediVal-Hi Tech-Homeopathics and Natural Pharmaceuticals-Physicican Cybernetic Systems-Dr. William Nelson, M.D.-Denver, Colorado-1998

G.C.I.Nutrients, Burlingame, CA.-1996

Herb Co.-Catalogue-North Hollywood, CA.-2001

Exsula Products Co.-Federal Way, Washington-2000

Grain of Salt-The Salt Society-Ashville, North Carolina-2001

The Health Cell-Natures Distributors-Fountain Hill, AZ.-2001

The Complete Book of Homeopathy-Michael Weiner, Ph.D., and Kathleen Goss-Bantam Books-New York-1982

The Bach Flower Remedies-Dr. Edward Bach, M.D., Dr. F.J. Wheeler, M.D., Keats Publishing Co.-New Canaan, Conn.-1979

Oxygen-Hydrogen Peroxide, Magnesium Peroxide, Chlorine peroxide-Kurt W. Donsbach, D.C., N.D., Ph.D.-The Rockland Corp.-1993

Tissue Cleansing Through Bowel Management-Dr. Bernard Jensen, D.C. And Sylvia Bell-Escondido, CA.-1975

Mental and Elemental Nutrients-Dr. Carl C. Pfeiffer, M.D.-Keats Publishing -New Canaan, Conn.-1975

Life Extension Companion-Derk Pearson, Ph.D.-Warner Communication Co.-New York-1984

Diet and Nutrition-a holistic Approach-Rudolph Ballantine, M.D.-Himalayan Institute-Homesdale, Penn.-1978

Between Heaven and Earth-a Guide to Chinese Medicine-Efrem Korngold, L.Ac., O.M.D. and Harriet Beinfield, L.Ac.-Ballantine Books-New York-1991

Food Enzymes the Missing Link to Radiant Health-Humburt Santillo, B.S., M.H.-Hohm Press-Prescott Valley, AZ.-1987

Proven Health Encyclopedia-American Publishing Co.-Montclair, CA.-1998

Peak Immunity-Luc De Schepper, M.D., Ph.D., C.A.,2nd Edition-Santa Monica, CA.-1990

Imagery Healing and Shamanism and Modern Medicine-Jeanne Achterberg, Ph.D.,-New Science Library-Shambala-Boston, Mass.-1985

Psychogenesis Everything Begins in the Mind-Jack Ensign Addington, Ph.D.-Dodd, Mead & Company-New York-1971

Ageless Body, Timeless Mind-Dr. Deepak Chopra, M.D.-Random House, Inc.-New York-1993

Nine Day Inner Cleansing and Blood Wash for Renewed Youthfulness and Health-I.E, Gaumunt, Therapeutic Researcher, Harold E. Buttram, M.D.-Parker Publishing Co,-West Nyack, New York-1980

Transformation-You'll See It When You Believe It-Dr. Wayne Dyer, Ph.D.-Nightengale Conant-Chicago, Ill.-1998

The Seven Spiritual Laws of Success-Dr. Deepak Chopra, M.D.-Amber-Allen-New World Library-San Rafael, CA.-1994

Living Beyond Miracles-Dr. Deepak Chopra, M.D., Wayne Dyer, Ph.D.,-Amber-Allen Publishing New World Library-San Rafael, CA.-1993

Your Erroneous Zones, Wayne Dyer, Ph.D.,-Nightengale Conant-Chicago, Ill.-1983

The Eye of Revelation-Peter Kleider-Borderland Sciences Research Foundation-Gaberville, CA.-1939,1989

Meta Your Meditation-Jerome Plotnick, Ph.D., N.D.-21st Century Energetics.com Publishing, Lake of the Woods, CA. 93225-2002

Meta Your Mind-Jerome Plotnick, Ph.D., N.D.-21st Century Energetics .com Publishing/Createspace.com-Lake of the Woods, CA.- Columbia, S.C.-2002,2015,2016,2017

Meta Your Nutrition-Jerome Plotnick, Ph.D., N.D.-21st Century Energetics.com Publishing-Lake of the Woods, CA.93225-2002

The 13th Step for Total Addiction Recovery-Jerome Plotnick, Ph.D., N.D., C.C.D.C.S.-C.A.D.D.E.21st Century Energetics.com Publishing-Lake of the Woods, CA.-93225-2002,2017

The 13 Spiritual Tao's From Ancient to Modern Day Masters-Jerome Plotnick, Ph.D., N.D.-21st Century Energetics.com Publishing-Lake of the Woods, CA.-93225-2000-2015,2017

Food Combining Handbook-Gary Null, Ph.D.-Jove Book, New York-1983

Healing With the Mind's Eye-Dr. Michael Samuels, M.D.-Summit Books-New York-1983

Health and Healing-Dr. Andrew Weil, M.D.-Houghton Mifflin-New York-1995

Is Modern Medicine Killing You?-Dr. Marcus Laux, N.D.-Naturally Well-Pontiac, MD.-1995

Chinese Healing Arts Internal Kung Fu-John Dudgeon, M.D.-William K. Berk-Unique Publications, Burbank, CA.-1986

Isoflavones and the Soy Concentrated Supplements-Phillip N. Steinberg, C.N.C.-Healing Wisdom Publications-New York-1996

The Therapeutics of Soybean Phytochemicals-U.S. Research Reports, Inc.-Metarie, LA. and Norcross Georgia-1996

Jude's Herbal Home Remedies-Jade C. Williams, M.H.-Liewellyn Publications-St. Paul, Minn.-1996

The Zodiac Homeopathic Remedies for the Sign Types-Dr. George Washington Carey, Inez Endora Perry-Samuel Wiser, Inc.-York Beach, Maine-1932

Secrets of Chinese Herbalists-Richard Lucas-Parker Publishing Co.-West Nyack, New York-1987

Healing With Chinese Herbs-Richard Hyatt-Healing Arts Press-Rochester, VT.-1990

Elementary Treatise in Herbology-Dr. Edward Shook, N.D.-Enos Publishing Co.-Banning, CA.-1993

The Celestine Prophecy-James Redfield-Time Warner Trade Publishing, Los Angeles,, CA.-1994

Miracle Medicine Foods-Rex Adams-Parker Publishing Co.-West Nyack, New York-1977

The Ecology of Commerce-Paul Hawkins-Harper Business Publishers-New York-1993

Bovine Colostrum Offers Broad Spectrum Benefits for Wide Ranging Ailments-Medical Journal report of Innovative Biologics-Morton Walker, D.P.M.-1999

The Red Clover Cure-Lauri M. Aeosph, N.D. Lets Live-New York 1998

Hydroxygen Plus-Ed McCabe-2002

Pau d' Arco-Louise Tenney, M.H.-Cancer News Journal, Spring Issue South American Cancer Cure-Excerpt from Spotlight-1982

Noni-EnGarde and Morinda Co.-2000

Excerpts for a Few Botanicals-The Little Herb Encyclopedia-Jack Richason, N.D.

Colloidal Silver-Health Science-Vol.1, Spring 1997

Amazon Rainforest Phytochemical Herbal Medicine-John Esterling, et al.-So. American Herb Co. Oct.-1994

Amazon Rainforest Natural Cancer Fighter-Health Sciences Institute.-Jan.-2001

Amazon and Peruvian Natural Treasures-Natures Natural Pharmacy-Article-2003

M.S.M.-Bill Rich and Health Sciences University-1980

Etherium Technology and Products-Etherium -Patrick Bailey-1996

Harmful Ingredients can Kill You-The Safe Shoppers Bible-2001

Alernatives-W.D.D.T.V.-Dangerous Ingredients-Harold Gaier, N.D., D.O. Hom D.-Oct.-1999

Toxic Toiletries-what the Medical Doctors Don't Tell You-Health Awareness-Vol.10#17 Oct.-1999

Graviola-Gravizon Clinical references:Koolman P., Structure of the galactomannans from seeds of Annona Muricata Feb.-1993

Frequently Asked Questions about Lifer Support's-Hydroxygen Plus (T.M.)-Ed McCabe-Jan.-2000

Squeaky Clean Intestinal-Colon Cleansing for Optimal Health-Holistic London Guide-Winter-1998-1999

Features and Benefits of OxyMoxy-EnGarde Health Products-1999

The Therapeutics of Soybean Phytochemicals-U.S. Research Reportrs, Inc.-P.O.Box 931104, Norcross, GA.-June 1996

IP6 Nature's Revolutionary Cancer Fighter-Dr. Abraham M. Shumsuddin, M.D.-Kensington Books-New York-1998.

The Complete Book of Homeopathy-Michael Weiner, Ph.D. and Kathleen Goss-Bantam Books-New York-1981

The Fungus Kombucha the Natural Remedy and its Significance in Cases of Cancer and Other Metabolic Diseases-Rosina Faching-Lich Upper Hessia, Germany-1985

Adjuvant Nutrition for Cancer Patients-Haelan-851-U.S. Research Reports-Metarie, LA.-Sept.-1996

Getting Started with Neurofeedback-John Demos, M.A.-1987

Vibrational Medicine-Richard Gerber, M.D.-Bear and Co.-Sante Fe, N.M.-1988

Magic Medicine of Plants-Readers Digest Association, Inc.-Pleasantville, N.Y.-1985

Acupressure Way of Health: Jin Shin Do-Iona Teegarten-C.M.Th.-Japan Publications, Inc.-1978

Pranic Healing-Master Choa Kok Sui-Samuel Wiser Co.-York Beach, ME.-1989

Super Immunity-Paul Pearson, Ph.D.-Random House-Ballantine Publishing Co.-N.Y.-1987

Proven Health Tips Encyclopedia-American Publishing Co.-1997

Amino Acids Book-Carlson Wade-Keats Publishing Co.-New Canaan, CT.1985

Life Extension & Companion Book-Durk Pearson, Ph.D. And Sandy Shaw-Warner Books, N.Y.-1989,1984

Mad Cow Disease-N.B.C. Dateline T.V. Show and Video-N.Y.-1997

Acupressure's Potent Points-Michael Reed Grouch-Batman Doubleday Dell Publishing-N.Y.-1990

Love, Medicine, and Miracles-Bernie S. Segiel, M.D.-Harper & Row Publishers-N.Y.-1986

How to use Nutritional Substances-Dr. Morter, D.C.-Morter Health System,Rogers, AK.-2000

Body Reflexology-Mildred Carter-Parker Publishing Co.-West Nyack, N.Y.-1994

Touch For Health Manual-John Thie, D.C.-Touch For Health Foundation-Pasadena, CA.-1975

Helping Your Health with Pointed Pressure Therapy-Dr. Roy Bean, N.D.-Parker Publishing Co.,West Nyack, N.Y.-1975

The Cure Conspiracy-Medical Myths-Alternative Therapies & Natural Remedies-FC and A Medical Publishing, Peachtree City, GA.-2005

Heinerman's Encyclopedia of Healing Juices-John Heinerman-Med. Anthropologist-Parker Publishing Co.-West Nyack, N.Y.-1994

Heinerman's Encyclopedia of Fruits, Vegetables and Herbs-John Heinerman-Med. Anthropologist-Parker Publishing Co.-West Nyack, N.Y.-1988

Natural Cures-Kevin Trudeau-Alliance Publishing Group, Inc.-Elk Grove, Ill.-2004

Buffalo Woman Comes Singing-Brooke Medicine Eagle-Random House Publishing Co. N.Y.-1991

The 40/30/30 Phenomenon-Ann Louise Gittman, M.S., C.N.C.-Keats Publishing Co.-New Caanan, CT.-1997

Biofeedback Practitioners Guide-Mark S. Schwartz, Ph.D.-Gulford Press, N.Y.-1987

The Biochemic Book Handbook-Leslie B. Colin-Thorsons Publishers Ltd.-England-1984

Vitamin Bible & Vitamins are Good for Your Body-Earl Mandell, Pharm, R. Ph.-Van Nuys, CA.-1979

Healing Juices-L.A. Justice-Globe Communications Co.-Boca Raton, FL.-1999

Homeopathy For Emergencies-Phyllis Speight-C.W. Daniel Co.-Health Science Press-Great Britain-1984

The Healing Foods=Patricia Heusman & Judith Benn Hurley-St. Martin Press-1989

Back to Eden-Jethro Kloss-Back to Eden Books-Loma Linda, CA.-1971

The 13 Steps From Illness To Health-APNBMPDR-Jerome Plotnick, Ph.D., N.D.-21stCenturyEnergetics.com, Lake of the Woods, CA.-Createspace.com-printer, Columbia, S.C./Amazon.com-distrubtor-2015

AFTERWARD V.
ALKALINE FOODS AND HERBS

Alkaline Foods: Shitake Mushroom (eaten raw), Papaya, Blueberries, Adzuki Beans, Purple Grapes, Watercress, Kale, Broccoli, Sweet Potato (with skin), Kelp, Coconut, Coconut oil, or Extra Virgin Olive Oil, and Lemon.

Alkaline Herbs: Turmeric, Basil, Nutmeg, Guggul, Tropical Rose Mallow, Cat's Claw, Ginger Root, Rosemary, Cinnamon, Parsley, Chamomile, Boswella, Chives, Cardamon, Licorice, Spirulina, and Cayenne.

Anti-Cancer Foods and Herbs: Bitter Melon, Graviola (Annona Muricata), Dandelion Root, Grape Seed Extract, Frankincense, Myrrh, Black Cumin, Sage, Marijuana Leaves and Oil, Hemp Seed Oil, Red Root, Paw Paw, Doenzang (Korean Miso Fermented Paste), Isoflavones from Soy (daidzein, genistein), Red Clover, Turmeric, and Ginger Root, D.M.S.O., Australian Thrush Tree Berry, and Vit. C.-Pine Needles, Dandelion root, and Galandal root.

Immune System Enhancing Foods and Herbs: Astagalus, Schizandra, Mushrooms: Reishi, Mataike, Shitake, Chaga, Coriolus, Cordyceps, Bovine Colostrum, Larch, and Eleuthro Siberian Ginseng Root.

Anti Radiation Foods and Herbs: Siberian Eleuthro Ginseng Root, Arctic Alginate, Bentonite Clay, Zeolite, the Homeopathic Remedy called Anti-Rad, or goEnergetix's.com Phyto-Rad homeopathic remedy.

Detoxifying Cell Scrubbers: Lemon-rind and Lemonene Essential oil.

Anti Virus, Bacterial, Fungal Parasite Herbs: Pau d' Arco, Una de Gato, Olive Leaf, Black Walnut, Pomegrante, Silica, and Wormwood.

Cell Protectors & E.M.F.: Folic Acid, Vit. A with Beta Carotene Activity, Vit C (ester), Vit E (d-alpha-tocopherol), Selenium, Silica, and Olive Leaf. (F.A.C.E.S)

Super Foods and Herbs, etc.: Kidney Beans, Adzuki Beans, Green Beans, Garbanzo Beans, Hemp, Chia, Flax, Sunflower, Sesame, and Pumpkin Seeds, Ghee, Extra Virgin Olive Oil, Coconut Oil,

Jerusalem Artichoke, Parsley, Cilantro, Broccoli, Pumpkin, Beets, Cauliflower, Tomato, Cabbage, Carrots, Sweet Potato, Red Onion, Garlic, Ginger Root, Mushrooms (all), Turnips, Kale, Romaine Lettuce, Chard, Watercress, Coconut, Walnuts, Almonds, Cashews, Brazil Nuts, Banana, Purple Grapes, Berries (all), CA. Figs, Dates, Peaches, Apricots, Cherries, Apples, Plums, Oranges, Pineapple, Lemons, Avacado, Papaya, Mango, Watermelon, Cantelope, Bitter Melon, Grapefruit, Kiwi, Green Tea, Twig Tea, Fenugreek Herb, Cinnamon, Nutmeg, Cumin, Turmeric, Stevia, Maple Syrup, Raw Honey, Bee Pollen, Royal Jelly, Quinoa, Aramanth, Oats, Millet, Buckwheat, Brown Rice, Kelp, Spirulina, Chlorella, Celtic Sea Salt, Cayenne, Wheat Berries, Red Rice, Rye Berries, Farro, and Nutmeg.

Note! Glycerin can be used in any topically used soap, skin care, solvent, food preservation, cough syrups, mouth washes, and sweetening agent.

AFTERWARD VI
TABLE OF CONTENTS FOR "CANCER WHAT'S THE ANSWER?"

AFTERWARD VII

CANCER WHAT'S THE ANSWER?

Alternative, Biological, Natural, Holistic Protocol for Detoxification, I.S., Balancing Body and Blood pH, Cancer Killing Foods, Herbs, Elements, and Prevention of Cancer in 45 Days.

This protocol is being successfully used by many existing cancer patients. Cancer cells exist in the blood of all mammals in the form of a polymorphic microbe. This microbe can change its forms from a bacteria, to a virus, to a fungus, and finally into a cancer cell. It has been seen under both regular microscopes and electronic scopes. It has been noted by many biologists since the 1800's. Both Medical Doctors: Royal Rife and Wilhelm Reich discovered and recognized its existence in the late 1920's to the 1950's. It recently was again reappeared and once again surfaced from the research work of Medical Doctor Rudolph Skelnar of Germany, Bergold, Nissle, et al., from the 1970's to 2017. It was also acknowledged by many other doctors world-wide since the late 1800's. See on pages 145-147 and on pages 179-181.

Cancer cells develop when a microscopic polymorphic organism that is found in the blood of all mammals proliferates. This organism (which can change its form from a bacteria, to a virus, to a fungus), eventually into a cancer cell, and begin to proliferate (metastasized) when the blood pH rises above 7.56 pH. I call it the cancer producing microbe the "Psora." It is called the Endobiont by many of the researchers. Reich called it the Bion and Rife the BX Bacillus. These doctors healed cancer in the 1920's.

Cancer Microbe Researchers, of the Past, and Present.

The history of the discovery of this cancer cell microbe in our blood has actually be known for hundreds of years. The following is a list of researchers who saw the microbe:
1890-Russel from England described "fuchsin" particles inside of cancer cells.
1898-Sanfelice pointed out the correlation of blastomyces with the development of cancer.
1899-Dr. Josef Koch found parasitic inclusions that he termed "Protozoon cancrosum" outside the cancer cells.

1901-Van Leyden described the so called bird's eye cells in cases of cancer.

1902-Borrel suspected a virus to be responsible for the cancer was triggered by parasites.

1903-Otto and Wolfgang Schmidt discovered vermicules and spores in cases of cancer.

1904-Doyan reported cocci in chains of tumorous tissue.

1914-Mori from Naples, Italy published his theory concerning the mycetic nature, an ultra-virus, and whose transformation he had originally witnessed in 1910.

1920-Enderlein discovered a microorganism' that he believed lead to cancer; he called it "Endobiont."

1925-Dr. Royal Rife discovered the cancer microbe with his Rife Microscope. Called it the Bacillus BX.

1926-Tissot mentioned a parasitic cancer elements as being amoeba-like forms.

1928-Heidenhain Tubingen talked about histological traceable microbe in cancer.

1930-Dr. Wilhelm Reich discovered microscopic entities that he said caused cancer which he called "Bions."

1931-Dr. Otto Warburg stated that cancer cell cannot exist in an alkaline or an oxygen rich cellular environment. [Cesium chloride]

1932-Van Neerguard called cancer a virus disease and termed the responsible virus "Siphonospora polymorpha."

1932-Nebel bred various growths from cancerous blood, tissues, and termed the virus he named "Onkomyxa neoformans."

1933-Dechow pointed out a variety of aspergillus as a cancer-causing organism.

1933-Gruner and Glower found and called "Cryptomyces pleomorpha" an organism in cancer.

1935-Von Brehmer's "Siphonospora polymorpha" was officially recognized as a new blood parasite by the Reichagesundheitsamt (German Ministry of Health), by commission of specially appointed clinicians and bacteriologists. The research findings of Dr. Von Brehmer are as follows: the cancer virus is the invisible stage of development of the microscopic forms of "Siponospora polymorpha," which "In vitro" can be made visible.

1948-Franz Gerlach published his monography Krebs and obligator Pilzparasitismus (Cancer and Obligatory Fungus-Parasitism) in Vienna. He also reported and maintained that cancer came from even uncivilized communities such as those in Africa. In other words cancer is not an affliction solely restricted to civilized countries.

1951-Lea Del Bo Rosslin of Milan, Italy published micro photographs of the tiniest species of fungi found in cancer.

1955-Villequez in Paris, France spoke about latent parasitism in blood cells.

1956-Scheller published case histories of microscopy in the dark field called "Von Viren, Mitochondrien und vom Krebs" (On Viruses, Mitochondria, and Cancer").

1957-Professor Stanley of Berkeley University talked about the correlation of viruses and cancer.

1958-Clara Fonti from Milan, Italy published her "Aeitopathogense des Krebes" (Aetiopathgenisis of Cancer), asserting her theory of cancer parasites with all its consequences. Dr. Scheller succeeded in triggering tumors in mice by means of sphonspora rods.

1970's-Professor Gerhard Sauer from the German Cancer Research Institute, Heidelberg, Germany stated in an article named Viruses in Accomplices, Cancer Research New Paths that after years of research he, and his collaborators had succeeded in proving that viruses play a vital role in triggering tumors. In the case of various types of papilloma viruses are involved; they are popova viruses, which are among the tiniest varieties.

1970's-Dr. Rudolph Skelnar, M.D. with his blood timed photographs or blood picture proved that there are four (4) stages of development of the blood parasite within the red blood corpuscles in both pre-cancerous and cancerous cases. Dr. Bergold et al.

1981-Weber from Erding, West Germany cultivated isolated cancer protozoa on freshly fertilized chicken egg. He displayed micro-parasites in their various forms of development by means of an electronic camera and shown on a T.V. screen.

1981-Mordes and Rossi at the University of Massachusetts in Worchester pointed out a substance circulating through the organism as the cancer-causing agent. When they linked up the blood circulation of tumor-free rats in parabiosis with animals suffering from cancer, they noted that the tumors were triggered in the cancer free rats.

1984-Bishop, Vormus in San Francisco, California, Gallo in Bethesda, Maryland, and the physicist Rosenberg in East Lansing, Michigan were all able to trigger cancer by means of the virus in apes.

Here are some of the important factors known to date about the development of cancer. There are four (4) stages of development that are as follows: 1. Primitive stage is the Protitie, measures one hundreth-thousandth of a millimeter and constitutes the original from of life itself. Note! It is not a cancer cell at this point. This living non assimilated protein colloid grows into a 2. symprotite ball, also called a mychite. 3. This grows into a mych, it develops into a polyvalent nucleus called a symmchon, or the chite comes into being, and constituting the original form of a bacterial cell. 4. It now becomes visible with the use of a microscope enlargement of 20,000 power. It is now a cancer cell.

This bacterial reproduction can result from simple division mitosis or sexually called myosis. The bacterial cyclogensis is the cycle of morphological development involving countless generations, from morphological uniformity, (mychite stage # 1) to morphological culmination and back again to morphological uniformity. This is a chronic complex development of "Endobiosis" and is found in the blood of all mammals including man. The culmination point of endobiotic cyclogenesis. i.e. The highest point of the development of parasites, is to be found in its fungal stage. All the previous stages pose no danger to man, but if it goes into the fungal stage it consequence such as cancer tends to ensue.

1. All chronic diseases including cancer are by no means infectious diseases in the traditional sense, because an infection is inconsequential. All the cells, all organs, tissues are infested by microscopic, invisible "unseen" to the naked eye, or barely visible primitive forms of the "Endobiont."

2. "Endobiont" is one of the noxious microorganism with the greatest resistance against all types of outside influences. It can survive temperatures of up to 590 degrees F, survive in a dry state, immune to chemotherapy, radiation therapy, and extreme cold temperatures as well.

3. Budde-Grawitz from Argentina even managed to revive it from ancient Egyptian mummies 10,000 years old. Also A. Cockburn and his research team from Detroit, Michigan succeeded in proving in tact proteins in Mummy Pum II from the Prolemeic Era. Even Enderlein was able to cultivate the light brown spores of Mucor Recemosus Fresen. Performed on a Karg scale from ancient sarcophagi in the catacombs near Rome, Italy. Even after a human death the proteins, too, are absorbed by the "Endobiont," and

gradually transform into spores called (endobiosis). Due to this the parasite cannot be conquered by conventional allopathic oncology, chemotherapy, and radiation methods.
4. But: It is one of the truths of biology, even a truism, that primitive bacteria are dependent on an alkaline environment, and fungi of all types are dependent on an acidic environment. Seen on a agar plate, disturb each others development, and prevent each others growth. In other words the cyclogenetic development of the microorganism cannot be enhanced by increased acidity of its nutritional base, on the other hand, it can be arrested (pH level of the blood; acidity-alkaline balance of the human blood). Based on this proven research work, Enderlein reaches the logical conclusion that the cure for cancer can only be solved by biologists, because living organisms can be combated by live matter only!

The work of Dr. Skelnar indicates that every chronic disease including cancer is preceded by a preliminary illness, resulting mainly in metabolic disorders. This increased metabolic waste, the feces including undigested proteins, carbohydrates, and fats. This creates an ideal environment where the Endobiont the primitive cancer microorganism (virus-bacteria-fungus), can develop through its four (4) main stages into cancer cells, and tumors. Digestion is important and essential factor concerning one's vibrant health or illness. Death begins in your colon. And 75% of your immune system is in the colon. The root cause cannot be purged by colon cleansers, herbs, foods, fasting, juices, and teas, but must be eliminated by:

No To Cancer: Alternative Biological Holistic Treatment Protocol.
1.] Herbal Detoxification that prepares the body for a complete detoxification such as goEnergetixs.com "Opening Channels" previously outlined on page 23 in this book. Body & Colon Cleanse.
1a.] Supercedes 1. Energetic Light Photon Detoxifcation. This is the energetic light photon detoxification program the "Liquid Needle Bath Soaks" Then treat topically your acupuncture points, meridians, and chakras with Liquid Needle Original topical energetic solution. I so outlined on pages 23-29 in this book. L.N. Bath Soaks advised for cancer are: Lympha-L-105, Gold-105EX, Coffee-130EX, CAN-133, LVR-105, NRV-105, PAR-134. Also pre use Liquid Needle's E.V.B. to raise the body's biofield MHz 4-6 times.

2.] Balancing the blood pH into a more acidic value but still alkaline. Keeping it below 7.56 pH. I advise a pH between 7.35-7.45 pH for body and blood. Advised is Kombucha Fungus tea. capsules @555 mg. from Pronatura Dr. Skelnar's original recipe. Kombucha is 3 pH., or G.T.S. Living Foods Kombucha. 1-877-735-8423

3.] Maintaining your digestion, assimilation, and metabolism. I advise goEnergetixs.com Cataslyst 7, U, FloraSynergyPlus, Amino Gest and Galt Immune. Also Glutaloemine-Oxymogen and Mutaflor.

4.] A proper balanced organic vegan preferred alkaline diet Ayurveda based. Highly recommended is proper food mixing, eating at proper times, eating and masticating the food slowly, a pleasant eating environment, and performing the Eating Meditation. See on pages 275-276.

5.] Treating all foods, water, and herbs with Liquid Needle Yellow to energetically detoxify your food in 5 minutes. Protects for 32 hours thereafter. Also ozone (03) treating foods, air, and water.

6.] Periodic detoxification with goEnergetix's.com "Opening Channels" and Liquid Needle Bath Soaks every three (3), four (4), or six (6) months. See pages 23-29 and pages 169,193,284-310

7.] Ongoing goEnergetix's.com enzymes Catalyst 7, or U, and goEnergetix's.com Flora Synergy for minerals. Eat mainly freshly picked organic foods raw, juiced, and steamed. If cooked maintain a temperature under one hundred eighteen (118) degrees F. The following is suggested for cancer patients: T.O.L. & Rick Simpsons Marijuana (R.S.O.) full extract essential oil with high dosage T.H.C.-C.B.D. The following are also suggested: mangosteen, beet, graviola, pau d'arco, turmeric, galandal, cayenne, dandelion root, ginger root, red root, echinacea purpurea, ozone-03 in water, air, foods, and oils, Kangen water or alkaline wands for alkaline H_2O, Halean 851,"Doenzang" miso fermented soy paste, O2, IP6+Inositol, Biosan's Vita-Flax seed-amino acid blend, and Gravizon from the Amazon Herb Co. Also a Truapur for H ions produced filtered water.

Due to the xneobiotic toxemia caused by anti-biotic use, E.M.F.'s, radiation, M.R.I.'s, T.T.E.'s, WiFi's, X-rays, chemotherapy chemicals, factory farmed heavy metal toxic food, G.M.O.'s, synthetic drugs, and toxic water. Rx: Goenergetix's.com Phyto-Rad or Apex Energetics- Radiation Anti-Tox N-4 and D.N.R., Inc., IN.-Liquid Needles-Coffee-130EX or Can-133 bath soaks. These toxins need to be all addressed using the aforementioned energetic detoxification program. This will eliminate the toxins, followed by nutrient replenishment, an organic alkaline vegan diet, daily meditation, and daily exercise, etc. Note! The most important factor is maintaining a blood pH below 7.56. this renders the cancer causing pleomorphic microorganism called the "Endobiont" dormant. This is the only true remission. It prevents any further cancer cell proliferation. Then one can proceed to kill off any cancer cells in the body or blood. Kombucha: G.T.S.- 877-735-8423

How to Kill Cancer Cells Naturally-Nutrition You are What You Eat.

1. To kill all cancer cells advised is <u>1</u>. full extract (Rick Simpson or Tree of Life high dosage T.H.C.-C.B.D. essential oil daily, <u>2</u>. an A2Z Aqua6 ozone generator for air, water, and oil-03, 02, Turapur for H ions. <u>3</u>. Graviola "Gravizon" an Amazon Herb Co. formula., <u>4</u>. cancer killing herbs and foods: red onion, dates, dandelion, turmeric, galandal, ginger, beets, chaga, reishi, jack fruit, mangosteen-noni, bitter melon, grape seed extract, MK-7-Vit.-K-2, Vit.-B-17-apricot kernels, bushwood tree berry, peaches, colloidal gold, colloidal silver, Vit.-D3, Vit. B-12 Vit-A with beta carotene, red root, boswellia, chaparral, and black garlic.

Dr. Skelnar states, "the causative organisms must be neutralized, vital agents of metabolism, immune system, and defensive reactions restored. Cancer is influenced by the intestinal bacteria. Unfortunately most medical doctors after prescribing anti-biotics usually fail to inform the patient to re-seed the intestinal flora friendly needed bacteria by taking pre and probiotics." I recommend pre biotics and the probiotics listed on pages 279-280. Most probiotics never make it out of your stomach.

Dr. Skelnar also states the following to be noted: "The substances of the vitamin B group do not have to be supplemented usually due to their production in a healthy intestinal tract. Vitamin synthesis mainly takes place in the colon; it is the function of the intestinal bacteria."

The fermentation splitting of heavy or indigestible carbohydrates which includes starch, pectin's, cellulose, cell fibers of plants as well as proteins, especially from plant cells; this is a vital of cell bacteria especially for herbivores. An antagonistic over function growth and increase of the pathogenic bacteria. This is how cell bacteria form anti-biotic active, protein like colicines (probiotics). Also advised is MK-7-Vit. K2 and Vit. D3. Olive oil based, and sublingual Vit. B-12.

The reduction of bilirubin in urobilin by intestinal bacteria does not occur when they are weakened, so the feces contain only bilirubin. Intestinal bacteria live in immune biologically balanced symbiosis. i.e. there is an immune-biological interaction between the organism and the intestinal bacteria. In the mucous membranes of the intestines the bacteria keep up a constant reciprocal metabolism among each other. If this is disturbed these bacteria trigger certain illnesses.

When the intestinal bacteria are weakened (Non-physiological, but not yet a pathological condition) the chemical, and the biological balance of the body suffers grave disturbances. Dehydration, causes sleeper minerals called the "Braddy Effect" where minerals deactivate, remain dormant, cannot perform its assigned bodily function(s), alterations of the electrolyte balance; it can even prevent the formation of antibodies against various viruses, and their metabolic products. Dandelion root extract and even caffeine can reactivate minerals. Vitamin K2 for instance is produced by the intestinal bacteria so it is necessary for prothrombin synthesis in the mitochondria of the liver. When the vitamin K2 synthesis is disturbed a secondary consequence is that of blood coagulation is also disturbed. Rx: goEnergetix's.com-Rehydration. Dandelion root, organic coffee with caffeine. MountHagen organic.

Vitamin K2 has been found in coli bacteria. The bacteria called (Escherichia coli) which are two kinds of asparaginases have been discovered. One is completely non effective against cancer cells and the other displays the most effective cancer cell-tumor-arresting qualities observed recently. Healthy intestinal bacteria dissolve various toxins that the liver can no longer handle. The liver and the intestines are in constant interaction. Seventy (70%) to eighty (80%) percent of defense cells are located in the intestinal wall. In order to to function properly against viruses they need contact with healthy intestinal bacteria. Combating cancer, other metabolic diseases, is directly correlated with a healthy intestine, and healthy intestinal bacteria. Professor Dr. Nissle describes the after-effects of a so called dysbacterium of the intestinal bacteria in the colon, he developed an excellent coli compound for healing, and stabilizing the intestinal bacteria in the colon.[Mutaflor] He defined dysbacterium as the degeneration of the intestinal bacteria, which results in physical disturbances of many kinds. The toxins emanating from the degenerated intestinal tract bacteria cause many frequent digestive disorders, I.B.S., U.C., affects the liver-gall system, migraine headaches, halitosis, rheumatic diseases, asthma, M.S.- multiple sclerosis, skin disorders such as psoriasis, eczema, C.F.S. Canadida, and cancer to name a few of the important ones.

The Research Work of Dr. Rudolf Skelnar, M.D. Germany.

The research work of Dr. Skelnar indicates that every chronic disease including cancer is preceded by a preliminary illness. Also see pages: 26-27 on the eight (8) stages of acute to chronic bio-accumulation (toxic load) and disease. Cancer is histological.

This results in mainly metabolic disorders. This increased metabolic waste(s) including undigested proteins, carbohydrates, and fats. And this creates an ideal environment where the cancer micro-organisms the polymorphic Endobiont can now begin to develop through its four (4) stages into cancer cells. So therefore digestion, assimilation, metabolism are a main factor concerning one's health, or illness. Death begins in the colon a true fact. Around 75% percent of your immune system is located in the intestinal tract. Therefore the root cause cannot be purged by colon cleansers or herbal teas but must be eliminated by the following:
1.] Herbal Detoxification using "Opening Channels" or currently superceded by and advised now is:
1a.] Energetic Detoxification-"Liquid Needle pre internal orally taken preparatory remedy E.V.B. followed by the post Bath Soak series of five (5) bath soaks. See pages:23-29,208-210,240,284-310
2.] Balancing the blood pH into a higher acidic pH value but still alkaline between 7.35-7.45 pH and must be under 7.56 pH according to Dr. Skelnar's research and discovery. This is performed by taking Kombucha Fungus tea in liquid or as I prefer in 555 mg. Pronatura, Dr. Skelnar's Original recipe caps, or use drinkGTS.com
3.] Maintaining assimilation, digestion, food metabolism taking enzymes such as goEnergetix.com Catalyst 7, or U digestive enzymes. Pre and pro biotics such as FloraSynergyPlus by goEnergetix's.com, or Complete Probiotics by 1MD, Mutaflor a Dr.

Nissle an e-coli formula, and Glutaloemine by Oxymogen both are available @Amazon.com or @Oxymogen.com See also on pages: 276-278
  4.] A proper alkaline pH diet with alkaline foods and herbs. Alkaline foods are essential for maintaining an alkaline pH and vibrant health. The best and normal pH values for the cells as well as the body fluids ranges between 7.35-7.45 pH. Acidic foods such as high protein meats, fish, poultry, cereals, and seeds render the pH to an acidic range. This causes many serious problems and various symptoms which are health debilitating. Foods that have the highest alkalinity are those between 8.5-9.0 pH. The foods with a pH between 8.5-9.0 are as follows: Mainly these are fruits such as: lemons, watermelons, mangoes, blue berries, and papayas. The vegetables are: seaweed, kelp, spirulina, dulse, chlorella, algae, kuduz root, and watercress. Then next there are the moderate alkalizing foods with a pH between 7.5-8.0. These are the fruits: mangosteen-noni, apricots, grapes, nectarines, peaches, unriped bananas, figs, dates, and grapefruit. The vegetables are: spinach, pumpkin, peas, cabbage, lentils, and sweet potato with the skin left on. Then there are the slightly alkalizing foods and herbs. These are: turmeric, basil, cinnamon, parsley, cats claw, cayenne, cilantro, tropical rose mallow, licorice, nutmeg, green tea, extra virgin olive oil, shitake mushroom, broccoli, guggul, garlic, ginger, cardamon, boswella, chives, and chamomile. The aforementioned foods, herbs will even tually bring a alkaline body and blood desired pH. Additionally an alkaline fruit punch can be made by using the following fruit juices:
lemon, nectarine, grapes, watermelon, peaches, unriped bananas, aloe Vera, mangoes, and papaya. Goenergetix's.com: Galt Immune and Amino Gest, Dr. Nissile's-Mutaflor, and Oxymogen's-Glutaloemine.
5.] Elimination of the existing cancer cells can be performed using the following:
a.] Full extract cannabis 16% or higher % of T.H.C.-C.B.D. marijuana R.S.O. or Tree of Life essential oil.
b.] The essential oils of Frankincense, Black Cumin, Myrrh, and Sage in exact doasges added to 3 more secret essential oils called X-Y-Z put into a carrier oil such as coconut. This can be implemented by using a plastic enema squirt bottle that you can squirt 1-2 squirts into the anal-colon-rectum or you can use a vaporizer a diffuser to breathe the formula into the lungs. A drop under the tongue or on the roof of the mouth also. Order Can Kill-

1 Formula from 21stCenturyEnergetics.com see on page 206. 2 oz.- $50.00

c.] With the use of a safe A2Z Aqua6 ozone generator for water, air, or oil ozonation. Ozone 03 kills cancer cells on contact. So if you ozone your distilled alkaline water, inside room air, all used oils like olive, coconut, and your foods. You will be ingesting 03 which will kill the cancer cells. A Turapir H ion water maker and filter pitcher is also suggested as H ions are the highest of all antioxidants, anti-inflammatory, and anticancer.
d.] Graviola also called soursop or annona muricata. This is known to kill cancer cells, only seeks out cancer cells, and is 10,000 times more powerful than chemotherapy chemicals. It is non toxic. The Brazilan version is called Paw Paw. Ginger root, beet root, dandelion root, galandal root, red root, and turmeric root.
e.] the following herbs, foods, elements, essential oils, chemical substances, radionics-frequency generators, and immune system modulated vaccines are also known for their cancer killing properties: Turmeric, dandelion, ginger, galandal, beet roots, bitter melon, jack fruit, wheat grass, marijuana leaves and buds eaten, red root-Jersey Tea, apricot kernels, dates, mangosteen-noni, bushwood tree berry, grape seed extract, peaches, Halean-851 isoflavones: genistein and daizdein, chaparral, black cumin or black seed, pau d'arco, una de gato (cats claw), colloidal gold-silver, chondriana, baking soda and coconut oil, the essential oils of: frankincense, myrrh, sage, black cumin, cayenne, hemp lavender, cannabis R.S.O.-16% T.H.C.-C.B.D, castor oil, coconut oil, IP6 and Inositol, Dr. Wilhelm Reich-orgone box (Faraday cage) and generator (box consists of five (5) or more layers a matrix of organic separated by inorganic material), Dr. Royal Rife-Frequency generator (replaced by John Crane's square wave generator), microwave modulated hyperthermia, calcium, vitamin K2-MK-7, vitamin D3, thymus extract, 02 stabilized oxygen, chondriana, carnavora, vita-flax seed and sulfur protein amino adids, silver colloid, interferon and interleukin, vitamin A with beta carotene, carbonate, cesium chloride, lypocodium clav, hydrazine sulfate, reviverine, flutamide, clondronate, oncotox, 1-IGH colostrum, immune modulation, Chinese herb paris 7 + cho ko and curcumin, eshcarotics black salve, and C.B.D. Hemp, or Cannabis oil for melanoma and other skin cancers, black cannabis 18% T.H.C., beplureum, antineoplastavis, fermented soy miso paste: Doenzang, and immune system modulated vaccines, etc. For a more detailed

description and analysis on all of the aforementioned go to pages 588-603 in The 13 Steps From Illness To Health-APNBMPDR book.

Cancer in the years 2016-2017 has the same fatal death statistics from the same allopathic oncology conventional treatments since the 1950's. This with all the traditional medicine research to date including: chemotherapy, radiation, and surgery. They have produced no improvement in cancer elimination nor life expectancy of cancer patients. The oncology based treatments are both barbaric and insufficient for a healing from this most deadly biological caused disease. In fact the cancer treatments given eventually kill you and not the cancer in most cases.

Finally after many years of denial The National Cancer Institute has stated and admitted that your diet is related to cancer. But unfortunately there is more to it than just your diet. Discovered is your body and blood pH, psychological factors caused by stress, negative thinking, a compromised immune system, and finally the environments toxicity. See pages 313-316 for N.C.I. statistics on cancer.

Although the conventional medical establishment has been given billions of dollars from donations and grants little if anything has been discovered. Some minor discoveries have been genes, interferon, and interleukin. There is a slow pace costing millions of dollars and relatively no real results. You may ask why? Because believe it or not they the cancer medical industry do not want their $124.6 billion dollar cancer industry apple cart upset. They are only attempting to suppress, or kill cancer cells, not get to the true biological cause that has been discovered, and hidden from the public. Although the researchers claim breakthroughs and progress. Where are they? If cancer is then a biological disease which it is, then it surely cannot be treated using conventional treatments. Biological treatment is the only true method of elimation and prevention. Answer is Naturea Medica.

So again to reiterate all of the research and billions of dollars spent has produced a minimal result. One out of every two Americans will have cancer. Besides as I stated cancer is a biological disease, the cancer polymorphic kleptic blood microbe called Endobiont, or as I call it the Psora. It is contained in the blood of all mammals. It goes through four (4) stages before becoming a cancer cell. It can be eliminated, prevented, with biological, and natural holistic treatment. There is no profit in natural cost effective holistic treatments. That's why "they" the big pharma, medical, and chemical industries "Do Not Want a Cure"! The $124.6 billion dollars of annual profits is the reason. They use misinformation, confusion, and disinformation as a tactic.

As famous comedian and actor Chris Rock states, "They ain't going to find a cure for nothing. Because if they did it would put them out of business." Further he stated, " all they are going to do I give you some kind of medicine that cures nothing but masks the symptoms because there is no money in a cure."

This is where I believe legitimate original natural proven cost effective holistic, naturopathic, anti-cancer remedies, and medicine comes into play. Naturopathic medicine and its practitioners believe and are interested in providing all of humanity with Naturae Medica (natural medicine). This is Nature-God created just as we are non toxic medicines which if and when are used properly have a 99.99% healing rate. Non toxic herbs, homeopathics, essential oils, elements, light photon frequencies, and organic foods, etc. They implement gentle and safe treatments. They are cost effective. They do not mask symptoms. I believe are created in nature for our use as the antidote(s) against all illnesses.

Also remember you are what you eat, what you think, breathe, and drink. If you are eating a toxic factory farmed food, G.M.O., non food chemical altered diet causing a extremely toxic physical body, stress, think negatively, shallow breathing, are drinking toxic water, or beverages. The results are apparent as billions of Americans are facing a multitude of illnesses and diseases. Most all are from man-made causes. As we become more and more toxic the bio-accumulation toxicity increases. It goes through eight (8) stages, from acute to the eighth stage the histological stage, and pre mature death from cancer, etc. See on pages 26-27.

Do you remember this famous statement?: "The doctor of the future shall give no medicine, but rather teach the patient the care of the human frame and mind." I am a doctor of the future except I do give advice on taking natural medicine, diet, and proper positive thinking. With this in mind I give you the cutting edge research information, successful natural holistic alternative cancer natural remedies, alternative, and holistic treatment(s).

Non Traditional Cancer Treatments.

I will now reveal to the American public the non traditional treatments that can enable healing ones self and prevent all cancers. The F.D.A., U.S.D.A., D.E.A., A.M.A., Quackwatch, big pharmaceutical, chemical, medical industries are the biggest impediment of progress in cancer research, and treatment. They do not want natural medicines as I said it would put them out of business. They exclusively want to control or have the corner on anything in the health field marketplace. There is no money in cures. But unfortunately there is big money in keeping people sick, on toxic chemicals, addictive toxic drugs, and medicines.

The arrest medical doctors, alternative holistic practitioners, take their licenses to practice, other evasive intimidation, harassment, and actions. They even want to control the natural known natural herbs, homeopathics, etc. Michael Taylor is the head of the F.D.A. He recently stated, "That T.H.C.-C.B.D. from cannabis that has shown a 100% cancer killing ratio is the exclusive property of big pharmaceutical companies, that plant molecules come under the F.D.A., and pharmaceutical governance." He ordered a ban against Hemp C.B.D.'s and Cannabis T.H.C.-C.B.D. Monsanto and other big pharmaceutical companies are manufacturing synthetic G.M.O. marijuana so it can be patented and sell for four hundred (400) times the profit. He also is going after homeopathic medicine claiming its a superstitious pseudo non science proven medicine. So there is a war going on against natural medicine. Who do you think appointed Mr. Michael Taylor, a former Monsanto C.E.O. to head the F.D.A.? Yes and non other than our former U.S. President Obama. Who by the way also signed into law, The Monsanto Protection Act." This act gives Monsanto freedom not to label G.M.O.'s, immunity from claims, and law suits arising from damages incurred by their chemical toxic poisons. It is being challenged.

Ask yourself this question just why such an overwhelming interest, attempts to block the uses of alternative natural medicines, and therapies? The answer is simple, not what the F.D.A. tells the public that they are protecting the public from non proven medicines, and treatments, etc. The answer is two fold as first the hospitals, clinics, private doctors that make millions of dollars with their traditional drugs, medicines, and treatments will lose their money. By the way talking about traditional cancer treatment that nets around $124-$200 billion dollars annually and heals almost no one. The fact is that eventually it kills you. Secondly, the pharmaceutical manufacturers of chemotherapy chemicals will also lose billions of dollars of profits. So you see its a lose-lose situation for them. The cancer industry medical establishment lives off death, misery of the lied to, and misinformed public. Many will lose their employment, hospitals will close, and put many companies out of business. So a non traditional out patient treatment for cancer that is more effective in costs and eliminating cancer is here now. Many cancer patients are self treating, healing naturally, holistically with the proven alternative medicines, and treatments. I will give them to you shortly. Remember that cancer is a biologically caused disease. It can only be eliminated and prevented biologically. Its the status quo of the medical establishment that perpetuates the dilemma, prevents the elimination of cancer, and maintains all of our toxic environmental issues as well.

For the most part people are the herd. They are products of the environment and creatures of habit. They for the most part believe what the medical establishment and the government tells them. Even when the allopathic treatments are completely harmful. Its all about the belief system. What one doctor may call a quack remedy another doctor calls it the magic curing silver bullet. After years of medical school, intimidation, and brainwashing it is no wonder that medical oncologists reject everything except what they are told is acceptable. Even when it is shown over and over again to cause eventual death. They are told to stay in line or lose the license to practice. I have even heard these medical doctors call other health practitioners superstitious quacks. They call Naturopaths, homeopaths, osteopaths, chiropractors, psychologists, herbalists, acupuncturists, even their own preventive holistic doctors, and environmental toxicologists quacks. Yet all the aforementioned alternative doctors have a very high success rate with patients they treat, or they would not be covered by health insurance companies, and they would be out of business. Have you noticed the amount of alternative natural remedies, medicines, essential oils, etc., in stores, pharmacies, and on line? People are using them with successful results or they wouldn't sell. Even these are being attacked currently by the F.D.A. and being called quackery. There are billions of dollars being spent on alternative natural medicine these days because it works successfully. It is cost effective, non toxic, and also prevents many illnesses before they manifest physically. The American public is disenfranchised with toxic synthetic poisonous chemicals that are called allopathic medicines, drugs, and the barbaric medical treatments. [Fact: chemotherapy, radiation, internal surgery for cancer is what mostly, and ultimately kills the cancer patient within a five (5) year life expectancy.] Note! Cancer is a $124.6 billion dollar annual business for profit. Over 77 holistic cancer docs murdered?

In America today, there is a large shift to non traditional alternative based natural, naturopathic medicine, holistic treatment of the whole person, and not just the symptom(s). There is now a large segment of the population seeking these new but old ancient healing methods. A holistic healing approach through mind, body, to spirit balancing. These include an organic vegan alkaline diet, vitamins, minerals, elements, herbs, homeopathics, essential oils, exercise, prayer, meditation, yoga, biofeedback and neurofeedback training, hypnosis, guided imagery, creative visualization, positive affirmations, self talk, aromatherapy, massage, Bach flower essences, Tai chi, Tajii, Chi Gong, yoga, Internal Kung Fu also known as Internal Exercises, deep breathing exercises, bio-energetic frequency based medicine, both touch and non touch healing, Pranic and Reiki healing, Touch For Health healing, aerobics, B.E.S.T. Chiropractic, A.K.-muscle testing and balancing, acupressure, needle-less acupuncture, Jin Shin Do, Shiatsu, Tui-Na, frequency radionics, and light photon frequency based solutions. Cancer is now being healed using T.H.C.-C.B.D. full extract essential oils. Note! I advise using only 16% R.S.O. and Tree of Life. High T.H.C. strain 18% is black cannabis.

It is my hope that after people read this chapter they will become informed, more knowledgeable about health rest-oral in general, using natural holistic medicines, and treatments. They will know how to better treat their illness holistically. How to re-balance their bio-field energy, strengthen their immune system, how to prevent cancer, treat cancer effectively, and naturally. The F.D.A. calls many natural remedies, treatments unproven quackery because it costs a minimum of around $2.56 billion dollars in most cases to properly test, and then publish the findings in a legitimate medical journal. Then another $312 million to post approve with trials, etc. Legitimate medical journal there is the first fraud. It also takes a minimum of up to ten (10) years to accomplish. The pharmaceutical company only wants patented medicines and drugs that will eventually return them high profits before they make the investment. Nothing in nature can be patented. But now the F.D.A. Head Michael Taylor an former C.E.O from Monsanto is claiming that all plant molecules belong to the pharmaceutical companies and under F.D.A. jurisdiction. He just issued an order outlawing all Hemp C.B.D. essential oils from being marketed. All while the pharmaceutical companies scurry, hurry along, to formulate synthetic C.B.D.'s so they can patent them, and sell them for four hundred (400) times higher profits.

The F.D.A. rule states that any substances used for prevention, treatment, cure, and the mitigation of disease shall be considered a drug. So if you use cabbage juice for constipation or Vitamin E for heart disease in this concept would be considered a drug. Therefore any drug needs to be F.D.A. approved. They control the marketplace on all drugs and treatments. This is how the F.D.A. big pharma, health insurance, and the A.M.A. control the system. I strongly believe this conspiracy must be eliminated through public education and our unwillingness to go with the establishment that will finally over turn their hold on the public. Through supply and demand ecomomics is how they keep their tight hold on the public. So once there is no demand for their toxic synthetic poisonous drugs, medicines, foods, treatments they will either be out of business, be forced to join the bandwagon for non traditional medicine, or become a dinosaur.

It is a matter or a question of economics, the supply and demand, and re-educating people. As the old generation dies off, as the baby boomers generation retires, I predict a massive switch to alternative natural medicine, and treatments. In fact as you are presently are seeing that the conventional allopathic medical doctors are going to have to learn holistic naturopathic methods such as nutrition, psychology, osteopathy, homeopathy, herbs, chiropractic, aromatherapy-essential oils, massage, hypnosis, bio-energetics, mind healing methods, healing methods such as Pranic, Reiki, touch and non touch, remote healing, bioenergetics, both E.M.G. Biofeedback and E.E.G. Neurofeedback training, shamanistic healing, acupuncture healing, chakra healing, Ayurveda healing, and all other presently effective modes of natural healing.

Cancer Causes Theories.

There are different theories on the causes of cancer. But in general cancer cells are cells that come from a polymorphic Endobiont a microbe found in the blood of all mammals. These are caused by a blood pH that rises above 7.56 pH. They are abnormal, anaerobic cell, that is, disorderly, and out of the normal biology that determines how a cell functions. The defect according to one theory is genetic and that the genetic code may instruct the cell to become a cancerous abnormal cell. The cell mechanism may have been altered by the genetic code to cause abnormality. The current research findings are that cancer cell blood microbes begin to proliferate when the blood pH rises above 7.56 pH, an initiator either genetic, and trigger or promoter a toxin then begins to proliferate the cancer cells. Also the intestinal flora negative bacteria decreasing the immune system function, nutritional deficiencies, energy deficiencies, stress factors that cause your immune system to be weakened, and compromise the immune system function. Code of Life is genetic and in the D.N.A. and transcripted by the-R.N.A.

Cancer cells may also be the result of chemical and E.M.F.'s electromagnetic influence on the cell causing it to be an abnormal mutated cell. Cancer is caused by an alien agent. This is the surveillance theory of cancer. It also proposes that cancer can be caused by a microorganism a polymorphic bacteria, virus, fungus, and found in the blood of all mammals. Since all cells both cancerous and normal cells require nourishment from the blood vessels to supply their accelerated growth. Cancer cells have a deficient genetic pattern for making these new blood vessels and causes them to be defective. This results in a increased blood supply to the cancer cells to increase their metabolic rate. The increased metabolism results in an increased demand for nourishment and an increased production of waste material. Cancer cells are anaerobic and feed off (sucrose-glucose) sugar. They do not need O2 to live. Note! Some cancer cells require no oxygen.

Normal non malignant cells in comparison are able to obtain sufficient nourishment, cell detoxification because they have an adequate blood supply, lymph causing nourishment, and detoxification to be adequate. Conversely, cancer cells are just the opposite. Cancer cells require large amounts of energy they obtain from glucose sugars in the blood. Certain substances can block the tumor cancer cell's ability to metabolize glucose. When starved of their energy supply and structure are disrupted. Then the cancer cells have less resistance to immune system attack. <u>This is why it is paramount to starve the</u> cancer cells and enhance the immune system. Also recent evidence reveals that our Endocannabinoid System (E.C.S.) <u>needs marijuana</u> T.H.C.-C.B.D. To <u>block sugar to the cancer cell that can kill and destroy the cancer cells</u>. Also certain therapies can control the cancer cell through nerve instruction. Microwaves can transmit normal neural intelligence to the cancer cells. It is also well known that certain viruses, bacteria, fungi are associated with tumor production, and growth. And again it is this that explains why cancer is a world-wide disease found every where across all countries borders. From Africa, Middle East, Mexico, Russia, China, and to the United States. Note! These cancer causing, destructive microbes are damaged, killed by 915 MHz microwave frequency energy, and when the Fahrenheit (F.) temperature reaches the cancer cells bio-critical temperature of 42 (C) degrees centigrade. Hyperthermia is a very effective cancer treatment.

There are also certain immune system (vaccines) modulator blueprints that have improved. The autogenous, hetrogenous vaccines, used to stimulate a cancer patients immune system, and kill the cancer cells. Medical Doctors: Virginia Livingston, Harvey Bigelesen, von Brehmer, Coley, Issels, Contreas, Alseben, and Enderlein have produced these anti-cancer vaccines being used mainly in Mexico. They are not F.D.A. approved. The Tri-Vac Modulator Blueprints, L.A.K. cells, stem cells, cytokines, anteoplastives, and Kombucha Fungus Tea. Hevleferon and pre-probiotics are believed to lead the field in cancer immunology. Certain genes, viruses, bacteria, fungus, negative intestinal tract bacteria flora, a blood pH over 7.56 are the main causes(s) of cancer, and are being currently researched. There are nearly a million new cases of cancer in the U.S. In the U.S. approximately one million people die of cancer each year even with all the available conventional oncology traditional therapy. The fact is that chemotherapy, radiation, internal cancer surgery kill you, and not the cancer in most cases. Cancer is the second leading cause of death in young people. Many causative destructive disease agents have been here over the millennium of time, yet mankind has survived, because of his immune system, and modern hygiene. When the immune system is competent it can destroy any newly developing cancer cells before they develop and grow into tumors. Preventing cancer cells from proliferating can be accomplished by taking daily Kombucha fungus tea which will keep the blood pH below 7.56 pH. Also taking R.S.O.- T.H.C.-C.B.D., Tree of Life, or black cannabis. An <u>incompetent immune system cannot</u> destroy cancer cells, viruses, bacteria, and fungi. This allows then to flourish and further undermine the body's resistance to all diseases. Note! Go to pages 462-466 in The 13 Steps From Illness To Health-APNBMPDR to learn how to highly, quickly regenerate, power, and enhance your immune system quickly. See pages 144-192 herein. Bio-energetics (radionics) and Microwave Modulated Hyperthermia. Microwaves are in the electromagnetic spectrum and can be dangerous only at lower frequency levels. Medical microwave frequencies for the most part are healing and less destructive. Since they are focused and non scattered to certain body areas. They deliver 915 MHz frequency beam into the cancer tumor. The tissue is heated up to 42 degrees Centigrade. Neural frequencies instructions are then transmitted into the tumor. These injure the tumor, the body can safely dissolve, and eliminate the toxins. This allows for slow and gradual tumor destruction so the body can detoxify and eliminate toxins at its own speed without overwhelming itself. The microwave antenna transmits a beam of sufficient diameter to have coverage of the tumor entirely. If greater areas need to be treated then two antennas are used to to have coverage of the tumor sites. There are two theories. One is that the frequencies generated are more important than the heat generated. The other is that the heat generated is more important. I believe they are both equally important. As you can't have one without the other. It is also known that that immune system enhancement is available no matter where the microwave beam is applied. Microwave therapy is beneficial by itself, but can be used in conjunction with other non traditional therapies, and natural herbal medicines such as marijuana R.S.O.-16% T.H.C.-C.B.D. full extract cannabis essential oil, or Tree of Life, etc. Hyperthermia is now being used to treat rectal-colon, vaginal, breast, lung, and prostate cancers. It can also be used for enlarged prostate problems. This according to a Mayo Clinic of a study performed of sixty (60) patients in May of 1992.

Recently in Canada and Mexico doctors have been treating prostate cancer with H.I.F.U. Or a high intensity ultra frequency device similar to Dr. Royal Rife's frequency generator that converts high frequency sound into heat which destroys the cancer cells. Only the cancer cells become affected and ultimately destroyed. This treatment is relatively new and is being current researched in the U.S. It is a form of hyperthermia treatment.

There are now many alternative clinics in both the U.S., Canada, Europe, and Mexico. They have a wide range of clinical evidence to support non traditional alternative holistic cancer treatment and natural medicines. One such clinic was shut down by the F.D.A. in Mexico. Hospital Santa Monica in Mexico was raided by the U.S. F.D.A. and closed because it used a pulse modulated microwave hyperthermia treatment. The Al-Don method was developed by Dr. Rudolph Alseben, M.D. in conjunction with Cheng Laboratories. The therapy which kills or damages cancer cells without damaging normal tissues. The tumor tissue is exposed with a 915 MHz frequency wave forms and this heats the tumor tissue to cancer cell critical temperatures. This is micro-transmission of neural healing encoded instructions to assist in tumor regression.

This method of controlled P.M. Microwave exposure of a cancerous tumor is effective in not only destroying the tumor mass, but in preventing the cancer cell's ability to survive, resist the immune system, and obtain nourishment. The hyperthermia heats the tumor or cancer cells to their bio-critical level. When at this temperature the cancer cell will become dysfunctional. Before I go any further I will explain how cancer cells develop, obtain nourishment, reproduce, resist immune system attack, chemotherapy, and radiation, etc. Cancer cells develop in four stages and thereafter begin to proliferate. Cancer cells develop when a polymorphic blood invisible to the naked eye microorganism go through the four stages: 1. bacteria 2. virus 3. fungus 4. cancer cell. It is called an Endobiont that I call the Psora. It metastasizes and which is present in the blood of all mammals. Note! For further detailed information see the book "Tea Fungus Kombucha the Natural Remedy and its Significance in Cases of Cancer and other Metabolic Diseases by Rosina Fasching the research and findings from the cancer case studies of Dr. Rudolph Skelnar, M.D. in Germany. The history of the discovery of the Endobiont the cancer cell microbe. It has been known and researched by many biologists, medical researchers for hundreds of years, and are given in this aforementioned book. This is the basis of the surveillance theory of cancer. It states that the "Endobiont" is in the blood of all mammals and remains dormant except and until the blood pH rises above 7.56 pH. This has been researched extensively and concluded as fact by Dr. Rudolph Skelnar, M.D. et al. Also see on pages 179-181.

Cancer Gene Theory.

The gene theory has been recently discovered and it indicates that people with a damaged gene that is genetically passed on through birth that can cause certain skin cancer (melanoma). A cancer cell can then be from different causes as the research indicates, but ultimately is linked to the blood microbe, the blood, the body pH over 7.56 pH, influenced by bio-accumulation toxicity called carcinogenic initiators, biofield cellular interference frequency, radiation-E.M.F.'s, a depressed immune system, stress, metabolic intestinal negative bacteria flora, and negative thinking as well.

When normal cells reproduce they replicate themselves in a duplicating process that should allow them to be the same as the previous cell. This is the genetic code the normal neural inlligence, of R.N.A., the chromosome information transcribed, and passed on into the D.N.A. When toxins or genetic defects occur "metzymes" are produced and formed which are defective genes. This alters the newly formed cell, causes deficiencies, and this is what becomes an abnormal cell. This cell then multiplies itself into further abnormal cells. This is the description of a cancer cell, a weak mutated cell that is abnormal, and is an anaerobic cell.

Negative Thoughts and Thinking Compromise Your Immune System.

The immune system is compromised through your mind with negative emotions, intestinal negative bacteria flora, stress, cellular, lipid toxins, and a toxic colon, etc. It can no longer destroy the weak anaerobic cancer cells. The cancer cells grow into clusters we call tumors which protect themselves from the immune system defenses. Chemotherapy and radiation completely destroy all of your immune system so there are no further defenses whatsoever. Keep in mind that your mind plays a very important role if healing from any disease including cancer. The mind is capable of enhancing your immune system responses against any illness. Numerous scientific studies support this fact. See pages 263,268

Calcium a Mineral, Vitamin D3, MK-7-Vit.-K2, and Cancer.

Calcium and Vitamin D3. Research indicates that in areas of the U.S. where there is at least sunlight on a yearly basis as compared to areas where there is less sunlight is directional proportional to the amount of certain cancers. City's such as N.Y.C., Chicago, Boston, Philadelphia, Pittsburgh, and Cleveland. They have the highest rates of breast cancer, and intestinal cancers. They have low annual sunlight. Conversely, the city's of San Joaquin Valley in California, Tuscon, Phoenix, Albuquerque, El Paso, Miami, Jacksonville, Tampa, and Orlando. These urban cities have the highest daily sunlight, the lowest breast, and intestinal cancer rates.

But it is not so much the Vitamin D3, but rather the Calcium related to decreased cancer rates. But the Vitamin D3 is extremely important in allowing adequate Calcium to be available and assimilated by the body. Also needed is MK-7-Vit.-K2 and the trace element Boron. Calcium makes up our bones and teeth. Only a small percentage amount around one percent (1%) of the total Calcium is found in the blood stream. This one percent (1%) us extremely important. Calcium is readily absorbed by the intestine when Vitamin D3 is present along with the trace element Boron. When the blood level drops, then extra Vitamin D3 is mobilized by the kidneys, and sent to the intestinal tract wall where it will attract more Calcium into the blood. If inadequate amounts of Vitamin D3 (sunshine) are unavailable then the para thyroid gland sends hormonal messages to the bones and teeth to release Calcium for the blood.

The importance of the blood level of Calcium involves the cell. Each cell uses Calcium as a messenger. With no messenger the cell cannot work well and will behave detrimentally. The rest of the extra-cellular fluid at a ratio of 10,000:1, with the one (1) being inside the cell. This ratio is so critical that even a minuscule of the internal cell level of Calcium will result in large changes of abnormal cell division, abnormal movement of the cell, and extra excitability of the cell. The bones contain over

1,000,000 mg. of Calcium; the blood only contains 200-400 mg. An excess of Calcium in the blood is just as serious as if there is a deficiency. When normal Calcium levels are reached the excess is deposited in the soft tissues, linings of the arteries, the brain tissues, and cells. Rx: K2-MK-7 non GMO and Vit D3 olive oil base.

Therefore a slight high blood Calcium level can result in serious problems due to the excess Calcium in the cell. A normal cell does not constantly divide because the communication with cells immediately adjacent. The communicator is Calcium which is in heavy concentration falls or the intracellular Calcium levels rise three (3) conditions occur: 1. Abnormal movement that causes hand and foot cramps . 2. Hyper excitability that cause muscular tremors, fibrillation, and a rapid heart beat. 3. Cell division without Calcium balance that can cause a communication breakdown results in rapid cell division. First the cells are benign and are rapidly destroyed by the immune system or may cause hyperplasia that is extra cell growth. If not destroyed by immune system factors then these cells may expand themselves to a certain size, encapsulate, and remain as a benign tumor. If the divided cells are invaded by any type of toxic carcinogens such as a virus, chemical toxins, radiation, etc., and which may then may distort the D.N.A. These are called iniators. Thereafter, an abnormal cell will be formed, which can be malignant cancer cells, and tumors.

To summarize, Calcium is mostly stored in the bones but a small amount and a very important amount found in the blood. The minute amount of Calcium (approximately 200 mg.) is responsible for the control of most all of the muscular action in the body. It controls heart function and is involved in all the important cell communication network. When it falls due to an inadequate amount of Calcium intake from food or lack of Vitamin D3, MK-7-Vit.-K2 and the trace element Boron two (2) orderly reactions occur.

1. Vitamin D3 is sent to facilitate Calcium absorption from the intestine. If this does not quickly yield the Calcium then. 2. The parathyroids secrete a hormone which leaches Calcium from the bones and teeth. An erroneous concept is that when one has normal blood Calcium levels that one has enough Calcium is wrong. The body will always attempt to keep the Calcium levels in the blood at the expense of the bones and teeth, etc. Another misconception is that Calcium deposits in the blood vessels exhibited as kidney

stones indicate an excess of Calcium. The opposite is actually true. The kidney stones signal a lack of Calcium and or Vitamin D3 with excess parathyroid activity that is releasing more Calcium from the bones than is necessary. This is the cause of osteoporosis and could cause sclerosis. There is also no danger in taking to much Calcium. There is also no danger in getting sunlight and Vitamin D3 prevents us from getting cancer. Some daily sunlight after three (3) P.M. is suggested daily. The best natural Calcium sources are: Kale, Carrots, California Figs, Rice Milk, and Calcium supplements from vegetable sources. Advised is Dr. Pinkus: Cal-Mag. Oyster shell and Coral Calcium are not easily assimilated as they are Calcium Carbonates. There are many false claims, hype from television infomercials by Dr. Robert Barefoot in the book Coral Calcium by Dr. Robert Barefoot, and Carl Reich. No proof claims that it heals cancer and gives longevity, etc. The claim points out a Japanese Okinawan man who is over one hundred (100) years old and has taken Coral Calcium over his lifetime. I believe there are many other more important factors that are more explainable for his long life such as: a non stress life style, clean air, water, a diet of sea vegetables, brown rice, mainly a vegan-vegetarian diet, non chemically treated contaminated foods, powerful immune system, and his genes.

A renowned world expert on Calcium from Japan disputes the claims made by Doctors Barefoot and Reich. Dr. Takuo Fujita, M.D. a world expert on Calcium that has performed fifty (50) years of research on Calcium including four hundred (400) scientific papers on the subject. He claims that Coral Calcium is not the panacea as claimed. He claims there are much better sources of Calcium than Coral Carbonate.

His research can be seen @ www.publishedresearch.com or at www.pub.med.com. Another good product that is recommended is Cal-Advantage. Another factor to be considered is that you should take Calcium in a ratio of 4:1 with Magnesium. Potassium, Vitamin D3, MK-7-Vit.-K-2, Boron to balance and make the Calcium readily assimilated, and distributed properly. I advise ionic minerals in the right proportions such as goEnergetix's.com-Spectramin, Life Supports-Hydroxygen Plus that contains ionic minerals, enzymes, and amino acids, Celtic Sea Salt, and Life Leaders-Ionic Minerals. For Cal-Mag Plus, or Cal-Mag 100, or Cal-Mag Zinc go to amazon.com For the highly recommended Physiologics.com balanced Calsorb, or

Osteologic 2000, Osteo Pro, Physio Soy all are excellent products sold to alternative physicians, and practitioners. The Physiologic Calcium products also contain a balance of Calcium, Magnesium, Phosphorous, Vitamin D3-olive oil base non G.M.O., Vitamin K2-MK-7-non G.M.O., Zinc, Boron, and Silica. Again, do not believe the hype, on T.V advertisements, and infomercials for health magic bullet products. Most are pure hype and pseudo science based. Do careful research as most are just attempting to sell you products that are not genuine nor do they meet the promises made.

Nontraditional Anti-Cancer 48 Remedies Include the Following:
1. Thymus extract. To stimulate the thymus gland which is part of the immune system and provides immune system function. Also recommended is Light Photon Liquid Needle's "Original"E-116 to topically apply to the thymus point. Thymus extract from disease free cattle from New Zealand and are protomorphogens which are freeze dried ground glands such as thymus, etc. See also Goenergetix's.com-Core Lapacho Blend. Liquid Needle's-Brown-B-111-EX, Original-E-116-EX and END, an H.B.H. series phytotanical.
2. Mushrooms. Shitake, Maitake, Ganoderma-Lucidium, Reishi, Moer, Coriolus, Cordyceps, and Chaga, etc. The herbs of Schizandra and Astragalus. These are immune system stimulators and enhance the immune system. Goenergetix's.com.com sells Core Mycelia Blend and Physiologics.com sells Immunene for immune system enhancement.
3. Ozone 03, Oxygen 02, H ions. these both kill cancer cells on contact. Purchase an ozone air, water, and oil A2Z ozone generator from Amazon.com also recommended as is Hydroxygen Plus, OxyMoxy, and Dynamo2 from Engardehealth.com. Cancer cells are anaerobic cells and normal cells are aerobic. Various studies have shown that when high amounts of oxygen (02) or ozone (03) are introduced into the cellular environment they kill cancer cells on contact. For intestinal tract, and colon use a product Colo2Zone from Engardehealth.com for a gentle 02 cleansing of the intestines, and colon. Uses Magnesium Oxide and releases a gentle cleansing with it used with Vitamin C intake. Also a "Turapur" Hydrogen ion water maker and filtering system. A super antioxidant. 1-866-444-1501
4. Graviola. Also called (annona muricata or soursop). An Amazon tree leaf, fruit that has been researched, and is reported in several studies to kill cancer cells. It is reported to be 10,000 times more powerful than chemotherapy and does not harm healthy normal cells. It is non toxic and only goes after and kills only cancer cells. Sold by many health companies but I recommend the

Amazon Herb Company.com in Juniper, Florida and their formula containing graviola called Gravizon that contains many other detoxifying and synergistic herbs that work in conjunction with the graviola. See on pages 284-285 for more detailed information.

5. <u>Hydrazine Sulfate</u>. Through the discovery of Dr. Otto Warburg, Nobel Prize in 1931 for the discovery of the difference between a normal healthy cell and a cancer cell. One cell required energy production and oxygen and the other cell did not. Cancer cells live on sugar glucose and are anaerobic in nature. These cells do require little to no oxygen. Normal cells require oxygen for respiration and function. The use of Hydrazine Sulfate is used to starve the cancer cell.

6. <u>Riviverine</u>. A Mexican manufactured herbal remedy used for its anti-cancer properties, immune system stimulator, and is used to treat cancer. Believed to contain a powdered version of Chondriana. Germanium Sesquioxide GE-132. ARG, Jarrow, Amazon.com

7. <u>Chondriana</u>. A discovery of Nobel Prize winner Dr. George Merykl, Ph.D. The chondriana were extracted from ancient rocks using Dr. Merkyl's cold fusion extraction. They are our ancient primitive T-Killer cells. They kill the cancer cells and tumors by attacking their roots and eating them thereafter. Dr. Merkyl's study's show them actually attacking and killing the cancer cell roots, thereafter it produced phagocytes that began eating the dead cancer cells, and them producing useable D.N.A. The chondriana is injected or orally administered into the person and would in a short time completely renew and revitalize the immune system. Once in the immune system it immediately goes after cancer cells and any other foreign invaders. To order the video on Dr. Merkyl's cold fusion experiment of the extraction from ancient rocks our primitive T-killer cells which are the ancient mitochondria. You can see the Dr. Merkyl's discovered mitochondria the primitive T-Killer cell called chondriana in action filmed under a microscope. A short video that you can order from 21stCenturyEnergetics.com

8. <u>Carnavora</u>. An extract from the Venus Fly Trap plant. It is used by Dr. Hans Nipper, M.D. of Germany. Dr. Nipper claims it kills cancer cells. It must be taken all your life.

9. <u>Colloidal Gold</u>. The high frequency of gold in colloidal form 10-60 p.p.m. is used to trap the cancer cells. Then use colloidal silver 1100 p.p.m. High frequencies (915 MHz) are anti-cancer and kill the weak cancer cells. This was exhibited and successful with the Rife frequency generator that emitted ultra high frequencies

and killed cancer cells. Colloidal Silver also has this ability. Use both gold first and then the silver. Atlantean Alchemy.com

10. Can Kill 1. A new anti-cancer prostate, ovarian, rectal-colon cancer formula based on the research, the case study findings of Dr. Terry Friedmann, M.D. Now using 7 main essential oils, and a carrier oil. 21StCenturyEnergetics.com to order. 2 oz. $50.00

11. Hemo-Pure. A blood purification alkaline purification formula. It is anti-cancer. It has been known for years that employees that worked for the C.N.R. Sugar processing company in Crockett, California where they process sugar cane into molasses and refined white sugar daily. It was noticed they had a very low if any cancer with the employees. It was discovered that employees at the plant that sipped molasses during the day had no cancer. It was discovered that the ingredient in the molasses that may be preventing cancer is potash. This one of the many ingredients in Hemo-Pure. Clean and purified blood with an alkaline pH below 7.56 pH will prevent cancer cells from proliferating. Non sulfured Black Strap Molasses is a detoxifier. Aids liver detoxifying.

12. Vita Flax. From Biosan a company in Arizona produces it. This is from the research of Dr. Johanna Budwig, M.D. one of the world's premier cancer researchers. She discovered that flax seed oil omega-3 becomes water soluble when mixed with a sulfured protein like cottage cheese or yogurt. This mixture causes the the oil to become highly assimilated into the body and even getting into the smallest blood capillaries. Dr. Budwig has had remarkable success with her research on cancer patients. So no matter what form of flax seed or oil you take it should always be combined with sulfured amino acids a protein containing food. If taking capsules of flax seed then eat some sulfur protein like cottage cheese, etc. Vit-Flax by Biosan contains organic flax seed and sulfur-containing protein in equal amounts for greater activity. Note! I use 4 Tsp. of organic flax seed oil or meal to 1 Tbsp. of sulfured amino acids. Advised: Bragg high sulfur amino acids.

13. Can-Cell-Kill. A researched remedy containing chondriana. Not F.D.A approved. The original remedy was outlawed and made by a researcher in Michigan. The second Can-Kill remedy was Dr. Terry Freidmann, M.D. His formula of four essential oils has healed many cancers. I added three (3) more essential oils to a new formula now called Can Kill-1. See on page 205 To order 2 oz. $50.00

14. Liquid Needle's Bath Soak detoxification Can-133 or 12-Can Shock. For detoxification of chemo chemicals, radiation, turns pre cancerous cells back to normal cells eliminates carcinogens, free

radicals, enhance T-Killer cells, and immune system. Go to D.N.R., Inc.com IN. 1-800-886-6222 or 1-317-543-4886 Dr. Ken Widgery, N.D.
15. <u>Interferon and Interleukin</u>. When a cell is infected with a virus it manufactures and secretes chemical messages that signal neighboring cells as how to defend themselves. These are called interferon's. Licorice an herb produces interferon. Colostrum 1-IGH contains interferon and interleukin. Go to Luckyvitamins.com
16. <u>Germanium Sesquioxide</u>. GE-132. It contains interferon compounds. Interferons can inhibit the growth of cancer cells. GoEnergetix's Core Mycelia Blend. Physiologics.com manufactures Immunene product. Germanium is a substance from Shitake mushrooms, aloe Vera, ginseng, and garlic. These plants (herbs and foods) are rich in Germanium that is an adjunct used in the treatment of cancer. Also a product formulated by goEnergetixs.com called Galt Immune. It contains pre digested amino acids and cytokines-T.N.F. probiotics needed for metabolic treatment of cancer (tumors). Also licorice, echinacea, cats claw, and astragalus.
17. <u>Flutamide</u>. Dr. LaBrie initiated the use of Flutamide in the treatment of prostate cancer and its metastatic after-effects with some extremely dramatic results.
18. <u>Beta Carotene and Vitamin A</u>. Recent university studies have indicated that dosages as high as 600,000 I.U. Are non toxic. Vitamin A with Beta Carotene activity are absolutely essential for the production of natural body made antibodies against cancer cells made by the Thymus gland. The Thymus is stimulated by Vitamin A with Beta Carotene activity and by Liquid Needle Original E-116 topical placed upon the thymus gland.
19. <u>Carbatine</u>. This therapy was developed by Dr. Demopoulas of Greece. It is based on the healing affect of urine on certain conditions. It appears that liver and bone cancers respond very well with the addition of carbatine to the treatment protocols. Carbatine contains urea and creatine hydrate both of which have been shown to have anti-cancer properties. Tumor matrix destruction by the use of hydrophobic breakers. A preliminary report, Clinical Oncology 1977,3,319-320 Malignant cells are known to consist of aggregations of cancer cells, the surfaces of which are rich in glycoprotein, and other macro-molecular surface active agents. The cancer cells are embedded in hydrophobic sites, surfactants form a highly structured matrix containing immobilized water, and electrolytes in which cancer cells are embedded. This matrix is disrupted by the ingredients of carbatine which leads to

interference with metabolic exchanges and replication processes necessary for on going uncontrolled abnormal cancer cell growth.

20. Oxygen-02. EnGardehealth.com OxyMoxy, Dynamo2, Colo2Zone, Life Supports-Hydroxygen Plus, and all other stabilized oxygen products. Certain research performed by Saske, Wakutani, Oda, and Yamasaki from the Tomari University School of Medicine, explores the fact that the therapeutic effect of radiation, and chemotherapy is enhanced by oxygen tension in the cell is increased. Institute Santa Monica when it was operating stated, "that the use of intravenous hydrogen peroxide infusions on fifteen maxillary cancer cases, eight (8) of the cases showed a complete disappearance of the tumors, six (6) cases demonstrated a partial reduction, and only one (1) had little change." In an oxygen rich cellular environment cancer cells are less virulent and are destroyed by the presence of oxygen. Hydrogen Peroxide infused (intravenous) or taken orally has the ability to increase the oxygen content of the blood. Hydroxygen Plus one of the aforementioned oxygen ionic products has the ability to increase the body's oxygen content four (4) times higher. A oxygen product called Life Leaders Oxygen Boost also highly increases the body's oxygen content but remains alkaline. The most cost effective are EnGardehealth.com oxygen products OxyMoxy, Dynamo2, Colo2zone for colon gentle detoxification, and cleansing using Magnesium oxide released into the colon by taking Vitamin C. OxyMoxy @amazon.com

21. Clondronate. Used for bone cancer to eliminate pain. It is side effect free, extremely effective in altering the outflow of Calcium, and prevents further metastasis.

22. Live Cell Therapy. This is where dying cells D.N.A. or "Code of Life" is imprinted in the D.N.A. When a cell dies it transfers this D.N.A. information an exact replica to the newly born cell. Certain toxins called metzymes weaken this D.N.A. Information passed on to the newly born cell. This will produce premature aging and cell dysfunction. It is called a "metzyme" which is an altered cell. The use of extracted D.N.A. From new born animal organs such as sheep are used because of the virgin immune system that has not had a chance to develop antibodies against all dangers; so the extract do not become antigens to elicit allergic reactions. When this extract "vaccine" is injected it acts as a natural stimulant to one's own individual D.N.A. A thirteen (13) organ and gland extract is indicated to overcome illnesses from weak D.N.A. Caused by metzymes. Note! The Hospital Santa Monica and the Issels Clinic for use of their L.A.K., Stem cell,

cytokines were both raided by the U.S.F.D.A., and closed down. They worked to well. By the way why is the U.S.F.D.A. is going into a foreign country Mexico and raiding a cancer clinic? Just whom are they protecting? The answer is the cancer chemotherapy $126 billion dollar industry.

23. <u>Micro Dose Chemotherapy</u>. The problem with large dose chemotherapy as it is implemented is that it not only kills the cancer cells, but also kills normal cells, and destroys the immune system. Using micro-dose chemotherapy is much more effective with little to no side effects. And afterward by using the cutting edge light photon frequency energetic detoxifying solutions as in #24.

24. <u>Liquid Needle's Can-133</u>. or (Can-12 Shock) Which will eliminate the harmful side effects caused by the chemotherapy. It eliminates radiation, carcinogens, chemo chemicals, toxins, enhances T-Killer cells, your immune system, and can turn pre cancerous cells back to normal. D.N.R., Inc.com IN. 1-800-886-6222

25. <u>Cyro Freezing</u>. A new method of cyrogenic therapy where the cancer cells are frozen to kill them. It is a non evasive method of tumor killing and removal. Call: 1-888-PYC-CRYO for further information.

26. <u>Shark Cartilage and Liver Extract</u>. The Shark liver extract was used in Sweden with cancer leukemia patients. There is some evidence that indicates it is effective and in other cancers as well. The researchers state that sharks do not get cancer. From this it was discovered that sharks do not have bones but only cartilage. Shark cartilage was discovered to inhibit the formation of new blood vessels which cancer cells need to grow. Physiologics, Inc.com sells a deodorized shark cartilage product.

27. <u>Visualization, Guided Imagery, E.E.G., and Hypnosis</u>. These have been used with success in treating cancer patients by O. Carl Siminton, M.D. at his Texas Clinic, Jerome Plotnick, Ph.D., N.D. At 21st Century Energetics in Lake of the Woods, California, Dr. Janet Harnicky, Ph.D. at U.C.L.A. Cancer Medical Center in Westwood, California, David Bressler, Ph.D. At the Bressler Center in Westwood, California references that validate this are in the following books: The 13 Steps From Illness To Health-APNBMPDR on pages: 27-28, 30-35, Meta Your Meditation, Meta Your Mind by Jerome Plotnick, Ph.D., N.D. Imagery in Healing-Shamanism by Jeanne Achterberg, Ph.D., Healing With the Mind's Eye by Dr. Michael Samuels, M.D. et al. Also see pages: 268-271

28. <u>Bio-energetics, Magnetics, Radionics, and Liquid Needle's Frequency Light Photons</u>. There have been many studies performed by

U.S., European and Russian researchers with the use of microwave-frequencies generated by bio-magnetic frequency generators that have the ability to destroy abnormal cancer cells and harmful organisms depending on the frequency used. Dr. Royal Rife's frequency generator or the after market version named John Cranes, Square Wave frequency generator. See the books: Body Electric, Cross Currents by Dr. Robert O. Becker, M.D., and other research conducted by Dr. Royal Rife, M.D. contained in the book The 13 Steps From Illness To Health-APNBMPDR by Jerome Plotnick, Ph.D., N.D on pages: 664-679. The research by Dr. Wilhelm Reich, M.D. and his books on orgone energy. Also the forgotten, but most important Nikola Tesla, his many experiments, and research. Mostly hidden by the power companies. Also Tanio Technologies and Etherium Co. Recently there is also much research, evidence of life force light photon frequencies imprinted by a frequency generator upon ionized mineral water crystals called Liquid Needle, Liquid Signals from a company called Developmental Natural Resources, Inc., or D.N.R., Inc. in Indianapolis, Indiana that formulates light photon solutions. Go to pages: 208-210, 240, 287-30, dnrsite.com, or D.N.R., Inc.com in Indianapolis, IN. by Dr. Ken Widgery, N.D. and his father Arthur Widgery for a complete products list also listed in The 13 Steps From Illness To Health-APNBMPDR book on pages: 64-74, 406-431. The Liquid Needle light photon bioactive frequencies help counter toxicity and eliminate toxins by helping the body's bio-field re-balance itself. It also counters adverse negative frequencies from the toxic bio-accumulation in the body's bio-field. These are the energetic frequencies called "foci" emitted by physical toxins. There are many different enactments or various applications used in light photon frequency solutions. It can be used to supply a person with the frequencies received from foods and herbs, or balance the brain waves, or promote a normal balanced organ and gland, or to assist the body in elimination of toxins, or heal bio-field energy keloid and scars that interfere with the bio-field, re-balance the entire acupuncture system in under one (1-2) minutes with no needles, or re-balance the eleven (11) major glands, and chakras in one-two (1-2) minutes use L.N. Original, detoxify water, food and herbs in five (5) minutes, provide energy-balance-vitality, detoxify your entire body in a series of five (5) bath soaks using only your skin (derma) as the elimination organ, or actually put you in a state of meditation, etc. Cancer patients who have had chemotherapy and radiation can use CAN-133 bath soak to completely detoxify and eliminate all radiation, carcinogens, chemo chemicals, other chemical toxins, enhance T-Killer cells cancer fighters, and the immune system function. See pages: 64-74, 406, 407,415,419,421-428, and 431 in The 13 Steps From Illness To Health-APNBMPDR book. Dr. Ken Widgery, N.D., C.E.O., D.N.R., Inc., Indianapolis, Indiana.

29. Oncotox. It contains an ortho-para-toulene-sul-fonamide compound with the organic formula: C9H1302NS. Oncotox is a non toxic at therapeutic doses has specific and measurable cancer killing, growth inhibitor effects both on IM, and oral routes. Mallory Institute of Pathology, Boston School of Medicine, states that Oncotox has been shown to enhance both B, T-Killer cells responses to mitogens, and enhance natural killer T-cell activity.

30. Hyperthermia. Pulse Modulated Micro Wave. Researched by Cheng laboratory, the Hospital Santa Monica, and Al-Don Medical research Institute. Dr. Rudolph Alseben, M.D. states it kills and damages cancer cells, starves cancer cells, and helps poison cancer cells without damaging normal tissues. The P.M. Microwave Hyperthermia there are three (3) dynamic therapeutic benefits possible: 1. Exposure of tumor tissue to 915 MHz ultra high frequency and wave forms; 2. thermal heating of tumor tissue to cancer cell bio-critical temperature; 3. Micro-transmission of neural-healing encoded signals giving specific instructions to assist in tumor regression. And as stated previously was raided in Mexico by the U.S.F.D.A. and shut down. The reason is obvious it works to well and was cutting into the cancer oncology industry's profits. The F.D.A. calls it unproven science. As if chemotherapy and radiation are proven science. There not. It is not proven except for quickening ones death from it.

31. Isoflavones. Haelan 851 and 951 is a fermented soy beverage with nitrogen in it. Researched in China at at the Beijing Hospital, in the U.S. by many doctors including Dr. Edleson, M.D. preventive, and toxicologist in Atlanta, Georgia. It contains: genestein, daidzein, nitrogen, and proven as highly anti-cancer in its properties. See U.S. Research Reports, Inc. P.O. Box 931104, Norcross Gerogia. 30093 the booklet contains various studies on the effects of soy bean phytochemicals and in particular Haelan-851. Also see the video "Therapeutics of Phytochemicals of Soybean" Lecture: by Walter Wainright, May 20, 1993. Write or call U.S. Research Reports, Inc. for a booklet or video. A collection of international research demonstrating the value of using the Biological Response Modifier capabilities of soy bean phytochemicals as an adjunct nutritional program to eliminate

protein calorie malnutrition, to support, extend, improve the quality of life for patients with cancer, cachexia, leukemia, H.I.V., (A.I.D.S.), and other chronic diseases. By the inducement of non toxic immune stimulation, anti-angiogenesis, and anti-viral serum conditions that are beneficial. Haelanhealth.com or at Lotstolivefor.com

32. Kombucha Fungus Tea. Researched in Germany by Dr. Rudolph Skelnar, M.D. Bergold, et al. It increases the alkalinity pH of the blood, it keeps the polymorphic microbe cancer cells dormant, and inactive below a 7.56 blood pH. from proliferating. It also helps balance the intestinal good flora, thereby increasing the immune system function, and is highly anti-cancer. For further information see the book Tea Fungus Kombucha the Natural Remedy and its Significance in Cases of Cancer and other Metabolic Diseases by Rosina Fasching from the research and findings of Dr. Skelnar, M.D. in Germany. Rx: Pronatura 555 mg. Kombucha caps.

33. IP6 and Inositol. Based upon the research and findings of Dr. AbulKalum M. Shamsuddin, M.D., Ph.D. See the book "Nature's Revolutionary Cancer Fighter by Dr. Shamsuddin, M.D. Also on various cancer case studies by various cancer researchers confirm its effectiveness. Puritan.com or Amazon.com or Luckyvitamins.com

34. Bovine Colostrum 1-IGH. It is found to stimulate and enhance the immune system. Case studies from all over the U.S. by M.D.'s, D.C.'s, N.D.'s confirm its effective use to power the immune system, and fight off disease. I recommend NOW foods brand Super Colostrum 500 mg. 90 vegetable capsules. LuckyVitamins.com

35. Cesium Chloride. The basic mechanism was outlined by Nobel Laureate Winner, Dr. Otto Warburg in 1931. He indicated that if the normal cell is disturbed by radiation or a carcinogen, then a free radical change takes place in the cell. This change prevents oxygen from entering the cell but glucose enters freely. This causes lactic acid to be formed in the cell. This causes an acid medium in the D.N.A. of the cell and this allows uninhibited reproduction of the cell. In other words an abnormal cell, a cancer cell. Dr. Keith Brewer, M.D. proposed that the use of cesium or rubidium would alter the pH of the cell without being toxic to normal cells and called his theory, "High pH Therapy for Cancer." Research from Texas University found that the use of cesium is most effective in the suppression and regression of a cancer called sarcoma. Dr. Hans Nipper, M.D. in Germany states he is very impressed by the use of cesium and says its the treatment of choice in any kind of tumor, particularly bronchogenic,

carcinoma with bone metastasis. American University of Washington, D.C., indicated that tumors treated with cesium weighed less than 9% than those tumors in animals not treated with cesium. The University of Wisconsin found a 97% suppression of colon cancer was achieved by the use of cesium. H.E. Aroti, M.D. found evidence of some shrinkage in tumor size in all cases in a study with human patients with cancer. He also reported pain relief.

36. <u>Lycopodium Clavatum</u>. A homeopathic remedy used by the famous Dr. James Taylor Kent, M.D, in the early 1900's. He used it to cure abdominal tumors with great success. See the book "The Complete Book of Homeopathy by Michael Weiner, Ph.D. and Kathleen Goss.

37. <u>Beplureum</u>. Researched by the Japanese to heal liver cancer. See the study in The 13 Steps from Illness To Health-APNBMPDR book on pages: 433-434 by The Institute of Traditional Medicine and Preventive Health-1996. Brion Herbs.com or naturalnutritionals.com

38. <u>Gravizon</u>. From the fruit and leaves of an Amazon tree known as "graviola," "annona muricata," and "soursop." The Brazil version is "paw-paw." Amazon Herb Co.com or net formula with synergistic Amazon herbs, the main herb ingredient is graviola known for its ability to seek out, and kill only the cancer cells. It is 10,000 times more powerful than chemotherapy and is non toxic with no side effects. It also contains Fiberzon a high fiber cleanser, Aquazon from sea plants that boost the immune system function, and increase energy. See on pages 284-286 for more information.

39. <u>Escharotics</u>. The use of American Indian Black Salve-Ointment belong to a group of compounds that are capable of producing a scab when applied to the skin. Used primarily on skin cancers the following sequence of results will occur. <u>1</u>. There will be mass destruction of the cancer cells but not the healthy normal cells. <u>2</u>. Pus will form with a scab forming over the area. <u>3</u>. There will be a sloughing off of the scab leaving a non cancerous cavity. <u>4</u>. This will eventually heal over time, leave a slightly di-pigmented area, and slight scar. The entire process will takes from five (5) to fifteen (15) days. The escharotic herbs usually are made of: sanguinaria (blood-red root), bittersweet, ginger root, galangal, creosote bush, and capsium. Also contains zinc chloride an antimicrobial. Inactive ingredients are any of the following: kerosene, glycerine, lard, metallic cobalt, olive oil, and water. To determine and see if a skin growth is cancerous you simply apply the escharotic salve over the suspected growth. You then observe it over a period of several days. If an "Eschar" (Pus

which scabs over) forms then it is cancer; if it doesn't the growth is benign, or non-malignant. Supportive products such as ozone salve can be applied after use of the escharotic to speed up the healing process. There is also current research on the use of escharotics for internal cancer. The research is presently ongoing and no final results are yet available except for a few cancer patients who have used it and obtained successful results. Note! See Quackwatch.com Dr. Barret, M.D. warnings before using. I don't know whether Dr. Barret's of Quackwatch's opposition or his claims of the damages using escharotic salve are true or not. So until a true factual analysis is determined I would advise using R.S.O. full extract cannabis 16% T.H.C.-.C.B.D. oil, red root salve, and the milkweed plant extract topically on the external cancer site. It should also be used internally. There are no known damages or corrosive substances in R.S.O. 16% T.H.C.-C.B.D. or Tree of Life cannabis oil. According to the sworn testimony of Rick Simpson who used his R.S.O. applied topically to three skin cancers that were eliminated in a few days after he topically applied his oil on them. Note! Quackwatch's Dr. Barret of allopathic medicine attacks all alternative medicine modalities and calls them all quackery. For a rebuttal of Dr. Barret's claims see: allnurses.com/general-nursing-discussion-any success-with-Dr. Budwig Tx for cancer. If you choose to use escharotics proceed carefully. Also use baking soda and castor oil or coconut oil.

40. <u>Chinese Herbs</u>. 7 Forests Chinese Herbal Formula called Paris 7 with Chih-ko and Curcumin has been used successfully with metastatic cancer of the breast, prostate, and melanoma. There are several other 7 Forest anti cancer herbs as well. They are: with tumor mass-Gynostemma Tabs, hard tumor mass-Sparganium 12, lung tumor-Balamcanda 15, breast tumor-Blue Citrus Tabs, and again all metastasized cancer-Paris 7. Chineseherbs: naturalnutritionals.com

41. <u>1-IGH Super Bovine Colostrum</u>. Now Foods contains the following: 1-IGH, olive leaf, astragalus, and larch. It stimulates the immune system, contains 1-IGH, and many natural immune factor enhancers. It is formulated from lactating mother cows and is used for nursing baby cows. It has been thoroughly researched and found to be a powerful immune system enhancer. It is used by many medical doctors, chiropractors, and naturopaths. All report its beneficial medicinal and healing benefits. It also contains interferon and interleukin. Luckyvitamins.com (NOW foods brand).

42. <u>Immune Modulation Therapy</u>. Dark field microscopic time lapse photos of fresh human blood from world experts such as Doctors:

Skelnar and von Brehmer in Germany, Villique in France, Fonti in Italy, Livingston, Coley, and Alseben in the U.S. have repeatedly viewed luminous microorganisms in the blood streams of patients suffering from cancer, and catastrophic diseases. These microorganisms have been isolated, identified, found to be related to various collagen, and tumorous diseases. Many of the previous observations have determined that the organisms exist only in different forms. This was also stated by Dr. Skelnar of Germany in the book by Rosina Fasching "Tea Fungus Kombucha the Natural Remedy and its Significance in Cases of Cancer and other Metabolic Diseases. This polymorphic microbe called the Endobiont which I call the Psora goes through four (4) stages of change and development into cancer cells. Some recent other names for it are: Bacillis Endoparactis, T-bacillis, and Progenitorcea Cryptocides. This organism has been cultured from tissues, bodily fluids of all tumor bearing hosts, both in humans, and mammal animals. The organism is pleomorphic. It is capable of assuming different shapes, forms, and depending on the environment where it lives in your body. It is found in the blood of all mammals of both humans and animals (Vertebrates and some invertebrates) as well. The organism seems to be present in all people world-wide. In some people the organism appears to be very scanty; only a few are observed under the dark field microscopy. Yet other people have and abundance of them that affect the red blood cells by their movement. These were also observed in the past by both doctors Wilhelm Reich, M.D. who called them bions and Dr. Royal Rife, M.D. who called it the BX bacillus. In 1934, Dr. von Brehmer isolated a specific organism from human blood which he called Siphonspora Polymorpha. He believed that this organism could be the very <u>basic cause of all illness</u>. In later years of research it was found that if the acid pH level of the blood became more alkaline, i.e. from 7.56 to 8.00, the organism became identified with tumor growth. This fact is also stated in the book: Tea Kombucha the Natural Remedy and its Significance in cases of Cancer and other Metabolic Diseases. This book is based on Dr. Skelnar's research and his findings. So a miniscule change in the blood's pH over 7.56 toward alkalinity and then the cancer cells metastisis (proliferate) and step one begins. This is why Dr. Skelnar uses Kombucha Fungus tea with a pH of 3.0 because it keeps the blood pH between 7.35-7.45 pH where the cancer microbe polymorphic microorganism remains dormant. This is in line with the surveillance theory of cancer. Dr. von Brehmer's was able to culture the blood from many human tumors as well as the blood with the person with the tumor. The more he investigated, the more places within the body the organism could be found. The organism is highly pleomorpic, capable of changing into mycellia fungal forms, sporangia, and spore forms. The stages of its development are. 1. bacteria form 2. virus form 3. fungal-spore form 4. cancer cell. It has survived extreme heating with temperatures over 1000 F, radiation, laser, and freezing below zero (0) degrees. It cannot be destroyed by these allopathic conventional methods. It is biologic in nature and can only be neutralized and prevented by biological means. It has been found in the mummies of Egypt in spore form. The only proven way to kill, eliminate, and prevent it is biological.

43. <u>Antineoplastons</u>. Dr. Burzynski, M.D, in Texas claims that his neo-plastastivs have a high cure rate. It is extremely expensive from over $100,000 for the first year of intravenous treatment. Most insurance companies will not cover its use. Both the National Cancer Institiute and the Japanese National Cancer Institute have reported that antineoplastons did not work in their studies. It is not F.D.A. approved and it is given now only after conventional treatment has failed as a clinical trial. The active ingredient is A10 and As-2 respectively, both work by inhibiting oncogenes, promoting apoptosis, and activating tumor suppressor genes. Also another factor that allows cancer cells to continmue to grow is the presence of abnormal enzymes, a by-product of D.N.A. methylation. In the presence of these enzymes, the normal life cycle of the cell is disrupted, and they replicate continually. Antineoplastons have been shown in the laboratory to inhibit these enzymes. But recent studies have shown that inhibiting histone deacetylase (HDAC) promotes the activation of tumor suppressor genes p21 and p53. Phenylacetic acid contained in the Antineoplaston AS2-1 mixture has been shown to be a weak H.D.A.C. inibitor. Antineoplaston (ANP) is a group of peptides, derivatives, and mixtures for which Dr. Burzynski claims have anti-cancer activity. These compounds have been administered by Dr. Burzynski, M.D. since 1976. So after considering all the known facts about antineoplastons it is still uncertain to its effectiveness. More research is needed to determine a healing rate from its use and morbidity or life span after antineoplaston treatments. He and the late Dr. Gonzalez his colleague also use nutritional support and herbs in their cancer treatments. Also read "Knockout" by Suzanne Somers a patient of both doctors and her curing her own cancer using natural treatments.

44. <u>Doenzang</u>. Fermented soy bean miso paste from So. Korea. The University of So. Korea indicates that it kills cancer cells as well as it prevents cancer cells. This may be due to the fact that it contains the isoflavones: genistein and daidzein the anti-cancer phyto-chemicals. So. Korean men have the lowest prostate cancer rates in the world. Doenzang is a daily food staple eaten in So Korea. Available @ Amazon.com. <u>Note!</u> <u>Only eat fermented soy</u>.

45. <u>Vaccines</u>. Dr. Harvey Bigelsen, M.D. et al. He uses immune vaccines, other cutting edge cytokines-T.N.F., L.A.K., Stem cells that work in conjunction with the patients immune system. The Biological Institute and the Issels Clinic in Mexico have used these with positive results. For further information: <u>www.drbigelsen.com</u> or call 1-(888)-943-8463. Doctors Skelnar and Alseben have researched these microscopic organisms for many years using dark field microscopy techniques and time lapse motion picture photography that revealed where they came from. Where they go and what they do in the meantime. These both doctors and many others as well have observed a family of nearly sub-microscopic forms of life in the blood of all cancer patients they have seen. They are convinced as well as myself that they are definitely directly associated with many degenerative diseases and especially cancer. These organisms seem to exist in all people, but only gather in force when they need energy that they cannot produce by themselves. If your internal biochemical environment supports their growth such as the alkaline blood pH from over 7.56 to 8.00 pH they will grow at the expense of your life. Therefore a must is to keep the blood pH below 7.56. The best way to accomplish this is with Kombucha Fungus Tea. I highly recommend Pronatura which is Dr. Skelnar's original Kombucha Fungus tea recipe in 555 mg. capsules which is also non alcohol and cost effective for 90 capsules. Pronatura Kombucha is available @ Luckyvitamins.com.

46. <u>Bushwood Tree Berry of Australia's Outback Wilderness</u>. Recently discovered and being researched. After injecting the berry juice into a cancer cell it simply kills it. More research is coming soon.

47. <u>Vitamin B-17</u>. This B vitamin which is known for killing cancer cells comes from a synthetic drug called Laertrile and is currently banned by the F.D.A. Laertrile is not approved by the F.D.A. and is a synthetically prepared drug. Therefore it has to be approved by the F.D.A. Since there has been no definitive phase III clinical trials on Laertrile, it has not been approved by them for sale, and, or use. It was used in the 1970's by doctor

Virginia Livingston, M.D. and she claimed as a great success. Note! apricot kernels can contain up to 3% of Amygdalin which is the natural form of Vit. B-17. You can eat apricot kernels in a powder or raw state without F.D.A. approval. B-17 is in reality not a vitamin as it is claimed as well. It has no vitamin properties. Dr. Contreas, M.D. in Mexico is the world's expert on B-17 states, "unequivocally that he knows of no one who has ever died from eating apricot pips." (seeds) He does not treat cancer patients with B-17 and he is neutral on the yeah or neh of its supposed cancer killing abilities. He claims that apricot pips alone are not a cure for cancer. Another fact is that no one who has been treated for cancer by Laertrile alone and has cured their cancer. Again, the same holds true for eating apricot pips (seeds). I advise eating the low amounts apricot seeds but I am opposed to any man made synthetic drug such as Laertrile.

48. <u>The Dr. Bach Flower Essences</u> "Fields of Flowers" contains all of the thirty eight (38) flower essences @ 30 C power in one bottle. Dr. Edward Bach, M.D. formulated the 38 flower essences from flower petals in the English contry side. These he determined were composed of ultra high frequencies (MHz) that can counteract the spiritual, mind emotional, and mental imbalances (negative frequencies), that he believed were the cause(s) of all physical manifastations of illness. He implemented them with all of his patients with wonderful successful healing results. From this he postulated that all physicial manifeststaions of all illnesses that first takes place in the spirit and mind. Thereafter it enters the physical body, with its symptoms, and physical ailments. I have them, the remedies, the causation he determined as from the unlearned spiritual lessons, the seven deadly sins, and the eleven mental terror states also listed on pages 34-38 in the beginning of this book in Chapter Three (3). The seven (7) deadly sins are: pride, cruelty, hate, self love, ignorance, instability, and greed. The eleven (11) mental terror states are: fear, terror, worry, others welfare, indecision, boredom, doubt, over-concern, weakness, self-distrust, impatience, and over enthusisam. Dr. Bach believed that all physical illness, disease comes from the ills of the heart, and spirit. The body's physical ills are just symptoms. The aforementioned causes called the seven (7) deadly sins, the eleven (11) mental terror states cause the suppression of the immune system, and the life force which subjects us to the invasion of illness. So simply put is heal your spirit, emotions, and then you will be able to heal your physical

body. This is especially important in eliminating cancer and preventing it. This is why I promote "How to Restore Your Health the Treatment and Prevention of Cancer Alternatively and Holistically Using Your Powers of Mind-Body to the Spirit." Heal your Spirit and it will then be able to heal your mind which can than be able to heal your body. Go to pages 256-280 in this book. I use extensively the following remedies along with mind and spiritual meditative exercises listed on the aforementioned pages. I also use extensively Fields of Flowers from goEnergetix's.com and from D.N.R., Inc. Liquid Needle's ExStress oral spray, topically applied Chi Gong, Original, L.N.T.B.-Liquid Needle Total Balance for brainwaves which are highly beneficial for elimination of stress, and Chi Gong for an instant meditative state induced by the captuured frequencies of the Chinese Master Chi Gong practitoner, and instructor in China.

Two Devastating Facts About the Cancer Causing Microbe.

There are two devastating facts about these microscopic life forms. If you can imagine trillions of microscopic cannibals eating away at your cells, bodily fluids, taking from your life force energies, giving you toxic waste by-products that weaken your cells, and their valuable nutrients. These kleptic microbes rob energy from your cells, they are toxic to every cell, and these microbes are capable also of altering our D.N.A.'s instructions-reverse transcriptase's within our tissue cells. When they colonize in the joint membranes the results will be rheumatic arthritis. If they attack the skin the result will be psoriasis, melanoma, or soft tissue sarcoma. If they attack an organ, gland, bone, blood, or lymph we have cancer. (Lymphoma and Leukemia)

More On Cancer Vaccines.

New breakthroughs in immune modulated blueprints can provide:
1. General cancer immune modulator.
2. Specific rheumatoid arthritis immune modulator.
3. Specific psoriasis immune modulator.
4. An autogenous vaccine or the precursor of the aforementioned deadly organisms called Progenitor Cryptocides the cancer related microbe identified by Dr. Livingston et al.
5. Purified antigen for cancer.

<u>What I Recommend Taking Daily as a Necessity for Cancer</u>.

I also highly recommend the following:
Take orally and daily:
1. <u>Kombucha Fungus Tea</u> which can be purchased in liquid or capsules. I use and advise Pronatura which is Dr. Skelnar's original recipe in 555 mg. 90 capsules and is cost effective. You can also make your own Kombucha with a starter kit available from various online stores: KombuchaAmerica.com, CulturesForHealth.com, www.Amazon.com, thrivemarket.com et al. For entire expose on all you want to know about Kombucha Fungus Tea read The 13 Steps From Illness To Health-APNBMPDR on pages 572-576. Dr. Skelnar's Pronatura 555 mg. 90 vege caps @ Luckyvitamins.com or drinkgts.com
2. <u>For Calcium: Kale and California Figs</u> that are high in absorbible calcium known for its anti-cancer properties. Kale also contains beta carotene. Note! Kale is hard to chew so lightly steam or juice it. Add some coconut or extra virgin olive oil and sea salt to season. Also advised is Cal-mag plus & MK-7-K2 and D3.
3. <u>Turmeric</u>. (curcumin) is an herb that provides extremely high anti-oxidant protection from free radicals and is cost effective.
4. <u>Organic Brown, Purple, Red, or Wild Rice</u> Note! Do not buy rice imported from China due to high arsenic levels discovered and plastic in the rice. It is the mainstay that one half of the worlds population that eat it daily. It is a high complex carbohydrate when combined with beans. It provides the body with the twelve (12) amino acids so our bodies can then manufacture the other (10) essential amino acids of the twenty two (22) amino acids for a complete protein. Brown rice also contains 02. Rice is a seed. U.S. white rice is either G.M.O. or factory farmed.
5. <u>Black Strap Non-Sulfured Molasses</u>. Is a blood cleanser and purifier that contains potash known for its anti-cancer. properties. It is made from sugar beets, has a high Chromium, Magnesium content, and we are currently Magnesium deficient in the U.S. Also advised is organic <u>maple syrup</u> an anti-cancer food.
6. <u>Apple Cider Vinegar</u>. Is a fat burning mild acid and a blood cleanser, and detoxifier.
7. <u>Honey raw organic certified</u>. An anti-bacteria (kills bacteria by eliminating their water) and a cleanser that provides antigens that prevent allergies. I also contains a high amount of vitamins and minerals. Also Bee Pollen and Royal Jelly. Most all U.S. honey has been found to contain toxic glyphosate. Monsanto's Roundup is the cause infecting the water tables in the U.S. The flowers that

the bees pollinate are toxic. Glyphosate is a carcinogenic toxic chemical compound.

8. <u>Non Fat Sulfured Cottage Cheese mixed with organic Flax Seed</u> in equal amounts that contains both sulfured amino acids, Omega 3.6, 9 e-fatty acids which have been demonstrated an ability to destroy cancer cell tumors according to the research, and findings of Dr. Johanna Budwig, M.D. of Germany. Biosan Nutritionals a company in Arizona, online sells a product premixed, and in equal proportions called Vita-Flax. I use 4 tsp. of organic flax seed oil to 1 cup of organic sulfured low fat cottage cheese. Note! I substitute the cottage cheese with high sulfured amino acid capsules.

9. <u>Wheat Grass and Barley Grass</u> juices both detoxifiers, anti-cancer, fatigue, infection fighters, and malnutrition. They are high in mineral salts. They can be bought in health food stores, Jamba Juice outlets, Trader Joe's stores or get some seeds at Amazon.com and grow your own indoors at home with a grow light.

10. <u>Parsley, Apple, and Carrot</u>. Their juices provide tannins, beta carotene, calcium, chlorophyll, pectin, minerals for health, and vitality. It also helps maintain a regular bowel movement and acts as detoxifiers as well. Aids the heart and lung function. A recent study revealed that Parsley taken is 96% effective in eliminating lung cancers.

11. <u>Pau d' Arco and Una de Gato (Cat's Claw)</u>. Two Amazon herbs that researched and proven for their anti-cancer properties. They are both anti-bacteria, anti-virus, and anti-fungal.

12. <u>Green or Black Tea</u>. Contains vitamin K2 and has anti-cancer properties. Green tea is a very powerful anti-oxidant.

13. <u>Wheat Germ, Lechitin, and Buckwheat (kasha)</u>. They contain high fiber, amino acids, omega 3, e-fatty acids, and are high complex carbohydrates. They all reduce the bad cholesterol, anti-cancer, and high in natural d-alpha-tocopherol Vitamin E an antioxidant.

14. <u>Lemon</u>. Rind, juice or essential oil lemonene. They all balance the body's pH. The lemon rind or skin contains lemonene oil known as an anti-cancer cell killer. Vitamin C and bioflavanoids.

15. <u>Tomato</u>. It contains lycopenes that are anti-cancer, a liver cleanser, and a heart enhancer.

16. <u>Cruciferous Vegetables</u>. Such as Broccoli, Cabbage, Cauliflower, and Brussels Sprouts especially when heated provide phyto-chemicals that are highly anti-cancer.

17. <u>Kombucha Fungus Tea</u>. Researched by German Medical Doctor Rudolph Skelnar for its anti-cancer properties by its ability to balance the blood's pH below 7.56 preventing the cancer microbe

the Endobiont from proliferating. It is also a digestive, and intestinal tract probiotic, aids the friendly flora, and metabolism. A must for all cancer patients to prevent further cancer cell proliferation and for those without cancer to prevent it. Rx: Pronatura Kombucha caps @ 555 mg. @ Luckyvitamins.com

18. Hydroxygen Plus. Renamed Oxygen Elements Plus. It contains ionic minerals, amino acids, and enzymes plus stabilized oxygen. It has anticancer properties, provides ionic nutrition to cancer patients who are suffering from Cachexia, or malnutrition. Life Support @ Amazon.com

19. OxyMoxy, Dynamo2, Oxiblast, Oxiboost, and Vitamin 02. all have anticancer properties as cancer cells do not survive in an oxygen rich cellular environment. We are oxygen deficient as the oxygen atmospheric percent has decreased from around 30 to 16 percent in the air we are breathing. Urban cities with chemical smog, chemtrails have also effected the oxygen levels. I highly recommend OxyMoxy, Dynamo2 that are both cost effective, and work well as I have personally researched them both for their effectiveness. OxyMoxy, Dynamo2 are sold by EnGardehealth.com, and amazon.com.

20. Colo2Zone a mild and gentle and highly effective colon cleanser. Magnesium oxide when mixed with Vitamin C releases oxygen into the colon for cleansing and detoxification. It is also cost effective. Sold by EnGardehealth.com It is based on a Nikola Tesla discovery.

21. Carnaovora (Pressed juice from the Venus Flytrap plant).

22. Reviverine and Life Crystals is the discovery of Dr. George Merykl, Ph.D. Physicist and Nobel Laureate Award winner who unlocked the door to genetic engineering by the hidden potential in the D.N.A. has been uncovered. Powerful reserves of energy and intelligence have been utilized in the basic building blocks of the D.N.A. These are A.T.P., G.T.P., and the five (5) penta carbon sugars. This discovery he made has led to the development of a health tonic which supplies the A.T.P., G.T.P., the five (5) penta carbon sugars named originally "Life Crystals," and now called "Renaissance." Derived from a natural source, delivers an abundance of vitality, instant energy, and promotes health in the body. This is for sale as an adjunct to the diet. For people with serious degenerative conditions. There is also available an injected clinical grade of Life Crystals. Note! Only is available to licensed Medical Doctors or Nurses.

23. Chondriana. If the health problem is a degenerative disease such as cancer then Chondriana another of Dr. Merykl's substances

222

is needed. Chondriana is a single cell primitive organism (it is your primitive macrophage a T-killer cell) which is a product of bio-engineering by extracting from ancient rocks our ancient mitochondria, or T-killer cell, and named Chondriana. The human gene was extracted in a process discovered by Dr. Merykl he calls a cold fusion process. Again, the human gene extracted from the ancient rocks is our primitive T-killer cell. Both the Life Crystals, Chondriana represent hidden, powerful resources of regeneration of all the cells of your body, enable a far superior immune system function within the building blocks of life, and our D.N.A. And harnessing the energy source of all life, in the genes.
24. <u>Milk Thistle (Silymarin)</u>. A liver detoxfier and cleanser. All of the body's blood passes through the liver for detoxification. Milk Thistle supports the liver function and is known for its anti-cancer properties. Keeping the liver functioning properly is a must for all cancer patients. Rx:Liquid Needle Bath Soak LVR-105
25. <u>Chondriana and Life Crystals called (Rennaissance)</u>.
The combination forms a very powerful synergy that provides the cells to regenerate themselves and enables the immune system to destroy any invaders including cancer cells. The Chondriana is our primitive T-killer cell. It is able to reproduce itself and provide you with a new powerful immune system. Several studies indicate that the Chondriana and Germanium Sesquioxide (GE-132) which is a naturally occurring trace mineral that works at the basic cellular level to strengthen the immune system by increasing the macrophage activity. It is found in high concentrations in essential oil and plants such as aloe Vera, garlic, ginseng, chlorella, comfrey, and shitake mushrooms. It was discovered in the 1960's by a Japanese scientist, Kazuhoko Asai. Studies indicate that Germanium Sesquioxide supplementation increases the level of gamma interferon, an immune system protein that simulates the immune system, and enhances healing. While the Chondriana helps increase the T-killer cells, multiplies them, and generally increases the immune system defense function. The Chondriana can instantly upon contact with any viruses, fungus, bacteria, and cancer cells completely destroying them within seconds. After destroying them it eats and produces phagocytes that engulf the invader. It then regenerates them and spews our usable substances such as D.N.A. for the body to use. The Life Crystals "Renaissance" are made by use of a solar still which receives the Sun's energy for around six (6) months while it ferments. The end product is a pure source of A.T.P. (adosine tri-phosphate),

G.T.P., and the five (5) penta carbon sugars. Drinking it daily provides the body's trillions of cells (mitochondria) that powers them and thereby energizes all of the body's thirty (30) trillion cells.

The Life Crystal tonic is a delicious tasting non alcoholic, high tech beverage, and a naturally made health rest-oral tonic. Ten (10) years of research resulted in the development, formulation of an advanced genetic energy, and health support tonic beverage.

If we provide naturally available A.T.P., G.T.P., it is possible to deliver optimum energy levels necessary for cellular, genetic growth, repair, and function. In Life Crystals the energy transducer is located within the A.T.P. and G.T.P. With the five (5) penta carbon sugars which provide the four (4) basic building blocks of life in pure forms. This ionic drink represents a highly stable concentrated energy reservoir of A.T.P. molecules. It contains nourishment for the genes in the form of the five (5) penta carbon sugars. These life enhancement ingredients are available to the body with oral sublingual ingestion. The dosage amount is one (1) to three (3) teaspoons daily under the tongue. Leave it under the tongue for two (2) to three (3) minutes then swallow it. Life Crystals: www.sunnation.com

The theoretical support for the Life Crystals tonic is that our cells age, mainly from antioxidant damage. This occurs to the mitochondria membranes of the cell. This degeneration in the D.N.A. and R.N.A. results in the production of metzymes that reduce and interfere with normal energy an maintenance physiology with the cells. This is the normal sequence of events leading to pre mature illness, acute, chronic illness, old age, and death. But, what if someone could repair, normalize the D.N.A., and R.N.A. Functions? Then it is quantitatively possible to postpone cellular respiratory function. This is based on the "Homeopathic Law of Similars." "Simila, Similus, and Currentor." This states that like cures like. It is now possible to nourish the D.N.A. and R.N.A. structures by providing them building blocks of these structures back to the body.

The Life Crystal tonic contains hemocrystals that now holds the promise of nourishing the D.N.A. and R.N.A. of our cells. If you nourish your body properly it will survive for a time. But if you nourish the genes then it will thrive for multiple of that time. Life Crystals contain A.T.P., G.T.P., the five (5) penta carbon sugars which are the basic building blocks of life, and with the characteristic Hydrogen bond of the D.N.A. molecule.

With properly <u>functioning enzymes</u> the body takes defensive measures against toxins and repairs all former damage. A disorder can be rectified by <u>rest-oral of the enzymes</u> that are suppressed. <u>Properly functioning enzymes</u> not only bring recovery but also rejuvenation. The research physicist and discoverer Dr. George Merykl. Ph.D. has actually replicated life with a more concentrated form of the Life Crystal solution. In many experiments the concentrated form of the Life Crystal solution has made it possible to manifest this precursor of our ancestors cells a nuclei and mitochondria that has been able to regrow organs. This has been accomplished through forward and reversed synthesis respectively. The synthesized organisms are known as Chondriana and may represent the greatest biological discovery in the history of mankind. Note! There are medical clinics around the world with the exception of the U.S. that are using the Chondriana in treating every known disease with astonishing results. Life Crystal tonic is now called "Renaissance." www.sunnation.com [Note! A.T.P.-the energy released by cleaving either a Phosphate (P) or a pyrophosphate (PPi) unit from A.T.P. or standard state of 1 M. A small molecule used in cells as a co-enzyme. Its main focus is intracellular energy transfer. It transports chemical energy within cells for metabolism. It is one of end products of photo phosphorylation, anaerobic respiration, fermentation, is used by enzymes, and structural proteins in many cellular processes. G.T.P.(cGTP)-Guanosine triphosphate-an organic chemical and energy carrier. It helps cyclic adenosine monophosphate (cAMP) activate cyclic nucleotide-gated ion channels in the olfactory system.
26. <u>Carnavora</u>. This is mentioned again and is the pure pressed juice of the Venus Fly Trap plant. It is being used in Germany by Dr. Hans Nipper, M.D. It eats and kills cancer cells and prevents them from spreading. Dr. Nipper uses it in his clinic and claims successful results. The Carnavora must be taken over a life time to prevent further metastasizing of the cancer cells.
27. <u>Reviverine</u> also called Rebiverina. This is a powder substance manufactured and produced in Mexico. It is use for reviving the

immune system function. It contains Germanium Sesquioxide and other anticancer herbs.

28. Olivir. This is an olive leaf extract that contains oleopein a chemical compound in olive leaf that was discovered to be a powerful immune system enhancer. Studies have shown that this compound interferes with certain amino acid production processes that are necessary to sustain some invader viruses. It prevents the virus from replicating themselves by penetration of the healthy uninfected cell walls. Oleopein is the compound that does this. It prevents the virus from reproducing called "budding." The oleopein provides cell wall protective shield so that the virus is unable to penetrate causing the virus to unable to reproduce itself and eventually die. Preliminary studies in vitro suggest it can limit the production of transcriptase's-enzymes that are essential to alter the R.N.A. of a healthy cell. Clinical data indicates that oleopein may also interact with the protein of certain types of cells, preventing them from shedding, budding, or assembling at a cell membrane site. Oleopein has also been shown in studies to stimulate phagocytosis which is an important immune system response. Original Olivir is available @Swansonshealth.com

29. Ukrane. A prescribed intravenous injected celandine plus other synergistic herbs (alkaloids) which is called a natural herbal chemotherapy used in Europe, B.V.C., Canada at a Naturopathic Clinic and here in the U.S. located at Sedona, Arizona, at a Naturopathic Health Clinic. It is being used mainly for treatment of cancer and Lyme disease. Note! First treat with SpiroX. pg.162

30. Colloidal Silver and Gold. Both are know for their upon contact killing of bacteria, viruses, fungi, and cancer cells. Only use 1100 p.p.m. Colloidal silver and only in a dark colored glass bottle. Use for seven (7) to ten (10) days only. Use as directed on the bottle. Take usually 18 drops sublingual under your tongue. Hold for one (1) minute then swallow. Drink a minimum of 8-8 ounce of pure distilled water daily when taking either colloidal silver or gold. Colloidal gold with its ultra high frequency @60 p.p.m. will trap cancer cells on contact. Then the Colloidal silver can kill 650 pathogens including cancer cells on contact. Only 1100 p.p.m. is adviaed. Atlantean Alchemy.com

31. Ozone 03. Purchase an A2Z Aqua6 ozone air, water, and oil generator or any other ozone air, water, and oil ozone generator. Infuse your drinking water, foods, air, and oils with it. Ozone taken daily in low dose will kill all bacteria, viruses, fungi, and cancer cells upon contact. Since your body is around 80%

water. If your oxygenate and ozonate your body fluids and cells you will be able to kill off all unfriendly invaders including cancer cells. This also enables your immune system to function much more efficiently without being over burdened.

32. <u>Can Cell 1</u> © 2009 USP&CO by JPPHDND. A health tonic and it is an anti-cancer remedy that contains the following ingredients: Doenzang extract 3X, apple seed extract 3x, Iredesca extract 3x, almond extract 3x, apricot extract 3x, Reviverine 3x (Violona 18 Ribavirina 400 mg.), chaparral 3x, Lypocodium clav 30x, beta carotene 1,000 I.U., Haelan-851 or 951 with isoflavones: daidzein genistein, and nitrogen, Olivir-olive leaf extract with oleopein 3x, collodial silver 1100 p.p.m. and gold 60 p.p.m. 3X, una de gato (cats claw) 3x, pau d' arco 3x, cinnamon 3x, echinacea purpea E 3x, garlic (allicin and germanium) 3x, turmeric 3x, walnut extract 3x, non sulfured black strap molasses (potash) 3x, Super Bovine Colostrum 1-IGH powder, dandelion root extract 3x, ginger root extract 3x, wild forest black berry leaves 3x, nutmeg 3x, Indian cardamon 3x, hibiscus flowers extract 3x, wild rose hips powder, roasted barley, and chicory root powder, blackberries juice, orange and lemon peel (lemonene) oil or powder, barley malt powder, lemon grass extract 3x, matte tea powder, cocoa leaves powder, myrrh essential oil 3x, frankincense essential oil 3x, sage essential oil 3x, black cumin essential oil 3x, R.S.O.- cannabis T.H.C.-C.B.D. essential oil, tri- flora tea powder, flax seed oil 3x, hemp oil 3x, IP6 + inositol powder, graviola (annona muricata) powder, rose essential oil @320 MHz, various secret light photon frequency solutions added to re-balance the bio- field(s) chakras and acupuncture, immune, nervous systems, and assist in detoxifying the body. © 2009-2016 by 21st Century Energetics: Jerome Plotnick, Ph.D., N.D. All of these aforementioned ingredients are known for their anti-cancer effects and immune system enhancement. A case study was performed on a cancer patient with lymphoma and the other with terminal melanoma. The cancer patient with lymphoma was given chemotherapy and radiation prior to using Can Cell 1 with no results and was given a very short time to live. Can Cell 1 formula is listed in The 13 Steps From Illness To Health-APNBMPDR book © 2009 U.S.C.P.O. Copyright Registration #: Txu 1-955-469 on 10-19-2009

33. Galangal root and Circumin called Turmeric. Galangal root contains the following: Emodin that suppressed tumors and improved immunity 2. Galangin killed colon cancer cells 3. beta sisterol has been researched and shown to kill cancer cells. Turmeric

contains turmeine that triggers programmed death with breast cancer cells. 2. targets destruction of cancer cell mitochondria cells 3. prevents D.N.A. damage. 4. targets cancer stem cells and leaves healthy cells alone. 5. halts replication of cancer are at the root of tumor formation and malignancies. Both Galangal and Turmeric are powerful anti-oxidants. Both are also powerful anti-inflammatory. They have been shown to kill throat, colon, lung, and prostate cancer cells. Add Dandelion, Beet and Ginger roots. 34. Bulgarian Formula. Ingredients are the following: 15 organic lemons, 12 organic garlic cloves, raw maleuka organic honey 35 oz., organic walnuts 14 oz., and wheat or any other sprouts 14 oz. Formulate: Take the wheat sprouts and place them in a large glass bowl to which you will add distilled water to. Then cover and let stand overnight. In the A.M. drain off all the water and rinse them off. Then remove the drained wheat sprouts and place into a bowl until you see the wheat sprouting. After that wait 24 hours until the wheat sprouts further. Then clean the garlic cloves. Mix them into the sprouted wheat. Then add the walnuts and grind the mixture. Then take 5 whole lemons with rinds and add them and grind the mixture once again. Then take the other 10 lemons and squeeze the juice from them into the mixture. Finally add the 35 oz. of raw maleuka organic honey to it and mix again. Take it and refrigerate it for 3 days. Thereafter if you are ill then take a Tsp. every 4 hours. For prevention take 1-2 Tbsp. in the A.M. Breakfast, P.M. Dinner, and 1 Tbsp. before you go to sleep.

Can Cell 1 a True Story.
Thereafter, and upon taking Can Cell 1 the cancer lymphoma patient lived another five (5) years, without any chemotherapy. or radiation. The upon the family member insisting that she should go back to taking chemotherapy and radiation the lymphoma cancer reappeared. She stopped the Can Cell 1 entirely and died shortly thereafter.

The other cancer patient with terminal melanoma was taking Can Cell 1 continually as a precautionary remedy before he even knew that he had melanoma. The melanoma was discovered and diagnosed by the V.A. doctors at the Supulveda Medical Center in Sepulveda, California. They were simply astonished and amazed that the fast spreading melanoma the patient had for several years remained in a limbo state. Normally a melanoma like this spreads quickly and causes death. This cancer patients immune system had stopped the spread of melanoma. The only remedy this patient ever took was the Can Cell 1 remedy previously to discovering that he had melanoma. The melanoma on the outer skin was surgically removed and no signs of melanoma have returned since then. This occurred in 1992 and he is still cancer free in 2017. The melanoma patient had taken Can Cell 1 for two (2) years prior to the finding of his melanoma. Can Cell 1 is being further studied for its anticancer properties and immune system enhancement.

35. <u>Herbs and Foods</u>. Black garlic, bushwood berry, graviola, bitter melon, pau d'arco, una de gato, flax seed, black cumin seed, noni, milkweed, chaparral, cannabis, parsley and oregano, cinnamon and ginger, dandelion, turmeric, and galangal. These all have shown their cancer cell killing ability. See pages: 247-255.

36. <u>Ultrashort Pulsed Laser</u>. This inactivates viruses or cancer cells by inhibiting viral replication and transcription to a host cell nucleus thereby stopping cancer cells from metastasizing.

37. <u>Laser D.N.A. Transcription</u>. Targeting D.N.A. repair pathways for cancer treatment. Also cancer treatment using a gene encoding of an R.N.A. replicase polyprotein self-replicating vaccine.

38. <u>Stem Cell Regeneration</u>. Scientists are now able to regrow your teeth using laser light and stem cells. If this is possible then after lets say chemotherapy, radiation that kill your immune, and healthy cells they now can be re-grown too.

39. <u>Sodium biCarbonate</u>. (Baking Soda) According to the unproven research and use of Baking Soda Dr. Simoncimi, M.D. Italy he has pioneered Sodium biCarbonate (NAHC03) therapy as a means to treat cancer. He postulates and claims that since Sodium bi-Carbonate, unlike any other anti-fungal remedy to which the fungus, (cancer cell and tumor) can become immune, that it is extremely diffusible retains its ability to penetrate the tumor, and kill the cancer cells. He further states, "that currently against any fungus which he states is what a cancer cell is that there is no other useful remedy other than, in my opinion, Sodium bi-Carbonate, and in fact they don't have the ability to penetrate the tumor mass." <u>I completely disagree</u> with Dr. Simoncimi to his claims about baking soda, in fact if overdosed it can cause acidosis, and kill you. Secondly, there is a Chinese herbal formula used to eliminate the biofilm of the borreliosis microbe of Lyme disease which can also be used to penetrate the tumor matrix. See Spirox on pages: 161 and 164. Also hyperthermia and bioenergetic light photon frequencies.

<u>The Endocannabinoid System and Cancer</u>. <u>Published Research Study's</u>.
Beginning in 1992, when the (A.E.A.) was first identified in the
porcine brain (Devane et al., 1992), numerous studies have
contributed to the current knowledge of the elements that form the
Endocannabinoid System (E.C.S.) (Maccaonne et al., 2010).
Endocannabinoids (eC.B.D.'s) are lipid mediators, isolated from
brain peripheral tissues that include amides, esters, and other
long chained polyunsaturated fatty acids that mimic the action of
A9-tetrahydocannbinol (T.H.C.) in different biological processes.
Until recently the most bioactive of eC.B.D.'s are anandamide
(archidonylethnolamide; (A.E.A.), 2-arachidonolyglycerol (2-Ag),
yet the family includes virodhamine, noladin ether,
A/arachidonoyldopamine (N.A.D.A.), besides homo-
linolenylethanolamide (H.E.A), and docosatetraenylethanolamide
(O.E.A.).

<u>Chemical Structural of Biologically Active eC.B.D.'s and of</u>
<u>eC.B.D. Like Compounds</u>.
eC.B.D."s on demand from membrane phospholipid pre cursors and
although not A.E.A. synthesis might be due to several metabolic
routes (Muccioli, 2010), N-acylphosphatidlethnolamine specific
phospholipase D (NAPE-PLD) is currently considered the major
enzyme responsible for A.E.A. production (Okamoto et al., 2009),
whereas a specific phospholipase C followed by the activity of the
sn-1diacylglercerol lipase (DAGL), and is responsible for 2-AG
synthesis (Ueda et al., 2011). The cellular uptake from the
extracellular to the intracellular space is ascribed to a
purported: Endocannabinoid membrane transporter (E.M.T.) that is
likely to take up both A.E.A. and 2-AG. However, while there is
wide experimental evidence to support the concept that the A.E.A.
transport across membranes is protein-mediated, no conclusive
evidence of its molecular identity is still lacking. For a
comprehensive review on alternative pathways of eC.B.D.'s see
(Rouzer and Marnett, 2011). eC.B.D.'s act principally through
cannabinoid receptors. That include type-1, type-2 (C.B.D.-1), and
(C.B.D.-2) receptors; more recently. It has been highlighted the
ability of some C.B.D. and non C.B.D. ligans to bind also to GPR55
(Gluckmann and Weich, 1999 et al). C.B.D. receptors are members of
the large family of heptahelical G protein coupled receptors
(G.P.C.R.'s) that activate Gi/o proteins (Pertweet et al., 2010).
Anatomical studies have revealed that these receptors display a
highly divergent pattern of distribution throughout the human

organism: C.B.D.'s are mainly present in the central nervous system (Herkanham et al., 1991), is mainly distributed to the peripheral, and immune system cells (Munro et al., 1993).
Due to the aforementioned P.P.A.R.'s are affected by the C.B.D.'s which then affects several physiological and pathological processes, such as lipid metabolism, energy balance, neuro protection, epilepsy, circadian rhythms, inflammation, addiction, and cognitive brain functions (Pistis and Melis, 2010). They also act as a modulator of other signal pathways neuro peptides and hormones. This highly complex network of interactions is reflected in the multifaceted modulatory effects of C.B.D.'s on the regulation of the brain and behavioral functions (Lopez-Moreno et al., 2008).

Physiological Actions of the Endocannabinoid System E.C.S. and Therapeutic Perspectives.

The presence of the E.C.S. in vertebrates, mammals, and humans implies a role in several physiological processes. These include appetite, cancer, cardiovascular disease, fertility, immune system functions, memory, moods, nervous system neuro protection, and pain modulation. (Ligresti et al., 2009).

The Endocannabinoid System and How T.H.C.-C.B.D. Kills Cancer Cells.

There are currently around 20,000 studies world-wide. Few researchers can deny the tremendous therapeutic potential of cannabis. Dr. Christina Sanchez, a molecular biologist at the Comprehensive University in Madrid Spain, has completed extensive research which led to the first discoveries that T.H.C.-C.B.D. in "cannabis sativa" marijuana does most certainly kill cancer cells. See page: 281 on how T.H.C.-C.B.D. kills cancer cells.

The Endocannabinoid System or E.C.U. is a group of cannabinoid receptors such as C.B.D.-1 and C.B.D.-2. These receptors located in the brain are responsible for many physiological process which include: appetite, pain sensation, mood, and memory. It also mediates many physiological processes, including motor functions, learning, synaptic plasticity, and appetite. See page: 281.

The Endocannabinoid System E.C.U. maintains and regulates our biological systems. It does this by regulation of each cell tissue. It uses Arachadonic Acid-Omega 6 to make Endo-

Cannabinoids: fatty molecules that communicate between cells. Dietary cannabis mimics the E.C.S. by providing Cannabinoids when there is an Atchadonic acid deficiency or a Cannabinoid deficiency. Note! Hemp C.B.D.'s and Marijuana C.B.D.'s are medicinal necessary herbs, food, and are much needed.

The early 1990 discovery of specific membrane receptors of marijuana's psychoactive component 9-tetrahydrocannabinol (T.H.C.) led to the revelation of a whole endogenous signaling system which is the Endocannabinoid system E.C.S.

The most incredible findings of the E.C.S. is that it appears to be within at least all vertebrate phyla, is present in the structure of receptors and their function, also in invertebrates, and thus implying its participation in vital functions in almost all organisms.

A concentrate or as its called a full extract essential oil made from the flowering tops of the cannabis herbal plant can produce a viscous oil containing large doses of active cannabinoids. The process in California was made popular by Rick Simpson, also called R.S.O., or Phoenix Tears. The ratio of compounds are typically 45-65% T.H.C.-C.B.D. and 7% to 12% C.B.D. Cannabinoid has been shown to reduce the intense side effects of T.H.C.-C.B.D. including the altered state of consciousnesses, anxiety, paranoia, and confusion. Also advised is Tree of Life T.H.C.-C.B.D. oil.

Cancer patients with different types of cancer have been able to use this oil topically and internally to force cancerous cells to kill themselves. R.S.O. has often had a higher success rate than chemotherapy and radiation therapy. While chemotherapy and radiation destroy cancer cells, they also destroy immune system, and healthy cells. They are unable to kill the cancer master regeneration cells. R.S.O. therapeutic essential T.H.C.-C.B.D. oil kills only cancer cells, leaves the healthy cells intact giving the patient a much better chance of survival, recovery, and cancer remission. R.S.O. Rick Simpson oil has also been used successfully as a therapeutic treatment of chronic pain, inflammation, muscle spasms, and intestinal tract disorders, etc. Note! Cancer patients that used chemotherapy and radiation on average have only a five year life expectancy. R.S.O. is also called Phoenix Tears.

The Endocannabinoid System: Is the Body Hard-Wired to Receive Cannabis?

Though we have the federal government and their agencies claiming that marijuana has no medical use. The D.E.A. still maintains that it is a schedule 1 narcotic and a gateway drug. Just the opposite is true. Because not only does marijuana (cannabis T.H.C.-C.B.D.) have many medicinal uses, benefits, but it is a fact that it kills cancer cells. But believe it many researchers non biased world-wide have overwhelming stated that it is also hard wired in our bodies to receive cannabis C.B.D.'s. It receives the C.B.D.'s through a system called the Endocannabinoid System. This is a scientific credible proven fact. Due to the D.E.A. Agency with its false claim that marijuana is a schedule 1 narcotic and a gateway drug much research has been lost. But thanks to new found legality by states who have legalized it as a prescribed medicinal medicine new research is blooming, and the results are astonishing.

It has been discovered that not only is the Endocannabinoid System merely a collection of receptors in the brain meant for getting a so called high, but is a complex matrix of binding locations throughout the central (C.N.S.), peripheral nervous systems (P.N.S.), the immune system, our organs, and whose main functions are to help us maintain homeostasis of our bodies. Scientists have also discovered that the Endocannabinoid System is present on all animals, mammals, and human vertebrates.

Endocannabinoids are not exactly the same as we find in cannabinoids that we find in marijuana like T.H.C.-C.B.D. One of the most amazing facts is its influence on neurogenesis. Neurogenesis, as the name infers, is literally the creation of new neurons. Because cannabinoids stimulate the Endocannabinoid System, and the Endocannabinoid System is responsible for helping in the creation of new brain cells. Logic would state that the introduction of phytocannabinoids to the body will help to stimulate in the creation of new brain cells. Recent evidence, suggests that short term memory is greatly affected, enhanced by our cannabis use, but now we also know that there are trillions of cells in the brain that are not responsible for memory function.

Synthetic marijuana has been around for twenty (20) years called "Dronabinol," under the patented name of Marinol. It is currently scheduled as a class III drug. Many of the health issues its prescribed for are identical to natural marijuana. The medical effects are designed to be the same as marijuana, it's synthetic T.H.C. It is F.D.A. approved and federally legal by prescription, yet natural marijuana remains classified as a schedule 1 dangerous narcotic, and with no "medical use." There have been over 16,000 published papers and articles in the last twenty (20) years that contain the word "cannabinoids." Despite the federal governments resistance, scientists every where world-wide are realizing that the medicinal effects of cannabis can not any longer be ignored. Its mainly the congress that are being bribed by the big pharmaceutical, alcohol, tobacco, private prison industry's, and the puppet F.D.A. agency headed and controlled by Monsanto former employees. So from all this non biased real factual evidence it is evident that are bodies are wired to accept and receive cannabis.

The Endocannabinoid System; An Overview.
Marijuana has been around for thousands of years and used as a medicine with evidence dating back to 2000 B.C. But only within the last few decades has it been researched and new discoveries on how it works. This has led to the discovery of the Endocannabinoid System, a unique biological system within the human body.

The Endocannabinoid System is a central regulatory system that effects a wide range of biological processes. It consists of a group of molecules known as cannabinoids (C.B.D.'s) as well as cannabinoid receptors that they bind to.

Although marijuana is a source of over sixty (60) cannabinoids (including T.H.C., C.B.D.'s), and the human body produces a number of cannabinoids as well. These endogenous cannabinoids include ananamide, 2-arachidonoylglycerine (2-A.G.), and these are present in all human beings.

Decades of scientific research on the Endocannabinoid System has resulted in the discovery of two (2) types of cannabinoid receptors called C.B.-1 and C.B.-2. These receptors are found in various parts of the body, but are not prominent in the brain and immune system. Note! So if you want to enhance your immune system take cannabis C.B.D.'s from hemp, or marijuana, and both are suggested.

Cannabinoid receptors act as binding sites for endogenous cannabinoids (C.B.D.'s) as well as cannabinoids found in marijuana. When cannabinoids bind to C.B.-1, or C.B.-2 receptors, and they act to change the way the body functions.

When cannabinoid receptors are primarily located in the brain and immune system, researchers have identified cannabinoid receptors in a variety of other body areas as well, including the peripheral nervous system, cardiovascular system, reproductive system, the gastrointestinal, and urinary tracts.

The Endocannabinoid System is not unique to human species. Research as shown that the system is common to all humans, mammal vertebrate animals, and even some invertebrate animals. This suggests its significance in the process of evolution. Experts believe that natural selection has conserved the Endocannabinoids System in living organisms for five hundred (500) million years.

Medical Applications.
The Endocannabinoid System's role in homeostasis comes from the research that has identified the cannabinoid receptor in tumor cells of various cancers, including lung cancer, breast cancer, and prostate cancer. Research has also revealed that tumor growth can be inhibited and even reversed when cannabinoids like T.H.C.-C.B.D. are administered.

Scientific experts believe that cannabinoid receptors is an indicator of the Endocannabinoid System's role as a biological defense system, providing strong support for the use of medical marijuana.

The research suggests that the defense system is not only useful in cancer, but may also be beneficial in the treatment of a wide variety of illnesses. The current evidence points to the Edndocannabinoid System as being a potential natural therapeutic target for the following illnesses, diseases, and disorders: A.I.D.S.-H.I.V., Alzheimer's Disease, Arthritis, Cancer, Chronic Pain, Epilepsy, Fibromyalgia, Glaucoma, Multiple Sclerosis, Sleep Disorders, Autism, Post Traumatic Stress Disorder (P.T.S.D.), Appetite, Psoriasis, Auto-Immune, Lyme Disease, and many more.

Review from the National Institute of Health (N.I.H.) 2006.

Summary.
"In the past decade, the endocannabinoid system has been
implicated in a growing number of physiological function, both in
the central, peripheral nervous systems and in peripheral organs,
modulating the activity of the endocannabinoid system turned out
to be a therapeutic promise in a wide range of disparate diseases
(illnesses), pathological conditions, ranging from mood and
anxiety disorders, motor movement disorders such as Parkinson's
and Huntington disease, neuropathic pain, multiple sclerosis and
spinal cord injury, cancer, stroke, atherosclerosis, myocardial
infarction, hypertension, glaucoma, obesity-metabolic syndrome,
and osteoporosis, to name a few."

Excerpt from (Pacher P., Baktai S., Kunos G. (2006) The
Endocannabinoid System as an emerging target of pharmacotherapy.
Pharmacol. Rev. 58, 389-462 goi:10.1124/pr.58.9.2

Recreational Use of Marijuana.
While the endocannaboinoid system has been thoroughly investigated
in the medical field, many still question its role in the
recreational use of marijuana.

Although its long-term effects continue to be debated, evidence
shows that marijuana is a surprisingly benign substance that poses
no risk of overdose, and minimal risk of addiction. Experts also
believe that the psychoactive properties of marijuana are most
likely to be temporary and pose no risk of brain damage over
a long period of its use.

Further, granted the use of marijuana should still be approached
with caution, evidence points and proves marijuana as ultimately
being much safer than most commonly available substances including
refined sugar, caffeine, nicotine, prescription opiates, and
alcohol. A recent study stated it did not seriously impair
driving.

T.H.C.V. Another Cannabis Sativa Strain Being Reserched.

The cannabis plant-herb makes most cannabinoids alike. The C.B.D. and C.B.C., out of C.B.G.-A. C.B.G-A appears in the plant which more rarely, and forms similar compounds except that they are only have small carbon trails (c3) instead of more common 5 carbon trails (c5). The (c3) carbon tailed cannabinoids are referred to as "Varins," such that the c3 version of the the T.H.C. (T.H.C.-c5)is named Tetrahydocannabicin (T.H.G.-c3.

Being closely related to the c3 version have very similar properties along with many unique qualities. For example, T.H.C.V. is more strongly psychoactive than T.H.C., but only has about one half (½) the duration of T.H.C. T.H.C.V. is also a protagonist of T.H.C. modifying its effects of T.H.C. The energetic effect of the T.H.C.V. is more prominent and stronger.

T.H.V.C. has been found to reduce and block Panic Disorder attacks and, as a result can be highly effective in the management of P.T.S.D. And other related disorders involving anxiety and stress as shown in research studies in Israel, where a great amount of cannabis research is performed. T.H.C.V. doesn't appear to suppress emotions, only the ability to panic, associated with the Fight or Flight Response. A nervous system response.

T.H.C.V. has been shown to reduce tremors associated with Parkinson's Disease along with disorders with motor control. There is also ongoing and promising research demonstrating reduction of brain lesions associated with Parkinson's Disease.

T.H.C.V. also stimulates bone, similar illnesses greatly, has the potential in the treatment of osteoporosis and similar illnesses, possibly can in the micro gravity of space travel, and to combat the loss of bone mass.

A side effect of T.H.C.V. That requires attention is its strong anorectic effect if a patient is already having difficulty in eating. The T.H.C.V. appetite suppression is an adverse detriment.

Tetrahydrocannabivarinic Acid (T.H.C.V.-A) is very similar to T.H.C.-A, and although it has yet to be properly researched, or studied, and it is assumed to be an anti-inflammatory. Originally

T.H.C.V. was most commonly isolated in land race sativa from the South Central Africa Continent. Until recently, T.H.C.V. was only available in small concentrations in sativa strains like Durban Poison, which an average yield was upwards of 0.5% T.H.C.V. In a T.H.C. dominant plant. Such herbal hybrid plants have a T.H.C.- T.H.C.V. Ratio of 20:1 or greater.

Several years ago, a strain named Pineapple Purple was created with a ratio of 3:1 and yielded 12% T.H.C. and 4% T.H.C.V. In the last year, a new strain, Doug's Varin was created with a ratio of 23% T.H.C.: 15% T.H.C.V. This is a first strain we have evaluated that has more classic tall lanky, narrow leaves sativa appearing variety. Black Strains: domina, widow, Jack, dog, rhino, diesel.

<u>The Rick Simpson's Story</u>.
Someday the name of Rick Simpson will be a household name. He will be known as the man who rediscovered the natural medicine for healing cancer by everyone. Rick's journey begins back in 2003. In 2003 Rick was diagnosed with basil cell carcinoma skin cancer. He had three spots of cancer on his body. Two on his face and one on his neck. Rick's decision on how to handle this diagnosis would be world changing.

After not having much success with surgery he decided to try something different. For almost a year he had been extracting essential oil from the cannabis herbal plant and ingesting it orally. He had been taking the oil for other health issues but the cancer diagnosis reminded him of something and gave him an idea. He remembered a radio headline he heard almost thirty years earlier. The radio headline had stated that the University of Virginia had found that cannabinoid in cannabis T.H.C. could kill cancer in mice. He figured if it killed cancer in mice it would kill his cancer too.

Rick's decision was to apply cannabis T.H.C. oil to his skin cancer. He applied his cannabis T.H.C. oil to some bandages and put them on the skin cancer. After four days of waiting he decided it was time to see if anything had happened under the bandages. To Rick's surprise the skin cancer was gone, His cannabis T.H.C. oil had cured cancer. Its called R.S.O. or Phoenix Tears.

Rick tried to tell his medical doctors but they wouldn't listen. He even went to cancer organizations and tried to get there help but nobody wanted anything to do with his discovery. At that point Rick took matters into his own hands. He started growing cannabis on his own land and producing his own cannabis oil. He gave the oil away free to anyone that needed it. Even after having his home raided multiple times and having over 2,600 cannabis plants cut down and taken by the R.C.M.P he still continued to produce the oil to help others.

In 2008 a film maker named Christian Laurette released the first free documentary on YouTube sharing Rick's discovery. The documentary is titled "Run From the Cure" If you haven't watched it you should, This documentary has been viewed millions of times world-wide and has helped millions of people. If not for Christian's documentary about Rick who knows where cannabis medicine would be today.

Its now been over ten years since Rick began his journey to tell others that cannabis oil can cure cancer. Rick has helped over five thousand (5,000) people personally with this amazing oil not to mention the countless others all over the world who have heard his story and have been healed. Rick was the inspiration for me to start CureYourOwnCancer.org and start helping others. The world owes this great man a thank you for his bravery, persistence in making sure that everyone everywhere knows about cannabis oil, and what it can do. Christian Laurette.

So on behalf of myself Jerome Plotnick, Ph.D., N.D., Gerard Joseph, Tim Bevan and all of us in the Alternative Holistic Cancer Ninja Fighting Warriors © 2016-2017, a forthcoming non profit organization. Dear Rick Simpson where ever you are our sincere blessings, gratitude and many thanks. Thanks to the many dedicated researchers I listed on pages 144-147 and on pages 179-183. Sincere thanks to Dr. Rudolph Skelnar, M.D. Germany, et al.

<u>Cancer Causing Foods Not to Eat & Man Made Chemicl Non Foods</u>.
All deli lunch meat, hot dogs, cold cuts, corn and corn products, dry-cured uncooked salami, milk, milk products, ice cream, yogurt, cheese, smoked fish, eggs, pork, ham, chicken, seafood, sushi, frozen fish, refrigerated pasta, beef, poultry, all shellfish, any raw egg foods like raw cookie dough, all enriched, bleached flour,

and grains, all white refined sugar products such as pies, ice cream, cakes, crackers, cookies, and G.M.O. soy, corn, and wheat.

Anti-Cancer Foods to Eat.
Whole organic grains like barley, spelt, quinoa, millet, aramanth, lentils. All green alkaline vegetables such as kale, spinach, leafy lettuce, chard, broccoli, cauliflower, asparagus, beets watercress, green peas. Root vegetables like ginger, red, radish, dandelion, beet, carrot, garlic, galangal, and black garlic. Herbs like cilantro, parsley, basil, etc. Other vegetables like cabbage, reishi, chaga, maitake, shitake, and moer mushrooms, sweet potato, red onion, radish, green onion, bell peppers, etc. Sea vegetables like kelp. sea weed, dulse, spirulina, chlorella, algae, etc. Fruits like avacado, lemon, watermelon, cantelope, grapes, mango, mangosteen, apples, jack fruit, banana, figs, dates, blue and all berries. Spices like turmeric, garlic powder, ginger root powder, cardamon, thyme, tarragon, oregano, nutmeg, cinnamon, cayenne, and black cumin. Nuts like coconut, almonds, and walnuts.

Adjuvant Cancer Nutrition.
A cancer patient must eat an adequate diet daily or they will suffer from malnutrition that leads to a condition called cachexia. The absolutely essential food health products recommended for cancer patients are: goEnergetix's.com: Galt Immune, Amino Gest, Biomatrix, Greening Powder, FlorsSynergy Plus, and Catalyst 7 or U, Exsula's-Iredesca, Mutaflor, Glutaloemine, Also highly recommended is Youngevity and all of Etheriums whole food energized supplements. Recommended for all cancer patients is an alkaline vegan organic diet listed in this book on page 175. These are all alkaline foods and herbs needed for a anticancer diet. Liquid Needle Green-120EX, MIN, VIT, and ENZ. See page: 183.

Alternative-Holistic-Bio-Energetic-Natural Protocol for Cancer.
By Jerome Plotnick, Ph.D., N.D. and also Ken Widgery, N.D.
My protocol for the elimination, prevention of cancer holistically, alternatively, biologically, and naturally.
A complete energetic light photon MHz frequency thorough D.N.R., Inc. detoxification using Liquid Needle's 1. Lympha-L-105 for cleansing, re-generating, and re-balancing the lymphatic system Bath Soak-$31.20 2. Coffee 130EX Bath Soak-$46.20 or 3. COFFEE-12-EX/shock $25.50 for 100% elimination of parasites, chemicals, chemo, heavy metals, all toxins, cleansing, and balancing. 4.

Gold- 105-GEX for yeast, fungus. 5. LVR-105-$46.20 or Shock-12-LVR for liver. 6. CAN-133-$45.00 or Shock-12-CAN-$25.00 for cancer. See #7 on pg. 240. 7. Pre detox use Liquid Needle E.V.B., for energy, vitality, and balance. Original-116-EX for re-energizing and balance of acupuncture points, meridians, chakras, and nervous system. Yellow-Y-118-EX for immediate detoxification of all foods, herbs, water, etc. Liquid Needle Green-G-120EX for all the signature frequencies of all vegetables, fruits, anti-oxidants, anzymes, vitamins, minerals, and amino acids. Liquid Needle Green-G-120-EX provides these frequencies to your cells, etheric energy body (biofield) as if you were eating freshly picked organic, non toxic, and non G.M.O. grown foods. Use: Place 5-7 drops of Liquid Needle Yellow-Y-118EX and Liquid Needle Green-G-120EX in a glass bowl filled with distilled water. Place foods in the bowl. Wait five to seven (5-7) minutes or longer, now your food is now detoxified, safe to eat as well, and re-energized to its maximum frequency energetic potential. See pages 287-310 Liquid Needle.

If you have been on allopathic, chemotherapy, and radiation treatments. 1. A complete energetic light photon frequency energy detoxification using Liquid Needle's CAN-133-$45.20 or Shock-12-CAN $25.50 for the 100% elimination of carcinogens, radiation, chemo chemicals, free radicals, helps boost the immune system, and enhances T-Killer cells. A series of five (5) bath soaks over fifteen (15) days. One bath every three (3) days. 2. L.N.-E.V.B. 3. To prevent any further cancer cells from proliferating in your blood and to keep the blood pH under 7.56 pH-Kombucha Fungus Tea capsules by Pronatura Dr. Skelnar's original recipe in 555 mg. 90 capsules-1-3 capsules daily. Can be ordered from Luckyvitamins.com 4. To immediately begin killing cancer cells and tumors: R.S.O. Rick Simpsons cannabis T.H.C.-C.B.D. full extract essential oil. Cannabis T.H.C.-C.B.D. also enhances the Endocannbiniod System receptor sites C.B.-1 and C.B.-2, immune, brain, and organ receptor sites. In California and most other states that have legalized the use of marijuana cannabis T.H.C.-C.B.D. oil a medical prescription-use card is necessary except in Colorado. Three (3) grams of R.S.O. is around $30.00. Also use Plus+ C.B.D. oil a whole plant Hemp oil balm and Tree of Life T.H.C. oil. 5. The following cancer killing herb is also suggested: graviola (annona muricata or soursop). I suggest purchasing a natural formulated formula from the Amazon Herb Company in Juniper Florida called "Gravizon." It contains pure graviola and other synergistic

herbs on one formula that assists in detoxification of the dead cancer cells. Graviola is claimed 10,000 times more powerful than chemotherapy, non toxic, only goes after, and kills cancer cells.
6. Purchase an A2Z ozone-03 air, water, and oil ozone generator. This will enable you to ozone your water, air, oils, and even your foods. Ozone 03 kills cancer cells on contact. If you ozone all your drinking water you will be killing cancer cells as your body is around 80% water. An A2Z aqua6 ozone generator is available from Amazon.com at around $70.00 Kangen alkaline water generator.
7. Purchase oxygen products: OxMoxy, Dynamo2, and Colo2Zone sold by EnGardehealth.com these sell for around $20.00 per product. OxyMoxy releases pure 02 into the body with every breath you inhale as is equivalent to one of those green oxygen cylinders you see people using with emphysema, and asthma, etc. It is for high altitudes also where the oxygen levels are decreased. Colo2Zone was a product initially formulated by Nikola Tesla. The modern version is magnesium oxide that when Vitamin C is introduced into the body begins to act upon the magnesium oxide that begins to gently release the oxygen into the colon to cleanse and detoxify. Another stabilized oxygen product I highly recommend is called Hydroxygen Plus. It contains ionic minerals, enzymes, amino acids, and oxygen. Purchase a Turapur-a hydrogen ion water maker. $44.95
8. From the research of cancer expert Dr. Johanna Budwig, M.D. Rx: 4 Tsp. of organic flax seed oil to 1 cup of organic sulfured cottage cheese or preferably 4 Tsp of high sulfured amino acids.
9. Then an organic vegan alkaline diet to produce an alkaline pH body between 7.35-7.45 pH. Cancer cells cannot survive in an overly alkaline environment. They are only survivable in an acidic pH and fed by sugar glucose. They are anaerobic weak mutated cells that went through four (4) initial stages the fourth stage they mutate into a cancer cell. Again they form with low oxygen, survive on blood sugar glucose, and an acid cellular environment. They are fermenting your body cells. In other words eating you up alive. The term is called cachexia or severe malnutrition caused by cancer cells. Also advised is Pronatura 555 mg. caps of Kombucha. Luckyvitamins.com, or Drinkgts.com Kombucha liquid.
10. Here are the main phyto chemicals, alkaline foods, and herbs: Foods Are: Black Garlic, (8.5-9.0 pH), Spirulina (8.5-9.0 pH), Kelp (8.5-9.0 pH), Reishi, Moer, Chaga, Maitake, Shitake Mushroom, Broccoli, Sweet Potato (7.5-8.0 pH), Blueberry, Papaya (8.5-9.0 pH), Green Tea, Extra Virgin Olive Oil, Lemon (8.5-9.0 pH), Mango (8.5-9.0 pH), Watermelon (8.5-9.0 pH), Seaweed (8.5-9.0 pH),

Chlorella (8.5-9.0 pH), Algae (8.5-9.0 pH), Kuduz Root (8.5-9.0 pH), Watercress (8.5-9.0 pH), Apricots (7.5-8.0 pH), Grapes (7.5-8.0 pH), Peaches (7.5-8.0 pH), Unripened Bananas (7.5-8.0 pH), Grapefruit (7.5-8.0 pH), Spinach (7.5-8.0 pH), Pumpkin (7.5-8.0 pH), Peas (7.5-8.0 pH), Garlic, Cabbage (7.5-8.0 pH), Beets (6.5-7.5 pH), and Red Onion-(5.30-5.88 pH highly anti-cncer)
Herbs are: Turmeric, Basil, Nutmeg, Guggul, Tropical Rose Mallow, Cat's Claw, Ginger Root, Rosemary, Cinnamon, Parsley, Cardamon, Chamomile, Chives, Cilantro, Graviola, Pau d' Arco, Boswella, Licorice, Cayenne, Red, Beet, Dandelion, and Galangal Roots. Alkaline foods and herbs are good for keeping your body in an alkaline pH. The best and normal body pH should be between 7.35-7.45 pH. This prevents inner inflammation and cancer. Avoid acidic foods such as high protein meats, sugar, and most cereals render the pH to an acidic range. This causes many serious health problems as there is a direct link recently discovered between an acidic pH, inner inflammation, and cancer. Note! The blood pH should always be below 7.56 pH as this prevents the cancer cell polymorphic microbe in the blood of all humans from proliferating.
11. Other cancer killing herbs are: cannabis marijuana T.H.C.-C.B.D., pau d' arco, una de gato, paw paw, chaparral, clary sage, black cumin seed, bushwood tree berry, Vit-B17 (apricot pips), germanium sequioxide, parsley, black garlic, frankincense, myrrh, (galangal, red, dandelion, ginger, beet, and turmeric roots).
12. Cancer killing elements are: oxygen 02, ozone 03, colloidal gold, colloidal silver, and bicarbonate of soda (NAHC03).
13. Cancer killing essential oil is: cannabis sativa-marijuana T.H.C.-C.B.D. see page 206 for Can Cell-1 essential oil formula.
14. Phyto-chemical alkaloids isoflavones that kill cancer are; genestein and daidzein. Found in fermented soy and red clover herb. In Halean-851 and in fermented miso soy paste "Doenzang."
15. Cancer killing detoxifying frequencies from D.N.R., Inc. light photon solutions are: Liquid Needle Bath Soak CAN-133, Lymph-L-105 COF-130EX, Yellow, Green, Original topicals. Immune system enhancers are: Eleuthro Siberian ginseng root, all other ginsengs (adaptogens) ashwanganda, astragalus, schizandra, moer, corlious, shitake, maitke, chaga, cordyceps, ganoderma (also called reishi or lucidum, and all other mushrooms, R.S.O. marijuana T.H.C.-C.B.D. or Tree of Life oil, Hemp C.B.D. oil, germanium sequioxide (interferon), bovine colostrum 1-I.G.H., black garlic, and super oxide dismutase (S.O.D.). For anti-stress Liquid Needle EXStress

and Chi Gong. Note! Recent research has indicated dates contain high amounts of polyphenols and a 59% cancer cell killing ability.

ALTERNATIVE-BIOLOGICAL-HOLISTIC CANCER FIGHTING NINJA WARRIORS a non profit organization. © 2016-17 by Jerome Plotnick, Ph.D., N.D.

Anyone with cancer currently or cancer in remission please accept my invitation along with Gerard Joseph and Tim Bevan to become part of our non profit group as a registered member. We are a forthcoming non profit organization with Alternative, Natural, Biological, Holistic Cancer information on self healing, treating cancer, and preventing it. Similar to Cureyourowncancer.org

We intend to form a non profit organization shortly to promote the education with non biased scientific credible information on all of the natural, alternative, holistic, remedies, treatments in the health rest-oral, and prevention of cancer world-wide. Conventional cancer oncology treatments that use chemotherapy and radiation are a one hundred twenty four ($124.6) billion dollar business. The success rates are minimal and usually a child or adult receiving the conventional treatment succumbs eventually to the cancer. The treatment kills your immune system and healthy cells. It cannot kill all of the cancer cells. Cancer is proven to be a biological disease, can only be eliminated usng biological remedies, and treatment. Fact: Life expectancy after chemotherapy is five years. This a non biological and suppressive treatment.

It is my hope that we can re-educate the public and give the masses a choice of treatments which are non toxic, highly successful, and cost effective. A total alternative, holistic, biological, approach to cancer, and remission. Anyone interested in our forthcoming non profit organization in the United States please contact either me Jerome Plotnick, Ph.D., N.D. or in India contact Gerard Joseph or E.U. contact Tim Bevan on facebook.com. Again, anyone interested is invited to join us. We intend to eventually become a non profit organization. In order to accomplish this we need your financial support. If you donate you will receive one of my books of your choice 1. The 13 Steps from Illness To Health-APNBMPDR-$20.00 2. Meta Your Mind-$10.00 3. Meta Your Health in 45 Days-$15.00 (with the 165 page chapter VII. entitled "Cancer What's the Answer?" Everything that a cancer patient or anyone wants and needs to know on how to prevent and eliminate cancer alternatively, by a powerful friendly flora intestinal tract producing a powerful immune system, an alkaline body and blood pH, herbs, foods, frequencies, detoxification, visualization (imagery), other mind healing methods, spiritual meditations thus allowing your body to heal itself as it was intended to biologically, and holistically. This is a mind-body-spirit connection for health rest-oral, well being, and longevity. The Tao of the Soul-Self-Slate a re-birthing (elimination of all erroneous zero order cognitive core erroneous beliefs), self healing of your mind-body-spirit (revitalizing and re-balancing your bio-fields (energy body's), (organs, glands, tissues, cells, acupuncture meridians, chakras, nadis-(nerves), and a how to begin a spiritual awakening). Plus healing sounds-vibrating frequencies tones, music, and chimes. Please contact me as we need your financial support to 1. obtain a non profit status 2. provide free alternative anti-cancer remedies for those unable to purchase them. 3. have a monthly news letter and website. Yours In Health, Jerome Plotnick, Ph.D., N.D.

CANCER CAUSING HOUSEHOLD, LAUNDRY, COSMETIC & FOOD PRODUCTS

1. Johnson & Johnson Baby Powder-contains TALC- a known carcinogen.
2. Cover Girl Replenishing Finish Makeup (Foundation) Proctor & Gamble-contains B.H.A.-carcinogenic, TALC-a known carcinogen, Triethanolamine T.E.A.-interacts with nitrites to form carcinogenic nitrosamines, Lanolin-D.D.T.-carcinogenic pesticide, Parabens-irritant causing contact dermatitis.
3. Crest Tartar Toothpaste-Proctor & Gamble-contains FD&C-Blue-carcinogenic, Saccharin-carcinogenic, Fluoride-carcinogenic.
4. Alberto VO5 Conditioner (Essence of Neutral Henna)-contains-Formaldehyde-carcinogenic, neurotoxin, contact dermatitiis, Polysorbate 80-contaminated with carcinogens-1,4 dioxane, FD&C Red #4.
5. Clairol Nice & Easy (Permanent Hair Color)-Clairol, Inc.-contains carcinogens Quaternium-15, Formaldehyde-carcinogen, neurotoxin, contact dermatitiis-Diethanolanise D.E.A.carcinogenic that interacts with nitrites to form carcinogenic nitrosamine, Phenylene-contact dermatitis, Propylene Glycol-contact dermatitis-Note! Evidence of a casual relalationship to non-Hodgkin's lymphoma, multiple myeloma, and other cancers.

6. Ajax Cleanser-Colgate-Palmolive, Inc.-contains-Crystalline Silica-carcinogen-eye, skin, and lung irritant.
7. ZUD-heavy Duty Cleanser-Reckitt & Coleman, Inc.-contains Crystalline Silica-carcinogenic-eye, skin, and lung irritant.
8. Lysol-Disinfectant Spray-Rickitt & Coleman, Inc.-contains Orthophenyphenol (O.P.P.-carcinogen and irritant.
9. Zodiac Cat & Dog Flea Collar-Sandez Argo, Inc.-contains Propoxor-carcinogen and a neurotoxin.
10. Ortho Weed B-Gon Lawn and Weed Killer-Monsanto, Inc.-contains Sodium 2,4 Dishlorphenoxyacetate 2,4-D-carcinogenic-evidence of a relationship to lymphnoma, soft tissue sarcoma, other cancers-neurotoxin, and reproductive toxin. Roundup contains glyphosate.
11. Beef Frankfurters-Oscar Meyer Foods Inc. et al.-contains unlabeled toxins-Benzenes hexachloride-carcinogen, Dacthal-carcinogen and can be contaminated with dioxins-irritant, Dieldrin-carcinogen, Xenoestrogen D.D.T.-carcinogen, Heptachlor-carcinogenic, neurotoxin, and reproductive toxin, Xenoestogen Hexachlorobenzene-carcinogenic, neurotoxin and reproductive toxin, Lindane-carcinogenic, neurotoxin, and damages to blood forming cells, Hormones-carcinogenic and feminizing, Antibiotics-carcinogenic, allergenic, and drug resistant.
Labeled Ingredient-Nitrates-interacts with the meats amines to form carcinogenic nitrosamines which is a major risk factor for childhood cancers. [leukemia]
12. Whole Milk-Crystal Dairy Farms, Borden, Lucerene et al. contain-D.D.T.-carcinogenic and xenoestrogen, Dieldrin-carcinogenic and xenoestrogen, Heptachlor-carcinogenic, neurotoxin, and reproductive toxin, Antibiotics-some are carcinogenic, cause allergies, and drug resistance, Recombinant Bovine Growth Hormone & IGH-1 aids for breast, colon, and prostate cancers. If your still going to drink milk then a safer alternative and advised is: rBGH-free raw organic. Advised is rice, almond, or coconut milk.
13. Most All Brand Named Laundry Detergents. Tide, etc. Proctor & Gamble all contain carcinogenic toxins. The reason that all toxic substances enter freely through your skin. A Clemson University study found that two percent (2%) of the fabric weight comes from laundry detergent. Since the skin absorbs seventy five percent (75%) of any fat soluble substance in comes in contact with within twenty six (26) seconds. Laundry Detergents may cause the following: skin problems like rashes, inflammation, severe itching, skin flaking or peeling, etc., allergies, headaches,

asthma, developmental disorders, infertility, birth defects, hormonal imbalances, and cancer.

Hidden Toxic Ingredients: Lineer Alkyl Sodium Sulfonate (L.A.S.S.)-carcinogenic, reproductive toxin, Petroleum (Petrol) Distilates-Carcinogenoic cause lung damage and inflammation to the mucous membranes, Phenols-toxic to the Central Nervous system (C.N.S.), heart, blood vessels, lung, and kidneys, Sodium Hypochloride (household bleach) reacts with organic materials in the environment-carcinogenic and toxic compounds are created that can cause reproduction toxins, endocrine, and immune system disorders. Polysorbate: blood clot, strokes, haart attacks, death. Note! Ralph Nader stated, "What is particularly galling about the "Dirty Dozen" is that these toxic chemicals don't have to be there. Yet these corporations continue to expose people to health hazards unnecessarily." Maybe its part of population elimination?

Current product labeling provides no warning for cancer or other chronic health issues. Food is labeled for cholesterol. But not for carcinogens. Cosmetics are labeled for major ingredients but not for those that are carcinogenic or contain carcinogenic compounds. Except for pesticides, household products contain no information on their ingredients. i.e. Proctor & Gamble.

Cancer rates are skyrocketing. Currently more than one third (1/2) of all of us will develop cancer in our lifetime. One quarter (¼) of us will die from the disease. It is predicted that eventually one (1) out of every two (2) people in the U.S. will develop cancer. Many cancers are due to avoidable exposure to industrial carcinogenic chemicals in the food we eat and all of the products we use. Cancer is preventable by biological natural treatment. Most cancer patients that receive chemotherapy, radiation, and internal surgery only have a five year life expectancy.

22 Herbs and Trees that are Cancer Fighters
1. <u>Astragalus</u>. (Huang Qi) a Chinese herb; an immune system enhancer, known to stimulate the body's natural production of interferon. It also assists the immune system in identifying rouge unwanted cells. The M.D. Anderson Cancer Centre in Texas conducted research indicating that Astragalus when having radiation therapy doubled survival times. What if you used it in conjunction with natural cancer alternative medicines?

2. <u>Berberis Family</u>. (Podophyllum peltanum) a slow active herbal purgative. Research has indicated these herbs to have a strong action against cancer and they are used especially with ovarian cancer. (In Cancer Watch March 2015). The ingredient berberine was also shown to out perform the brain cancer drug called Temozolomide in vitro. It was also shown to act synergistically with the drug and improve its efficacy.

3. <u>Blood-Red Root</u>. (Sanguinaria canadensis) Research indicates consistent neoplastic activity. It has been shown to be effective against cancer tumors, by shrinking them. It is one of the herbs used in the anti-cancer poultice called Black salve against both breast, skin cancers, and also with sarcoma cancer.

4. <u>Butchers Broom</u>. (Ruscus sculeatus) The active ingredient of the herb has been found to be called Ruscogenins which have tumor-shrinking and anti-estrogenic abilities. It can be used effectively with breast cancer.

5. <u>Cat's Claw</u>. (Uncaria tormentosa) also called Una de Gato) An adaptogen and very powerful immune system stimulant, it enhances the W.B.C. white blood cells clean up process called (phagocytosis). It is an excellent companion when used with astragalus, curcumin (turmeric), and echinecea. Research has indicated it can reduce tumor size, particularly with skin cancers. It also helps with the side effects of chemo and radiation therapy. It is anti-bacterial, viral, and fungal.

6. <u>Chaparral</u>. (Larrea mexicana) The Cancer Watch covered a major research story in the U.S. which confirmed the value of this herb. It boosts the immune system, stops metastases, and reduces tumor size. It seems positive when used with breast cancer and is another ingredient in Black salve. It is also an anti-oxidant, anti-microbial, and with low toxicity.

7. <u>Curcumin</u>. (Turmeric) This so called spice (Curcuma longa or Turmeric root) has been shown to have a significant anti-microbial and anti-inflammatory actions. This alone should be enough of a reason to use it in certain U.S. hospitals in the treatment of polyps and colon cancer. New research is indicating it can both shrink cancer tumors and inhibit the blood supply needed to grow tumors. It is also a very powerful antioxidant with liver protective benefits. The research also indicated that It out performs all anti-inflammatory used drugs without any side effects.

8. <u>Dang Shen Root</u>. (Codonopsis pilosula) This herb increases blood cells. This can be extremely important and helpful to cancer

patients receiving chemo, or radiation therapy, or in general to cancer patients whose cancer disease diminishes both white, and red blood cell levels.

9. Echinacea. (Echinacea purpurea) This herb is another immune system enhancer and also a cannabinoid. It gained recognition in treating the common cold. There is current research that its cannabinoid compounds in it that it is helpful in treating brain tumors apart from its ability to increase the levels of certain white blood cells in the body's immune system.

10. Feverfew. (Tanaceyum parthenium) This herb was researched by Rochester University in New York state and shown to be more effective than the drug cytarabine in killing leukemia cancer cells. The U.S. F.D.A. put the active ingredient called parthenoide, on its fast track program. Nothing currently has been heard. Why would it? As the puppet F.D.A. controlled by big pharmaceutical and two former Monsanto C.E.O.s do not want natural cost effective non toxic cures. Its on fast track to the garbage.

11. Goldenseal. (Hydrastis canadensis) One cause of stomach cancer can be the bacterium Helicobacter pylori. This bacteria burrows into the mucous lining of the stomach to hide from the gastric acids, then causes irritation, acid reflux, ulcers, and even cancer. Goldenseal is anti-microbial and is used in the South East Asia and the Caribbean against parasites. Golden seal taken along with the mineral Bismuth will help kill the bacterium Heliobacter pylori. Animal veterinarian doctors know this even though medical doctors don't. There is Berberine in Goldenseal. Goldenseal is also a powerful anti-inflammatory.

12. Milk Thistle. (Silymarin) It is an herb known for years as a liver detoxifier, enhancer, and this herb is now being shown to be able to protect the liver during chemotherapy. Research in the U.S. indicated that leukemia cancer patients who took Milk Thistle has reduced liver toxicity and chemotherapy side effects.

13. Pau D' Arco. (Taheebo) The Amazon tree bark was originally thought to be a strong anti-cancer agent, its actions have been re-clarified as an anti-bacterial, anti-viral, and anti-fungal. It is used in many So. American countries like Argentina in the treatment of cancer. New research on the differing of the ingredients has indicated that quinoids possess immune system strengthening abilities, are helpful in blood, and lymph cancers.

14. Red Clover. (Trifolium pratense) This herb is being researched and used by a number of cancer treatment centers including Royal Marsden. It has shown its potential as a part of a treatment

program against estrogen driven cancers from breast to prostate. One active ingredient in the so called herb of Hippocrates is the anti-estrogen compound called Genistein, which Professor Powles of the Royal Marsden named "the anti-estrogen," and hormone balancer.

15. <u>Sheep's Sorrell</u>. Used and one of the ingredients in Essiac formula and many other herbal remedies. It is a cleanser and aids in a healthy tissue regeneration. There is some suggestion from research that it helps normalize damaged cells and tissue. It is also a highly praised "vermifuge" used for expelling worms and other intestinal parasites.

16. <u>Skullcap</u>. (Scutellaria lateriflora) Research has shown it has action against many cancers. Especially lung, stomach, and intestinal cancers.

17. <u>Sutherlandia</u>. (Cancer bush) research has indicated that this herb is anti-inflammatory, anti-viral, and anti-fungal. It helps enhance the immune system, inhibits Tumour Necrosis Factor, known to drive the wasting away "cachexia" of the cancer patients body.

18. <u>Thorowax</u>. (Hares ear or Bulpleurum scorzoneraefollum) research has indicated its ability to enhance the production of natural interferon, has shown its effectiveness in curing liver cancer, and with bone cancers. See page 433 in The 13 Steps From Illness To Health-APNBMPDR book Japanese Research study on the effects of the Chinese herb Bupleurum on liver cancer by the Institute for Traditional Medicine and Preventive Health Care-1996.

19. <u>Wheatgrass</u>. (Cotyledons poaceae) One shot of wheat grass daily gives you the chlorophyll of 12 kilograms of broccoli. It is being used in one prominent South East Asia hospital due to its medicinal benefits of it being freshly juiced. It acts as a blood purifier (detoxifier). Also a liver and kidney cleansing agent. In recent research it after two weeks of using it has shown a significant increase in blood, tissue oxygenation levels, and also blood circulation.

20. <u>Sweet Wormwood</u>. (Artemeisia annus) This is another Chinese herb that has out-performed certain used anti-malaria drugs and is being used extensively instead of the drugs. It is highly anti-microbial, anti-yeast (fungal), and can be used as an effective part of an anti-candida diet program. Also certain cancer treatments cause excesses of yeasts to form, (for example, in leukemia treatment), and threatening the patients health further. Excess yeast (fungal) are even felt by many cancer experts to be one of the causes of cancer. Current research indicates that the Endiobiont cancer causing polymorphic microbe is the third stage

of development before the fourth stage where it becomes a cancer cell. In some current research wormwood has indicated to have direct anti-cancer properties. The fungal stage is the third (3rd) stage on becoming the fourth (4th) stage which is the cancer cell.
21. Cannabis. (Cannabis sativa or marijuana) Recent research has indicated that this herb being used currently called medical marijuana kills cancer cells effectively without harming healthy cells. The cannabinoid compound in it called T.H.C.-C.B.D. is the agent that destroys cancer cells. It also is used by the recently discovered Endocannabinoid System E.C.S. By uptake into C.B.D. receptor sites in the body. Brain, immune system, and organs have these receptor sites. It also is being used to treat autism, H.I.V.-A.I.D.S., and other chronic diseases successfully. Pg. 281.
22. Pine Tree Needles. (Coniderous evergreen or pinus strobus) Pine Needle tea is a cancer killing, health tonic, and cancer preventive though immune system enhancing. Pine needles have been used for thousands of years by Native Americans for health benefits. However, it is not a go-to-for alternative medicine these days though it certainly should be. In fact, it can help provide mental clarity, conquer diseases, and even combat cancer effectively. Pine needles are actually more potent in Vitamin C than even orange juice, was used extensively by the early American settlers to avoid Vitamin C deficiency disorder, scurvy, since pine needles also have a very high content of anti-oxidants, and it is also helpful for boosting immunity.

Herbs and Edible Plants-Foods that Contain Cannabinoids E.C.S.
1. Coneflower. (Echinacea purpurea)) The many medicinal benefits of this herb-plant are well known. They are fighting the common cold to relieving anxiety, fatigue, arthritis, and migraines, etc. They are similar to what marijuana (cannabis sativa) also does. So what do both have in common? Yes they both contain cannabinoids. Some species of echinacea contain cannabimimetics. The herbal cannabimimetics are a slight bit different than the cannabinoids found in marijuana plant, but they engage the Endocannabinoid System E.C.S. just as well. The primary cannabinoids in echinacea are called N-alkyl amides or (N.A.A.s). The echinacea canabiboids (cannabimimetics) interact most with the E.C.S. at the CB-2 receptor. This particular receptor is responsible for regulating the immune system, pain, and inflammatory response. In marijuana, the psychoactive C.B.D. is T.H.C., and is the the primary stimulator of the C.B.D. receptor called CB-2. Pages: 229-239,281

2. <u>Oxeye Plants</u>. (Heliopsis helianthoides) These plants are also known to have these types of cannabinoids.

2a. <u>Electric Daisy</u>. (Acmella oleracea) This Amazon herb or plant is also known and called the toothache plant. It can be made into a powerful pain killing gel. Trials of it were conducted at Cambridge University and found that the herb was successful in blocking pain receptors located at the nerve endings. Cannabinoid like compounds known as N-Isobutylamides act upon the CB-2 receptor, making this odd looking flower a very powerful painkiller, and as well as anti-inflammation fighter. Its so powerful that many dentists are now using it as the drug of choice when working with patients with impacted wisdom teeth and even tooth extraction.

3. <u>Helichrysum umbraculigerum</u>. This daisy is found in South Africa and contains a large amount of cannabigeol (C.B.G.) It has antidepressant, mood stabilizing, and anti-inflammatory properties. At an annual meeting and lecture of the International Cannabinoid Research Society, the Italian natural product chemist Giovanni Appendino, stated, "that Helichrysum was used like hemp, to make fumes in ritual ceremonies in African pharmacology." He also suggested that compounds in the plant may have a psychotropic effect that is similar to cannabinoids like marijuana.

4. <u>Liverwort</u>. (Rodula marginata) There appears to be another version of T.H.C. called Liverwort found in New Zealand. It contains a large amount of perrottetinenic acid. It was discovered in 2002, this perrottetinenic acid is remarkably similar to T.H.C. It acts upon the CB-1 receptor of the E.C.S. The CB-1 receptor is the primary binding site for T.H.C. and is what gives the compound its psychoactive effects. Although there have been no reported psychoactive effects to date the from this lichen plant. The plant has been used for a natural treatment of bronchitis as well as gallbladder, liver, and bladder problems.

5. <u>Chocolate</u>. (Theobroma cacao) A well know fact among marijuana smokers is that if you consume dark chocolate before smoking, it will increase dramatically the psychoactive effects. This is because chocolate contains a variety of compounds that interact with the Endocannabinoid System E.C.S. Similar to non psychoactive C.B.D. found in marijuana, chocolate contains compounds that interact with a particular enzyme in the body. This enzyme is known as F.A.A.H. F.A.A.H.'s is responsible for the breakdown of the endocannabinoid which is known as anandamide in our bodies. Anandamide is our natural version of T.H.C. Compounds in chocolate

de-activate these enzymes, increasing the amount of anandamide in the body. This makes us feel happy, relaxed, and in a good mood. In 1996, researchers from the Neurosciences Institute of San Diego found that anandamide and two (2) other separate compounds in chocolate that act as cannabinoids, although chocolate is no where near the potent psychoactive that T.H.C. is, it definitely also has an impact on the brain, and body more than you might expect.

6. Black Pepper. (Piper nigrum) There are some marijuana strains like Hash Plant that have a peppery taste and aroma. The reason is that they contain a high level of a particular terpene called beta-cayophyllene (B.C.P.). A terpene is an aroma molecule that's found in plant essential oils. Unsurprisingly, this distinct aroma and flavor is found heavily in black pepper. It was recently discovered that B.C.P. actually functions as a cannabinoid. Like many other plant compounds the B.C.P. has a binding affinity with the CB-27 receptor. Research has also suggested that the anti-inflammatory compounds of this terpene make it therapeutically valuable for treating arthritis and osteoporosis. Other research has confirmed, indicated that B.C.P. can increase the efficacy of any anti-cancer drug, or natural remedy.

7. Peruvian Maca. (Lepidium meyenii) Maca root grows in the mountains of Peru at high altitudes of 7000 to 11,000 feet, making it the highest altitude plant in the world. Maca is a radish-like root vegetable that is related to the sweet potato family, is tuberous, and round in form. The root itself is around three (3) to six (6) centimeters in length. There are four (4) different types of maca root based on the color of the root. Root colors are creamy yellow, or light to dark purple, or black. Chemically it contains significant amounts of amino acids, carbohydrates, minerals including calcium, phosphorous, zinc, magnesium, iron as well as vitamins B1, B2, B12, C, and E. It also contains a number of glyocides. It has generalized tonic effects in the enhancement of the biochemical functioning of the body. It has an effect on the endocrine function. This system includes all of the body's glands (pineal) etc., and the hormones they secrete. That exist in the body that control such conditions as fertility, sexual function, epilepsy, digestion, brain, nervous system physiology, and energy levels. Hormone regulation is responsible for all of the physiological functions. These are sexual arousal, physical activity, and mental states of being. Maca root is an adaptogen, which increases the body's ability to defend itself against both mental, physical weakening, and protect one for potential illness.

It does this by supporting both adrenal and pituitary gland health. Its many uses are it helps relieve symptoms of P.M.S. and menopause. Decreases symptoms like hot flashes and night sweats. It enhances a mans fertility and sexual function. It also increases libido, sex drive, energy, stamina, and promotes a general feeling of well-being. For cancer driven hormone related breast cancer maca may be one way to naturally balance the hormones. Note! Red Clover herb also balances the hormones.

8. <u>Chinese Rhodoendron</u>. (roododendron arboreum) It is used as an effective cure for the following: anorexia, kidney disease, cancer, lung cancer, eczema, and menstrual problems. It is an anti-inflammatory, stomatic, astringent, and digestive herb. It contains the following: alkaloids, glycosides, steroids, anthraquinones, phlobatannins, tannins, flavinoids, saponins, and terpenoids. Note! The leaves are poisonous. Note! Do not take in high doses. The flowers and petals are used. It is an evergreen. It grows in a tropical climate. It grows as high as 12 meters. It is best used for kidney disease. India, Burma, Mongolia, China, and Nepal. It is also used to treat dysentary and diarrhea. The Greek translation of its name means rose tree and is the national flower of Nepal. There are 30 species of it. The leaves are used as incense in Buddhist Monasteries. Its flowers are used as offerings to pay-homage and for decoration on social occasions.

9. The following herbs-spices-leaf are known cancer fighters: black garlic, oregano, cloves, cayenne pepper, cinnamon, ginger, basil, nutmeg, rosemary, parsley, cardamon, chives, cilantro, boswellia, licorice, cayenne pepper, tropical rose mallow, guggul, cat's claw, green tea (Vit. K2) and turmeric. Turmeric effects can be increased significantly when combined with black pepper, (red, ginger, dandelion, beet, and galangal roots), and graviola.

10. The following organic vegetables are known cancer fighters: broccoli, tomato, sweet potato with skin, red onion, watercress, kelp, spirulina, beet, chlorella, kudiz root, ginger root, dandelion root, horse radish, sauerkraut, shitake, reishi, moer, and black chaga mushrooms.

11. The following fruits are known cancer fighters: lemon, purple grapes, brown spotted banana, papaya, mango, jack fruit, blue and black berries, bitter melon, cantaloupe, avacado, mangosteen (noni), dates, and the bushwood tree berry.

12. The following oils are known cancer fighters: organic pure extra virgin olive oil, frankincense, myrrh, sage, black cumin,

hemp, cannabis oils, flax seed, and organic pure coconut oil. Also in Ayurveda medicine "Ghee" or also called clarified butter.

13. The following minerals are known cancer fighters: Celtic sea salt or Himalayan pink salt.

14. The following elements are known cancer fighters: ozone-03 and oxygen 02 and hydrogen H ions. Also advised are colloidal silver @ 1100 p.p.m. and gold @ 60 p.p.m. or higher if available.

15. The following food of organic flax seed, organic sulfured cottage cheese combined used and proven by Dr. Johanna Budwig, M.D. to heal cancer, and many other diseases. Use high sulfur amino acids instead of cottage cheese and orgnic flaxseed oil.

16. Essiac Tea an anti-cancer herbal formula. Essiac tea spelled backward is Caisse, the surname of Rene Caisse a nurse who was from North Carolina, and came upon a Canadian Indian medicine man who's herbal tonic was used for woman's breast cancer in the late 19th century. Rene Caisse met the one woman that had cured her breast cancer while in a nursing home decades before. So Caisse decided to collect the herbs in the formula and began to heal people from cancer in 1920. This began by word of mouth and after some time many more people began coming to her. Her cancer healing formula soon evolved, she eventually ended up in Bracebridge township, and it was there that she was provided a building which was an old hotel.

She treated patients there for over eight years and this is where her Essiac formula gained medical recognition from several of the cancer patients that were healed, she had many M.D.'s endorse her Essiac tea in the 1930's to 1940's. She charged no one, all the patients had to be pre, and post diagnosed by an M.D. Rene Caisse had healed many thousands of cancer patients. Before her death she signed her rights away on the Essiac formula to a Canadian company called Resperin Corporation, Ltd. for one dollar Canadian. The deal was included that promised to keep the secret formula pure and to keep it accessible for everyone. In 1995 Resperin signed it the formula over to Essiac, Canada International which is currently a provider of the formula. The formula contains a blend of organic wild crafted non irridated burdock root, slippery elm bark, Turkish rhubarb root, and sheep sorrel leaves with the roots used as part of the Essiac tea. www.essiac-canada.intl.com

AFTERWARD VIII

How to Restore Your Health. Treatment and Prevention of Cancer.
Alternatively, Holistically, and Using Your Mind-Body-Spirit.
My other book the 13 Steps From Illness To Health-APNBMPDR lists the following on mind-body to spirit connections and healing ones self. I use these in this book as well. I listed various well known proven scientifically facts and methods to use the spirit to allow the mind to heal the body. Enhance and power your immune system and once you are able to heal the spirit it will then be able to heal the mind so you can effectively heal your body. It all begins with your spirit. "S-P-S-N-I" © 2009-2017 JPPHDND

On page 14 is <u>Spiritual-Magnetic-Belief-Faith-Placebo Healing</u>. Whatever you believe truly believe and have faith it will manifest. If you believe it you will see it. And if you believe it has already happened it certainly will. Your mind acts as a two edge sword. The subconscious mind that is always conscious accepts your thoughts, beliefs, and manifests them in your life whether they are good, or bad. Therefore your mind can be a Healer or a Slayer. The choice is up to you Healer? or Slayer?

On page 15 is <u>Shamanistic-Visualization-Belief Healing</u>. Shamans world-wide have around an 85% success rate in healing all sickness. They employ a variety of altered mind states such as belief, prayer, rituals, visualization, herbs, repetitious drumming, and rattling sounds to accomplish their healing people.

On page 22 are <u>The Bach Flower Essences</u>. The 38 listed Bach remedies he used to heal the spirit-mind (emotions and inherited miasms) that he believed were the cause(s) of all physical illnesses. He was a medical doctor in England who practiced both allopathic and homeopathic medicine. He discovered that certain flower petals in the English country side produced frequencies that were able to eliminate what he called the Seven (7) Deadly Sins, the Seven (7) Mental Terror States (wrong virtues) that were what he believed the basis, and the direct cause of all physical illness. He formulated and extracted using pure water from the various flower petals the essences he used to literally cure 100% of all his patients that were ill physically. He actually gave up his very successful allopathic and homeopathic practices to exclusively treat his patients with the Bach flower essences. <u>The (7) Seven Deadly Sins are</u>: <u>1</u>. Pride <u>2</u>. Cruelty <u>3</u>. Hate <u>4</u>. Self-love 5. Ignorance 6. Instability 7. Greed. The (7) Seven Mental Terror States are: 1. Fear 2. Un-certainty 3. No interest in the present 4. Loneliness 5. Over sensitivity to outside influences 6. Despondency 7. Overly concern with the welfare of others. He also formulated the Five (5) Principles which are: 1. Spirit and soul-the body is the recognition of a creator-a higher power. 2. Removal of wrong virtues. 3. Our time on earth is a speck of the eternal evolution of our soul-spirit. 4. Harmony of the soul-spirit and inner peace. 5. Unity of everything. "All is one and one is all. All one God Creator and Universal Unity. The Law of One. See also on page 263.

On page 27 is Mind Over Matter. It is a fact, well known that your mind has the ability to cure any disease, and illness when it is in proper functioning. The universe according to the latest Quantum Theory is that the human being or physical matter, the (seen), and the unseen or invisible non-matter is not divided equally. The human being's physical body is nothing more than a template called a bio-field or a vortex (blueprint-hologram) which is moving (vibrating) at various rates of frequencies, wave forms which constitute our human physical seen form, and invisible unseen thoughts from our mind. The mind is an extension of our brain akin to wave frequencies that are emitted from it. Thoughts that are unseen, are in reality both real, can cause health, or illness. When viewed in its correct state it is easy to determine that so called disease (illness) is no more than an interference, or a disturbance in the bio-energy field of a particular body system, organ, and gland, etc. On the higher aspect of the universal energy flowing into our physical body there are the bio-field causal energy bodies called the physical, etheric, mental, and astral, etc. There also levels of mind: mental, spiritual, instinctive, and intellectual. The Ayurveda system of the 11 major chakras, the other minor chakras, acupuncture points, the nadis or nervous system also can be viewed as when they are blocked, disturbed cannot power the body correctly, and this is the cause of all physical illness. Prana the life force is needed to power our mind and body so we can maintain a healthy vibrant state. So on a cellular level of understanding it is a direct interference of the communication system between our trillions of cells that make up our tissues, organs, glands of our physical body, and the life force prana that powers our body. The mind has a large role in this because it is known that whatever you are thinking, saying, and in other words communicating to your trillions of cells will actually cause a certain result. i.e. A person says, "you are making me sick to my stomach" and this is heard by the subconscious mind for enactment. This also causes a low frequency stress that can actually put (HCl) hydrochloric acid into the stomach. When there is no food for it to act upon and digest the results are a peptic ulcer. This is where the mind, its state of consciousness, thought, e-motion-feeling, altered, normal states of consciousness have an effect on the body's timing, and proper function. So be careful of what you say, feel, think as these can effect your health, and well-being. So begin to realize where these negative thoughts are originating from and cancel them. Say to them "cancel-cancel". You cannot separate your thinking (mind) from your physical (body).

Your state of consciousness and your "Yi" a Chinese word for total focus, concentration, and intention. In a study that was being performed by scientists looking for the subatomic particles called leptons. It was only when they fully intended to see them, in other words they completed focuses, and concentrated on seeing them were able to see them. Others who did not do this were unable to see them even though the both groups used the same electronic microscope. See Vibrational Medicine by Dr. Richard Gerber, M.D.

On page 29 is Psycho the (mind)-Soma the (body) Neuro the (nervous system) Immunology the (immune system) or P.S.N.I. Which means the following the mind controls the body, which controls the nervous system, and the immune system. I recently added to this Spiritus © or the spirit is over the mind. Heal the spirit, it will heal the mind, then the mind can be able through the nervous, and immune systems heal the body. "S-P-S-N-I-L-E-E-A-C." (c) 2000-2017 by JPPHDND. Added is Lymphatic, Endocrine, Endocannabinoid, Acupuncture, and Chakra systems. See Vibrational Medicine by Dr. Richard Gerber, M.D.

On page 32 is Mind Healing Programs. Healing oneself by using the mind is not anything new and has been used by the masters for centuries. Christ said,: If ye see what you desire in your mind as if it has already happened, it will." Dr. Kenneth Pellitier wrote a famous book in which he stated, "Mind is a Healer, or Mind is a Slayer." Have you heard the term positive thoughts in, then positive thoughts out, or conversely negative thoughts in, then negative thoughts out. In other words the mind will respond to whatever you feed into it. Its akin to the virgin soil, if you plant corn the earth will return to you in abundance the corn you planted. But if you plant nightshade a deadly poison the earth will also return to you in abundance nightshade the poison. The mind is like the earth, it does not care what you plant, it just acts, and returns to you on what you feed it. Put positive thoughts in and positive outcome will be returned. Conversely, if you put negative thoughts in then negative outcomes will be returned to you. So again the choice is up to you Positive Healer? Or Negative Slayer? What is your choice?

The wonder of the mind is that it is not tangible as you cannot see it. But it exists and has tremendous power to heal if used correctly. The mind is an invisible extension of our brain. An extension if you will where your thoughts, thinking, and all our daily activities take place. There are our senses, data sensing, unconscious, conscious functions that take place in the brain, and are realized by you in your mind. The mind works in concert with your subconscious minds belief system. This is called the zero order cognitive core belief system. Also if you see it in your mind, you will believe it, and manifest it. If you truly believe it, you will also see it, and manifest it in your life. The trick is to truly be able to see it and believe it. The mind's eye your third eye "ajna" chakra is the pineal gland and the center of imagination. Its also called your minds eye. This is the minds screen when you close your eyes such as in meditation, self or hetero mediation awareness called hypnosis, biofeedback, or neurofeedback training. It is the alpha state of brain frequency and altered consciousness state. It is here that the forces of belief, intention, and the mind's eye imagination meet to create in reality the desired visualization, or picture on the screen in, or on your minds eye. As an example in E.E.G. neurofeedback training we train the person over time to enter what is called the hypnogogic window (this is a state of deep contemplation or a state of reverie) noted by long term meditation practitioners. The window is where the brain wave frequencies of alpha and theta meet, creating an opening in the subconscious mind where all visualizations, and suggestions are acted upon almost immediately. So here is where what we see, say, think goes deep into the mind, and creates it in reality. Also the third eye center "ajna" chakra to it whatever you place there is to it your reality.

Imagination and reality are one in the pineal gland the third eye chakra. We affect it when we perform self and hetero hypnosis, any meditation, or E.E.G. Neurofeedback alpha-theta brainwave training also called electronic Zen. See: Bioenergetic, Mind & Natural Medicine, Meta Your Meditation Volumes. 1 & 2, Meta Your Mind, Mind-Memes-Miasms, Virus Takeover to a Mind Healing Makeover, Meta Your Manifestation books and audio the Tao of the Soul-Self-Slate by Jerome Plotnick, Ph.D., N.D. Other study's performed also indicate the minds ability to enhance our immune system and healing from illness. Dr. David Hall, Ph.D. Psychologist demonstrated that when patients pictured their W.B.C. white blood cells increasing in number they were successful. Doctors Wayne Smith and John Schneider experimented with volunteers that imagined one type of white blood cell, the neutrophil, left the bloodstream to fight germ invaders inside the cells of various organs. What they found was the neutrophil blood levels dropped, but not at the levels of the white blood cells. The mind control is much greater than once believed and it is also extremely precise. Confirmed by Doctors Carl O Simonton and Janet Harnicky.

Here are some of the <u>Quotes From Famous Healers</u>:
"If you perceive it, then conceive it, then believe it, you will achieve it." Mary Baker Eddy-Mind Science. "If you believe it you will see it." Dr. Wayne Dyer. "Mind is a Healer, Mind is a Slayer-Dr. Kenneth Pellitier. "Take your positive mental vitamins daily."-Dr. Nathan Fink. "Imagery in Healing-Shamanism in Modern Medicine."-Dr. Jeanne Achterberg. "Think and Grow Rich"-Napolean Hill. "The Power of Positive Thinking." Dr. Norman Vincent Peale. "As a man thinketh all day long in his heart he becometh." James Allen. "We come from an invisible field that all our dreams are made of. The Field of all Possibilities." Dr. Deepak Chopra. "Duty makes us do things well, but love makes us do them beautifully." Zig Zigler.

On page 50 is <u>Mind-Memes-Miasms</u>. Recent research evidence showed that there is a part of the brain that contains the negative factors of passed on inherited toxins called miasms or currently held negative thoughts called miasms. These are the mind's spiritual toxins that are the cause of fear, depression, negative sub conscious thinking, anxiety, constant worry, and even mania (manic thoughts). Once realized and understood these all can be eliminated or neutralized by the use of a homeopathic remedy called Apex Energetics Miasm Tox, goEnergetix's.com-"Fields of Flowers that are the Bach 38 Flower Essences in one (1) bottle at 30C power, and also by D.N.R., Inc.com IN.-Liquid Needle's-ExStress, Chi Gong, L.N.T.B., NRV, Original-E-116 light photon solutions. Besides the aforementioned there are many brain nutrients, essential oils, and a variety of herbs that can be used for these inherited miasm toxins. See Apex Energetics Miasmtox. A homeopathic remedy for miasm(s) elimination. Miasms are inherited.

Miasms are passed on multi generational imperfections from your ancestors. These are passed on genetic information in your D.N.A. chromosomes from your grandparents, parents, and your family tree. This affects your present state of health and well-being. It effects the way you think currently. These so called miasms which are based upon your zero order cognitive core beliefs are the spiritual "viruses"-toxins that form the energetic foci that interfere with your brain (mind), body (soma), and spirit (shen). Just like a computer can become infected with a virus so can you. Again, let me state that miasms are frequency interference (energetic interference) that block or interfere with brain, nervous system, cellular communications, the cause of many emotional, and mental problems. This is the basis of negative thinking and behaviors. This causes many undetectable symptoms and the direct cause of many illnesses. Miasms are also on the physical plane of passed on diseases like psoriasis, syphillis, and gonorrhea, etc. Remember that just one negative thought can and does compromise your immune system. This is a proven and researched scientific fact. Cancer can be brought about by stress, negative thoughts, thinking, and it decreases your immune systems ability to fight off invaders like a cancer cell. A proven fact is that just one negative thought can depress your immune system.

On page 50 is <u>The Holistic Approach to Health</u>. Holistic health views the person as a whole and this includes their life styles, belief systems, and attitude. If a person focuses on illness (disease) rather than health they cannot manifest health. Holistic promotes healthful patterns of positive thinking, focusing on health, followed by positive attitudes, and behaviors will govern a person's state of health. The mind, body, and the spirit connection. If one heals the spirit then the spirit can heal, the mind, and the mind can heal the body.

When we say we need to heal ourselves then we are just talking about feeling no pain and having no illness symptoms. But the holistic approach to health is about a human being on all levels of being or as many state, "a spiritual being in physical form having a human experience." Again let me state that treating symptoms of an illness does not have anything to do with the healing of one's self. It is only masking the cause(s) of illness.

"Ka" is a spiritual entity an aspect of a person, believed to live within the body during life, and to survive after physical death. Remember the most important role of the spirit (shen) has over the mind and in health. Your peace of mind (inner peace), soul harmony is the greatest aid in recovering from any illness, and including cancer. In many instances the hypertension, the stress of daily modern everyday life directly interferes with our peace of mind, soul harmony causing us to have a compromised, very decreased immune system, and thereby unable to fight off illness. Here is my daily mantra I begin each day with, "I am a wave of tranquility and calmness (Peace of God) in an ever negative changing sea of chaos. My number one goal is inner peace and soul-spirit harmony." So again holistic or holism means the whole. And that means the whole of you which is the inter relationship between the mind, body, and the spirit. An Act of Forgiveness is required. Pg.100-01

Again, this relates to cancer as using chemotherapy, radiation alone destroys, kills your immune system, when coupled by negative thinking, and all of the aforementioned factors you cannot be healed. You need your immune system to survive and stay healthy. Another factor is the daily stress that actually is imagined and it compounds itself in the body. Hypertension the unseen killer keeps you in a state of fight, flight, or mental exhaustion. So in the treatment of cancer one must not only be concerned with physically taken remedies, but most importantly be concerned with a positive mind, and a balanced healed spirit.

On page 54 is The Bach Flower Essence Remedies. When a person has fear, worry, tension, frustration, hate, aggression, or negative emotions as pointed out by Dr. Edward Bach, M.D. These cause us to have the seven deadly sins which are: 1. pride, 2. cruelty, 3. hate, 4. self-love, 5. ignorance, 6. instability, 7. greed. These will produce the physical illness to manifest. As long as a person has one of the seven deadly sins then one cannot restore their health and well-being. These and the mental terror states of: 1. fear, 2. uncertainty, 3. no interest in the present circumstances, 4. loneliness, 5. over sensitivity to influences, 6. despair, 7. despondency, 8. over concern for others welfare, 9. negative ideas, etc. These he believed were the reason, the cause of all physical, and mental illnesses. These he also believed were the cause of a diminished immune system function. After he treated his patients with his Bach Flower essence remedies he discovered that they all would heal quickly. He believed that all disease was directly caused by these unbalanced states of mind and spirit. This is why I also believe as Dr. Bach and highly recommend a remedy called "Fields of Flowers" that contains all thirty eight (38) of Dr. Bach's flower essences in one bottle at thirty (30C) power. It is available at goEnergetics.com and is cost effective. You will use only what essences you need. Again, I strongly believe, highly recommend any cancer patient, or anyone with any illness to begin taking it. Also on pagea: 261,263

On page 55 is <u>The Mind-Body Connection</u>. There has been other confirmed research in this area that states that 60% or more of all illnesses involve a psychosomatic promoting factor. This began a new field called <u>Psycho</u> (mind), <u>Somatic</u> Soma(body), <u>Neuro</u> (nervous system), <u>Immunology</u> (immune system). I added to it <u>Spiritus</u> (spirit-shen), <u>Endocrine</u> (glands), <u>Lymphatic</u> (lymph system), <u>Blood</u> (W.B.C.-basophils,neutrophils), <u>Chakras</u> (prana centers), and <u>Endocannabinoid</u> (C.B.D. receptors). So what I am saying is that is that the spirit (shen), has control over the mind (psyche), the mind has control over the body (soma), which includes the nervous system (neuro), and the immune system (immunology). The new field of Spirit-Psycho-Somatic-Neuro-Immunolgy-Blood-Lymphatic-Endocrine-Endocannainoid-Acupuncture-Chakra © 2017 JPPHDND has arisen with proof that there are dramatic effects of the emotions on the immune system, nervous system, and the endocrine-endocannbinoid systems. In the research on cancer patients doctors O. Carl Siminton, at his cancer clinic in Texas, and Janet Harnicky, Ph.D. a specialist at U.C.L.A Medical Center in psycho-somatic-neuro-immunology b oth have been able to achieve remarkable cancer remissions, and recovery. This was through the use of a combination of visualization, relaxation, cognitive behavior modification techniques, hypnosis, and meditation as an adjunct to conventional cancer treatment. My approach has been with the added use of E.E.G. Neurofeedback, deep states hypnogogic training, and hypnotherapy. The use of visualization, suggestions are vital in both E.E.G. Neurofeedback alpha-theta brainwave training, and in hypnotherapy. S.P.S.N.I.B.L.E.E.A.C. © 2016-2117 by J.P.Ph.D., N.D. Read Dr. Bernie Segiel's book. "Love, Medicine and Miracles."

Your Thoughts Effect Your Immune System Study.
Here is a past study that indicates just how powerful your mind and your thoughts are concerning your immune system. A double blind study used three groups of people. The groups were given pre and post testing or measurement of their W.B.C. white blood cell count an immune system component. One group the control was given negative stimulus in the form of negative words, insults, and were yelled at. The second group had nothing done to it. The third group the experimental group received positive stimulus in the form of hugs, positive words, and affirmations. The pre-test results were nearly all the same concerning the W.B.C. Count. The post-test W.B.C. Count results were as follows: Group one the control group that were given negative stimulus has a very extremely low W.B.C. count and lower immunity. The second group that received nothing remained all about the same W.B.C. count. The third experimental group that received positive stimulus had a very high W.B.C. White Blood Count and a very high immunity. The study results strongly indicate the power of the mind, mental, and emotional in the white blood cell count that is an indication of your immunity. The higher immunity group given the positive stimulus, this influenced and raised their W.B.C., and immunity. Conversely, the lower W.B.C. count group that was influenced negatively has lowered their immunity. This study indicates the direct correlation between the mind and the immune system function. Again, I believe as many other experts state, that the mind plays a most important role in your immune system function, and the healing of any disease.

On page 57 is The Spiritual Connection. The spiritual aspect of any illness can be viewed as spiritual degeneration. The soul-spirit has a definite purpose for us, but when we neglect it, or get away from that purpose, which is usually our minds, not our hearts, and this is where we become spiritually sick. There is your Dharma or your meaning and purpose in life and when you are not full filling it you have chaos followed by disappointment. It is called heart break. You are not in spiritual alignment and you are going against Divine Will. This is where you believe you are in control (ego) and not Divine Creator Universal Consciousness that we call (God) by many different names. This is what Dr. Bach called it when you are not aligned with your souls divine purpose and will for you. Dr. Wayne Dyer put it this way when he sang, "Row, row, row your boat (you) gently down the stream (go with the flow of nature), merrily, merrily, merrily (happy in harmony and healthy), life is but a dream (no mind bliss, joy, and contentment).

If you try to row your boat hard up Niagara Falls against the current then life becomes a struggle, a nightmare, and a hardship. Then stated by James Redfield, your soul is like a ship going on a definite destination. If you sail it with a definite purpose, use your rudder, and chart the path you will achieve your destination. If you let your ship leave the harbor without a rudder or destination then you will go anywhere the winds of chance take you. You will sail aimlessly and never reach your intended universal destination. And, so it is with your spiritual self, your soul. It has a divine definite destination for you and you need to let it guide you there. Rx: Daily meditation.

The universe will always guide you if you ask it to, then wait for it to respond, confirm to you its divine path, and will for you. Here is how you can ask the universe the Divine Mind Intelligence to guide you. Go out into nature, then relax yourself. Then ask for guidance and direction. Wait and be patient. Soon you will receive an answer. Allow whatever happens to guide you. The answer will eventually come so be open for it. Remember if you have to try at something and you fail constantly this is not your Dharma, or meaning, and purpose. When you are aligned with your Divine will and purpose everything is easy. You don't have to struggle, it is natural as in nature. The grass grows, the sun shines, there is no struggle, and it just is. And so it is with your souls will for you. It is so easy, simple, and uncomplicated you begin doubting it. That is because you always had to struggle being out of alignment with your soul.

This is a most important aspect of your health because if your mind, body is not in synchronicity with your soul-spirit (shen), then you cannot have health, and well being. Most all the experts believe and state that every illness is a direct result of negative thinking. All illness is a direct result of spiritual degeneration that manifests in all of the physical symptoms.

On page 76 is The Mind-Body to Spirit Connection. All is one and one is all. You cannot separate the physical body from your higher self, the spirit, which overseas the mind, and your thinking. This is why I believe a spiritual program of recovery is essential in any healing program. Daily prayer to a Higher Power, meditation to connect to that Higher Power is essential to heal yourself. Also discovering your true Dharma meaning and life's purpose for you. Then there is Arma or your service to humanity this helps you to achieve the understanding of unity and unconditional love. You must also free yourself of all resentments, fears, hate, and judgment of others. No retaliation or getting even with anyone. Eliminate all negative Karma. Rx: An Act of Forgiveness. Pg.100

This is Advised to Say and to Pray Daily for all Cancer Patients. Affirm and pray:
"God or Higher Power or Divine Universal Mind Creator: "Help my mind from thinking negatively and constantly about everything, release me from cravings to straighten out everyone else's affairs. Help my mind free itself of endless details; get to the point of things immediately. Seal my lips, do not complain about aches, and pains. Help my my mind from clashing with others; give me humility, and less cock-sureness. Give me the ability to see good things everywhere and especially in unexpected places, let me see the talent in unexpected people, give me gratitude, grace to tell them, and praise them. Make me a sweet and gentle loving person, make me a good listener because even who you may consider ignorant has something interesting and meaningful to say, always be interested, and appreciative of what others have to say. Help me from being sensitive about my age, looks, or rights. Allow me to appreciate, understand and extract what I need, when I need it from life. I ask for others what I ask for myself, I prosper, they prosper, I go in blessings of peace, harmony, and prosperity, they go too, may everyone be blessed, and may all things work out for the greatest good of all concerned. My goal is always "Inner Peace of God" and soul-spirit harmony. With full faith: Christ, Krishna, Shiva, Buddha Consciousness," Aum, Namaste, A-Men, So Mote It Be.

On page 145 is Spirituality and Illness. All illness is an inner reflection of the patient. Illness has a definite purpose and the symptoms are manifested in the mind, body, to spiritual imbalance. In many illnesses such as cancer the person has an unresolved emotional issue that blocks them from healing. Some people make themselves sick as their mind (psyche) is the slayer or because of secondary gains of getting attention they need. This is all taking place on a subconscious level of mind. A cancer patient was asked if she really wanted to cure her cancer? She answered NO! This woman realized that if she cured her cancer, that she would lose all those secondary gains. Her husband had quit his work overtime just to be with her. Her three daughters that never visited her were now visiting her regularly. Then she was informed that it might be possible for her to receive attention in some other way. By doing volunteer work, and by being cancer free she could visit her three daughters regularly. Now she no longer needed to have cancer to get attention. Afterward she recovered from her cancer in three months. All illness is a warning sign that there is a lesson to be learned from it. When something is wrong physically, emotionally, or both. In most cases we only deal with the symptom and not the underlying cause. This is why modern allopathic oncology cancer treatment for the most part is a failure. They only treat the symptom and not the cause. Since cancer is a biologically caused disease, then only a biologically mind-body to spirit holistic, and biological treatment can heal it. So we miss the lesson, but the body will find another way to warn us by creating another symptom.

We are lacking in life and health if we are in the following situations:
*Loneliness
*Lack of sleep
*Lack of rewards
We need to do introspection and ask ourselves the following:
*Do we express ourselves or suppress our worries and anxieties?
*Do we stress ourselves and is there never enough time?
*Do we plan our day and do a blessing upon awakening?
*Do we set goals and priorities?
*Do we have happiness and prosperity?
*Do we reflect our day before sleep?
*Do we count our blessings daily?
*Do we feel content of what we have?
*Do we think positive no matter what happens?
*Do we compliment others and practice being non judgmental?

*Do we reflect on nature and beauty and positive things?
*Do we believe in compromise and everyone prospering?
*Do we believe it then see it?

On page 147 is <u>Positive Mind Reprogramming Placebo Belief & Effect</u>.
Mind is a healer or a slayer. Which one do you choose? The mind plays an important role in health and illness. There is much scientific research and proof that fear, anxiety, worry, tension, other negative emotions, negative thinking weakens the immune system, and makes us susceptible to disease like cancer. Dr. Janet Harnacky at U.C.L.A. After 15 years of study has discovered and postulated that cancer patients have a long standing belief system that keeps them in a state of emotional pain. Some of the things they do is distance themselves from people close to them and from nature. They do not like to play or have fun. They tend to harbor resentments, self-pity, and have a great deal of difficulty in long term meaningful relationships. Your belief, faith in the treatment whether conventional, or holistic, and alternative in nature. Whether from a doctor or self treatment will greatly influence the final outcome. The belief system is the strong power that eventually determines the outcome. This is the placebo effect. The treatment can be an active or an inactive placebo. Your belief and the doctors belief in the treatment and the patient will cause the cancer patient to believe more in the treatment, doctor themselves, and to heal. The doctor is the teacher, a guide to ensure the cancer patient has a more loving positive attitude, is receptive to the treatment, and which will permit the body's regenerative forces to work more effectively. Again, these are the active placebo effects necessary for a true healing. The cancer patient believes in the healing program and believes in the doctor. The holistic practitioner believes in the healing program and the patient. The patient must perform An Act of Forgiveness.[Pages: 269-270 100-101] This is essential in any healing program so that the person lets go of resentments, etc. This allows the body to 100% detoxify and heal itself. To greatly affect the placebo effect you must also use visualization, or guided imagery where you see the affected area being healed, or see the medicine healing you, or see your immune system visualized as a warrior with a powerful laser-ray gun, aiming it at the cancer cells or tumors, and destroying them.

Also the use of affirmations (self talk) such as: "I AM Healing Myself, I AM Healthy, and Full of Energy, etc." I also strongly suggest that a cancer patient learn self-hypnosis awareness meditation. In self hypnosis one frees their mind from all outside distractions. Then the mind then will be powerful just like a laser beam that can cut through concrete and steel. The mind can be used to kill the cancer cells and empower the immune system to its highest potential. My other book entitled: Meta Your Mind has step by step instructions on how to perform self hypnosis, be able to accomplish the aforementioned killing cancer cells, and immune system enhancement, etc. The Meta Your Mind book is available @ Amazon.com/books, Barnes&Noble.com/nook/books and at 21stcenuryEnergetics.com. Also advised is the audio program for self healing, self hypnosis, re-birthing, spiritual alignment, and awakening: The Tao of the Soul-Self-Slate.

Also recently discovered by Tanio Technologies is that cancer has a frequency of 42 MHz. A health state was measured at 62-68 MHz. So if a cancer patient wants to increase their bio-field frequency to 62 MHz. Just two (2)-(20) twenty minute meditation sessions daily will increase their bio-field twenty (20) MHz into the health state. It will provide four (4) hours of restful sleep. Also Earthing walking barefoot in Nature and Liquid Nesdle's E.V.B. Raises the Body's MHz. four (4) to six (6) times higher.

On page 467 is <u>An Act of Forgiveness</u>. An act of forgiveness is essential for a 100% detoxification and any healing program. You cannot hold on to any resentments, or negative thoughts against yourself, and all others. You must be able to forgive yourself and them too. This is the spiritual way to heal thyself. If you hold these unforgiving thoughts you will not be able to allow your spirit to heal your mind and body. Forgiving is healing, elimination the detoxification of the spirit to the mind, and to the body. See pages: 100-101, 269 in this book.

<u>An Act of Forgiveness</u>.
"I forgive now and forever all persons, places, situations where I had resentments, anger, and fear. I am now holding a rope between me and those people. I see each person I resented and now there is a rope between me, that person, situation, or place. I now cut the rope that binds me to them or it, and when I do, I release immediately for now, and forever all resentments between us or it.

I cut the rope, now I let them, or it go in peace, and blessings. They prosper, so do I, now I let go, now and forever, and all negative thoughts towards them, or it. They go in peace and harmony as I do too. I forgive. I let all things go, so that the greatest good for all concerned manifests. Love, peace, harmony, and blessings forever. Aum, A-Men, Namaste, I AM. So Mote It Be.

The Three (3) Steps for Self-Hypnosis Meditation Training are:
1. The first (1st) step in creating the awareness meditative state of self hypnosis is to find a physical stimulus. This a word that will create the ego sensations or physical change. i.e. You can visualize your arms and legs getting heavy. Then apply this to your physical body and feel it. Then add a positive thought to it. The Law of Attraction.
2. The second (2nd) step is affecting your emotions. You must sense and feel an emotion such as happiness. Then add a visualize image into your mind's eye, the third eye chakra "Ajna." of what the word means to you. The word happy relates to being free of fears and tension. This connects the words and visualization together. The Law of Association.
The third (3rd) step is affecting your intellect. This is the most important part of the self-hypnosis conditioning induction. The word will be the same for everyone, is the word sleep, or deep sleep. The Law of Attraction and of Repetition is very strong when associated with sleep. You have been conditioning yourself since birth to go to sleep a basic daily need. Every night you prepare to sleep and your subconscious mind always allows your unconscious to take control and you drift into sleep. This is also what you do on the practice of self-hypnosis as well.
The Law of Repetition.
Once in the meditative self-hypnosis state you can suggest and visualize the following: Always begin with I or I AM: happy and in harmony, feel fine, accomplishing my dreams, a doer and a achiever, attract health, attract peace, positive, finish whatever I begin, healing myself, mean what I say, have meaning and purpose in my life, give everyone forgiveness, eat to live healthy, meditate and pray daily, have faith, hope and belief, a giver, do things so all works out for the greatest good, spiritual, and the inner peace of God, etc.

<u>Spiritual Exercises to Restore Health and Eliminate Cancer</u>.
<u>Daily meditation</u> for twenty minutes (20) two (2) times will rise
your body's biofield 20 MHz. A cancer patient biofield is measured
at 42 MHz. Meditating will raise it by 20 MHz to the health state
measured at 62 MHz. Any Eastern or Western meditation is advised.
The meditations are in my forthcoming book Meta Your Meditation
and they are as follows: Smiling, Micro Cosmic Orbit, Safe Harbor,
Noise to Noise, Mini, Sensory, Iron Shirt, Tai Chi Chuan, Chakra,
Single Point, Color, 1000 Petal Lotus, Breath, Zen of Doing, Zen
of Anything, and Trsanscendental Meditation (T.M.) There are many
others as well. Anyone of these will do.

<u>Yoga</u> especially Hatha or any yogic practice that opens the root
chakra such as Kundalini, etc. Bakti, Hatha, Bhagwan ji Kundalini,
and Raja, etc. These are Hindu yoga practices from India.

<u>Tantra</u> exercises to eliminate any negative attributes. In tantra
one become the thing they want to change such as hate to love, et
al. Vigyana Bhairava, Breath a Bridge to the universe.

In order to change as an example hate to love. You must become the
hate fully, be with it for a time, and then become one with it.
When you do it will transform to its opposite which is love. The
Tantra exercises are: Vigyana & Harara, Love, Sex, Nirvana,
Awareness, Breath a Bridge, Breathing, and Breath. These are all
in my forthcoming books Meta Your Meditation Vol.1-124 pages and
Meta Your Meditation Vol.2-350 pages. Also the 5 audios: The Tao
of the Soul-Self Slate. Audio program for rebirthing (elimination
of the erroneous xero order cognitive core beliefs), self healing,
(rebalaning spirit, to mind, and body), spiritual awakening
(opening your higher spiritual chakras), frequency tones and
chimes to heal one's self, enter higher altered spiritual states
of consciousness, balance acupuncture points, meridians, chakras,
nervous, lymphatic, endocrine, endocannbinoid, and immune system.
This is used in conjunction with Liquid Needle Total Balance,
E.V.B., Original, Yellow, Green all Extra Strength, Chi Gong, and
Exstress light photon frequency solution remedies. Pages: 287-310

<u>Internal Kung Fu</u> (internal exercises). These meditative exercises
will stimulate the acupuncture meridian system, nervous system and
chakras. For further information read the book Chinese Healing

Arts-Internal Kung Fu Originally translated by Dr. John Dudgeon, M.D. and edited by William R. Berk. Also Jin Shin Do and Shiatsu. The Original Five Tibetan Rites of Rejuvenation. These are yoga like exercises for rejuvenation. Read The Eye of Revelation by Peter Kelder or is in both books Meta Your Meditation Vol.#1 & Vol.#2

Nei Kung Breathing Exercises. These are: The Revitalizing Breath, The Inspirational Breath, The Perfection Breath, The Vibro-Magnetic Breath, The Cleansing Breath, The Grand Rejuvenation Breath, and Your Own Spiritual Breath. Read my forthcoming book Meta Your Meditation, Volumes 1, and 2 that contains these revitalizing breathing exercises.

Meditation. The following meditations are advised: The Safe Harbor, The Noise to Noise, Mini, Single Point, Waiting, Sensory, Tai Chi Chuan, The Zen of Doing, The Zen of Anything, Color, Chakra, 1000 Petal Lotus, Progressive Relaxation, Autogenic, Transcendental (T.M.), Smiling, Micro Cosmic Orbit, Chi Massage, Iron Shirt Chi Gong (Kung), Little & Higher Bliss, Breath, Eating, Thought to Thought, A-Z, Walking, Putka (Hara point), and Six Healing Sounds. Tajaii. Qigong, Chi Kung (Gong), Iron Shirt, Chinese Shaolin Boxing, Tai Chi Chuan, Yin and Yang "Chi," and a energy martial art movement spiritual meditative exercise.

Buddhist Spiritual Exercises. The Eight Spiritual (Shen) Disciplines The Eight Fold Path, Buddhist Act of Forgiveness, and The 9 Miyamoto Musasho Strategies. See Page 101.

Taoist. Tao Te Ching-Lao Tuz, Tao of Jeet Kune Do, Artless Art, The Wisdom of Kung Fu-Master Bruce Lee, Tai Chi Chuan, or the Primal Beginning, or The Great Ultimate, and Internal Kung Fu.

On page 51-52 is Chiropractic, A.K. Acupressure, Muscle Testing, Touch For Health Techniques, Non and Touch Healing. All of the above aforementioned physical body methods of restoring balance and the life force energy. Both John Thie, D.C., Dr. John Diamond, M.D., Doctors: Goodheart, Riddler, Stone, and Perry, D.C. are pioneers in applied or bio-kinesiology (A.K.). This is testing muscles that are connected to your organs and glands. The muscle testing techniques were authenticated by Dr. John Diamond, M.D. in his book called Bio-kinesiology. The Touch For Health muscle testing methods and acupuncture, lymphatic, neuro vascular massages, acupressure holding techniques are used to re-balance the physical structure-the body, and the mental-emotional mind. Mind heals the body and the body heals the mind. This is accomplished through first muscle testing a person to find weak muscle groups. This indicates if they need re-balancing through the touch for health methods of muscle testing, acupuncture meridian balancing, using acupuncture touch on specific points and acupressure, lymphatic massage, neuro vascular holding point touch to improve structural balance, reduce physical, mental pain, and tension. Hypertension is the number one killer.

Thereafter, once the mind, body are in harmony, balance, and then spiritual aspect can be added. Hence the holistic balancing of the mind, body, and to spirit. Remember that treating symptoms does not have anything to do with truly healing one's self. Remembering the important role of the spirit (shen), mind has in health, and disease is paramount. Your peace of mind (inner peace), harmony with the soul (soul harmony), is the greatest aid in recovering from any illness, and especially cancer. It is essential in regaining your health. In many instances the hypertension, stress of our everyday modern life interferes with our peace of mind, harmony with the spirit (soul) which then causes a compromised deficient immune system, and thereby out of ease, or disease. It is essential to use the Touch For Health techniques, chiropractic B.E.S.T. adjustments that will hold, A.K., Doctors. Morter, D.C., and Williams, D.C. acupressure and all of the touch massages. Once in physical and mind balance you can then be in alignment with your spirit. Jerome Plotnick, Ph.D., N.D. Cert A.K., Touch For and Health Instructor-Practitioner, Acupressurist, Jin Shin Do, Shiatsu, Needle-less Acupuncture, and Bioenergetic-Pranic Healer.

On page 15 is Shamanistic: Visualization, Belief, Placebo Healing. Shamans are the medicine men of all indigenous people's world-wide that use a variety of altered mind states such as placebos, belief, prayer, rituals, visualization (imagery), herbs, power animals, amulets, crystals, earth entering, repetitious rattling, and drumming sound frequencies to heal illness. They heal their patients with around an 85% success rate no matter what continent or country where they reside. American Natives, South American Indians, Eskimos, Siberian Tangu Natives, and others world-wide. They extensively use nature, natural plants, flowers, herbs, trees, rituals such as chanting, power animals, sweat lodge, essential oils-aromatherapy, visualization (imagery), meditation, prayer, drumming, rattling sounds, touch, massage as their healing milieu. Also herbal medicine, hypnotic trance suggestions, massage, essential oils, mud baths, mineral baths, sauna were used in ancient civilizations of Egypt, Greece, India, China, Tibet, Mongolia, Africa, and Europe for many centuries B.C.-A.D. Then it came to America through our American Native Indians and then passed on to us. It was used in the 1700's-1800's with great success. It was in the 1900's that most all of herbal, homeopathic, chiropractic, shamanistic healing was attacked by the chemical, pharmaceutical, and medical industry that wanted higher profits. There are no high profits in healing people naturally. Shamanistic healing is used in many modern day forms now called by many different names. It is still being practiced in many places in the world with great success. Books to read are: Imagery in Healing Shamanism and Modern Medicine by Jeanne Achterberg, Ph.D., Healing With the Mind's Eye by Dr. Michael Samuels, M.D., Vibrational Medicine by Dr. Richard Gerber, M.D., Touch For Health by Dr. John Thie, D.C., Meta Your Mind by Jerome Plotnick, Ph.D., N.D., The 13 Steps from Illness To Health-APNBMPDR by Jerome Plotnick, Ph.D., N.D., Meta Your Health in 45 Days by Jerome Plotnick, Ph.D., N.D., Bioenergetic, Mind, and Natural Medicine by Jerome Plotnick, Ph.D., N.D., Meta Your Meditation Volumes 1 and 2 by Jerome Plotnick, Ph.D., N.D., Meta Your Manifestation by Jerome Plotnick, Ph.D., N.D., Mind Memes, Miasms, and a Viruse Takeover to a Mind Healing Makeover by Jerome Plotnick Ph.D., N.D., Visualization The Uses of Imagery in the Health Professions by Dr. Errol Korn, M.D. and Karen Johnson, M.A., Pranic Healing by Master Choa Kok Sui, Esoteric Healing Vol. IV by Alyce A. Bailey translated from Jwahl Khul the Tibetan. Plus Vibrational Medicine by Dr. Richard Gerber, M.D. and other books.

From the book Esoteric Healing: The Great Invocation...
"From the point of Light within the Mind of God, Let Light stream forth into the minds of men and women. Let Light descend on Earth. From the point of Love within the Heart of God. Let love stream forth into the hearts of men and women. May Christ, Buddha, Shiva, Krishna et al., return to earth. From the centre where the Will of God is known. Let purpose guide the little wills of men and women. The purpose which the masters know and serve. From the centre which we call the race of human kind. Let the Plan of Love and

Light work out. And may it seal the door where evil dwells. Let Light, Love, and Power restore the Plan on Earth."

The above invocation or prayer does not belong to any person or group but to all humanity. The beauty and strength of the invocation lies in its simplicity, its expression of certain universal central truths which all humanity, innately, and normally accept-the truth of existence of a basic Universal Intelligence to whom we vaguely give the name of God-the motivating universal power of Love.

NOTE! All of the aforementioned spiritual practices will be written about extensively in the forthcoming book entitled: Meta Your Meditation Vol.#1. 124 pages and Meta Your Meditation Vol.#2 which will be available fall in 2017, and Vol.2 winter 2017.

My books are all available @Amazon.com/books and world wide EU, UK, Barnes&Noble.com/nook/books and @21stCenturyEnergetics.com

The Eating Meditation.

Eating your food should be a spiritual experience because it is an encounter with the body your holy temple. The holy temple is the God self identity within you and the mind-body to spiritual connection. When you eat food you are feeding your holy temple, the God within that is your God self. Prepare to eat your meal with a nice dish, the decorated with flower arrangement, or a plant. Light an incense or a candle to glorify the experience. Play some soft music in the back ground. Prepare the food meal so it looks, smells, and tastes heightens your senses. Have the meal with a loved one if possible. Make small talk about peaceful and positive things. Realize that this is a holy event and take notice of how you feel. Begin the meal with a prayer of thanksgiving, blessing, or other invocation. Begin the meal 15-30 minutes before it with a piece of fruit as it will start the digestive enzymes to enhance digestion such as Lipase, Bromelain, Papain, snd Amylase, etc. Think pink loving thoughts, Begin and chew our first bite of food slowly for a few minutes until it dissolves in your mouth. Notice its flavor mixed with the saliva and then swallow it. See it, smell it, chew it, and then swallow it. Do this with all of the food and eat small amounts until all the food is eaten. Afterward, you have your desert. Do not drink 45 minutes before, during and and wait until one half to an hour after the meal as it retards digestion. When you focus on eating slowly, appreciation of the senses, food, the surroundings, and until you become with the eating. Become the eating as a meditation, the ceremony of it, and go with it until you transcend it. You will really love, appreciate yourself, and everything much more when you become one with the thing your doing. Then after you transcend it, take charge, and focus on what really is on a higher spiritual level. This then now becomes a spiritual encounter with the God Self.

The Smiling Meditation.
This meditation is also called The Inner Smile. It is a sitting meditation that takes twenty (20) minutes to perform. You begin by practicing breathing from the spinal cord nine (9) to thirty six (36) times. This will help activate the cranial and sacral pumps, as well as the thyroid, parathyroid, adrenals. and thymus gland. Now place your hands in the lap with the right palm over the left palm. Knees and hips at the same level. Now become aware of the cosmic particles (prana) around you as the Inner Smile attracts this energy. Now picture a smiling face in front of you. A then begin to smile as well. Then spiral, draw the life force cosmic energy particles flowing around this face into your pineal mid eyebrow, and eyes. Allow the smiling energy to to flow down the nose and cheeks relaxing them as your jaw muscles become loose. Now consciously create a real smile all over your face. Now smile down at your neck, throat, and send loving energy down to your body as you smile down to your thymus gland. This will greatly strengthen the immune system by helping the thymus gland to produce T-killer cells to help to ward off and fight off diseases (illnesses). Now smile down to your heart, feel joy, wisdom, serenity, passion, peace, happiness, love glowing from your heart, and expanding outwardly. Think of a positive affirmation to enhance this as you smile and shine to all other organs. When smiling at your chakras feel the creative power or consciousness the sexual and healing energy. As you feel it growing draw it up into the navel "putka" chakra, then allow it to expand and move outward to all of your organs, and glands. Assist you in your function of decision making because they are the source of your e-motions. The immune system enhances the positive qualities and characteristics of each organs energy. Each day emphasize a different positive e-motion. Always focus on the organ associated with each e-motion. Courage-Lungs, Kindness-Liver, Fairness-Spleen, Gentleness-Kidney, Love-Heart, and Creative Growth-Sex Organs. Also as you meditate thank your digestive system for its functions and move your tongue to swish the saliva in your mouth to charge it with prana (chi) life force energy. The saliva is the

essence of the cosmic force and it combines easily with the universal prana (chi). Follow the saliva down to your stomach, small intestine, large intestine (colon), rectum, and anus. Smile into your spine, pineal gland (3rd eye chaka), and pituitary (crown chakra). Your eyes should look inward and then upward. Now smile into your left brain hemisphere and then your right brain hemisphere. Now move your eyes again inward and smile at your brains hypothalamus, corpus collusum, limbic, cerebellum, medulla, and grey matter. Smile down to your coccyx. Now return your concentration (Yi) to your hara point (putka).

The Six Healing Sounds.
Lungs sound is-Ssssss; Kidney sounds is-Whooooo; Liver sound is-Shhhhh; Heart sound is-Hawwwww; Spleen sound is-Wooooo; Triple Warmer sound is-Heeeee

Blessing the Earth and Sentient Beings With Loving Kindness.
From the Heart of God, Let the entire earth be blessed with loving kindness. Let the entire earth be blessed with great joy, happiness, and divine peace. Let the entire earth be blessed with understanding, harmony, good will, and the will-to-good So Be IT! From the heart of God, Let the heart of all sentient beings be filled with divine love and kindness. Let the hearts of all sentient beings be filled with great joy, happiness, and divine peace. Let the hearts of all sentient beings be filled with understanding, harmony, good will, and the will-to-good. With full thanks, So Be IT! By Choa Kok Sui, Master Pranic Healer.

Buddhist Anapanasati Yoga
Whenever in and out breath in that instant you touch the energyless filled center called the hara point or putka. The fusion point is your center. Zen mystics say that that point is the center. When at your center your energized, happy, and blissful. At your center your never tired, in the now, and totally vibrant. Take a deep breath in and at the point before the exhale place your focused attention "Yi" right there. Feel your center.

A Prayer of Light.
~Eternal Universal Divine Mind Creative Consciousness "I AM"~
I ask now, once again, for the Light of the Glorious Holy Spirit. The Light of the Christ, Buddha, Shiva, Krishna all asended Masters, and The Light of God to be Present here with Me.

I ask that this Divine Light...Surround~Fill~Guide~Protect~and Uplift Me, Allow Only That Which Is for the Highest Good To be brought Forward to Me, Now, and throughout this Day.
I ask for the God Presence, the Love, the Guidance of the Holy Spirit~Protector Consciousness~and Any other Ascended Masters of Light. That would guide, Assist, and Uplift Me.
I ask for Healing on all levels of my Beingness, that Any Karma or Negativity Which can be released, Be taken, and Transmuted Into the Highest Realms of Light.
I ask All in Perfect Love, And Perfect Understanding, Keeping Clear My Destiny on the Planet~ I AM always Willing~and Grateful To be of Service~
And I ask for More Opportunities to be of Service, And to perceive them, and a Loving Consciousness in which to Manifest that Service. Though, Ever Thy Will Be Done.
And I ask that My Will be as Thine, And that Jesus the Christ, Buddha, Shiva, Krishna, All Masters of Light Dwell in My Beingness~Now, and All the Days of My Life. ~So Be It~ ~"I AM"~

Autogenic Exercise

Begin with a deep breath and then saying to yourself inwardly or outwardly the following: 1. "My arms and legs are heavy." Feel your arms and legs become heavy. 2. "My lungs are brathing me." Feel the inhale and then the exhale of your breath and breathing. 3. "My forehead is cool" Feel your forehead as if a cool breeze was flowing across it. 4. "My abdomen is warm." Feel your abdomen is warm like after you were eating hot soup. 5. "My heart beat is calm, normal, and regular." Feel your heart beating. 6. I am now in connection with my mind, body, and spirit. My life is love, I am in control of all my bodily, and mind functions. And this shall be the same for now on...My life is love, health, and I am now functioning at my optimal level of being. The object of an Autogenic exercise is to tune in and connect, with your mind, and body. It is a mind body interplay. This will cause you to be aware of body organs and mind consciousness. This also is a relaxation meditative exercise.

HEAL YOUR INTESTINAL TRACT WITH FRIENDLY FLORA HEAL & ENHANCE YOUR IMMUNE SYSTEM = HEAL YOUR BODY FORMULA. © 21stCenturyEnergetics

Ideal Internal Environment for a Powerful Immune System-Anticancer The following foods, herbs will replenish your intestinal tract (gut), thereby enhancing a powerful immune system that will eliminate all illnesses, and heal your body. Your intestinal tract friendly flora are the bacteria that compromises around 75% of your immune system. Most of the nutrients contain high amounts of polyphenols and other phyto-chemicals. Pre and pro biotics. Advised in Liquid Needle Green, Yellow, ENZ, MIN, VIT, and INT. These are the suggested organic foods, herbs, and vitamins: 1. black current 2. high-low bush blueberry 3. dates 4. artichoke heads 5. organic coffee 6. sweet cherry 7. strawberry 8. black berry 9. plum 10. red raspberry-rhubarb 11. flax seed meal or oil 12. dark organic chocolate 13. chestnut 14. black tea K2 15. white tea 16. green tea K2 17. apple 18. rye 19. chicory 20. hazelnut 21 red wine extract 22. organic cocoa-cacoa powder 23. banana 24. black beans 25. pomegranate 26. spinach 27. pecans 28. red onion 29. broccoli 30. pycogenol (pine bark extract) 31. bitter melon 32. mulberry 33. cloves 34. star anise 35. Mexican oregano 36. celery seed 37. black choke berry 38. Gymnema sylvestre 39. Vit. B-12, B Complex Brewers Yeast 40. slippery elm 41. probiotics from the following foods: sauerkraut-fermented miso-organic yogurt-kombucha-kimchi-kefir-acidophilus-organic raw buttermilk. 41(a). Probiotic supplements advised: #1. Complete Probiotics by 1MD-A+, #2. Renew Life Ultimate Critical Care 50 billion by Renew Life-B+ #3. Culturelle Digestive Health Probiotic Capsules by Culturelle-B+ #4. Align Probiotic Supplement by Meta-C #5. Trubiotics Daily Probiotic Supplement by TruBiotics-C-Other Probiotcs highly recommended are: #6. LiveWell Pro45 Probiotics by Livewell-Labs-B+ Also: Glutaloemine, Mutaflor, FloraSynergyPlus. NOTE! For bowel assistance: 1. L-acidophilus-This strain boosts the treatment of respiratory infections, helps relieve I.B.S., decreases the frequency of yeast infections (candida), reduces the growth of pathogens in the digestive tract, and produces lactase which helps break down the sugar lactose in milk. 2. L.casei-This assists with digestion issues that include Chron's disease, ulcers, and other gastrointestinal problems. 3. L.plantarum-Plantarum helps treat I.B.S., Chron's disease, and colitis. It also preserves critical nutrients, vitamins, and antioxidants.

4. <u>L.salivarlus</u>-Salivarius makes enzymes that kill bad bacteria, including the bacteria responsible for bad breath. It also helps with flatulence and bloating.

<u>For digestion help</u>: #1. <u>B.longum</u>-This strain stops bad bacteria and prevents them from growing. Longum also breaks down carbohydrates and reduces the symptoms of seasonal allergies. #2. <u>Bacillus Coagulans</u>-This strain helps to stop the growth of bad bacteria. It also prevents various digestive disorders such as I.B.S., diarrhea, and stomach ulcers. #3. <u>L.rhamnosus</u>. This strain aids in the prevention of urinary tract infections U.T.I. Especially those caused by anti-biotics. It also helps to enhance the immune system, assists in digestion of dairy products, and helps to fight against digestive tract illnesses.

<u>For immune function</u>: #1. <u>B.lactis</u>-This strain helps to increase immune function, helps to fight against infections, makes faster recovery times possible, and helps prevent diarrhea. #2. B.bifidum-Bifidum helps to stop the increase of bad bacteria, enhances the immune system, and aids digestion process. #3. <u>L.bulgaricus</u>.-Bulgaricus works in your intestinal lining (mucous membranes) as an enforcer by eliminating toxins. This strain also creates its own natural anti-biotics.

<u>For weight loss</u>: #1. <u>L.gasseri</u>. This strain reduces abdominal fat and supports weight loss. It also helps ease the pain of menstruation and helps lower bad L.D.L. cholesterol

<u>Pre Biotics</u>: the following foods are indicated: bananas, blueberries, artichoke, onions, chicory, dandelion, all greens, spinach, collard, chard, kale, wheat grass, spirulina, chlorella, and broccoli. Also advised are: Mutaflor, Glutaloemine, FlorsSynergyPlus, Amino Gest, Cataylist-7,or U, Galt Immune, BioMatrix, Exsula's-Iredesca, Life Crystals, Greening Powder, and Liquid Needle's: Green, ENZ, VIT, MIN, and E.V.B.

Afterward X
Physiology of how exactly T.H.C.-C.B.D. from Cannabis Sativa Marijuana kills cancer cells.

T.H.C.-C.B.D. blocks the lipoxy genase pathway to directly inhibit tumor growth. Note! If a healthy cell becomes cancerous, yet it is programmed to create cannabinoid receptors (CBR) as a last resort, then the cell would become more susceptible to be apoptosis-inducing effects of anadamide. It is likely that the anandamide is killing the cancer cell(s) before they have time to replicate and spread. Summary: All in all there are hundreds of scientific non biased studies indicating that T.H.C.-C.B.D., other non psychoactive cannabinoids like echinacea purpera that kill cancer cells, and research showing that endocannabinoids are produced by our own bodies also kill cancer cells. Note! Those persons with stronger endocannabinoids C.B.D. receptor systems have a better cancer survival rate. Note! Cancer cells need an adequate blood supply and sugar to survive otherwise they cannot survive. This is how the T.H.C.-C.B.D. kills the cancer cells by blocking the blood pathway snd sugar wihin it. Cancer cells need sugar to live.

There are hundreds of people reporting that the T.H.C.-C.B.D. cannabis extracts have helped treat their cancer or control other extremely serious diseases. i.e. Dr. Margaret Gedde found that eight (8) out of eleven (11) epilepsy patients she is treating have experienced a 98-100% reduction in seizures, most within the first month of treatment. Note! For a medicine to work that well, that fast, in cases where nothing else had worked, and is miraculous in itself. Even the other three (3) patients experienced good results. 1. with a 75% reduction and 2. with a 20-45% reduction in seizures. Even that result is amazing, and they are likely to improve with modification of dosing and more time. By Justin Kinder, Phoneixtears.org www.medical marijuana directory news 12/18/2013. Also see black Indica strains of cannabis as this grows in darker light and becomes dark purple then black. There is black widow, beauty, disiel, domina, Jack, and Russian, etc. It contains a high T.H.C. amount of 18%. www.medicalmarijuanastrains.com

Afterward XI
Physiology on the latest research on Dandelion Root and its cancer cell killing "apoptosis" ability.

The latest information according to Dr. Siyaram Pandray, Professor of Chemistry and Biochemistry at the University of Windsor, Ontario, Canada. Dr. Pandray is the principal research investigator for the project. Dandelion root has definite cancer cell killing potential.

How does it work? This Dandelion root extract causes the cancer cell(s) to go into apoptosis, a natural cell process where a cell acivates an intracellular death program because it isn't needed anymore. In brief, Dandelion root extract causes the cancer cell to "commit suicide," without influencing, or harming healthy normal cells. NOTE! It is important to mention that the concentration of the extract is much higher than the ones currently available. Even though trials are still rendering, this high dose of Dandelion root extract may be the future of cancer treatment.

Dr. Ovadje a research assistant in the Dandelion extract trials, etc. 1."We have had information from an oncologist, a collaberator here here in Windsor, who had patients showing improvement after taking Dandelion root extract. And so, with a phone call, we decided to started to study what was in this extract that makes cancer patients respond to it, so we started digging up Dandelions." 2. "I was quite suspicious in the beginning not because it was an-all natural source. I figured dandelion are very plentiful here and if there was something to it, people would have found this already, she explained. We should be gald to hear that the researchers have started studies on Dandelion root extract and its effects on cancer, as the results are amazing." 3. "Since the commencement of this program, we have been able to successfully assess the affect of simple water extract of Dandelion root in various human cancer cell types in the laboratory and we have observed its effectiveness against human T-cell leukemia, chronic myelomacytic leukemia, pancreatic, colon cancers, and with no toxicity to non cancer cells. Furthermore, these efficacy studies have been confirmed in animal models (mice) that have been transplanted with human colon cancer cells. Dandelion root extract was approved for human trials in Feb, 2015. Now it is Phase one

(1) trails and the stage for blood related causes such as leukemia and lymphoma." by Dr. Ovadje, Univ. of Windsor, Ontario, Cananda.

Bibliography references:
Dr. Siyaram Pandray, Ph.D., Univ. of Windsor, Ontario, Canada
Dr. Ovadje, Ph.D., Univ. of Windsor, Ontario, Canada
www.davidwolfe.com
www.lovingtraditionally.com/dandelionroot-cancer
www,naturalnews.com
www.cbc.ca/news/cancer/calgary/calgaryanticancer

The Physiology of CL-4 and How it Kills Cancer cells.
CL-4 a New Cancer Cell Apoptosis Death "Apatamer."

Nucleic acid apatamer have been developed as a high affinity ligands that may act as antagonists of disease-associated proteins. Apatamers are non immouogens and characterised by high specificty and low toxicity thus representing a valid atteuractive to anti-bodies or soluble ligand receptor traps-decoys to target specific cancer cell surface proteins in clinical diagnosis and therapy. The epidermal growth factor receptoe (EFGR) has been implemented in the development of a wide range of human cancers including breast, giloma, and lung. The observation data is that inhibition can interfere with the growth of such tumors has led to the design of a new drugs including monocloned anti-bodies and tyrosine kinase inhibitors currently used in clinc. However, some of these molecules can result in toxicity and acquired resistance, the need to develop novel kinds of EFGR target drugs with high specifity and low toxicity. Here we generated, by a cell-systamtic evolution of ligands by exportified enrichment (SILEX) approach, a nucleus resistant R.N.A.-apatamer that specifically binds to the EFGR with a binding constant of 10nM when applied to the EFGR expressing cancer cells. The apatamer inhibits the EFGR mediated signal pathwyas causing a selective cancer cell death (apoptosis). Furthermore, at low doses it releases apoptosis even of cancer cells that are resistent to the most frequently used EFGR's inhibitors such as gefinib and cetoximab, and inhibits tumor growth a xenogiaft model of human non small-cell lung cancer. Interstingly combined treatment with cetximob and the apatamer shows clear synergy in including apoptosis in vitro and in vivo. In conclusion, we demonstrate that this neutralizing R.N.A. Apatamer is a primary bio-molecule that can be developed as a more effective alternative of already existing EFGR inhibitors. Con't on page 286.

AFTERWARD XII
Physiology of Graviola (Annona Muricata) the phyto-chemicals called "Annonaceous Acetogenisis" and how it kills cancer cells.

Graviola also named guanabana, custard apple, cherimya, and paw paw.

The medicinal uses are: the juice reduces fever. It counters diarrhea, dysentary, and is anti parasitc (worms). Also the seeds are anti-parasitic and anti-lice. The bark, leaves, roots are used for medicinal tea, sedative, and are anti-spasmodic. It is slso used for high blood pressure. The bark reduces fever and is a wound healer. The unripened fruit is a digestive aid. In Peru, the Andes mountains, graviola leaves are brewed and drank to discharge mucus, and also soothe inflamed mucous membranes. It is also used for stabilizing the blood sugar, a heart, liver tonic, arthritis, and rheumatism.

The Manhatten, N.Y. City Sloan Kettering Cancer Center-affirmed the effectiveness of the plants beneficial properties. A neurological study published in 1998, found graviola helps the capability to stimulate the brain receptors for seratonin, and may also have an anti-depressant effect. [Cassileth, Barrie-8-2008]

Side effects. Animal studies indicate that it dialates blood vessels and lowers blood pressure, so if you have low blood pressure it is not suggested to use. Consult with your physician before taking. Note! Large doses can cause nausea and vomiting. [Taylor, Leslie-2005]

Graviola's purported anti-cancer potency comes largely from its ability to reduce the supply of adenosine-tri-phosphate or A.T.P. to the cancer cells. A.T.P. provides the metabolic energy to healthy cells as well.[Taylor, Leslie 2005]

NOTE! If your taking graviola then stop taking CoQ10 as that increases A.T.P. to cells. [Taylor, Leslie-2005]

The N.C.I. National Cancer Institute studied it in 1976 and did not release its findings although it was found highly successful. So much of the subsequent research has been conducted at Perdue University in Indiana. [Bluestein, Chuck 3-2009]

The studies at Perdue University concentrated on the anti-tumor properties and selective toxicity of graviola's chemical compound annonaaceous acetogensis. In 1997 the Purdue University researchers stated that these phyto chemicals of graviola, in studies, appeared especially effective in destroying cancer cells that has survived chemotherapy. Such cancer cells can develop resistance to several anti-cancer agents called M.D.R. Multi-drug-resistant. Usually, less than 2% of cancer cells have M.D.R. Properties. NOTE! But a small amount of the cancer cells can quickly multiply after the chemotherapy, rendering subsequent rounds of chemotherapy useless. Expelling the anti-cancer agents requires large amounts of cellular energy which M.D.R. Cancer cells acquire from the chemical A.T.P., Acetogenins in graviola inhibit A.T.P. Transfer, retard their functions in a process called apototsis that eventually leads to cancer cell death. This biological process bypasses the normal healthy cells, which do not require infused of the A.T.P. [Taylor, Leslie-2005]

These research findings have found graviola as a viable anti-cancer herb-one study indicated that graviola is 10,000 times more effective against cancer than chemotherapy drug Adriamycin. Ralph Moss, a respected cancer writer who has been critical of main stream oncology, that even without no F.D.A. necessary millions of dollars to prove it works that graviola is of potential importance in the future of medicine. [Moss, Ralph-2-2009]

NOTE! And as usual big pharma is attempting to manufacture a synthetic so they can patent it and make (400) four hundred times the profit. As natural plants and herbs cannot be patented. So some companies have succeeded in reproducing several anona acetogenis in their labs. They are presently tinkering with the chemical structure with the goal of creating a synthetic acetogenis unique enough to patient and effective enough to market. [Moss, Ralph-2-2009]

My take and professional educated opinion is don't be fooled as only the natural graviola is what you need. No man-made for high profits so called medicine are what anyone needs. Graviola only goes after cancer cells and leaves all healthy cells in tact. It is a non toxic natural botanical. [Plotnick, Jerome-6-12-2017]

Sources.
Moss, Ralph www.findarticles.com March 9, 2009
www.graviola.com March 8,2009
Memorial Sloan-Kettering Cancer Center March 7,2008
www.amazon.botanicals.com March 8, 2009
Bluestein, Chuck www.graviolaleaves.com March 7, 2009
Cassileth, Barrie www.cancerntework.com Sept. 2008
Taylor Leslie www.raintree.com/graviola/html
Plotnick, Ph.D., N.D. Jerome-www.21stCenturyEnergetics.com The 13
Steps From Illness To Health-APNBMPDR 2009-2017, Meta Your Health
in 45 Days-2017, Bioenergetic, Mind & Natural Medicine-2001-2017
Paaov Airola, N.D. Are You Confused? 1971

Con't CL-4 from page 283. Summary and Results of CL-4 Apatamer.
By using differential whole cells SELEX on human NSCLC we
identified a set of five families of sequence related 2'-
fluoropyridmes (2'FPy) R.N.A.-apatamers that distinguish A549
cells (resistant to cell death induce by trial, cisplatin
praclytaxel) from the more sensitive H460 cells. CL-4 full length
(FL) is the best candidate apatamer from this selection,
efficiently binds to A549 cells within apparent dissociation
constant (Kd) calue of 46nM. Based on the preficted secondary
structure of the original molecule, we designed a shorted apatamer
of 39nM (here indicated as CL-4). Regulation of EFGR promotes
tumor processes including ongonegenesis and metastasis and is
associated with poor prognosis in many human malignancies
including giloma, lung, and breast cancer. The prevalence of this
receptor in well established cancers has elicated many studies and
discoveries leading to generations of multiple F.D.A. approved
agents including monodnal anti-bodies (as cloximob and panitommds
for treatment of correctal cancer. NSCLC, and squamous cell
carcinoma. In essence after a cancer patient completes chemo
therapy it does not kill the master cancer cells. These are
responsible for new regeneration of cancer after chemotherapy. By
use of CL-4 these cells are also destroyed preventing further
cancer cell proliferation. Then use of the alternative treatments
such as getting the blood pH below 7.56 pH and a natural holitic
approach in this chapter will eliminate and prevent cancer.
Sources: Exposito, Assera, Longabardo, Condorelli, Marota et al.
http//doi.org/10.1371/journal pone 0024071 Sept. 6, 2001
A Neutralizing R.N.A. Apatamer Against EFGR Causes Specific
Apoptosis Cancer Cell Death.

AFTERWARD XIII

The Liquid Needle Story. Liquid Needle Light Photon Frequencies. Why we need them? What they are? How they are formulated. What they do to restore your health and well-being? Physiology of Liquid Needle. Excerpts from the D.N.R., Inc. Liquid Needle D.V.D.

Introduction of Liquid Needle.

D.N.R. Liquid Needle energy-based solutions are made from water. Water is an excellent conductor of electricity. Since the body reuires electrical energy to move signals from one place to another, water becomes an essential element for carrying life sustaining signals. Up to seventy percent (70%) of the body is composed of water-fluids. Over ninety percent (90%) of the nutrient carrying blood is composed of water.

The body depends on its water base to sustain the electrical potential of the neuron as well as each cell's electrical voltage or current.

The cells depend on this electrical current to facilitate the movement of impulses. These electrically stimulated impulses trigger or signal all of the body parts to carry out their vital tasks.

Capsules, pills, powders, and tablets are not considered good conductors of electricity. Manufacturers have not considered the body's electrical needs when they make substances that act as carrying agents for drugs, medicines, vitamins, minerals, herbs, and other dietary substances. These substances carry virtually no positive electrical charge or voltage. In fact, water carries a negative charge of approxitmately forty five (45) millivolts.

Nerve cells require a positive electrical potential of + seventy (+70) to + ninety (+90) millivolts of electricity to move the neuro-transmitters and hormones throughout the body.

Each of the D.N.R.'s Liquid Needle energy-based solutions (formualtions) can hold and exert a positive electrical charge between + seventy (+70) and + two hundred fifty (+250) millivolts.

D.N.R., Inc. has developed a proprietary technique of boosting and maintaining the electrical anergy on all its water based solutions. The boosted electrical chrage enables each lipid formualtion's ability to unblock the natural energy pathways.

By boosting the base electrical charge of the water four (4) to six (6) times higher than the normal body electrical MHz frequency potential, staff technicians are able to encode (imprint) thousands of light photon wave frequencies into the energy-based solution(s). The combined frequency signals of each formulation have been selected to meet the needs of specific areas and conditions of the body.

The entire body depends on its communication system and its ability to send and receive messages (sometimes called signals or impulses). When a sending message is weak due to toxins interfering with the communication, a malfunction can result, and some health consequencies (symptoms) may occur. When there is a blockage of natural energy, some organs, or glands will feel the loss of the required energy signal.

When messages, impulses and signals are weak, they need support. When they are blocked, they need unblocking. D.N.R. Liquid Needle energy-based formualations are generated to send up to two hundred and fifty (250) millivolt signals of electrical support to weak and blocked energy signals. Each D.N.R. Liquid Needle energy-based formulation provides an electrical vehicle that can carry the select light photon wave signals to well parts of the body. Often times these areas of the body are undetectable to conventional means.

The human body conveys and processes some thrity thousand (30,000) signals per second. With our toxic and energy depleted bodies, is it any wonder the body hungers for all the electrical, and signals it can get?

D.N.R. Liquid Needle energized solutions are derived from nutritional. herbal, homeopathical, botanical, other natural resources the body requires for balancing, and healing.
Note! <u>Remember that only the body has the ability to heal and repair itself</u> once cleared of cellular communication blockages caused, by toxins, and weakened electical potential in the cells, organs, and glands. D.N.R. Liquid Needle products are always safe, generally fast acting, and simple to use.

<u>Usage Guide</u>. <u>The Eight (8) Balancing Points</u>.

Your body has Eight (8) Balancing Points. These provide maximum protection benefit from application of all Liquid Needle Rebalancer Topical ® solutions. Apply to all parts of the body at least two (2) times daily. Below is a simplified explanantion of the points and their relationship to other parts of the body.

<u>Point One (1)</u>. Located at the center brow above the eyes, this point is associated with the pineal gland and the pituitary gland. It governs the nervous system, the brain (logic side), the eye (sight), ears (hearing), and nose (smell). This major point is related to the bslanced production of melatonin and the neuro-transmitter, seratonin. Melatonin is essential in supporting the immune systems ability to fight cancer and regulate restful sleep. Seratonin is the brain master impulse modulator for all our emotions and drive. It especially keeps aggression in line.

<u>Point Two (2)</u>. Located approxitmately two and one half (2 ½) inches below the bottom of the throat on adults, this point is associated with the thymus gland. This point has a direct action on the heart, lungs, throat, and thyroid gland. Stimulation helps stabilize the body's energy. Activation and stimulating the thymus gland can assure the production of T-cells which are essential in activating and supporting the immune system.

<u>Point Three (3)</u>. Located at the middle of the hairline, this point is associated with the pituitary gland, and a controlling point for the brain. It is responsible for receiving and directing messages or impulses to brain areas of the brain, and body. It is one of the five (5) points of the head for balancing and stabilizing the energies of the body. The pituitary gland is known as the master gland, controls balance, production of hormone to the thyroid gland, adrenal cortex, testes, ovaries, breast, muscle, bones, and skin.

<u>Point Four (4)</u>. Located at the crown (top center of the head), this point is associated with the pineal gland, physical balance and energy, governs the organs, brain, and right eye. This point is a major point of all the positive energies. It has a direct effect on memory, feelings, and influences the psycho-emotional balance.

<u>Point Five (5)</u>. Like Point three (3), it is a major controlling point of the brain. Located approxitmately two and three quarters (2 ¾) inches behind the crown point. It is responsible for receiving, directing messages to and from all areas of the head brain for balacing, and stabilizing the energies of the body. This point is associated with the hypothalamus the switch board for all communications in the body.

<u>Point Six (6)</u>. Located between C-6 and C-7 (cervical vertebras) (largest extending vertebra at the base of the neck), this point is the meeting point of all the bodies positive energy. This point is used to build up and generate the positive energy of the body and help destroy pathological conditions. It is considered a major body protection point.

<u>Points Seven (7) and Eight (8)</u>. These points are located in front of the ears where on extending half circular extrusion is located. These points are related to the corpus collosum. The vital tissue that divides and separates the the brain hemispheres. When the corpus collosum is out of balance the right side, and the left side of the brain hemispheres seem to function in a reversed manner causing confusion, and mental frustration. These are major points used to balance mental, emotional, and memory capabilities.

NRV-105 and its H.B.H. companion NRV-SYS and NRV-EX are used as directed is formulated to where the body's ability to deal with these toxins throught its heightened use of cellular communications at the sub-atomic level.

By raising the body's vitality and clearing energy pathways directly related to the nervous system, they can promote many tasks that the body most take to ensure less irritability, anxiety, depression, confusion, and shock.

The brain relies on the rest of the neural pathways to carry its signals to other parts of the body without blockages from toxins that can distort and interfere with its messages.

<u>Helpful Hints About Using All Body Detoxification Bath Soaks</u>. If you have never taken a D.N.R. Liquid Needle body soak, you should begin with E.V.B. (Energy-Vitality-Balancer) regular

strength three to four (3-4) days prior to the taking your first bath soak. All body soaks should be taken at night, before bed, except Liquid Needle body soak Blue. If your scheduling requires morning or afternoon soaks, leave time to rest after the soak, and then shampoo 3 times daily. Soak for thirty (30) minutes each bath soak. Bath water should be warm not to hot in summer months, cold baths are acceptable. For best results, soak the top of your head for ten (10) minutes during each soak. To remove toxins held in your hair, wait, four (4) hours minimum after the soak, and shampoo three (3) times daily. Afterward put drops of lemon juice or concentrate mixed with the shampoo will help release the toxic buildup on the hair. If you desire the benefits of two (2) different soaks they are Blue and Clear. For basic soaks are: (Blue, Clear, and Amber). Alternate soaks for advanced protocols are (Lympha, Cof, and Cig, etc.) Always completre one (1) protcol before beginning another.

The most effective re-soak protcol is to add four (4) oz. of body soak before bed for the first (1st) two (2) soaks, and eight (8) oz. per bath for the next three (3) soaks. With two (2) days between soaks. If you prefer you can use half (½) the amount with one (1) day between soaks.

For those who have been experiencing ill health or feel they are surely free may feel comfortable using: two (2) oz. of body saok instead of the four (4) oz. for the next three (3) soaks. Soaks can be controlled at four (4) oz. or increased to eight (8) oz. thereafter.

Important Read
Whenever D.N.R. Liquid Needle energy-based products experience any discomfort, or unnecessary side affects-feelings after taking a bath body soak, or any oral application, any of the following conditions may exist. The body is severly out of balance; or a combination. Sometimes there may be a conflict with a drug or strong supplemewnt being raken. Usually, discomfort or pecular feelings take place after the soak or application. If they persist reduce tha amount number of oz. in the soak, reduce oral dosage, or discontinue use while taking medicine, or just supplements.

Release of Toxins.

The body uses the lungs, kidneys, colon, skin to extricate harmful toxic chemicals, and substances from the body. The skin being the largest organ of the body, offers billions of individulent pores that open up to allow toxic debris to naturally, slowly, and steadily disperse. NOTE! Often the kidneys, lungs, and colon are not capable of dealing with the synthetic man-made chemicals.

Product Protocols and Regimens.

While these protocols are particulary recommended as written, they may require personalized usage instruction. Follow these protcols exactly to attain the results desired. If you have never used D.N.R. Liquid Needle energy-based products you should begin with taking first E.V.B. (Energy-Vitality-Balance) regular strength three to four (3-4) days prior to using any other Liquid Needle product.

Prostate Urinary Difficulty.

Begin with the following: STA-506, K.B.L.-514, and GLA—519. Add five (5) drops each to six (6) drops of water, or juice, and drink it all, three (3) times per day. Use extra strength Liquid Needle products for more severe/nagging conditions.

One (1) week after starting with these supplements begin using URI-SYS Pour one (1) Tsp. into one (1) oz. of water or juice in the morning (A.M.). Swish in the mouth for thirty (30) seconds and then swallow. Repeat at lunch or dinner if needed.

Duration of Protocol: Follow as long as necessary. You can enhance the performance of this protcol by applying Liquid Triggers [Item-#-L-4] to the appropriate vertebra lumbar L-4 three (3) times per day.

Blood Pressure.

Begin with HEA-508, K.B.L.-504,, GLA-519, ExStress, or ExStressEX. Add Six (6) Drops of each to three (3) drops of water or juice, and drink it all, three (3) times per day. Use extra strength Liquid Needle products for more severe/nagging conditions. Some people prefer six (6) sprays of oral ExStress, spray three (3) times per day or as needed. One (1) week after starting with these supplements begin using Liquid Needle Body Soak Clear-105-C and follow the directions on the container. Ten (10) days after starting with these supplements begin using CAR-SYS-EX. Pour one (1) tsp. into one (1) oz. of water or juice in the morning (A.M.). Swish in mouth for thirty (39) seconds and swallow. Repeat at lunch or dinner if needed.

Duration of Protcol: Follow for as long as necessary.

Liver Detoxification Cleanse.
Begin using nine (9) drops of K.B.L.-514-EX in three (3) oz. of water, three (3) times per day for eight (8) weeks. After four (4) days of taking the K.B.L.-514-EX drops take one (1) tsp. of LVR-604-EX two (2) times per day for the eight (8) week period. Then begin LVR-Detox Bath Soak by adding four (4) oz. to warm bath water and soak for thirty (30) minutes every other night for two (2) soaks. Then use eight (8) eight (8) oz. for the remaining soaks three (3) times per week until the two (2) quarts have been used completely. Note! If the bath water is still dark and cloudy after the first two quarts, continue the entire regimen for an additional two (2) weeks.

Duration of Protocol: Forty five (45) days {Note! You can enhance the performance of the Liquid Needle product by applying Liquid Needle Trigger [Item-#-Thoracic-T-5] to the L-5 thoracic vertebra two (2) times daily.

Allergies.
Begin with ALL-519-EX, COL-515-EX, and VIR-515-EX, add six (6) Shampoo Drops to three (3) oz. of water or juice, and drink it all, three (3) times per day. Use extra strength Liquid Needle Topical Original-E-116 on the eight (8) balacing points, three (3) times per day as indicated on the container. Ten (10) days after starting these supplements begin using RES-SYS-EX. Pour one (1) tsp. into one (1) oz. of water or juice in the morning (A.M.). Swish in the mouth for thirty (30) seconds and then swallow. Repeat at luch or dinner if needed. Use Liquid Needle Body Soak RES-105 for more cleansing.

Duration of Protocol: Seasonal or as long as necessary.

A.D.D., A.D.H.D., L.D., Mental Focus, Concentration, Anger, and Mood.

Begin with Liquid Needle Total Balance L.N.T.B. Topically applied to the eight (8) balancing points as indicated on the container. After one (1) week, use orally, or topically, or use Liquid Needle Total Balance Oral Spray as desired. Add three (3) drops in three (3) oz. of water, three (3) times daily and drink all. In severe cases use ExStress or ExStress extra strength. Add three (3) drops in three (3) oz. of water, or juice, and drink all, three (3) times daily. One (1) week sfter starting with ExStress, begin using ExStress Bath Soak-105-EX as directed on the container.

Duration of Protocol: As long as necessary. Note! see my double blind study on the effects of Liquid Needle Total Balance (L.N.T.B.) in cases of A.D.D., A.D.H.D., L.D. (dyslexia), children using Liquid Needle Total Balance (L.N.T.B.) and E.E.G. Neurofeedback Fourier Analysis of the brain waves after use. In this book on pages: 309-310. See the study results on page 417 of my other book: The 13 Steps From Illness To Health-APNBMPDR.

Chronic Indigestion.

Use Liquid Needle Yellow Y-111 and Liquid Needle Green G-120 orally. Add five (5) drops of each in three (3) oz. of water, or juice, and drink all, three (3) times per day. If Liquid Needle Yellow and Green are not entirely within ten days then begin STO-601, or INT-612. Pour one (1) tsp. into one (1) oz. of water or juice in the morning (A.M.). Swish in the mouth for thirty (30) seconds and then swallow. Repeat at lunch or dinner if needed.

Duration of Protocol: as long as necessary.

Parasite Activity-Parasite PAK Program.

Begin with PAR-534-EX. Add ten (10) drops to three (3) oz. of water and drink all, three (3) times per day for twenty one (21) days. Plus SKN-525-EX. Add three (3) drops to three (3) oz. of water, or juice, and drink all, three (3) times per day. One (1) week after starting, the above supplements, begin using PAR-134 Liquid Needle Body Bath Soak once (1) time weekly.

Chronic Fatigue Syndrome (C.F.S.) And Fibromyalgia.

Use Amber Plus Body Soak-105-Plus or Body Soak Blue-105 Blue as directed on the container. Use extra strength Liquid Needle

Topical Original E-116-EX on the eight (8) balancing points, three (3) times per day for best results. Use Checkmate Spray C.M.-105 on all areas of concern.

Duration of Protocol: As long as needed. Note! [you can use Liquid Trigger Cervical C1-C6 Item-#-C1-C6] to the C-1 and C-6 appropriate vertebras two (2) times per day.

Depression or Stress Related Issues of Hypertension, Anxiety, and Worry, etc.

Begin with ExStress or ExStress-EX. Add six (6) drops to three (3) oz. of water, or juice, and drink all, three (3) times per day. Use Liquid Needle Brown Topical Label B-111 on your eight (8) balancing points as indicated on the container three to four (3-4) times per day. One (1) week after starting ExStress begin using ExStress Body Soak-105-EX as directed on the container.

Duration of Protocol:As long as necessary.

Colds, Flu's, and Sinus.

Begin with COL-515-EX, VIR-513-EX, and ALL-510-EX. Add six (6) drops of each to three (3) oz. of water, or juice, and drink all, three (3) times per day. After one (1) week after starting with the above supplements begin using Liquid Needle Body Soak Amber-105 as directed on the container.

Duration of Protocol: Begin whenever your symptoms first occur and continue as long as necessary. Note! [You can enhance the performance of this protocol by applying Liquid Trigger [Item-#-C1 & C2 to C1 & C2] appropriate vertebras, two (2) times per day.

P.M.S., Pre Menopause, Menopause, or Post Menopause.

Use MEL-502, PRO-503, and ExStress or ExStress-EX. Add three (3) drops of each to three (3) oz. of water or juice and drink all, three (3) times per day. After the first (1st) increase to six (6) drops frequency. Use Liquid Needle Brown Label Topical on your eight (8) balancing points, three (3) times daily if necessary. One (1) week after starting these supplements, begin using Liquid Body Saok Clear-105-C, or ExStress Soak depending on your stress level, and as directed on the container.

Duration of Protocol: continual. You can enhance the performance of the protocol by applying as Liquid Trigger [Item #-Lumbar L-5] to Lumbar-5 the appropriate vertebra, two (2) times per day.

Chemical & Heavy Metal Toxicity Detoxification Cleansing Protocols.

Use COF-130-EX Whenever the D.N.R. Scientists develop a product to perform particular tasks, they rely on light wave frequencies to signal, and trigger precise response(s). These response(s) take place first at the sub-atomic level. The same is true with COF-130-EX Body Soak and Oral Drops 9COF-520-EX. Their charged and energized particles activate response(s) using light wave generated signals to stimulate, trigger detoxification-cleansing, and other desired actions within the cell. After adding the COF-130-EX Body Soak to the bath water, you simply relax as the charged water molecules, send their coded signals to the parts of the body that have been experiencing imbalances, or blockages of natural energy movement. As localized balance returns to these areas.

Add four (4) drops of COF-520-EX to two-three (2-3) oz. of water, and drink all, three (3) times per day. Continue the rest of the entire protocol. Body soaks use as directed on the container COF-130-EX, leaving two (2) days between soaks for all the rest of the twenty one (21) soaks. Use four (4) oz. for the next two (2) soaks. Use eight (8) oz. for the remaining soaks.

Important Detoxifying Regimen Tips.

1. E.V.B. regular strength water energizing should be used by those who have never used D.N.R. Liquid Needle energy-based products. E.V.B. soaks should also be added to drinking water for thirty (30) days prior to and during the COF-130-EX product protocols. This allows the body to establish balance, be prepared for the side effect sensations of the accelerated actioins of the released energy, and vitality that normally comes from the first (1st) soak.

2. It is important that your diligent in the process. There may be times during the protocol that your body may be relea
sing excessive amounts of toxins, so may you feel sleepy, fatigued, and
even light headed. This is a natural part of detoxifying-cleansing.

3. It is recommended to leave the head submerged for approxitmately ten (10) minutes. This allows for the natural removal of chemical toxins or metallic toxins that may be isolated in the jaw, gums, or head. The sticky toxic debris held in the hair can be removed by using lemon juice to the shampoo lather as you shampoo your hair.

Special D.N.R. Liquid Needle Protocols.
D.N.R. Liquid Needle products have many uses. The following list of protocols outlined suggestions for many situations.
A.D.D., A.D.H.D., L.D., Anger, Mental, Focus, Concentration, and Moods, etc.
1. Liquid Needle Total Balance (L.N.T.B.) oral or topical, three (3) times per day.
2. In severe cases ExStress-525, three (3) drops in three (3) oz. of water, three (3) times per day.
3. Use ExStress Body Soak-105-EX

Basic Health Starter Kit.
What everyone needs to stay healthy, every day, energy balance, nutrition protection.
1. E.V.B. Energy-Vitality-Balance energized water.
2. Fabric Shield Wash F-109 add to wshing machine water for protection against E.M.F.'S and T.S.E.'s.
3. VIT-506 for fourteen (14) plus vitamins
4. ENZ-507 digestion forty four (44) sources of enzymes and twenty amino acids.
5. MIN-521 derived from seventy (70) minerals and trace elements
6. ENC-527 antioxidants from twenty (20) plants rich in natural tocopherols.
7. Liquid Needle Yellow Y-118 eliminates, countera and neutralizes pesticides, chemical toxins, desensitizes toxin, parasites, and indigestion.
8. Liquid Needle Green G-120 for forty four (44) vitamins, seventy (70) minerals, trace elements, antioxidants, and enzymes.
9. Shampoo Drops S.D.-121 for energy balance protection use with a natural shampoo.

Lymphatics-Immune System.
The health of the entire body depends on the full time actions of the lymphatic system. The lymphatic system is what is responsible for carrying antibodies to body areas being attacked by viuses,

negative bacteria, and toxic agents. Lympha-105 Soak and Lympha Drops help the body:
* Initaite drain age and cleansing.
* utilize cancer fighting cells.
* restore youthful healthy appearance.
* increase lymph flow.
* balance all immune system activity.
1. Lympha Drops L.D.-528. Three (3) drops to three (3) oz. of water, three (3) times per day.
2. Thirty Five (35) days later Lympha Body Soak-105-L every third (3rd) night or as needed.

Metabolism,
Good for cleansing, firm skin, and cellulite. Metabolism balancing and energy. Higher metabolic, maximizes energy utiliztion, and minimizes dietary cravings. Cleanse away toxic buildup from skin, tissues as it tightens, and firms the body. Helps release the unsightly appearance of cellulite and stretch marks.
1. TAB-153 Body Soak.
2. TAB-153 Oral drops.
3. Trim TAB Oral Spray T.T.-140 helps the body deal with "snack cravings."

Neutra Spray.
The hair protection spray. Deals with the second most toxic area of your body. Developed to counter toxic poisons accumulated and derived from chemicals in most hair sprays, shampoos, conditioners, colorings, and permanents, etc. By spraying over the hair on the head. Neutra Sprays powerful mist can help correct any polarity imbalances and help counter chemical toxicity brought on by synthetic chemicals application to the head.
1. Use Neutra Spray N.S.-136 each morning before starting the day. If possible also after lunch.

Parasite Acrivity.
You can be literally eaten alive by prasites. Recent medical research studies estimate eighty five to ninety five pecent (85%-(95%) of the North American population have one (1) or more types of parasites living in their bodies.
1. PAR-534 or PAR-534-EX Ten (10) drops to three (3) oz. of water three (3) times per day for twenty one (21) days.

2. SKN-524-EX Three (3) drops to three (3) oz. of water, three (3) times per day for one hundred and twelve (112) days.
3. CLN-603-EX One half (½) Tsp. into one (1) oz. of water, two (2) times per day for forty two (42) days.
4. PAR-534-EX Body Soak three (3) days per week for three (3) weeks or twenty one (21) days.

Blood Pressure.
Helps the body build a balanced working cardiovascular and circulatory system.
1. HEA-508, K.B.L.-504, GLA-519, and ExStress STR-525 six (6) drops in water taken three (3) times per day.
2. One (1) week later Body Saok Clear-105-C).
3. Ten (10) days later CAR-SYS-EX take one (1) Tsp. in water one to two (1-2) times per day.

Breast Implants.
Provides maximum detoxification benefits for toxic chemicals suxh as silicone. Use at night.
1. Body Soak Gold-105-G. When the bath water no longer has color, begin Body Soak Blue-105-B or Body Soak Clear-105-C

Cancer-Toxins.
Chemotherapy chemicals and radiation (E.M.F.'s) both have a debilitating effect on the body and it's ability to get rid of them both. The immune system also shuts down.
1. CAN-133 Body Soak-helps bring the body back into balance so the immune system can function. (CAN-Shock-12).
2. CAN-509-EX oral drops derived from Black Walnut, Wormwood, fifty two (52) other natural botanical sources for antioxidants, and elimination of free radicals (E.M.F.'s).

Chi Gong.
Peace-Tranquility-Harmony-Chinese healing meditative exerxise centered around the body's Chi. Qi Gong (Chi Kung Iron Shirt) has been used by the Chinese Taoists, Buddhists, Shaolin practitioners for thousands of years as a method (Tao-way) to provide salf-healing, energy Chi-Qi restoration, and longevity.
1. Chi Gong Topical (Chi-131) enjoy a feeling of centeredness.
2. Chi Gong Body Soak (Chi-105) no sticky residue left in hair. Balancer and mild detoxifier. It washes away feelings of anger, frustration, and anxiety.

Cold-Flu's-Sinus.

COL-515-EX was developed especvially for preceding and during the cold and flu season. Targets sinus congestion, flu attacks. VIR-513-EX supports, and energizes the immunme system. Enhances the body's own natural action when dealing with infection. ALL-502-EX supports the body's ability to deal with allergy symptoms.

1. COL-515-EX, VIR-513-EX, and ALL-510-EX. Six (6) drops into three (3) oz. of water, three (3) times per day.
2. One (1) week later, Body Soak Amber-105-A or Body Soak Blue-105-B.

Fabric Shield Spray & Fabric Shield Wash.

Counters harmful toxic chemicals and materials in our environment. Formulated for use on carpets, upholstered futniture, mattresses, car upholstery, any other synthetic material, etc.

1. Dilute one (1) part of F.S. Spray F.S.-114 to six (6) parts of water in a spray bottle and lightly spray onto fabrics. One (1) eight (8) oz. bottle will make forty eight (48) oz. of Fabric Shield Spray.
2. Add one (1) Tblsp. Of F.S. Wash F-109 or F-109-EX to the final rinse cycle of the washing machine. Provides a "balancing shield" for your body. Treat upholstery and items such as clothing, under garments, and bedding.

Fibromyalgia/Fatigue.

For those individuals severly out of balance due to symptoms of pain and stress. Helps the body deal with stress, deep pain, and localized pain. Amber Plus Pain Body Soak is for those suffering from pain resulting from fibromyalgia, rheumatoid arthritis, osteoporosis, and M.S., etc. Amber Body Soak Plus is for those suffering from fatigue resulting from the out of balance condition of the body.

1. Amber Plus Body Soak-A.P.-105.
2. Liquid Needle Original Extra Strength E-116 applied onto the eight (8) balancing points, three (3) times per day as indicated on the container.
3. Shampoo Drops S.D.-121, three (3) times per week.
4. Check Mate Spray C.M.-135.Body Soak Blue-105-B.

Firm & Tighten Skin.
Begin with your first (1st) soak, Dynique tightens, tones, and firms loose skin. Helps increase circulation. Use Dynique to firm stretch marks as a bust firmer/lifter, neck, and chin lift, etc.
1. Dynique Solution D-106 can help create a healthier more youthful and trimmer appearance.
2. Dynique liquid Pearls D.L.P.'s tightens up and firms saggy areas around the eyes and chin. Use over night to help smooth our fsacial lines and wrinkles.
3. Dynique face, neck and chin Lift Kit. Helps eliminate face, neck, and chin puffiness.
4. Slender Body Enhanced Soak S.B.-111 Dynique Soak with added frequencies for the skin balance.

Foot Soak. A detoxifying soak without a bath.
Balance, vitality, pain, stress, hormone, endocrine. For those individuals unable to soak in a bath tub, or for those needing help with the feet, ankles, and toes. Provides balancing benefits of body soaks Clear, Blue and Gold. A very powerful soak product
1. Liquid Needle Foot Soak L.N.F.S.

H.B.H. Herbal-Botanical-Homeopathic Series.
Derived from the energies (signature frequencies found in nature) of all three (3) sources of herbal, botanical, and homeopathic remedies. Promotes the body's ability to unblock energy and neutralize cellular toxicity. Avsilable in extra strength (faster actions, quicker results, and more potent).
There are H.B.H. Photanical solutions for: Colon, Intestines, Nervous System, Endocrine System, Cardio-Vascular System, Respiratory System, and Urinary System.

Heavy Metal Detoxification.
The averge person has two hundred (200) toxic chemicals in their body fat. Detoxification for lead, radiation, aluminum, cadmium, and other radiated heavy metals. Excellent support protocol for those with heavy metals, toxic, poisonous accumualtions, and including free radical advancement.
1. COF-130-EX Body Soak. Safely cleans outwardly through the pores of the skin.
2. COF-520-EX Oral Drops. Stimulates toxic release.

Joint & Pain Inflammation.
Enhances the body's ability to deal with pain and inflammation
from arthritis, injury and pain in joints, muscles, tendons, and
ligaments.
1. CheckMate Body Soak-C.M.-105 covers the entire body with all
the benefits of CheckMate spray.
3. CheckMate Spray C.M.-135 Spray spray on muscles, ligaments,
tendons, and joints for instant relief.

Liquid Triggers Kit.
For Massage Therapists and body healing practitioners, Osteopaths,
Chiropractors, and Physical Therapists. The spine is the
electrical junction box for the entire body, every system, organ,
and function of the body is directly linked to one (1) or more
vertebras. Liquid Trigger solutions are:
1. Send select combinations of impulses through the nervous syetem
to targeted areas of the body.
2. Trigger the signaling capabilities of the body's vital organs,
glands, and soft tissues.
3. Transfer subtle energy with coded siganls to the appropriate
body areas being influenced by blocked energy or imbalances.
* All twenty six (26) Liquid Triggers C1-C7, T1-T12, L1-L5,
sacrum, and coccyx.

Liver Cleanse.
Excellent for cleansing and neutralizing, engages the body's own
natural diuretic action.
1. K.B.L.-514-EX Six (6) to nine (9) drops to three (3) oz. of
water, three (3) times per day for eight (8) weeks.
2. After four (4) days LVR-604-EX One (1) Tsp. in one (1) oz. of
water, two (2) times per day for the rest of the eight (8) weeks.
3. Also start LVR-105 Body Soak, two (2) soaks at four (4) oz.,
for thirty (30) minutes every other night. Then eight (8) oz. for
three (3) times per week until the two (2) quarts are used. If the
bath soak water is still dark, continue the regimen for another
two (2) weeks.

Parasitic Prevention.
Once you have gotten rid of the parasites infecting your body
stay free of them. They are prone to return. To keep parasite
infection from recurring.

1. PAR-504 or PAR-504-EX and CAN-501-EX Six to nine (6-9) drops to three (3) oz. of water per day.
2. One (1) week after PAR-134 Body Soak One (1) or two (2) times per month.

P.M.S. Menopause.
MEL-502 has signals from melatonin and seratonin sources. Helps the body deal with sleep disorders, anxiety, and depression. PRO-503 has signals from progesterone, estrogen, testosterine to help men and women whose bodies are over dealing with mid life changes.
1. MEL-502, PRO-503, WOM-512, Ex Stress STR-525 three (3) drops each to three (3) oz. of water, three (3) times per day.
2. Liquid Needle Brown Topical B-111 on six (6) balancing points indicated on the container, three (3) times per day.
3. One (1) week later Body Soak Clear-105-C or ExStress Body Soak-105-EX depending on the level of stress.

Respiratory.
Almost all lung conditions and disease are brought about by three hundred (300) allopathic synthetic medicines including prescribed drugs, air pollution, and tobacco smoking. Your respiratory system is one of the body's most valuable assets. Toxic coatings on the lungs inner surafce can hamper the body's ability to dispose the CO_2. The least little imbalance or freedom of blood flow caused by toxicity can result in permanent damage to the lungs. To help the body restore your energy balance and to maximize the respiratory system function.
1. RES-SYS-EX One (1) tsp. in one (1) ox. of water, two (2) times per day.
2. Three (3) days later RES-105 Body Soak. Take nine (9) soaks for eight (8) weeks if toxic.

Smoking & Drug Detoxifier Cleansing.
Assists the smoker in maintaining their will power and energy necessary in dealing with "quitting" smoking addiction. Helps the body clean away accumulated chemical of tobacco toxins.
1. CIG-131 Body Soak.
2. CIG-522 Oral Drops. Note! The TAB protocol will assist in not gaining weight while going through the process of "quitting" smoking.

Sports.
When used twelve (12) to twenty four (24) hours before prior to an athletic event or activity, it will help the body establish, maintain maximum balance, and performance. Helps the body maximize its energy, concentration, stamina, and vitality during strenuous activites.
1. Sports Soak Physical S.S.-P prior to the activity.
2. Sports Topical Physical S.T.-P prior to the activity.
3. Sports Soak Mental S.S.-M prior and after the activity to cleanse, loosen tendons, and muscles.
4. Sports Topical Mental S.T.-M prior and after the activity to cleanse, loosen tendons, and muscles.

Stress & Depression.
Derived from St. Johns Wort and Ginseng with Valerian, Evening Primrose, Kava-Kava and other natural herbal remedies. Non habit forming. ExStress users have expressed feelings of wellness, relaxation, hypertension, and cases under stressful situation.
1. ExStress STR-525 Six (6) drops to three (3) oz. of water, three (3) times per day.
2. Liquid Needle Brown Label Topical B-111 applied on your eight (8) balancing points, three (3) times per day.
3. One (1) week later ExStress Body Soak-105-EX

Swelling/Trauma Injuries.
Designed for animals, DRAW can be administrated through a localized soak. A wrap or a spray. Used on muscles, tendons, ligaments and soft tissue. Good for trauma to a muscle, tendon, ligament, or soft tissue. NOTE! Can also be used on humans.
1. DRAW Soak W-105.
2. DRAW EX Strength Soak W-105-EX.
3. DEAW Plus Spray W-105-S

Urinary-Prostate-Adrenals.
The body can better deal with prostate conditions when a natural balance is established. When in balance, natural function of the adrenal glands become more natural, and in balance.
1. STA-516, K.B.L.-514, GLA-519 Six (6) drops to three (3) oz. of water, three (3) times per day.
2. One (1) week later Body Soak Amber-115-A.
3. Ten (10) days later URI-SYS One (1) Tsp. in one (1) oz. of water, three (3) times per day.

Yeast-Candida-Fungus.

When the balance of good and bad bacteria in the intestines is lost, yeast and candidia can ensue. Especially formulated for those with chronic yeast type called G-105-EX. Works quickly and effectively to restore digestive balance. Fortifies the body's ability to fight off, overcome the spread of fungus, and candid-yeast infection.

1. Body Soak Gold Extra Strength-105-GEX.
2, INT-602-EX One (1) Tsp. in one (1) oz. of water, three (3) times per day. Later take two (2) tsp. per day for future protection.
3. Skin Gel GEL-105 topically applied for any outbreak of the skin caused by yeast or candidia fungal infection. Highly concentrated, has no fragrance.

Liver Detoxification Cleansing Protocol.

1. Begin taking six to nine (6-9) drops of K.B.L.-514-EX in three (3) oz. of water, three (3) times per day for eight (8) weeks.
2. After four (4) days taking K.B.L. Drops begin taking one to two (1-2) Tsp. of LVR-604-EX, two (2) times per day for eight (8) weeks.
3. After taking the K.B.L., begin adding four (4) oz. of LVR Detox Soak to a warm bath water and soak for thirty (30) minutes every other night for two (2) soaks. Then use eight (8) oz. for the remaining soaks, three (3) times per day until two (2) quarts have been used completely. If the bath water is dark color and cloudy after the first (1st) two (2) quarts continue with the entire regimen for an additional two (2) weeks.

For the best results when using D.N.R.'s Liver Cleansing Program.
* Drink sixty four to one hundred twenty eight (64-128) oz. of pure water with added E.V.B. regular strength as directed on the label container for best results.
* Reduce consumption of all meats and fats. Soak all vegetables and fruits in Liquid Needle Yellow Y-118-EX and Green G-120-EX in water. Five (5) drops each and soak for fifteen minutes.
* Stretching exercises like Hatha Yoga, Tai Chi, etc, can be helpful.
* Minimize use of dietary supplements, homeopathic, and herbal remedies.
* Extended sleep, meditation, nap, and rest periods sre helpful.

Chemotherapy & Radiation Protocol.

For those being treated for breast and prostste cancer with chemotherapy, radiation needing balancing, and detoxification support.

1. Drink E.V.B. Added to between sixty four to one hundred twenty eight (64-128) oz. of water per day. (preferably one hundred twenty eight oz. equal one (1) gallon.

2. Shampoo Drops S.D. three (3) times per day for emotional, mental, physical balance, and energy throughout the day.

3. Fabric Shield F.S. for everything washable for balance, fortifying the engagement of the immune system throughout the day, and especially while sleeping.

4. ExStress. Five (5) drops five (5) times per day for emotional and hormonal balance.

5. STA-515-EX. Ten (10) drops five (5) times per day, but not after six (6) P.M. Preferably at two (2) hour inteverals for centering the actions of the adrenal glands, and or the prostate.

6. CAN-519-EX Ten (10) drops five (5) times per day when taking STA-516-EX for minimizing the effects brought on by the use of toxic agents and assisiting their release.

7. CAN-133 Bath Soaks every M.-W.-F. Nights. Use four (4) oz. for the first (1st) two (2) weeks and then eight (8) oz. thereafter for balancing, increase of vital energy, and cleansing toxins accumulated through past treatments.

Eight Week Heavy Metal Toxicity Cleansing Protocol.

When it comes to detoxifying heavy metals D.N.R. Liquid Needle is number one (1) in simplicity, safety, and efficacy. The eight (8) week heavy metal cleansing protocol consists of two (2) one half (½) oz. COF-520-EX oral supplement, five (5) thrity two (32) oz. Body Soak COF-130-EX Note! First (1st) time D.N.R. Liquid Needle users will use two (2) eight (8) oz. E.V.B. energized water regular strength as described on the container.

Liquid Needle Tips are as follows:

1.Drops. Add four (4) drops of COF-5120-EX for three (3) to five (5) oz. of water and drink all three (3) times per day. Continue for sixty one (61) days of protocol.

Body Soaks. Always use as directed on the container of COF-130-EX leaving two (2) days between soaks for a total of twenty one (21) soaks. Then use four (4) oz. for the next two (2) soaks).

Thereafter use eight (8) oz. for each of the remaining nineteen (19) soaks.

Important COF-130-EX Protocol Tips.
* E.V.B. Energized regular strength should be used by those who have never used and D.N.R. Liquid Needle energy-based-activated water product. E.V.B. should be used and added to your drinking pure water three (3) days prior and during the COF-130-EX soak regimine. That allows the body to establish balance and be prepared for the side effect sensations (Herxheimer reactions, or healing crisis) from the accelerated movement of renewed energy, and vitality that comes from the first (1st) soak.
* It is important that your diligent in this process. There may be some protocol that your body may release excessive amounts of toxins. So you may feel sleepy, fatigued, and even light headed. This is a natural part of cleansing (detoxifying).
* It is recommended to leave the head submerged approxitmately ten (10) minutes. This allows for the natural removal of chemicals or metallic toxin(s) that may be isolated in the jaw, gums, or head. The sticky toxic debris held in the hair can be removed later by adding lemon juice to the shampoo lather as your shampoo your hair. Note! Only organic non toxic shampoo is advised.
Note! Drink E.V.B. enerized regular strength with all of the protocols. E.V.B.-137, E.V.B.137-R., E.V.B.-137-EX, and E.V.B.-137-OR

Protocols, Products, & Regimens.
While the written protocols are recommended, they also may require personalized usage instructions. Follow these protocols exactly to obtain the best results desired. If you have never used any of D.N.R.'s Liquid Needle energy-based products, you should begin with E.V.B. energized water regular strength three (3) to four (4) days prior to using any of the protocols.

Prostate-Urinary Difficulty.
Begin with STA-516, K.B.L.-514, and GLA-519. Add six (6) drops of each to three (3) oz. of water, or juice, and drink it all three (3) times per day. Use extra strength products for more severe/nagging conditions. One (1) week after starting with these supplements begin, using Body Soak STA-105 as directed on the container. Ten (10) days after starting with these supplements begin using URI-SYS. Pour one (1) Tsp. into one (1) oz. of water

or juice in the morning. (A.M.) Swish in the mouth for thirty (30) seconds and then swallow. Repeat at lunch and dinner if needed.

Blood Pressure.
Begin with HEA-518, K.B.L.-514, GLA-519, and ExStress-EX. Add six (6) drops of each to three (3) oz. of water or juice and drink it all, three (3) times per day. Use extra strength products for more severe/nagging conditions. (Some people prefer six (6) sprays of the ExStress Oral Spray three (3) times per day as needed). One (1) week after starting with these supplements, begin using CAR-SYS-EX. Pour one (1) Tsp. into one (1) oz. of water or juice in the morning (A.M.). Swish in the mouth for thrity (30) seconds then swallow. Repeat at lunch or dinner if needed.

Duration of Protocol: Follow as long as necessary.

Liver Cleanse.
Begin taking six (6) to nine (9) drops of K.B.L.-514-EX in three (3) oz. of water, three (3) times per day for eight (8) weeks period, then begin LVR-Detox Soak by adding four (4) oz. to a warm bath, and soak for thrity (30) minutes every other night for two (2) weeks. Then use eight (8) oz. for the remaining soaks three (3) times per week until completely used. Note! If the bath water is dark colored after the first (1st) two quarts, continue the entire regimen for an additional two (2) weeks.

Duration of Protocol: Forty five (45) days. (You can enhance the performance of this protocol by applying Liquid Triggers Item-#-T-5 on the 5th thoracic vertebra two (2) times per day.

Allergies.
Begin with ALL-510-EX, COL-515-EX, and LVR-513-EX. Add six (6) drops each to three (3) oz. of water, or juice, and drink all, three (3) times per day. Use extra strength Topical Orginal O-116-EX on the eight (8) balancing points, three times per day. Ten (10) days after starting, with these supplements begin using RES-SYS-EX. Pour one (1) Tsp. into one (1) oz. of water or juice in the morning (A.M.). Swish in the mouth for thity (30) seconds and swallow. Repeat at lunch or dinner if needed. Use Body Soak RES-105 for more cleansing.

Duration of Protocol: Seasonal or as long as needed.

<u>A.D.D., A.D.H.D., Mental Focus, Concentration, Anger, Moodiness</u>.
Begin with the Liquid Needle Total Balance to your eight balancing
points, three times per day as indicated on the container.
Excerpts from the 13 Steps from Illness To Health-APNBMPDR book on
page 418. E.E.G. Brainwave Study of the Effects of Liquid Needle
Total Balance Topical Light Photon Solution on Attention Disorder,
A.D.D., Attention Defecit Disoordered Hyperactive, A.D.H.D., and
L.D. Children. See the study on pages 309-310.

Jerome Plotnick, Ph.D., N.D. Is a Clinical-Counseling-Cognitive-
Health-Holistic Transpersonal Behavioral Psychologist located in
California. He has specialized in E.E.G. Neurofeedback training
for children and adults with Attention Deficit Disorder, A.D.D.,
Attention Deficit Hyperactivity Disorder, A.A.H.D., and Learning
Disabilities, L.D.. Since 1995, Dr. Plotnick is also a Naturopath,
Holistic Health Practitoner-Counselor and a Drug-less
Practitioner, has specialized in bioenergetic stimulation using
D.N.R.'s Liquid Needle light energy frequency formulations
exclusively as the foundation of all his healing programs.

From May 20, 1998 to August 31, 1998, Dr. Plotnick performed a
double blind study using three (3) children ages ten (10-13)
through thirteen, diagnosed with A.D.D., A.D.H.D., and dyslexia.
The study monitored brainwave activity recorded on graphs on a
Bio-Comp 2001 Neurofeedback Device.

Each child was given a standard brainwave mapping analysis and
determined to have both a Beta and Theta brainwave deficiencies.
The Bio-Comp 2001 has diverse functions. Its major function is to
establish and monitor brainwave activity and the implemantation of
Neurofeedback training.

After monitoring and mapping brainwave activity of the three (3)
children subjects, all were hooked up to the Bio-Comp 2001 for
analysis, and two were hooked up for the Neurofeedback training.

After several training sessions with the Bio-Comp 2001, the first
child's brainwaves remained in the same frequency range as
established readings prior to the training. The second child
[control model] went through several training sessions and there
was a gradual re-balancing of the Beta, and Theta brainwaves. The
third (3rd) child [experimental model] was hooked up to the Bio-

Comp-2001, but instead of administering brainwave training sessions, D.N.R.'s Liquid Needle Total Balance (L.N.T.B.) was topically applied to the brainwave training sites. Immediately and without any neurofeedback brainwave training, the Bio-Como-2001 monitor, mapping chart reflected the Alpha, Beta, and Theta brainwave frequencies establishing instant maximum balance.

The third (3rd) child [experimental model] received three (3) more sessions using only D.N.R.'s Liquid Needle Total Balance (L.N.T.B.) topical administered applications on the brainwave training sites. Again, without any brainwave training, there was an immediate indication of brainwave re-balancing of the Alpha, Beta, and Theta brainwaves. There was also immediate corrective behavior and positive attitude changes noted at school, at home, during these training sessions, and the following two (2) weeks where Liquid Needle Total Balance (L.N.T.B.) was used in conjunction with E.E.G. Neurofedback training. These changes were noted by teacher, parents, and the neurofeedback training therapists.

A nine (9) month follow-up study was performed and the third (3rd) [experimantal model] child using L.N.T.B. daily remained in balance, a normal range for the Alpha, Beta, and Theta brainwave state. There was no further A.D.D. symptomology.

Jerome Plotnick, Ph.D., E.E.G. Neurofeedback Clinician (brain-trainer) now uses D.N.R.'s Liquid Needle Total Balance (L.N.T.B.) exclusively in all of his E.E.G. Neurofeedback training sessions with all A.D.D., A.D.H.D., L.D. children, adults with this, all other learning, addictive recovery, and brain related disorders.

Liquid Needle Total Balance (L.N.T.B.) placed on topically to the brainwave traing sites, head, face, and the eight (8) balancing points per the instructions for use. This dramatically effects the users Alpha, Beta, Theta brainwaves, placing them in complete, and normal balance.

Once accomplished the person (user) has a positive behavioral attitude towards learning, focus, concentration, and motivation. Jerome Plotnick, Ph.D.,N.D., Cert. E.E.G. Neurofeedback, Aug. 1998 Sources: D.N.R., Inc., Dr. Ken Widgery, N.D. and Arthur Widgery Developmental Natural Resources, Inc. IN. 1992-2017.

A CONDENSATION & SUMMARY OF DR. MAX GERSON, M.D. CANCER THERAPY

Dr. Maz Gerson, M.D. observed in his cancer clinic in the 1930's through 1955 certain characteristics associated with cancer patients he treated. From this he formulated the Gerson Therapy.

In his therapy (treatment) the patient is taught and learns how to fight their own cancer. The main components are 1. be totally aware and control of what your eating and what your body is eliminating. 2. a strict vegetarian diet. 3. nutritional supplements, enzymes, liver detoxification, and liver rebuilding.

Currently as well the patient is also immunotherapy for immune system enhancement. The Gerson therapy (treament) is rooted in the belief is a disease of the whole organism, the tumor (cancer cells) are only a symptom of a digestion imbalance, dysfunctional immune system, and intestinal metabolism. The goal is to bring back the body to its normal metabolic state.

Gerson observed that cancer patients exhibited degenerated organs, especially the liver, caused by toxins of a unknown type that cancer produces. He also noted that the cancer became much worse after chemotherapy, radiation, and probably because they produced more toxins that entered the blood stream. So the Gerson therapy (regime) centered upon helping the liver rid itself of these toxic substances while restoring healthy liver functioning. He stated, "during detoxification that results from the Gereon diet, that the liver became more over-burdened as the body rids itself of these toxic substances from the breakdown of cancer cells." So he prescribed coffee enemas, pancreatic enzymes, and a crude liver extract to deal with the burden of releasing toxic sunstances.

Hence the idea of controlling of anything eating and leaving the body. 1. teaching and learning the body. 2. a strict vegeatarian diet. 3. nutritional supplements and enzymes. The diet is six (6) weeks of specific fruits, vegtables eaten raw, or stewed in their own juices. No animal protein. Only whole grains like oatmeal and flaxseed due to the high Vitamin A content. No fats, salt, or pepper. A daily glass of fresh squeezed fresh vegetable, or fruit juice with high potassium, and low sodium. Gerson prepared supplements, potassium solution, Lugol's Solution (potassiuniodine), CoQ10, flax seed oil, pancreatic enzymes, pepsin, and coffee enemas.

The following are statenments made by the N.C.I. (National Cancer Institute):
To date there is no scientific evidence to support it and in some certain instances it can be very harmful to your health. So again the Gerson dietary therapy by itslf will not be able to enable one to heal themselves from cancer.

N.C.I. also states about the Gerson Therapy:
<u>1</u>. It treats cancer in dietary intake.
<u>2</u>. with an organic vegetarian diet plus, vitamins, enzymes, and enemas.
<u>3</u>. The regimen is designed to detox the body especially the liver, enhance the liver, immune system, and raise the potassium in the cells.
<u>4</u>. Based on Dr. Max Gerson, M.D. and his clinical observations from 1930 to 1955.
<u>5</u>. There are no scientific laboratory facts for humans or animals reported.
<u>Summary</u>. The Gerson Therapy for cancer is rooted in the belief that cancer is a disease of the whole organism. The tumor or cancer cells are only a symptom of the diseased body, dysfunctional immune system, and body metabolism. The intended goal is to bring the body back to its normal functioning.

My opinion is that it is in part correct but only part of the whole picture. As I have aforementioned in this chapter according to new evidence from Dr. Rudolf Skelnar and others the cancer microbe is found in the blood of all mammals. There is also evidence that this blood cancer microbe will proliferate if the blood pH goes over 7.56 pH. Also there are now recently discovered many natural cancer killing herbs, elements, etc. I believe as I stated that he was right in some of his suppositions about cancer. I strongly believe in a vegan alkaline diet, and whole body not just liver detoxification. Diet is essential in any healing program. (a raw vegan alkaline diet to bring the body pH between 7.35-7.45. is essential). As an after note!. The N.C.I. has hidden for example the amazon herb graviola, studied scientifically, and know to kill cancer cells 10,000 times more powerful than toxic chemotherapy. Non toxic too. They kept this from the public. Why?

National Cancer Institute and Center For Disease Control
Statistics

Here are statitics on cancer dated 2013. Two (2) out of every five Americans will develop cancer in their lifetime. One (1) out of every five (5) will have their death cetificate writtn died of cancer. Half of all cancers are diagnosed in people under age sixty seven (67). U.S. men are less likely to die of cancer then men in the U.K., Germany, France, and Italy. But nothing like women because they lead the world in breast cancer deaths. Four (4) major cancers are: breast, colon, lung, and prostate. They account for one quarter (¼) of the estimated cancer deaths.

Fruits and vegetables compared to people who only eat two (2) or more fewer fruits and vegetables daily to those who eat five (5) or more daily have about a forty percent (40%) decrease in lung, colon, stomach, esophagus, or oral cancers states, Tim Bymes of the Center of Disease Control and Prevention C.D.C. In Atlanta, Georgia. That is fairly a big effect and a fairly achiveable change in diet. Lung cancer strikes fewer people than prostste, breast, or colon cancer. But its the biggest cancer killer because its only thirteen percent (13%) that only live more than five (5) years after being diagnosed.

Who's most at risk? Cigarette smokers contribute to an estimated eighty five percent (85%) of lung cancer deaths. Radon, asbestos, arsenic, radiation, second hand smoke, and air pollution cause the rest. Smokers who eat fruits and vegetables, especially those rich in beta carotene supplements for five (5) to seven (7) years have had no lower cancer risk. An even with an optimal diet the National Cancer Institutes (N.C.I.) Regina Ziegler states, "smokers would still cause a ten (10) fold, rather then a twenty (20) fold increase of lung cancer."

Warning signs of lung cancer are: persistent cough, bloody sputum, chest pain, recurring pneumonia, or bronchitis.

Colon Rectal cancer. One (1) out of every three (3) cases of cancer when the cancer is found localized, which means the patient has a ninety percent (90%) chance of surviving five (5) years or more.

Who's most at risk? People who eat diets high in saturated fats, mainly on red meats, low on fruits, and vegetables. Anyone with a family history of colon, or rectal cancer, polyps, or I.B.S. In a recent study, beta carotene, Vitamin E, and Vitamin C <u>did not</u> cut the risk of potentially pre cancenrous polyps.

Warning signs of colon rectal cancer are: rectal bleeding, bloody stool, and change in bowel habits.

Breast cancer. Who's at risk? The risks are with age, family history of brest cancer, early menarche or late menopause age at which the first child is born, never had children, higher education and income, obesity, possible hormone replacement therapy, and oral contraceptives. The typical American saturated high fat diet may also increase the risk. Even moderate alcohol drinking is linked to breast cancer.

Warning signs are: any lump, thickening, dimpling, skin irritation or pain, or discharge from the breast.

Prostate cancer. One (1) out of very eight (8) en will get prostate cancer in his lifetime. Half ½ of the deaths are in men seventy seven (77) or older.

Who's at risk? African American men are twice as likely to die of it. People who eat diets rich in saturated fats especially red meats, have a greater risk in some studies. A recent study indicated that Vitamin E-50 I.U. Protected Finnish men smokers.

Warning signa are: difficult, painful and frequent urination, bloody urine, pain in lower back, pelvis, or upper thighs.

Pancreas cancer. Its the worse cancer to get. Only three (3) out of one hundred (100) patients survive for five years. Smokers have a double the risk of non smokers, but smoking only accounts for about a one quarter (¼) of the risk. But a typical patient survives for three (3) months. Remember Michael Landon the famous movie actor?

Warning signs are: none until it has spread that"s why its so deadly.

Next is stomach cancer. World wide deaths from stomach cancer is second only to death from lung cancer. But the U.S. death rate is only one quarter (¼) of what it was in the early 1900's. Unfortunately tumors of the upper stomach are rising in white America men.

Who's at risk? For lower stomach cancer its smokers. African American men, people with a family history of stomach cancer, and those who have stomachs infected with Heliobacter pyloris bacteria have a higher risk. Highly salted, cured, or smoked foods containing nitrates, and sulfates, etc. These may also increase the risk by by creating cancer causing nitrosamines in the stomach although its never been definitively demonstrated in humans. As for the upper stomach its unknown presently, what causes it in white men.

Warning signs are: gas, bloating slight nausea, heart burn persisting over weeks, or months.

Ovary "Ovarian" cancer. Often there are no warning signs. So less then one quarter (¼) of the cases are detected early. Only forty one (41) out of every one hundred (100) patients are alive after five (5) years after they have been diagnosed.

Who's at risk? A family history of ovarian cancer is the strongest factor, but it only counts for three (3) out of every one hundred (100) cases. Infertility increases the risk especially on a woman who has been taking fertility drugs. Pregnancies, whether failed or successful cut the risk, as do oral contraceptives, tubal ligations, hysterectomies, and bresat feeding. In a recent study, woman with ovarian cancer reported eating diets with high saturated fats, low in vegetables, and fruit. Also recent evidence of young woman taking Gardisil a vaccine that is supposed to prevent ovarian cancer actually can and has caused it.

Warning signs are: enlarged abdomen, vague persisitent digestive problems of gas, and bloating.

National Cancer Institute Statistics from 2016.
In 2016, an estimated 1,685,210 new cases of cancer will be diagnosed in the U.S. and 595,690 people will die from the disease.

The most common cancers in 2016 are projected to be breast cancer, lung and bronchus cancer, prostate cancer, colon and rectum cancer, bladder cancer, melanoma of the skin, non Hodgkins lymphoma, thyroid cancer, kidney and renal pelvis cancer, leukemia, endometrial cancer, and pancreatic cancer.

The number of new cases of cancer (cancer incidence) is 454.8 per 100,000 men and women per year (based on 2008-2012 cases).

The number of cancer deaths (cancer mortality) is 171.2 per 100,000 men and women (based on 2009-2012 deaths).

Cancer motality is higher among men than women (207.9 per 100,000 men and women). It is highest in African American men (261.5 per 100,000) and lowest in Asian/Pacific Islander women (91.2 per 100,000). (Based on 2008-2012 deaths).

The number of people living beyond a cancer diagnosis reached nearly fourteen and a half (14.5) million in 2014 and is expected to rise to almost nineteen (19) million by 2024.

Approximately 39.6% of men and women will be diagnosed with cancer at some point during their lifetimes (based on 2010-2012 data).

In 2014, an estimated 15,780 children and adolescents ages 0-19 were diagnosed with cancer and 1,960 died of the disease.

National expenditures for cancer treatment and care in the U.S. totaled nearly $125 billion in 2010 and could reach $156 to $200 billion in 2020.

Sources are; N.C.I. www.cancer.gov/about-cancer/understanding/statistics
C.D.C. Tim Rymes and Regina Ziegler www.cdc.gov

NOTE! SOME AFTER THOUGHTS. AFTERWARD XVI

Two medical doctors Royal Rife and Wilhelm Reich were healing cancer in the 1920's to the 1950's. They both used frequency generators and were healing stage four (4) terminal cancer patients. Dr. Rife was using his Rife frequency MHz generator which took an average of thirty days to kill all the cancer cells he called ths Bacillus. Dr. Rife was curing terminal cancer patients at the U.S.C. Medical Hospital located in Los Angeles, California in the late 1920's, and Dr. Wilhelm Reich actually cured a bone metastasized stage four cancer in less than thirty days and the patient walked out of New York City's Manhattan's Bellevue Hospital. Dr. Reich used his orgone accumulator frequency generator and his orgone box to accomplish it. They were both scorned, called crazy, and admonished by their own medical profession. Both of their inventions, papers, patents, had disappeared after they were raided, and all of their professional possessions were taken by the U.S. government. Dr. Wilhelm Reich was imprisoned for contempt of court and placed in a federal prison where he was mysteriously found dead in his cell.

Be aware that the establishment of conventional medicine, big pharmaceutical, and the government do not want a natural cure for cancer which has existed for many years. The cancer industry makes an estimated annual profit from treating cancer with chemotherapy, radiation, and surgery of around one hundred twenty four ($124.6) billion dollars. They do not want their apple cart upset. They don't want a natural cure that has already existed and currently exists that is cost effective that eliminates, prevents cancer alternatively, naturally, and holistically. Cancer is a biological disease and can only be healed biologically which is a holistic and natural method. Cancer can be naturally healed for under $1,000 dollars a patient. It can be prevented daily for pennies a day.

All healing takes place at the sub atomic levels and molecular levels of your energy body called the biofields. This is why it is essential to completley eliminate the toxic "foci" negative frequencies that are in your energy body. These counter negative frequencies are what causes the interference between your trillions of cells and this causes a breakdown in your bodily functions on your physical level. Treating the physical level cannot eliminate these harmful toxic interferences and the cause of your illness. This is why it is imperative to first do a complete energetic detoxification using the D.N.R. lighty photon frequency solutions I have listed in this book. These specific solutions are called Liquid Needle and they specifically aim at: 1. An energetic detoxification bath soak that takes 15 days to complete. Only your skin is used to eliminate the toxins. 2. They also contain counter frequencies aimed at assisting your body's immune, lymphatic, nervous, endocannabinoid, endocrine, blood, acupuncture, and chakras to function at their highest optimum levels thereby helping your physical body to be able to heal itself. 3. Detoxify all foods, herbs, and water, etc. in a few minutes. 4. Your body once free of toxins has the ability to then heal itself. 5. Liquid Needle has frequencies in it that are four times higher than a measured healthy body. This allows for continuous re-balancing, repair, regeneration of your sub atomic, and molecular levels that preceed your physical body. Go to pages:206,208-10,239-40,242,259,287-310 for Liquid Needle Light Photon frequency solutions. So in my deepest and earnest sincerity I have hopefully given anyone whether a cancer patient, or not the information they need for a better choice in the healing of cancer, and all other diseases. Again, to reiterate that cancer is a biologically caused disease. Therefore it can only be healed by a biological treatment program. I have added one hundred and sixty five (165) pages in the Afterward VII entitled: "Cancer What's the Answer"? This book is an adjunct to any preventive medical, environment toxicology, and alternative healing programs. Therefore it is an educational and health rest-oral based book. The information contained herein is based on the authors professional experience, knowledge, research, and opinion(s). Lastly, the choice is always up to you. Healer or Slayer? Which do you choose? Namaste (Hindu means One Universal Law-Intention), Mahalo and Aloha (Hawaiian means Hello and Goodbye and I Am Thankful, Gratitude, Admiration, Praise Regards, and Respects), Ho'omaika Ana (Hawaiian means Congratualations on Your Great and Special Accompishments), Wakan Tanan Nici Un (Lakota means): May You Walk With the Great Spirit), Benedictions Salat (means The Spirit of God is Upon You and You are the Salt of the Earth and Bring Light to the World), Zhufu (Madarin Chinese means Wish You Well, Bless You), Aum-OM Shiva (India mantra which means The External Universal Source and Many Spiritual Blessings, Yours In Health, Your Greatest Wealth Is Your Health, It Is Your Birth Right..."I AM" ~JereOM~. Jerome Plotnick, Ph.D., N.D.

AFTERWARD XVII
BIBLIOGRAPHY For "CANCER WHAT'S THE ANSWER?"

www.wakeupworld.com 09-2014 The Endocannabinoid System & How T.H.C. Kills Cancer Cells

www.wakinggames.com 2014 The Endocaanabinoid System & How T.H.C. Cures Cancer

www.nobl.nim.nih.gov The Endocannabinoid System Modulation in Cancer

www.onlinelibrary.wiley Endocannabinoid System & Cancer: Therapeutic

www.preventdiseases.com The Endocannabinoid System & How T.H.C. Cures Cancer

www.nature.com The Endocannabinoid System in Prostate Cancer

www.projectcbd.org The Endocannabinoid System Project C.B.D.

www.cureyourowncancer.org

www.macycenters.org

cannabisdigest.ca/what-is-rick-simpson-oil?

www.emeraldcompassionus/rso/html

ocgreenrelief.org/medication/full-extract

The 13 Steps from Illness To health-APNBMPDR 2009-2016 Alternative Natural Cancer remedies & treatments for the Prevention & Health Restoral-Elimination of Cancer-pages-509-602, 664-677 by Jerome Plotnick, Ph.D., N.D. Amazon.com/books, Barnes&Noble.com/nook/books

Marijuana Chemistry-Genetics, Processing, Potency by Michael Starks-Ronon Publishing, Berkeley, CA. 1977, 1996

The Safe Shoppers Bible McMillan/IDG 1995 N.Y., N.Y. (800-434-3472)

The Politics of Cancer Revisited by Epstein, S.S. East Ridgecress Press 1998 Hankins, N.Y. (845-887-6407)

http://smartklean.wordpress.com & http://preventcancer.com

bestherbsforhealth.com 08-29,2015

http://www.realfarmacy.com/top-12-cancer-causing-products-average-home

http://canceractive.com/cancer-active-page-link-aspr?-354

www.wakinghtimes.com 05-19-2016

www.curenaturalcnace.com & www.cancertutor.com

Steep Hill Media May 9,2014 Rev. Dr. Kymron de Cesare Chief R.O.

Meta Your Mind (Techniques for conditioning your mind in a positive and effective manner) by Jerome Plotnick, Ph.D.,N.D. 12-2009-10-2016 Amazon.com/books and Barnes&Noble.com/nook/books

<u>Gerson Therapy</u>, N.C.I.com, Gerson.org., amazon.com
<u>The Tao of the Soul-Self-Slate Audio-a self healing, rebirthing & elimination of all erroneous zero order cognitive core beliefe and a spiritual awakening for true enlightenment</u> by Jerome Plotnick, Ph.D. Behavioral, Health, & Counseling Psychologist-1992-2017, N.D., Naturopath-1976,2000-2017, Meditation Instructor of Eastern & Western Meditationa, Cert. Touch For Health Practitioner-1976-2017, A.K. & Needle-less Acupuncture Th., Shamanistic and Mind-Body-Spiritual Healer, Cert. Pranic Healer-1995-2017, Visualization & Guided Imagery Practitioner, Cert. Master Hypnotherapist-1976-2017 H.E.C., Cert. E.M.G. Biofeedback-1992-2017 & Cert. E.E.G Neurofeedback Clinician-Trainer-Therapist-1998-2017, Cert. Chemical Recovery Counseling Specialist-1992-2017, C.A.R.R.D-1980., N.A.C.-1980, C.A.D.D.E-1992. Amazon.com/books, Facebook.com, 21stCenturyEnergetics.com, Barnes&Noble/nook/books
<u>Esoteric Healing</u> by Alyce Bailey Vol. IV Lucas Publishing, N.Y.-1984
Vibrational Medicine by Dr. Richard Gerber, M.D. Bear & Company, Sante Fe, New Mexico, 1954,1988
Antineoplastons-Dr. Burzynski, M.D. http://www.burzynskiclinic.com
Moss, Ralph-www.findarticles.com March 7, 2009
<u>www.graviola.org</u> March 8, 2009
Memorial Sloan-Kettering Cancer Center March 7, 2009
Amazon Botanicals <u>www.amazonbotanicals.com</u> March 8, 2009
Bluestein, Chuck <u>www.graviolaleaves.com</u> March 7, 2009
Cassileth, Barrie <u>www.cancernetwork.com</u> Sept. 2008
Taylor, Leslie <u>www.raintree.com</u>./graviola-html 2005
D.N.R., Inc. Liquid Needle D.V.D. information by Dr. Ken Widgery, N.D. and Arthur Widgery D.N.R., Inc.com Indiana 2005-2017
National Cancer Institute. N.C.I.com 2017
Center for Disease Control C.D.C.com 2017
https//doi.org/10.1371/journal pone 0024071 Sept. 6, 2011 "A Neutralizing R.N.A. Apatamer Against EGFR Causes Specific Apoptosis Cancer Cell Death." Exposito, Cassera, Longbardo, Condorelli, Marola, and Affuso et al.

BOOK INDEX FOR CANCER WHATS THE ANSWER?

P

Proctor & Gamble-247
progentor cryptocides-219
proliferates cancer-196,199
proliferates illness-197,202
Pronatura-220,241
Prostate cancer-198,206
protein-182,183,185,187,189
protite-182
protomorphegens-204
protozoa-179
psora-179,190
psuedo science-192
psyche-267
psychoactive-230,252
psychologists-193,195
psychology-190,195
P.T.S.D.-235
published research-209,229,230
pulse modulated hyperhermia-210
pumpkin-188,242
punch, alkaline fruit-188
puritan.com-212
pus-23
pyrophosphate-225

Q

quackery-214
quacks-193
Quack Watch-214
quinoa-239
quinoids-249
quotes from healers-260

R

radiation-200,210-11,241,244
radiation antitox-184,211
radionics-189,199,209
radioactive E.M.F.'s-183,200

R

radish-240,254
Raja yoga-271
ratio of CA:MG-203
raw egg products-239
raygun visualization-268
R.C.M.P.-239
reality-259
rebirthing-269
recovery-310
recreational use of
cannabis-236
red blood cells-248
red clover-249
Redfield, James-265
red onion-240,242,279
red root-189,213,240,242
248
Reich, Dr-180,189,215
Reiki-195
reishi-204,242,254
relaxation-263,276,278
remedies, anticancer-191
remission of cancer-185
244,263
remote healing-195
Renaissance-223-225
replicate cells-208
reproductive toxin-246-
247
reprogrammimg-268
resentments-268
resistance-246
Resperin, Inc.-255
reverie-259
reverse transciptase-219
Reviverine-189,205,225-
226
rheumatic disease-187,
219,253
rhodoendrum-254

332

<u>NOTE! DISCLAIMER</u>   <u>AFTERWARD XIX</u>

This book and it's contents have not been approved by the F.D.A. The book has been written for educational purposes only. The program herein is for actors, professional athletes, martial artists, other qualified persons desiring mental fitness, and peak performance. Always check with your duly licensed medical doctor before performing any health, or wellness detoxification, and health rest-oral program. This is in accordance with the present law in the U.S. Also and especially if you are under a medical doctors care for a preexisting or current health problems. Again the contents of this book are to be used as an adjunct to any medical or alternative health rest-oral program. The author, publisher, book distributors online, and retail stores are not liable for all or any damages that may occur if you perform the books program without Medical or Naturopathic consent. This book and program are only for the aforementioned professionals, other interested people, health professionals, for educational purposes, and health rest-oral only. Again, under the U.S. Constitution Bill of Rights: Freedom of Speech, Press as I am voicing my opinions, and conclusions that I have written about in this book. Only a licensed medical doctor can diagnose or treat disease. This book and my other books are for health restoral, spiritual enhancement, and educational purposes only.

For further information on this book and program described herein please contact:
Jerome Plotnick, Ph.D., N.D., 21st Century Energetics, 6132 Frazier Mt. Pk. Rd. #45, Lake of the Woods, CA. 93225 Phone: (661) 245-3616 M-Sa. 9 A.M.-5 P.M. P.S.T. E-mail: plotnickj@yahoo.com
Websites:21stcenturyenergetics.com, 21stcenturyenergetics@fb.com, createspace.com, linkedin.com, amazon.com-books/kindle, bing.com, manta.com, biopharma.com, jeromeplotnickphdnd@facebook.com, Jerome Plotnick, Ph.D., N.D.@google.com, amazon.com/EUR, & GBP, Barnes&Noble.com/nook/books, and all other book store outlets you may have to ask them to order it for you. The book will also be available on a F.D. We accept PayPal, Master Card, U.S.P.M.O., Checks from a verifiable bank account made out to cash and then your order will be shipped when the check clears. Please don't send cash. Thanks for your cooperation.

IBSN-10#:-1451593171   © 2010-17 USCPO
J.P.,Ph.D.,N.D/@21stCenturyEnergetics.com
IBSN-EAN 13#:-9781451593174   U.S. $40.00

Made in the USA
Columbia, SC
21 February 2018